*M*agellan

We shall not cease from exploration
And the end of all our exploring
Will be to arrive where we started
And know the place for the first time.

T.S. Eliot
Four Quartets

The boast of heraldry, the pomp of power
And all that beauty, all that wealth e'er gave,
Await alike the inevitable hour.
The paths of glory lead but to the grave.

Thomas Gray
"Elegy Written in a Country Churchyard"

MAGELLAN

Tim Joyner

International Marine
Camden, Maine

First paperback printing Fall 1994
Published by International Marine®

10 9 8 7 6 5 4 3 2 1

Copyright © 1992 International Marine, an imprint of TAB Books. TAB Books is a division of McGraw-Hill, Inc.

Library of Congress Cataloging-in-Publication Data

Joyner, Tim.
    Magellan / Tim Joyner.
      p. cm.
    Includes bibliographical references and index.
    ISBN 0-07-033128-6
    1. Magalhães, Fernão de, d. 1521. 2. Voyages around the world.
I. Title.
G420.M2J69 1992
910'.92–dc20
                                                  91–42835
                                                    CIP

Questions regarding the content of this book should be addressed to:

International Marine
P.O. Box 220
Camden, ME 04843

Typeset by A&B Typesetters, Inc., Bow, New Hampshire.
Printed by Fairfield Graphics, Fairfield, PA.
Design by Edith Allard.
Production by Molly Mulhern.
Edited by Jonathan Eaton and Tom McCarthy.

Printed on acid-free paper.

Contents

List of Illustrations

Foreword *by William Manchester*

Magellan!

His name ricochets down the canyons of nearly five centuries – ricochets, because the trajectory of his zigzagging life, never direct, dodged this way and that, ever elusive and often devious. We cannot even be certain what to call him. In Portuguese documents his name appears alternately as Fernão de Magalhães and Fernão de Magalhãis. Born the son of a fourth-grade nobleman, in middle age he renounced his native land and, as a Portuguese immigrant in Spanish Seville, became Fernando de Magallanes. Sometimes he spelled it that way, sometimes as "Maghellanes." In San Lúcar de Barrameda, before embarking for immortality on September 20, 1519, he signed his last will and testament as "Hernando de Magallanes." Cartographers latinized this to Magellanus; we have anglicized it to Magellan. But what was his real nationality? On his historic voyage he sailed under the colors of Spain. Today, Lisbon proudly acclaims him: "*Ele e nosso!*" – "He is ours!" – but that is chutzpah. In his lifetime his countrymen treated him as a renegade, calling him "*traidor*" and "*suo rege trânsfuga*" – "turncoat."

One would expect the mightiest explorer in history to have been sensitive and proud, easily stung by such slurs. In fact he was unoffended. By our lights, his character was knotted and intricate. It was more comprehensible to his contemporaries, however, because the *capitán general* of 1519–1521 was, to an exceptional degree, a creature of his time. His modesty, for example, arose from his faith. In the early sixteenth century individualism, and pride in achievement, were reserved for sovereigns, who were believed to be sheathed in divine glory. Being a lesser mortal, and a pious one, Magellan assumed that the Madonna was responsible for his accomplishments.

At the time he may have underrated them. That is more understandable. He was an explorer, a man whose destiny it was to venture into the unknown. What he found was, therefore, new. He had a fairly good idea of its worth but lacked accurate standards by which to measure it. Indeed, he couldn't even be certain what he was looking for until he had found it, and the fact that he had no clear view of his target makes the fact that he hit it squarely all the more remarkable.

At the outset his sponsors had seen his goal as very different. If the pos-

sibility of circumnavigating the globe had crossed his mind, he left it un-
mentioned in his royal audience with Carlos I, sovereign of Aragon and
Castile, who, as the elected Holy Roman Emperor Charles V, was to play a
key (if largely unwitting) role in the great religious revolution which split
Christendom and signaled the end of the medieval world. Carlos's commission to Magellan was to journey westward, there to claim Spanish possession of an archipelago which was then in the hands of his Iberian rival,
Manuel of Portugal. These were the "Spice Islands"–the Moluccas, lying
between Celebes and New Guinea. Now they are an obscure part of Indonesia, unshown on most maps, but then they were considered priceless.
Officially, the *capitan general*'s motive lay in the king's pledge to him. Two
of the islands would become Magellan's personal fief–he would receive five
percent of all profits from the archipelago, thus making his fortune.

But this Moluccan plan was, as Dr. Joyner notes, "a scientific failure and
a diplomatic disaster." Indeed, as the leader of the expedition, Magellan
was killed before he could even reach there. Meanwhile, however, he had
landed in the Philippines. This was of momentous importance, for east-
bound Portuguese had reconnoitered the Spice Islands nine years earlier.
Therefore, in overlapping them, he had closed the nexus between the
123rd and 124th degrees of east longitude. His voyage had encircled the
Earth.

Yet his achievements were slighted. Death is always a misfortune, at
least to the man who has to do the dying, but in Magellan's case it was
exceptionally so, for as a dead discoverer he was unhonored in his own
time. The Spanish sovereign–displaying the same lack of judgment which
had marked his confrontation with Martin Luther at the Diet of Worms–
chose to lionize the surviving seaman who had conned the fleet's one remaining vessel back to Seville. The same man had mutinied against the
capitan general off the coast of Patagonia. Even Magellan's discovery of the
strait which bears his name was belittled. Only a superb mariner, which he
was, could negotiate the treacherous, 350-mile-long *Estrecho de Magellanes*.
In the years after his death, expedition after expedition tried to follow his
lead, but they couldn't do it; all but two were shipwrecked or turned homeward, and those two met disaster in the Pacific. Frustrated and defeated,
skippers decided that Magellan's exploit was impossible, and they broad-
cast the slander that it was a myth.

Had fortune and a viceregal role in the Moluccas been Magellan's real
motive, he would have been, by his own lights, a failure. But the true drives
of a man may be hidden from him. That was true here. Magellan's vision
may have been cloudy, but his real inspiration had been larger than greed.
The profit motive does not exalt, and throughout his epic voyage he had

been a man transformed. Now we know that he had actually triumphed—had, in fact, provided the first empirical evidence that the world is round.

In so doing, he had done much more. He had provided a linchpin for the men of the Renaissance. Philosophers, scholars, and even learned men in the Church had begun to challenge stagnant medieval assumptions, among them Vatican dogma on the shape and size of the Earth, and its position in the universe. Magellan had given men a realistic perception of the globe's dimensions, of its enormous seas, of how its landmasses were distributed. Others had raised questions. He had provided answers, which now, inevitably, would lead to further questions—to challenges which continue on the eve of the twenty-first century.

He was a commander, but he lacked commanding presence. Despite his high birth, his build was that of a peasant—short, swart, with a low center of gravity. His skin was leathery, his black beard bushy, and his eyes large, sad, and brooding. Bearing scars of battle, he walked with a pronounced limp, the souvenir of a lance wound in Morocco. He had acted recklessly then, and would again, in the last twenty-four hours of his life, but he was seldom impulsive. On the contrary; his reserve approached the stoical. A man who lived within, he saved the best of himself for himself, relishing his solitude. As a commander he could be ruthless—"tough, tough, tough," in the words of a fellow mariner. Yet even officers critical of him conceded that he was always quick to reward men who performed well, and he was generally admired below decks.

Proud of his lineage, meticulous, fiercely ambitious, stubborn, driven, secretive, and iron-willed, the *capitan general* was guided by an inner beacon which he discussed with no one, for there was a hidden side to this old seaman which would have astonished his men. He was imaginative, a dreamer; in a time of blackguards and brutes he believed in heroism. Romance had become a muted theme, though not altogether dead. Malory's tales of King Arthur were enormously popular, and even if Magellan had missed them he would have been aware of Camelot; the myths of medieval chivalry had persisted, passed along from generation to generation for a thousand years. Arthur himself was a genuine if shadowy historical figure, a mighty British *Dux Bellorum* who won twelve terrible battles against Saxon invaders from Germany and was slain at Camlann in A.D. 539. Less real, but also enchanting to children like Magellan, was the paladin Lancelot du Lac, introduced in 1170 by the French poet-troubadour Chrétien de Troyes. De Troyes was also celebrated for his *Perceval, ou Le Conte Grall*, the first known version of the Holy Grail legend, which was retold in 1203 by the German poet Wolfram von Eschenbach as the story of *Parzival*.

Both de Troyes and von Eschenbach were translated into other European languages, including Portuguese. And there were others. At his death in 1210 Gottfried von Strassburg left his epic *Tristan und Isolde*; in 1225 France's Guillaume de Loris wrote the allegorical metrical romance *Roman de la Rose*, distantly based on Ovid's *Ars Amatoria*—Chaucer translated it in the next century—and in 1320 *Sir Gawain and the Green Knight*, a poetic parable of Arthur's elegant nephew, appeared in England.

Magellan, a man of boundless curiosity, found reality equally enthralling, devouring the works of Giovanni de Plano Carpini, who traveled east to Karakorum in 1245, and Marco Polo's account of his adventures in the Orient, dictated to a fellow prisoner in 1296. More important, the commander of the armada which would encircle the world had been inspired by the feats of Columbus and the discoverers since him. Other Europeans dreamed of following their lead. What set Magellan apart was his unswerving determination to match them and thus become a hero himself. Erasmus and his colleagues were admirable, but they were writers and talkers. Magellan had learned that deeds are supreme; he knew Meredith's "terrific decree in life" that "they must act who would prevail." And in his struggle for dominance his most valuable possession was his extraordinary will. He could endure disappointment and frustration with an almost inhuman patience, but he could never submit to defeat. He simply did not know how.

Some twenty-five degrees from the south celestial pole, two luminous galaxies, easily visible to the naked eye, span the night sky. These companions of the Milky Way are the Magellanic Clouds, trails of glory which arouse awe, give the heavens grandeur, and testify to the immensity of the universe. So high are they that their distance can be grasped only by a mighty sweep of the imagination. A ray of starlight from there, traveling at its speed of over 186,000 miles per second—six trillion miles a year—cannot become visible on Earth for 80,000 years. Thus the illumination which was leaving the Clouds when Magellan emerged from his Strait and crossed the Pacific will not reach this planet for another 795 centuries, a cosmic perspective which would have pleased him.

He was not the wisest man of his time. Erasmus was. Neither was he the most gifted. That, surely, was Leonardo. But Magellan became what, as a child, he had yearned to be—the era's greatest hero. The reason is intricate, but important to understand. Heroism is often confused with physical courage. In fact the two are very different. There was nothing heroic about Magellan's death. He went into that last darkness a seasoned campaigner, accompanied by his own men, and he was completely fearless because as he drew his last breath he believed—indeed *knew*—that paradise was imminent. Similarly, the soldier who throws himself on a live grenade, surrendering his life to save his comrades, may be awarded the Medal of Honor. Nevertheless his deed, being impulsive, is actually unheroic. Such acts, no more reflective than the swift withdrawal of a blistered hand from a red-hot stove, are involuntary. Heroism is the exact opposite – always deliberate, never mindless.

Neither, if it is valor of the first water, may it be part of a group endeavor. All movements, including armies, provide their participants with such tremendous support that pursuit of common goals, despite great risk, is little more than ardent conformity. Indeed, the truly brave member is the man who repudiates the communal objective, challenging the rest of the group outright. Since no such discordant note was ever heard around the round table, young Magellan, had he been enchanted by the tales of Arthur or El Cid, had been gulled. It follows that generals, presidents – all leaders backed by blind masses – are seldom valiant, though interesting exceptions occasionally emerge. Politicians who defy their constituents over matters of principle, knowing they will be driven from office, qualify as heroic. So, to cite a rare military instance, did General MacArthur when, protesting endless casualty lists with no prospect of an armistice, he sacrificed his career and courted disgrace.

The hero acts alone, without encouragement, relying solely on conviction and his own inner resources. Shame does not discourage him; neither does obloquy. Indifferent to approval, reputation, wealth, or love, he cherishes only his personal sense of honor, which he permits no one else to judge. LaRochefoucald, not always a cynic, wrote of him that he does "without witnesses what we would be capable of doing before everyone." Guided by an inner gyroscope, he pursues his vision single-mindedly, undiscouraged by rejections, defeat, or even the prospect of imminent death. Few men can even comprehend such fortitude. Virtually all crave some external incentive: the appreciation of peers, the possibility of exculpation, the promise of retroactive affection, the hope of rewards, applause, decorations – of emotional reparations in some form. Because these longings are normally very powerful, only a man with towering strength of character can suppress them.

In the long lists of history it is difficult to find another figure whose heroism matches Magellan's. For most sixteenth-century Europeans his *Vorstellung* – to circle the globe – was unimaginable. To launch the pursuit of this vision, he had to turn his back on his own country, inviting charges of treason. Before his departure Portuguese agents repeatedly tried, with some success, to sabotage his expedition. When he did sail, his hodgepodge crews couldn't even communicate in the same tongue, and the background of the captains assigned to him almost guaranteed mutiny and treachery, which indeed followed. Unable even to confide in anyone else after his crushing disappointment at the Río de la Plata, he stubbornly continued his search for the strait he alone believed in, and when he had at last found it, deserters fled with his largest ship and the bulk of the fleet's provisions. Of his other four vessels, three could not complete the voyage. During the armada's crossing of the Pacific, an epic of fortitude, it was its commander's inflexible will which fueled morale and stamina. His discovery of the Philippines dwarfed his original goal—the Moluccas—and he died trying to bring them into the modern age.

The shabby circumstances of his death are troubling, representing flagrant deviance from his code of conduct. They may be partly explained by his exhilaration after sailing around the world, and partly by the fact that, living in a God-ridden age, he was distorted by its imperatives. Yet the distortion in him was slight when measured against other chief figures of his time. The hands of contemporary popes, kings, and reformers were drenched with innocent blood. His were spotless. Granted that his misjudgments on Mactan isle were unworthy of him, the fact remains that few men have paid so high a price for their lapses. He lost not only his life, but, of even greater moment, the triumphant completion of his voyage and vindication in his time.

His character was, of course, imperfect. But heroes need not be admirable, and indeed most have not been. The web of driving traits behind their accomplishments almost assures that. Men who do the remarkable—heroic and otherwise—frequently fail in their personal relationships. This unpleasant reality is usually glossed over in burnishing the images of the great. So many eminent statesmen, writers, painters, and composers have been intolerable sons, husbands, fathers, and friends that they may fairly be said to have been the rule. Lincoln's marriage was a disaster. Winston Churchill's charm concealed a broad streak of cruelty. Franklin Roosevelt, to put it in the kindest possible way, was a dissembler.

They were achievers. Genuine paladins are even likelier to have been objectionable. Yet their flaws, though deplorable, were irrelevant; in the end their heroism shone through untarnished. Had Ferdinand Magellan met Jesus Christ, the Galilean might have felt a pang of disappointment—which the *capitan general* might have shared—but Magellan, like the Nazarene, was also a hero. He still is. He always will be. Of all the tributes to him, therefore, the Magellanic Clouds are the most appropriate. Like them, his memory shines down upon the world his voyage opened, illuminating it from infinity to eternity.

Author's Note

For readers who may wish to know how this book came to be written, this is how it happened:

About twenty years ago in the Seattle Public Library, I came across a copy of *Conqueror of the Seas: The Story of Magellan*, a translation of Stefan Zweig's 1938 work, *Magellan: Der Man und Seine Tat*. I took it home, devouring it in one sitting, for it was a rousing good story. Then, in 1973, while aboard a U.S. oceanographic vessel crossing the Pacific from New Zealand to South America, I received a radiogram from my boss in Washington, D.C., asking me to check on rumors that fishermen were catching wild salmon in the Strait of Magellan. Debarking at Valparaiso, Chile, I flew to Punta Arenas, a bustling port on the strait, where I discovered that the "salmon" were huge brown trout occasionally caught by sportsmen. The fish had been introduced from Germany at the beginning of this century, and a sea-run population had developed in the numerous channels and fjords of the region, where they came to be known as *"salmón."*

In a parklike square in downtown Punta Arenas stands a heroic bronze statue of Ferdinand Magellan, discoverer of the strait. At its base are figures representing the region's principal native peoples. Locals say that if a visitor rubs the shiny bronze toe of one of the figures, he will return to the strait. I did, making four subsequent visits, one of which was a fisheries assessment cruise through the strait and adjacent channels on a Chilean naval vessel. Sailing through these spectacular channels on a motorized ship with modern charts and navigational equipment, I was led to wonder how it must have been for Magellan and his companions in their clumsy square-rigged *naos*, probing without charts or channel markers or even knowing where any of these seemingly countless waterways led, searching for safe anchorages and having to claw off sandbanks and rocky reefs in the treacherous currents and fierce winds that often whip the waters of the strait into a seething, whitecapped fury.

My interest in the subject was stimulated again in 1985, when I found another copy of Zweig's book in the library of a small college in Sitka, Alaska, where I was a visiting faculty fellow. After rereading it, I used it as the basis for an evening seminar at the library. Probably because on that rainy winter night in Sitka there was not much else to do, more than a few

students, faculty, and guests showed up. The discussion following my summary of the story revealed that what they knew about Magellan came, for
the most part, from the limited information in school history books and
encyclopedias. The historical significance of his achievement was little appreciated. Gratified by their interest in learning more about the subject, I
searched for additional sources of information, but aside from the Zweig
book, there was little more of substance in the libraries of Sitka. Then one
day, rummaging through the books I had brought with me from Seattle, I
came upon Samuel Eliot Morison's *The European Discovery of America: The
Southern Voyages*, published in 1974. I had purchased the book several years
before coming to Alaska, but had not yet read it. To my delight, it contained a well-researched, well-annotated chapter on Ferdinand Magellan.
There were other chapters about Columbus and the explorers who followed in his wake, but Zweig had predisposed me to Magellan. Morison's
treatment of him got me thoroughly hooked.

When I returned to Seattle, I read everything I could find about Magellan in the public, university, and government libraries, using Morison's
notes and citations as a starting point. Much of what I read was in Spanish
and Portuguese, and some was in French and Italian. I barely remembered
the Spanish and French I had studied in high school, but fortified by Ro-
mance-language dictionaries and grammars, I plowed through the available
material. Exhausting that, I discovered that librarians armed with com-
puters now have access to information from anywhere in our country and
from much of the rest of the world. Thanks to their skill and helpfulness, I
was able to consult copies of priceless documents, the products of archival
research spanning at least four centuries, and works by generations of historians, geographers, and biographers from Europe and North and South
America who have used these materials.

I had undertaken this research simply because I was fascinated by the
drama of Magellan's life, but after I started, I became intrigued by recently
developed evidence that some of the records of the Magellan expedition
reflect the work of the "spin doctors" of his time. This practice of deliberately distorting records to serve diplomatic and political ends continues unabated today, and history is ill served by it. Underneath the fluff and sham
insinuated into the early accounts of Magellan's life and the great enterprise
with which it ended lies a story of immense vitality. Like Coleridge's Ancient Mariner, I sought out my relatives and friends to tell them about it.
As I eagerly launched into my favorite subject, the eyes of most of them
would glaze over, and they would excuse themselves at the earliest opportunity. A few, more charitably, urged me to buy a word processor so that I
might vent my obsession on paper. To save myself further embarrassment,

I took their advice. The results that survived the scrutiny of my constructively critical, extraordinarily patient editors are presented on the following pages.

Acknowledgments

I am indebted to many good people for their encouragement and guidance in what for me was unfamiliar territory: writing about history. Gertrude and Peter Hopkins were the first to suggest that what I had learned about Magellan was worth writing. The next was William Manchester who, when I expressed doubts about it, told me: "Go for it!" Since I first began writing the story, Lawrence Vivian has been a continuing source of encouragement and valuable help. Professor Dauril Alden steered me to the pertinent material in the library of the University of Washington and alerted me to sources in libraries and archives worldwide. The staff and publications of the John Carter Brown Library in Providence, Rhode Island, were excellent guides to the documentary and cartographic treasures in that priceless collection. Mateo Martinić of the Universidad de Magallanes provided much valuable information about the history and geography of the Strait of Magellan, and a careful critique of my treatment of Magellan's passage through the strait. The staffs of two institutions on Okinawa, the Prefectural Library and the Prefectural Museum, supplied information and illustrative materials about 16th-century Ryukyuan maritime trading activity, imperfect knowledge of which may have influenced Magellan's choice of a course across the Pacific.

Special thanks are due to the librarians at the Northwest and Alaska Fisheries Centers in Seattle, who tracked down and obtained research materials without which this book could never have been written. They are: Patricia Cook, Marilyn Magnuson, Valerie Schultheiss, and Sarah Galiger. The Seattle Public Library has been an excellent source of maritime history books and "quick information" by telephone. I will be forever grateful to my wife, Sumiko, for her tolerance of my obsession, and for sustaining me throughout this effort. The author bears the sole responsibility for the interpretation of information contributed by others for this work.

Prologue

September 6, 1522, San Lúcar de Barrameda, Spain. A weather-beaten, barnacle-encrusted sailing ship with an emaciated crew of eighteen Europeans and four Malays, its hold crammed with spices, hove-to off the bar at the mouth of the Guadalquivir to pick up a pilot. Victoria, *the last of a fleet of five ships that had put to sea nearly three years before, had circumnavigated the planet. For the first time, mankind had a realistic basis for estimating the Earth's true dimensions and the hitherto unsuspected extent of its oceans. The measure of the forbidding seas having been taken, Europeans were now poised to move over them in unprecedented numbers.*

In the age we know now as the Renaissance, European artists, scholars, and a few bold churchmen, statesmen, and sailors began to question many of the premises upon which medieval society had been built. Among these were church-approved concepts of the shape and size of the Earth and its position relative to the heavens. The sparks that ignited the intellectual fires of that age were struck by soldiers, pilgrims, and merchants who came in contact with the reality of Islam.

A militant religious movement of tremendous power and appeal, Islam had spread from the Near East westward into North Africa and the Iberian Peninsula, and eastward to Persia, India, the Malay Archipelago, and China. It lay astride the land and sea routes that from ancient times had provided tenuous connections between Europe and the Far East. In this position, Islam served as a conduit for the exchange of goods and ideas between the eastern and western extremes of the known world.

In the Near East, European crusaders and pilgrims acquired tastes for Far Eastern spices and silks brought there by Arab traders, and a lust for these luxuries quickly developed among the nobility and wealthy merchants of Europe. Merchants in the Italian city-state of Venice, growing rich at the end of the Arab trade routes from the Far East, were the envy of merchant bankers elsewhere in Europe, especially in the Iberian kingdoms and in Flanders and Germany. Luxury goods from the Far East were distributed throughout Europe by the merchants of Venice, and along with the goods came a flood of ideas that were to change forever the European world.

The world that the eighteen ragged European survivors of the first circumnavigation had left behind, and to which they returned when they debarked in Seville, had few of the comforts we now enjoy. Making their reentry into a society barely removed from the stultifying ignorance, cruelty, and prejudices of the Middle Ages, the penitents staggered, half-starved in their tattered shirts, to the Church of Santa María de la Victoria, and then to another, Santa María de la Antigua, giving thanks to the Holy Virgin for their deliverance.

At the time of the *Victoria*'s return, communication, even between adjacent villages, was nearly nonexistent. Overland travel between towns was confined to the sorry remnants of Roman roads in disrepair for more than 1,000 years; rural paths followed the traces of prehistoric hunters and herdsmen between seasonal pastures. Whether on old Roman roads or ancient trails, travelers without armed escort could expect to be set upon by murderous outlaws. Such laws as existed protected the property and rights of the mighty, but were enforceable only within a few days' march from their strongholds. Men and women were indifferent to squalor, filth, suffering, and cruelty even in their most obscene manifestations. The Church, begun in Roman times as a refuge for the powerless, while preserving a pretense of concern for the humble poor and dispossessed, had evolved into a rich, elaborate edifice competing with kings for temporal power. The Inquisition, a dark stain on the Church's history, was a desperate attempt to stem the diffusion of ecclesiastical power that was an inevitable consequence of the enlightenment accompanying the Renaissance. In the aftermath of the plagues that had devastated Europe in the previous century, farms were abandoned, and manpower was scarce in the depopulated villages.

In Spain, the accession of Charles I, although unpopular at first, had stabilized the precarious union of Aragon and Castile achieved by the marriage of Ferdinand and Isabella. But when Charles, a Hapsburg, succeeded his grandfather Maximilian as Holy Roman Emperor, his attention to Spanish affairs was diluted by his responsibilities in an empire whose German states were seething with the religious and political unrest stirred up by Martin Luther. The diversion of the young monarch's attention from Spain would prove a serious impediment to Magellan's developing project, which Charles hoped would become the keystone of the worldwide empire he dreamed of building.

Magellan's enterprise was handicapped from the start by a high command overloaded with arrogant, ill-disciplined courtiers, almost all of them landlubbers. For its achievements, won at such a terrible cost, we must credit the unshakable determination of the expedition's Portuguese captain general and the iron discipline he imposed on his fractious subordinates. Credit also is due to the unsung heroes who sailed with Magellan: the professional mariners whose skilled seamanship and unending fortitude made his achievements possible.

This is the story of that expedition and the controversial figure who conceived it and, against incredible odds, led it halfway around the world. It is also the story of his shipmates: those who supported him, those who bedeviled him, those who perished, and those few who, by completing the first circumnavigation of the earth, transformed their deceased leader's vision into firsthand knowledge of the size of the world and the extent of its oceans. Though it cost him his life and the lives of most of his shipmates, the single deed for which Magellan is remembered constitutes the most magnificent chapter in the history of exploration.

PAIRT

*D*own to the Sea in Ships

And then went down to the ship,
Set keel to breakers, forth on the godly sea, . . .
Ezra Pound, "Canto I"

In 219 B.C. Chinese junks made passages to the Isles of the
Blessed, thought to have been Japan, and by the second
century A.D. Arab chronicles tell of junks on the Euphrates
River. Chinese seafarers made use of such things as rudders
and magnetic compasses long before either was known in
Europe.

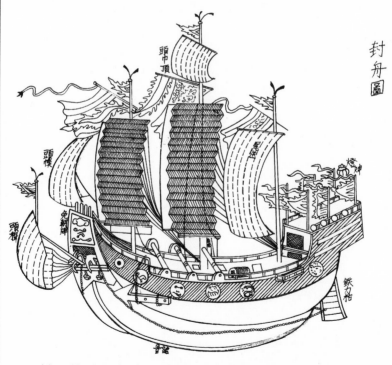

Adapted by the author from a drawing in the Okinawan Prefectural Museum.

5

1

$\mathcal{E}$arly Seafarers

The origins of blue-water sailing are hidden in the mists of prehistory. Legends tell of voyages before the first millennium B.C. into the oceans beyond the Pillars of Hercules and the Horn of Africa by sailors from the eastern Mediterranean, where the emergence of prosperous city-states created a demand for metals, timber, food grains, fiber, spices, fragrances, and dye-stuffs, stimulating the development of maritime commerce.[1] The search for new sources of valued commodities led these merchant sailors along the shores of the Indian and Atlantic oceans. On such journeys, they stayed close inshore. Offshore were neither landmarks nor soundings to guide a pilot.

Far to the east, between 2500 and 1200 B.C., a less numerous people, for whom there is no written history, were passing through the islands of Indonesia and Melanesia. They are known to us now only by shards of pottery and the derivatives of their ancestral language. In the island-studded seas between the tropical Pacific and Indian oceans, they developed seafaring skills that made it possible to transport entire communities to distant islands across vast reaches of both oceans.

Polynesians

Before 4000 B.C., a population of pottery-making agriculturalists lived along the coasts of Indochina and southern China.[2] Perhaps threatened by invaders from the north and west, they left their continental homelands for Taiwan and the islands of the Malay Archipelago. Such displacements were not unusual at the periphery of the Eurasian continent. Competition among nomads for shifting pasturage in the marginal grasslands of the Cen-

7

tral Asian steppes propagated waves of migration to the east, west, and south, displacing settled populations in their paths.

For perhaps 500 years—twenty-five generations—in the islands of Melanesia, they dwelt among an ancient Australoid population, with whom some linguistic and genetic exchange seems to have taken place.[3] By 1500 B.C. the ancestral Polynesians had become adept at building and sailing swift, maneuverable watercraft beautifully adapted to the sea-girt environment into which necessity had driven them. In search of less populous islands, they moved eastward, transporting groups of related families, domestic animals, and plants from island to island in large double canoes whose stability, seaworthiness, speed, and ability to sail to windward represented a remarkable achievement in design. Sailing beyond the easternmost islands of Melanesia and crossing hundreds of miles of blue water, they became the first humans to reach Fiji. By 1300 B.C. they had reached Tonga, and by 1000 B.C., Samoa. Between 200 B.C. and A.D. 1000 they had settled in the Marquesas, Society, and Hawaiian islands, Easter Island, and New Zealand.[4]

The last three destinations meant voyages of well over 1000 miles across open ocean, requiring organization, logistical planning, a reliable system of navigation, and the ability to carry many weeks' supply of water and food for passengers, crews, and domestic animals. In addition, plant cuttings for starting gardens had to be kept alive during the journey.

Three mechanisms have been proposed to explain how a people without writing or access to metals accomplished such remarkable migrations: drift, blowaway, and deliberate voyages.[5] The first two give little credence to the possibility that the preliterate Polynesians developed a system of navigation suitable for long-distance, blue-water voyaging. The last theory has emerged from an increasing appreciation of Polynesian origins and culture derived from advances in archaeology. The idea of deliberate migratory voyages gained support from the successful completion, in 1976, of a voyage from Maui to Tahiti in a double canoe constructed using ancient Polynesian boatbuilding techniques. The canoe, navigated without charts or instruments, carried seventeen people, water, traditional Polynesian foods, livestock, and garden plants to the planned destination in thirty-five days, covering a distance of 3,000 nautical miles.[6]

When Europeans first entered the Pacific Ocean, the Polynesians had long since settled the islands within a huge oceanic triangle twice the area of the United States, with apexes at Hawaii, Easter Island, and New Zealand. In their great double canoes, skilled navigators who carried star maps in their heads and had intimate knowledge of the oceanic environment used the sun and stars, wave patterns, winds, currents, drifting seaweed, and migrating birds to determine position and course on the high seas.[7] Behind the legends of great voyages led by mythical heroes lies the reality that the Polynesian migrations were carefully conceived and elegantly executed.

Egyptians

Fragmentary records dating from about 3000 B.C. tell of an expedition from Egypt to the land of Punt that returned with a cargo of myrrh (an aromatic resin), precious metals, and valuable woods. The location of Punt is not identified, but the precious metals probably were loaded on the southeastern coast of Africa near the mouth of the Zambesi River, more than 4,000 nautical miles from the Red Sea coast of Lower Egypt.[8] The journey must have taken several years and used the seasonal monsoons of the Indian Ocean. The building of seagoing ships began in Egypt about 3500 B.C. and accelerated with the discovery of cedar forests in the Levant, about 300 nautical miles northeast of the Nile delta.[9]

Phoenicians

The Phoenicians, a Semitic people, lived along the coast of the Levant. From the Egyptians they learned to build ships with their native timber. Soon surpassing their teachers in shipbuilding and seafaring, they used these skills to develop a thriving maritime commerce that was the envy of the ancient world.

One of the earliest accounts of Phoenician seafaring comes to us through Jewish history. From his wife, a daughter of the Egyptian pharaoh, Solomon, king of Israel from 972 to 939 B.C., learned the location of Punt, by then the source of much of Egypt's gold. Eager to enrich his coffers with shipments of that precious metal but handicapped by his small kingdom's lack of ships, Solomon turned to his northern neighbors, the Phoenicians, for a joint venture. They provided the ships and sailors; Solomon revealed the location of Punt and provided a port of embarkation on the Red Sea.[10] After completing the voyage and learning the location of Punt, the Phoenicians broke off the joint venture and conducted the gold-shipping business independently.

Around 450 B.C., Herodotus, a Greek historian from Ionia in southwestern Asia Minor, wrote of Phoenician sailors who, while in the employ of the Egyptian pharaoh Necho II 150 years earlier, had circumnavigated Africa. They returned to Egypt in the third year after their departure, passing through the Pillars of Hercules (Gibraltar) from the Atlantic. Although he did not believe it, Herodotus related the sailors' story that, as they rounded

Libya (Africa), they beheld the sun on their right. Since in Ionia when Herodotus faced west, the sun always was on his left, the sailors' story seemed incredible. The effects of his disbelief on the geography of his and later times are well known. For Ptolemy, a Greek geographer writing from A.D. 127 to 151, and for generations of geographers who followed him, the Indian Ocean was a closed sea. We now know that when one faces west in the southern hemisphere, the sun is on the right, just as the ancient Phoenician sailors reported.

From 2000 to 1400 B.C., the Minoans of Crete, a rising sea power, competed with the Phoenicians for maritime commerce in the Mediterranean and the Atlantic.[11] After Minoan civilization was devastated by a catastrophic volcanic explosion on the island of Thera near Crete, the Phoenicians undertook to finish the job.[12] From their North African colony of Carthage in 530 B.C., the Phoenicians attacked, captured, and destroyed the Cretan colony of Tartessus, a copper and tin mining center in southwestern Spain and a commercial rival of the nearby Phoenician port of Gadir (Cadiz). (The Romans evened the score in 146 B.C. when they wiped out Carthage, fulfilling Cato the Elder's admonition to the Roman Senate: "Carthage must be destroyed!")

From North Africa and Spain, Phoenician traders reached out into the Atlantic. By 600 B.C. they were sailing to Britain, attracted by the tin mines of Cornwall.[13] In the Madeira and Canary islands the enterprising Phoenicians discovered rich resources of *Murex*, shellfish from which they extracted a pigment used in the manufacture of Tyrian purple, a valuable dye.

About 530 B.C., Hanno, a Phoenician admiral, set out from Carthage with a fleet of sixty galleys to establish outposts in the Canary Islands and along the African west coast. This accomplished, he followed the coast south to Sierra Leone. Turning east into the Gulf of Guinea, Hanno and his crews witnessed a spectacular volcanic eruption on Mt. Cameroon.[14] Along the way, they encountered creatures described as manlike and covered with hair, probably lowland gorillas. The sailors killed a few, skinned them, and brought the hides back to Carthage.

Greeks

Despite their destruction of Tartessus, the elimination of Cretan competition, and closing the Strait of Gibraltar to vessels other than their own, the Carthaginians were not without competitors in the Atlantic. From their colony at Massilia (Marseille), the Greeks had developed inland routes to ports at the mouths of the Loire and Rhine, providing access to the Atlantic and the North Sea.

In 325 B.C., Pythias, a noted geographer of Massilia, set out to reconnoiter the lands bordering the northern seas. In one of the most remarkable voyages of antiquity, he sailed around Great Britain and visited Thule, where he was probably the first southern European mariner to encounter pack ice. The location of Pythias's Thule has been debated for centuries. His astronomical observations indicate that its latitude was about 64° N. He also stated that it was six days' sail (about 600 miles) north of Britain. At that latitude there are two possibilities: Norway and Iceland. Each has its advocates.[15,16] It is likely that one of the objectives of Pythias's expedition was the study of the tides around Britain. These were extremely hazardous for Mediterranean sailors unaccustomed to tidal ranges of such magnitude. Although it has been lost, *On the Ocean*, Pythias's work containing the observations made on his northern voyage, was well known to later Greek geographers, who quoted it extensively.

Timosthenes of Rhodes was the next Greek sailor-scholar in the tradition of Pythias.[17] In Alexandria, Ptolemy II, king of Egypt from 285 to 246 B.C., appointed him chief pilot of the Egyptian navy. For his *periploi* (books of sailing directions), he devised an elegant system of twelve winds which, subsequently simplified to eight, became the wind rose still used on nautical charts.

Eratosthenes, a mathematician and astronomer at the Library of Alexandria, was a contemporary of Timosthenes. In preparing his well-known work on geography, he relied heavily on one of Timosthenes's ten periploi, *On Ports*. By applying the principles of Euclidean geometry to measurements of the altitude of the sun at noon at two locations on the same meridian, the distance between them being known, Eratosthenes arrived at an estimate for the circumference of the earth more accurate than that used by the geographers of the Renaissance.[18] If they had accepted Eratosthenes's figure, it is unlikely that Columbus and Magellan would have undertaken their famous voyages.

Romans

Alexandria became a Roman province toward the end of the first century B.C. Among the many assets acquired by Rome from this conquest was the profitable maritime trade with Persia and India carried on by the Alexandrian Greeks. A book written in A.D. 60 by an anonymous Graeco-Egyptian author provides sailing directions for the Red and Arabian seas. Hippalus, a Greek shipmaster, was credited with making the first direct blue-water voyage from the Red Sea to India. Because he used it, the southwest monsoon was named "Hippalus" in his honor.[19] The Romans were quick to capitalize on the Indian Ocean trade. In addition to Graeco-Egyptian shipmasters, they employed experienced Arab and Indian pilots whose ancestors had for centuries used the monsoons for two-way voyaging on the Indian Ocean. When the Romans entered the trade, the number of ships making voyages to India soared from around 20 to about 120 annually, including passenger vessels on regularly scheduled runs.[20] In India, Roman traders purchased goods from Ceylon, Indonesia, and China, and wealthy upper-class Romans eagerly bought silks, jewels, and fine pottery from the Orient.

Indonesians

Not all the Austronesians had headed eastward into the Pacific Ocean from the Indonesian Archipelago. Some went west across the Indian Ocean. By the beginning of the first century A.D., they had crossed the 4,000 miles between southern Indonesia and Madagascar, bringing with them yams and bananas. Later introduced to Africa, these crops became staple foods in the humid tropics of that continent.[21]

Although there are no records to show how this stupendous migration was accomplished, the presence of strong genetic and linguistic components linking the Malagasies of Madagascar to the Malays and Polynesians provides compelling evidence that it did occur.[22] Arab geographer Al-Idrisi (1099–1166) noted that Javanese traders visited Madagascar regularly "on barques and large ships and export their wares, for they understand one another's languages." The Austronesian ancestors of Madagascar's Malagasies probably sailed across the Indian Ocean in craft not unlike those used in the migrations to the islands of Polynesia. The southeast monsoon reinforces the southeast trade winds during the summer in the Indian Ocean south of the equator, providing fair sailing along the route from Java to Madagascar.

Much of the maritime commerce passing through Indonesia from the seventh through the tenth centuries was between China and India. Ships traversing the Malacca and Sunda straits were subjected to taxes levied by local sultans.[23] By the ninth century, shipwrights on the north coast of Java were constructing two-masted oceangoing cargo ships with massive hulls stabilized by large outriggers.[24] Probably evolved from the double canoe, these Javanese trading vessels also were influenced by Chinese, Indian, and Arab ship designs.

Chinese

Although seafaring began early in China, it was rarely more than peripheral to the concerns of the administrators of the empires that rose and fell on the great landmass. However, because China's mountainous topography hampered the overland transport of goods between north and south, there was a need for reliable water transport along the reef-studded coastline. Responding to this need, Chinese shipwrights developed the junk.

The term "junk" (Portuguese "junco") comes from the Javanese "jon," meaning ship. Variations of this term are also used in southern India, China, and Japan.[25] Junks apparently evolved from the ubiquitous flat-bottomed sampans that swarm over China's inland waterways.[26] With no keels, and with wedge-shaped bottoms, junks draw little water, and their watertight bulkheads and specialized superstructures make them adaptable to various uses at sea, including cargo and passenger hauling, fishing, and fighting. Their sturdy masts support battened sails that can be trimmed for sailing close to the wind. The rudder, developed in China long before it appeared in Europe, could on some junks be retracted to pass through shallow water.

Chinese records tell of an expedition over the sea, in 219 B.C., to the "Isles of the Blessed," thought to have been Japan. By the second century A.D., Arab chronicles tell of Chinese junks on the Euphrates River at the head of the Persian Gulf.[27] Trade with the Arabs flourished, and by the ninth century A.D. there was a growing Arab community in Canton.[28]

Maritime trade in China boomed during the Sung Dynasty (A.D. 960–1279). By then, the magnetic compass had become standard equipment on seagoing junks, its principle having been known in China as early as the Han Dynasty (206 B.C.–A.D. 220). Arabs in contact with China during the Sung Dynasty may have brought knowledge of the compass to Europe,[29] but there is a strong tradition in Italy that the mariner's compass was developed independently in Amalfi early in the second millennium.[30]

In the thirteenth century, Kublai Khan, the Mongol Emperor of China, promised the Ilkhan of Persia a Mongol princess for a bride. An overland mission having failed to deliver her, Kublai Khan decided to send her by sea, and in 1272, he assembled a fleet comprising 14 junks manned by 600 crewmen and armed soldiers with supplies for two years. The Venetian travelers Niccolo, Maffeo, and Marco Polo were in the entourage as escorts for the princess, charged with responsibility for her personal safety. Although the Polos managed to deliver the princess to the Persian court in 1275, the voyage was not an easy one. Many of the six hundred who embarked with them perished en route.[31]

The Mongolian aptitude for land warfare did not carry over to war at sea. In 1274 and 1281, their attempts to land seaborne troops in Japan failed disastrously. Their final assault was dispersed by a great storm, giving rise to the Japanese legend of the *Kamikaze* (Divine Wind). Mongols mounted a similar invasion against Java in 1293. Although troops were landed successfully, the difficulties of supplying them by sea over such a great distance proved insurmountable, and the Mongol army had to be withdrawn.[32]

Chinese sea power reached a zenith in the Ming Dynasty (1368–1644). Between 1405 and 1433, with no ostensible purpose other than to demonstrate the splendor and munificence of the Celestial Empire, huge fleets were assembled and dispatched to those parts of the known world that could be reached by sea. Under the command of Admiral Zheng He (Cheng Ho), seven expeditions sailed into the East and South China seas, the Indian Ocean, the Persian Gulf, and the Red Sea, visiting nearly every inhabited land in that vast area.[33] The size of these expeditions was unprecedented, with the largest comprising 317 ships carrying 37,000 persons. Among these were interpreters trained in the languages of all the lands to be visited en route. Zheng He's junks, with their great size and unique construction, presented an awesome sight. The largest, a treasure ship, measured 444 feet overall with a beam of 180 feet. With a multitiered superstructure above the main deck, it carried nine masts and a rudder blade with an area of 450 square feet. The smallest ship of the fleet was a five-masted warship 180 by 68 feet, considerably larger than the ships used by Columbus and Magellan. Navigational equipment included compasses and elegant charts showing compass bearings. Little is known about Zheng He except that he was a Muslim and a eunuch. Being a Muslim, he could have learned much in the Arab communities in China about the places his fleet would visit.

When the hard-headed civil servants in the Ming bureaucracy compared the costs of the project with its benefits, they were dismayed. With his army bogged down in an expensive campaign in Indochina, the Mongols again threatening from the north, and domestic projects putting a strain on the imperial budget, the emperor was persuaded to forgo the extravagance of Zheng He's navy. In 1433, all further expeditions were cancelled abruptly. China withdrew from deliberate contact with the rest of the world and turned inward.[34]

Arabs

During the early Middle Ages, war and piracy kept the Mediterranean sea-lanes in constant turmoil;[35] while in the comparatively peaceful Indian Ocean, profits from maritime commerce stimulated the Arabs to develop swift, capacious sailing dhows and navigational techniques based on the astronomy and geography of the Alexandrian Greeks. The Indian Ocean became for Arab seafarers a familiar, well-traveled highway linking the Orient to the Middle East and Africa.

By the middle of the eighth century, the forces of Islam had conquered Syria, Mesopotamia, Persia, North and East Africa, much of the Iberian Peninsula, and India's Malabar Coast. In the wake of conquest, Arab merchants, shipowners, and seafarers poured into the Malabar ports where, encouraged by the Brahmin aristocracy, they soon became the dominant economic force. Forbidden by the rules of caste to engage in seafaring and profit-yielding commerce, the Brahmins were pleased to enlist the eager, capable Arabs as proxies.[36] Early in the tenth century, Arab seafarers had sailed across the Bay of Bengal and through the Strait of Malacca to Indochina, China, and beyond—as far as Korea and Japan.[37,38]

The vessels that carried the Arabs and their cargoes over the Indian Ocean probably were derived from earlier Egyptian and Phoenician hull designs.[39] Unlike the latter, which were held together with pegs and nails, Arab hulls were stitched together, through holes drilled in the planking, with ropes of oiled or tarred coconut fiber. During the tenth century, Arab shipbuilders in the Persian Gulf experimented with iron nails, but this construction did not prove popular with shipowners.[40] Although hulls constructed with nails required less-frequent maintenance, on long voyages the crews found it easier to make emergency repairs to the stitched hulls.[41] The application of lateen sails to deep-keeled, sharp-stemmed hulls gave the Arab ships of the Middle Ages exceptional speed and windward sailing ability, even for carriers of bulk cargo. Such ships were known to European sailors as dhows (from the Arabic *dawa*).

Before he was seventeen, Persian geographer Al-Biruni (A.D. 973–1062) had invented an improved device for measuring latitude, probably the ancestor of the *kamal*, an instrument used by Arab navigators in the fifteenth century. In later life, Al-Biruni felt confident enough in his knowledge of the world to challenge Ptolemy's concept of a closed Indian Ocean. Al-Biruni's world map showed the Mozambique Channel (which he did not consider navigable) connected with the "Ocean" (Atlantic) through a gap in the mountains to the south.[42]

During the fourteenth century, a Moor from Tangier, Ibn Battuta, traveled extensively over Arab trade routes in the Indian Ocean, visiting India, the Maldive Islands, and Ceylon. Taking passage from India to China on a Chinese junk, he served in that country as the ambassador for an Indian sultan. Accounts of his travels circulated widely throughout Islam; in the West, he became known as the "Muslim Marco Polo."[43]

One of the greatest of Arab navigators was Shihab'ud-din Ahmad bin Majid (Ibn Majid), whose career spanned parts of the fifteenth and sixteenth centuries, and who wrote widely on navigation and nautical astronomy. Some of his works were in verse,[44] and he was held in such high esteem as to be considered a saint by Arab mariners of his time. By a strange coincidence, he happened to be in Malindi, on the east coast of Africa (Kenya), when Vasco da Gama arrived there in 1498 with a Portuguese fleet seeking a sea route to India. Comparing notes with Gama and the Portuguese pilots, Majid was fascinated to learn that these "Franks" (the Arab term for Europeans) had entered the Indian Ocean from the Atlantic, thus proving Al-Biruni's hypothesis. Probably to demonstrate the sophistication of Arab geographical knowledge, Majid showed Gama detailed Arab charts of the Indian coast. Realizing that he could get no better guide, Gama somehow persuaded Majid to pilot the Portuguese fleet to India. While the Portuguese say that Majid went along because he was fascinated by the foreigners and their strange ships, Arab historians, outraged that one of their heroes had been instrumental in guiding the Portuguese to India, claim that Gama got Majid drunk before sailing off with him,[45] an odd claim for a man considered a saint.

Celts and Norsemen

From ancient times, the Celts of northwestern Europe made sea voyages in *curraghs*, skin boats not unlike Eskimo umiaks. About 600 B.C. a Carthaginian sea captain reported that such boats often made the 300-mile crossing from Brittany to Ireland.[46] In the early Middle Ages, many of the rocky islands to the north and west of Great Britain were settled by hermits and small communities of monks seeking solitude for their meditations, who reached these islands in curraghs that could be either rowed or sailed.

In A.D. 825, the monk Dicuil described islands two days' and two nights' sail north of Britain, probably the Faroes. The monks who had been living there had fled from Norse pirates, leaving behind only their sheep. Dicuil also reported that certain clerics had told him that between February and August of A.D. 795, they had been in Thule where, "in midsummer, there was enough light at midnight to pick the lice out of one's shirt." The Thule reported by Dicuil probably was Iceland, 240 miles north of the Faroes. When the Norsemen arrived in Iceland in A.D. 870, they found *papar* (Christian clergy) already living there.[47]

The Isle of Man, the Hebrides, and the Orkney Islands lie within a day's sail from the nearest point on the Scottish mainland. The highest peaks on the Shetlands and the Faroes can be seen at sea from the distance of a midsummer day's sail. Flights of birds probably provided clues to the presence of the Faroes and even of Iceland from the offshore islands north and west of Great Britain.[48]

The Irish legend of St. Brendan (sixth century A.D.) and the Welsh story

of Prince Madoc (circa A.D. 1170) both mention landfalls highly suggestive
of North America. While it is possible that they may contain a core of historical truth,[49] no one has yet presented evidence sufficient for upgrading
either story from the status of legend to history.

There are no such doubts about the voyages of the Norsemen that
brought them from Norway to Iceland (A.D. 870), Greenland (982–986),
and Labrador and Newfoundland (986–1000). Their descendents still live
in Iceland, where the old sagas describing these voyages are revered as a
link with the distant past. The settlements in Greenland died out at the
end of the fourteenth century, victims of the combined onslaughts of cli-
matic cooling, bubonic plague, and hostile Eskimos. The settlements in
North America were beset with internal dissension, treachery, and murder.
By 1020, the last remnants had returned to Greenland. While the Norsemen may have been the first European settlers in North America, they
cannot properly be said to have "discovered" it.[50] Although "discover" can
mean to see, find, or to gain knowledge of something heretofore unseen or
unknown, in its deeper, original sense, it means to reveal or to make generally known. The Norsemen did not do this with their ill-fated ventures in
North America.

Whatever may be history's final judgment of the voyages of the Norsemen in the North Atlantic, one cannot fail to be impressed by the audacity
of these sea rovers. They sailed without charts or compass into a frigid
ocean blanketed with mind-numbing fogs, bordered by treacherous shores
of rock and ice, and whipped by furious storms. Like the Polynesians, the
Norsemen developed vessels superbly adapted to their environment.
Their longships and knorrs were crafted with overlapping planks curving
gracefully upward to join high, recurved bow and stern posts. The latter
were securely joined to a keel hewn from a single piece of oak. Ribs, cross-
members and, in some cases, partial decking gave these sleek hulls the
strength to withstand the worst Atlantic storms. Powered by oars, the longships cut through the water smoothly and swiftly, conserving the energy of
the rowers. A steering oar was mounted on the starboard side aft. A square
sail suspended from a single yard could be mounted on a short, vertical
mast amidships for use in a following wind. With the wind slightly ahead of
the beam, the sail could be braced to windward with a pole so that forward
progress could be made without rowing.[51] The narrow longships were used
primarily for raiding; the beamier knorrs for cargo and passenger transport.
The latter very likely were the ships of choice for voyages to the Norse
settlements in Greenland and North America.

Norse navigators, like their Polynesian counterparts, did not use charts,
compasses, or instruments for observing the sun and stars. Although their

navigation was not as elegant as that of the Polynesians, it too depended on familiarity with the flight patterns of birds, the drift of seaweed, the temperature, color, and smell of the sea, and the character and abundance of marine life along the routes traveled.[52] Unlike those of the Polynesians, the routes followed by the Norsemen were studded with high, readily visible islands separated by relatively short distances of open water. Island hopping eventually led them all the way across the Atlantic. Yet once their destination was identified, the Norsemen were able to steer a direct course over the 1,500 miles of open water between Norway and Greenland.[53] To do this, they steered a westerly course by the sun, keeping between the Shetland and Faroe islands, which they could see in the distance. The abundant marine life over the edge of the shelf south of Iceland gave them another fix as they continued west toward Greenland, a huge target that was difficult to miss.

The Merchants of Venice

During the late Middle Ages, the Eastern Roman Empire began to crumble. As its power declined, Byzantium was unable to sustain the naval strength that for centuries had ensured its control over maritime trade in the eastern Mediterranean and Black Sea, and the Italian city-states of Venice and Genoa became the dominant sea powers. Genoese interests were focused on the Aegean and Black seas. There was a Genoese colony on the island of Chios in the Aegean, which Columbus visited;[54] his family is thought by some to have had roots there.[55] Venetian interests centered on the eastern Mediterranean, where huge profits were made by shipping Oriental merchandise into Europe from Turkish-held gateways in Syria and Egypt. As their Christian city was often at war with the Muslim Turks, Venetian merchants had to remain constantly on guard against attacks on their shipping, which were as likely to come from Barbary pirates as from Turkish naval forces.

Nevertheless, the mercantile interests of Venice required a practical accommodation with Muslim traders and with the Turkish and Arab officials through whom imported goods would have to pass on their way to Europe. Therefore, Venetian merchants developed far closer relationships with Islam than did other Christian states during three centuries of fruitless attempts to recapture the Holy Land from the infidels. Illustrative of this was the fictional characterization of a Moorish general in the Venetian army in Shakespeare's *Othello, The Moor of Venice*. Another was the alliance of Christian Venice with Muslim Egypt and Gujarat (a principality in northwest India) in a vain attempt to oust the Portuguese from India.

In England in the late Middle Ages, Venetian galleys docked along the River Thames, exchanging cargoes of Oriental silks and spices and Italian manufactured products for woolen broadcloths. After the birth of printing in the mid-fifteenth century, Venetian ships also brought books from Italian presses, among which was a novella by Giraldi Cinthio, printed in Venice in 1565, that inspired Shakespeare to write *Othello*.[56]

Fierce competition in the Mediterranean sea-lanes led to naval warfare between Venice and Genoa. A major stimulus for the European "Age of Discovery" in the fifteenth and sixteenth centuries came from an unlikely coincidence resulting from a battle fought in the Adriatic Sea in 1298. Genoa was victorious in a furious sea fight with the Venetians, and among her prisoners was the commander of a Venetian war galley, Marco Polo. In a Genoese prison Polo became friendly with another prisoner, Rustichello (Rusticiano) of Pisa, a writer of romances.[57]

Fascinated with Polo's tales of his travels in Asia, Rustichello committed them to writing, aided by Polo's success in getting his notes delivered to the prison from Venice. Rustichello's story, embellished to fit the form of the medieval romances with which he was familiar, is the only record of Marco Polo's remarkable adventures. The story, read by Christopher Columbus, a Genoese sailor of a later generation, triggered his ambition to reach by sea the riches of Asia that Marco Polo had described so vividly to his cellmate.

2
~~T~~he Iberians

 In *China, the Mongol Dynasty gave way to the Ming in 1368.* With the breakup of the Mongol Empire continuing into the fifteenth century, chaotic conditions in Central Asia prevented caravan travel along the Silk Road, stifling overland commerce between China and the Near East.[1] Oriental goods still arrived in the Near East by sea, but in 1453 the Turks captured Constantinople, gaining control of the sea route to Persia through the Black Sea. The Turks also controlled Egypt, another bottleneck for ships and caravans carrying merchandise from the Orient to Europe. The prices for silks, spices, and other Oriental luxury goods soared, severely draining Europe's gold and silver reserves. Each year, about $12,000,000 in gold was shipped from Venice to Alexandria.[2]

The last Moorish invaders had been driven from Portugal by the middle of the thirteenth century, but dynastic struggles on the Iberian Peninsula threatened the independence of the little kingdom. With valuable help from a contingent of English archers, Portuguese forces decisively defeated a Castilian army at Aljubarrota in 1385. A treaty signed in 1411 assured Portugal's independence from its powerful neighbor.

In addition to the help from the English, there were other important factors in the Portuguese victory. A former military monk and founder of the royal House of Avis, King João I enjoyed the support of two important segments of Portuguese society: the rural knights of the minor nobility, and the merchants and artisans of the cities and towns. The former formed the core of his army; the latter helped him to finance his military campaigns. Some of Portugal's most powerful nobles despised Dom João, considering him a usurper, and sided with the Castilians. The rural knights fought valiantly at Aljubarrota, and Dom João rewarded them with land grants and sinecures. They in turn taught their sons to respect the ideals of medieval chivalry that had earned for them the gratitude of their warrior king. For generations these ideals, exemplified by the legendary deeds of the Knights of the Round Table, continued to inspire the minor nobility of rural Portugal.[3] To sophisticated courtiers in Lisbon, however, such values had become laughable relics of a bygone age.

According to a popular story, Dom João, seeking an appropriate outlet for the exuberance of his sons, proposed an international tournament featuring jousting and other contests of martial skills. The young princes, deeming a mere tournament a dull way to test their manhood, proposed instead an attack on the Moorish fortress of Ceuta across the strait from Gibraltar. A holy crusade against the infidels would give them a better opportunity to prove their mastery of the arts of war. The English-born Queen Philippa, proud of her sons' crusading zeal, gave to each of the three eldest a piece of the true cross to wear in battle.[4] It makes a good story, and there may be more than a little truth in it, but there was also an economic motive for the attack: Ceuta was a terminus for caravans bringing West African gold across the Sahara into the bustling markets of Morocco.[5]

The Infante (Prince) Enrique was the third son of João I and Queen Philippa. In charge of assembling the fleet to carry the army to Ceuta, he also played a prominent role in the successful attack on the Moorish fortress. When they captured the city in 1415, the Portuguese seized a rich booty of gold and other precious commodities. Upon his triumphal return to Portugal, Enrique was knighted and made duke of Viseu and lord of Covilha. In 1420 he was elevated to the post of Grand Commander of the Order of the Knights of Christ, and made governor of the Algarve (the southern coast of Portugal) and Ceuta.

After Ceuta fell to the Portuguese, the caravans bringing gold across the Sahara were diverted to Tangier and other North African ports. As governor, Enrique was left with the profitless task of defending the North African citadel against repeated counterattacks. Wearying of defensive strategy, he decided to attack Tangier, a move that proved disastrous. As the attacking force withdrew, the defenders seized Prince Fernão, Enrique's younger brother, and held him hostage. The handsome, popular prince died in captivity when his brother was unable to raise the ransom demanded for his release. This tragic episode, and the accession of his nephew, Afonso V, to the throne of Portugal, sharply diminished Enrique's influence at court. He retreated to his estate at Sagres on Cape St. Vincent, the southernmost promontory of Portugal. There, adopting the asceticism of a scholarly monk, Enrique began the work for which he is best remembered. He became Prince Henry the Navigator.

Although the Ceuta campaign proved costly for the Portuguese, it did confirm for them the existence of a source of gold somewhere south of the Sahara, adding new stimulus to the dream of locating the mythical Prester John. Long sought by crusaders as an ally in their war with Islam, the Christian Kingdom of Prester John at first was thought to be in Central Asia. The notion probably was inspired by a twelfth-century Turkic tribal alliance whose leader was a Nestorian Christian.[6] After the failure of the Second Crusade in 1148, belief in the myth got a boost from a letter addressed to the pope and the principal kings of Europe. Signing himself Prester (Presbyter) John, with an appalling lack of modesty the writer proclaimed himself ". . . Lord of Lords and I surpass all the kings of the whole earth in riches, mercy and omnipotence." The letter was clearly a hoax, but the idea of a powerful Christian ally behind the enemy's lines was too appealing to be discarded easily, even though the Kingdom of Prester John had failed to materialize when Central Asia opened to travelers during its century and a half of Mongol rule. Then, Venetian traders heard rumors of a Christian kingdom (Ethiopia) somewhere to the south of Egypt. The notion that it might be the lost Kingdom of Prester John appealed to Queen Philippa of Portugal, who transmitted her enthusiasm with the idea to her sons.[7] The knowledge that the caravans bringing gold into North Africa came from the south, coupled with the idea that its source might be the Kingdom of Prester John, provided Prince Henry with an incentive to send ships southward along the West African coast in search of the elusive kingdom and its gold.

The rediscovery of the Atlantic islands in the fourteenth century by Genoese sailors attracted settlers from Italy, Mallorca, Normandy, Castile, and Portugal.[8] The Canary, Madeira, and Azores islands had been known to Carthaginians; the Canaries to Greeks and Romans.[9] Pliny the Elder referred to the latter as *Canaria*, after the large dogs found there. As it was the westernmost point of land known to him, Ptolemy drew his prime meridian through the Canary island of Ferro (now Hierro).

Prince Henry developed a strong interest in the Atlantic islands. In 1424 and 1427, he sent colonizing expeditions to Grand Canary to back up Portugal's territorial claims, but the native Guanches defended their territory with such unexpected vigor that the colonists were unable to win a foothold. These attempts were resented in Castile, which claimed sovereignty over all the Canary Islands. In the Treaty of Alcáçovas of 1479, Portugal finally recognized the Castilian claim.

Prince Henry's efforts to promote Portuguese settlement in the Madeira and Azores islands were much more successful. The wood, wine, grain, wool, fish, and livestock produced by the settlers found ready markets in Europe. Ships returning from voyages down the African coast stopped over in the islands to replenish their supplies of wood, water, and fresh food. For outbound ships sailing southwest along the African coast, the northeast trades provided a following wind. Returning required a long northwest tack to pick up the westerlies near the Azores. Then, with the wind astern on an easterly heading, the ships had clear sailing back to Portugal. Sailing far offshore into the Atlantic gave Portuguese mariners a familiarity with oceanic wind patterns unmatched by sailors from other parts of Europe.

It also gave rise to a new type of oceangoing vessel. Designed at Prince Henry's urging for exploratory voyaging, the caravel was a hybrid. With lateen sails like those on Arab dhows, caravels could sail close to the wind. In hull form they resembled the sleek, shallow-draft workboats used on rivers such as the Douro. Usually about 70 feet long and 25 feet in the beam, Prince Henry's caravels displaced about 50 tons, and with ample space for storage, they were able to carry supplies to sustain a crew of about twenty for voyages lasting many weeks.[10]

With adventure-seeking young noblemen, mariners, geographers, and makers of nautical charts and navigational instruments converging on Prince Henry's estate at Sagres, and the kingdom's best shipwrights building caravels at the nearby port of Lagos, the entire complex might be considered a precursor of the oceanographic institutes of our time. The personal fief of a crusading prince, its resources had been diverted from holy war to maritime exploration. The motives behind Prince Henry's search for gold and the Kingdom of Prester John were economic, military, and religious—virtually the same as those underlying modern oceanographic research (if scientific and religious motives may properly be considered analogous).

Prince Henry's caravels quickly penetrated beyond Cape Bojador. At 26° 15′ N, Bojador had been a psychological barrier to progress along the coast of West Africa. The sailors feared the fierce currents that could drive a coasting vessel onto the shallow sands of the dry, barren coast between Capes Noun and Bojador. Once the caravels proved that they could sail past the cape and return safely by tacking to the northwest until they could ride the westerlies home, voyages down the once-feared coast became routine.

Beyond Bojador lay Cape Blanco (*Branco* on Portuguese maps), where in 1444 Gil Eannes, one of Prince Henry's captains, obtained 200 black slaves. These caused a sensation in Portugal and improved Prince Henry's standing among those royal counselors who had criticized his previously profitless ventures as a waste of manpower and treasure that Portugal could ill afford.[11] It was the beginning of an unconscionable trade in human beings that would last for more than 400 years.

Beyond Cape Blanco, the land grew greener and more thickly populated.

A great river, the Senegal, was discovered, and then the Gambia. A captain named Nuno Tristão sailed into the mouth of the Senegal in 1444. Two years later, he sailed up the Gambia, where he and most of his crew were killed by tribesmen using poisoned arrows. Led by an apprentice seaman, seven of his crew, including several wounded, survived and were able to sail their caravel back to Portugal.[12] In addition to slaves, subsequent expeditions to the area brought back gold dust, ivory, and a kind of pepper known as the Guinea, or *malagueta* variety. By 1457, Alvise Cadamosto (Cà da Mosto), a Venetian merchant employed by Prince Henry, had discovered the Cape Verde Islands and sailed up the Senegal and Gambia rivers. His reports provide an entertaining account of African exploration in Prince Henry's time.[13]

After Prince Henry the Navigator died in 1460, his nephew, King Afonso V, found a way for the crown to profit handsomely from exploratory voyaging while investing very little. He leased trading rights to Fernão Gomes, a wealthy entrepreneur who, at his own expense, pledged to explore farther along the African coast by one hundred leagues (300 nautical miles) each year for five years. In return, the crown received a percentage of his profits. Under these terms, Gomes explored the West African coast to just below the equator. When Gomes's contract expired, the trading rights in West Africa were awarded to the crown prince. A new, exciting era of Portuguese discovery would begin in 1481 with the latter's accession to the throne as King João II.

During the reign of Afonso V, there seems to have occurred a curious event for which the evidence, while suggestive, is not strong enough to be accepted as historical fact. Nevertheless, it exemplifies how linkages between the closely related royal families of Europe stimulated the events that led to the great geographical discoveries of that era. Prince Henry is known to have received from his uncle, Eric VII, king of Denmark, a map of the North Atlantic drawn in 1427. In 1473, Pining and Pothorst, two German captains in the service of a later king of Denmark, Christian I, set sail from Iceland to explore the lands to the west. Afonso V of Portugal is said to have sent an observer, João Corte Real, to accompany the Danish expedition.[14] Although there is no direct evidence that he went on the expedition, Corte Real was given the governorship of Terceira, in the Azores Islands, as a reward for his discovery of "Stockfish Land." That term suggests knowledge of lands adjacent to the great codfish grounds of the northwest Atlantic. Is it only coincidental that the sons of João Corte Real, Gaspar and Miguel, made at least three voyages to explore these lands in the northwest Atlantic, and claimed them for Portugal? The results of their explorations appear on the Cantino world map of 1502, which shows forested land to the southwest of Greenland.[15]

By the time his lease expired, Fernão Gomes had explored the coastline of the Gulf of Guinea as far as two degrees south of the equator. The ensuing trade in gold, ivory, pepper, and slaves from this region proved immensely profitable. By the end of the fifteenth century, about $8,000,000 in West African gold arrived in Portugal each year;[16] much of it was gold dust sifted by tribesmen from riverbeds in present-day Ghana.

The Portuguese tried to prevent news of their African discoveries from leaking to the rest of the world, but the effort was in vain. Moving freely across national boundaries was a body of merchants, pilots, and professional mariners, more loyal to their employers and profession than to any king or country. Many were Italians, among them Christopher Columbus. A Genoese married to a well-born Portuguese lady, Columbus had lived and worked in Lisbon and in the Madeira Islands. In 1482–1483, he sailed on a ship carrying work crews and materials to construct São Jorge da Mina (Elmina), a Portuguese fortress on the Gold Coast.[17] It probably was there that he caught the gold fever that obsessed him for the rest of his life.[18] When the word spread in Castile that gold had been found in West Africa, poachers and pirates began to cut into the Portuguese monopoly. After war broke out between the two kingdoms in 1475, Queen Isabella of Castile legitimized the piracy by licensing privateers to raid the Portuguese treasure fleets.

The war between Portugal and Castile ended in 1479 with the Treaty of Alcáçovas. While the treaty recognized the legitimacy of the Portuguese trade monopolies in West Africa, it forced Portugal to renounce in favor of Castile all claims to the Canary Islands. After ascending the throne of Portugal in 1481, João II sought to protect his West African monopolies by building a chain of forts on the Gulf of Guinea, the largest of which was Elmina. During his reign, Dom João proved as enthusiastic for maritime exploration as his great-uncle, Prince Henry.

In December of 1481, Diogo Cão, an experienced sea captain in the service of Dom João, set sail from Lisbon for Africa with several caravels. He carried with him a number of *padrões* (stone crosses) to erect at prominent headlands along the coast, marking them as Portuguese territory. One, erected by Cão on a subsequent expedition, was found late in the nineteenth century and brought to Berlin. It reads: *"6685 years had passed since the creation of the world, 1485 since the birth of Christ, when His Most Illustrious and Serene Highness King João of Portugal ordered this pillar to be erected here by his knight, Diogo Cão."*[19] Stopping first at Elmina, Cão then crossed the Gulf of Guinea to Cape Lopez. From there he sailed south to the mouth of the Congo River, where he erected his first padrão and sent a scouting party upriver. When the scouts failed to return, he set sail again, heading south. A second padrão–found in 1892 and taken to Lisbon–was erected on a headland between 13° S and 14° S. Cão then returned to the mouth of the Congo to search for the men he had left behind. Failing to find them, he took aboard four native dignitaries and returned with them to Portugal, arriving in 1484.

In Lisbon, Cão claimed that he had reached the southernmost cape of Africa. Stirred by the prospect of reaching India by sea, King João rewarded him with knighthood and other high honors. The following year, Cão was given command of a second expedition and charged with entering the Indian Ocean by sailing eastward past the terminal cape he claimed to have found.[20] At the mouth of the Congo, Cão repatriated the native dignitaries who had accompanied him to Lisbon on the return from his first expedition. There to greet the ships from Portugal were the men of the lost scouting party. Failing to find their ship when they had returned from their journey upriver, they had taken shelter with Africans. Evidence of their travels on the Congo are still visible in inscriptions on a rock wall 80 miles above its mouth.[21]

After leaving the Congo, the expedition continued south. They left a padrão on a headland at 16° S, and another (the stone cross now preserved in Berlin) at Kaap Kruis at 21° 50' S. At this point, Diogo Cão disappears from history. He is thought to have perished somewhere near Kaap Kruis, but there is no reliable evidence to indicate what became of him. Whatever happened, the mission was aborted and the expedition returned to Lisbon, temporarily frustrating the hope of João II that his ships might reach India by sailing around Africa.

Determined to find a practicable route to India, the king decided on an undercover operation. He chose two knights of his court, Pedro de Covilhão and Afonso de Paiva, both fluent in Arabic, to travel to Egypt and the Near East. Disguised as Arab merchants, they were to gather intelligence about trade routes to India and the whereabouts of Prester John's kingdom. They departed in May of 1487 with a letter of credit from the Lisbon branch of the Marchioni, a banking house in Florence.

From Lisbon the pair proceeded to Rhodes, purchasing along the way a large quantity of honey. From Rhodes they sailed for Alexandria, representing themselves as honey merchants. After making their way to Aden, the two split up. Paiva headed for Ethiopia to look for Prester John, but stricken by some illness en route, he returned to Cairo, where he died. Covilhão went by sea to Calicut, on India's west coast. Heading north to Goa, he observed the flourishing trade in spices, precious stones, Arabian horses, and cotton. Leaving Goa, he sailed to Ormuz (Hormuz), noting its strategic location on the Persian Gulf. Taking passage on an Arab dhow, the intrepid Portuguese agent sailed to East Africa, where, following the coast to the south, he got as far as Sofala, the port from which gold from the mines of Zimbabwe had been shipped since ancient times. From the Arab captains and pilots with whom he sailed, Covilhão gleaned information that convinced him that farther south along that coast the Indian Ocean would merge with the Atlantic.[22]

Eager to get his information to his king, Covilhão made his way to Cairo, where he was met by two of Dom João's agents, Portuguese Jews fluent in Arabic and able to travel easily in the Near East. Having learned that Paiva had died before he was able to reach Ethiopia, the king had sent them to find Covilhão and to instruct him to continue the search for Prester John.

One of the agents, a shoemaker named João de Lamego, went back to Lisbon with the intelligence Covilhão had gathered in India and East Africa. The other, a rabbi from Beja named Abraham, accompanied Covilhão to Ormuz. Collecting all the intelligence that he could about the defenses of that strategic gateway to the Persian Gulf, Covilhão gave it to his companion to take back to King João. Abraham joined a caravan bound for Syria and eventually made it back to Portugal.

Apparently relishing the risk, Covilhão then traveled to Mecca, the holy city of Islam forbidden to all but faithful Muslims. From there he went north to Sinai, where he visited the Monastery of Saint Catherine. From Sinai he made his way to Zeila on the Somali shore of the Gulf of Aden. Heading inland across the Afar Plain, he climbed a steep escarpment onto the high plateau of Ethiopia, eventually arriving at its capital, Aksum. There he was welcomed by the Negus, the Coptic Christian ruler, who definitely was not Prester John, but who so esteemed his Portuguese guest that he refused to let him leave. Covilhão prospered in Ethiopia, married a noblewoman, and raised a family. In 1520, thirty years after his arrival, he was on hand to welcome the first Portuguese embassy to that country.[23]

To continue the search for a sea route to India, João II chose Bartolomeu Dias de Novais. A knight of the royal household who earlier had commanded a caravel on an expedition to the Gold Coast, Dias was given command of two caravels and a large store ship, with instructions to find out whether India could be reached by sailing beyond the farthest point reached by Diogo Cão. The expedition sailed from Lisbon in August of 1487, carrying aboard a number of Africans who were landed at various coastal villages as the ships sailed southward. In a sheltered bay (probably Baia dos Tigres at 16° 30' S, the storeship anchored while the two caravels continued on. After passing Kaap Kruis, the southernmost point reached by Cão, they put in at Angra Pequeña (Luderitz Bay) at 26° 35' S, where they rested five days, celebrating the Feast of the Nativity. Beating out of the harbor against a stiff northwest wind, they continued southward, holding well offshore. Dias shaped his course due south, keeping the wind, now at gale force, on the starboard quarter. The coast fell away to the east, and they soon lost sight of land. After thirteen days, the wind slacked and then shifted to the west. Changing course to the east, they ran before the wind for several days. Failing to raise land, Dias altered course to due north. Finally, on February 3, 1488, a lookout sighted land on the horizon ahead. By sailing far offshore to about 40° S, Dias's two caravels had cleared the southern capes and passed from the Atlantic into the Indian Ocean.

By this time the crews were in a state of panic. The gales and cold of the high southern latitudes terrified them, their food stores were nearly exhausted, and the coast ahead looked inhospitable. Landing near Mossel Bay, a shore party was attacked by natives. The crews wanted to turn back, but Dias insisted on following the coast to the east, erecting a padrão on a headland east of Algoa Bay. Because the coastline there trends to the north of east, Dias was convinced that he had rounded Africa's terminal cape, and that the way to India lay ahead. To the dismay of his crews, who implored their officers to convince him to turn back, Dias refused. Finally, off the mouth of a river thought to have been either the Great Fish or the Keiskama, the officers informed him that the men would go no farther. Dias reluctantly gave the order to turn back, but only after each of the officers signed a statement urging him to do so.[24]

Buffeted by gales and forced to take refuge in a sheltered bay behind the headland we know as the Cape of Good Hope, Dias sourly named it the "Cape of Storms." After doubling the stormy cape, the two caravels returned to the storeship at Baia dos Tigres, where they found only three of the nine crewmen left to tend it still alive. One of the three, sick with fever, died from the excitement caused by their arrival. Stripping the storeship of supplies that they could carry in the caravels, the crews burned the hulk and resumed their journey homeward, stopping at Principe Island and Elmina before finally entering the harbor at Lisbon in December 1488.

Dom João was disappointed that the expedition had turned back when the way to India lay before them, and he was less than generous in rewarding Dias for his accomplishment. To encourage other captains to do better, he changed the name of Dias's Cape of Storms to the Cape of Good Hope. Years later, on March 9, 1500, Dias sailed with a fleet headed for India under the command of Pedro Alvares Cabral. Ironically, a violent storm struck the fleet as it rounded the Cape, and Dias's ship vanished without a trace.

When Dias returned from his voyage around Africa, Christopher Columbus was present at the royal court in Lisbon. Probably helped by his wife's influential family, in 1483 Columbus had been granted an audience with João II to present his plan for sailing west to the Orient.[25] After listening politely to Columbus's proposal, the king referred it to a group of scholarly advisors, who unanimously recommended its rejection. Later, when his efforts to promote his project in Castile seemed to be bearing no fruit, Columbus applied to Dom João for another hearing. Cordially invited back to the Portuguese court, he arrived just in time to see his hopes dashed by Dias's discovery. With good prospects for reaching India by sailing around Africa, any interest the Portuguese may have had in a westward route evaporated. Returning to Castile, Columbus found that Queen Isabella had not yet made up her mind about his project. Like Dom João in Portugal, the queen had referred his proposal to a group of learned counselors who advised her to reject it.

Frustrated, Columbus prepared to go to Paris to present his plan to the king of France. In 1492, just as he was about to depart, Isabella finally decided to back his project. Although it is widely believed that she was swayed by Columbus's personal charm and powers of persuasion, she also was influenced by Luis de Santangel, an official of her husband's court, who saw potential for profit in Columbus's venture.[26] The queen's husband, King Ferdinand, a crafty and suspicious monarch, was not nearly as sanguine about its prospects, but in deference to his wife's wishes, he swallowed any objections he may have had.

On August 3, 1492, Columbus sailed from Palos on his epochal voyage. Another event occurred on that date that also would have a profound effect on the development of the Spanish nation. From Cadiz, sixty miles southeast of Palos, the last of Castile's Jews sailed into exile. Thus, while Columbus's voyage would lay the cornerstone of a vast Spanish overseas empire, the banishment of its Jews would stunt that nation's economic growth by robbing it of many of its finest minds, most skilled craftsmen, and most energetic entrepreneurs.

After his initial voyage of discovery, Columbus was certain that he had reached the island outliers of Asia. Three more voyages over the next twelve years, during which he explored the islands of the Caribbean and parts of the adjacent mainland, may have convinced him otherwise, but prudence probably prevented him from voicing any such doubts to his backers.[27] While Columbus's initial interpretation of his discoveries caused much excitement in Castile, it aroused little more than mild curiosity in Portugal. King João's savants did not consider the islands in the Caribbean to be outliers of Asia, but midocean islands such as the fabled Antilia, with which cartographers had filled empty spaces on maps and globes since the fourteenth century.

Rodrigo Borgia, a Spaniard as dissolute, extravagant, and unscrupulous as any of his infamous family, was elevated to the papacy in 1492 as Alexander VI.[28] Indebted to the Spanish sovereigns, in 1493 he jarred Portuguese complacency with a series of papal bulls acknowledging Spanish ownership of the lands discovered by Columbus, and reserving for Spain any lands west of a meridian drawn 100 leagues west of the Azores and Cape Verde Islands.[29]

Outraged at the possibility that the Spaniards might beat him to India just as he was preparing to exploit Dias's discovery, Portugal's João II protested vigorously. Unable to sway the pope, he entered into direct negotiations with the Spanish sovereigns. The outcome was the Treaty of Tordesillas of 1494, in which the line of demarcation was moved an additional 270 leagues to the west.[30]

The Spanish euphoria over Columbus's discoveries did not last long. After Columbus returned from his second voyage in 1496, the new lands in the west were visited by other explorers such as Ojeda, La Cosa, Pinzón, Vespucci, and Cabral. Their reports cast increasing doubt on Columbus's assertions that these lands were part of Asia. In both Spain and Portugal the realization dawned that there was a land barrier of considerable extent blocking a westward passage to Asia. With the new Caribbean colonies not producing profits of the magnitude Columbus had led his backers to expect, Spanish interest began to focus on the search for a passage to the Orient through or around the land barrier in the western Atlantic.

The Portuguese did not share the Spanish enthusiasm for finding such a passage. The long-sought eastern sea route to India had been opened by Vasco da Gama, whose expedition had reached Calicut and returned in triumph to Lisbon in 1499. Little more than a decade later, the lands bordering the Indian Ocean were being wrested from their Muslim and Hindu rulers by Portuguese sailors, soldiers, and seaborne knights. Among the latter was a gallant young nobleman, Ferdinand Magellan.

PART II

The Making of a Discoverer

The wreck of a Portuguese ship near Goa. Between 1501 and 1508, according to some estimates, eighty-one ships carrying 7,000 men sailed in six convoys from Lisbon to India.

Courtesy of the Newberry Library. Edward E. Ayer Collection.

3

ℳagellan's Early Years

From the obscurity of a quiet backwater, Ferdinand Magellan (*Fernão de Magalhães* in his native Portugal) was drawn into the maelstrom of Renaissance Europe. Like an eddy in a current, he quickly vanished, but not before generating a vortex that removed from the mainstream of geographic thought obsolete concepts like those that had deceived Columbus. Until recently in the land of his birth, Magellan was damned as a defector. In Spain, his adopted land, his accomplishments were belittled and a native-born hero was given most of the credit for their major consequences. Neither Magellan nor any of his immediate family lived to savor his achievement. Although the significance of the first circumnavigation was quickly appreciated throughout Europe, it remained for later generations to recognize the seminal nature of Magellan's contribution to it.

The precise time and place of Magellan's birth are unknown.[1,2] A claim filed by a relative after the discoverer's death states that, as a youth, he had lived in Nobrega, a district in northwestern Portugal where lands bordering the Lima River had been a fief of the Magellan clan since the eleventh century. Upon his arrival in Castile, Magellan registered as a *vecino* (resident) of Pôrto, a seaport at the mouth of the Douro River. Whether this implied that Pôrto was his birthplace, or merely the place where he had last resided, is not entirely clear;[3] but it is reasonably certain that Magellan was born between 1470 and 1480, and as a child lived in northwestern Portugal. Then as now, Pôrto was the principal commercial center of the region, and nearby Braga, with its ancient cathedral, the seat of the archdiocese.

The Magellans were descended from an adventurous French crusader who fought in the Iberian campaigns of Duke Eudes (Odo) of Burgundy toward the end of the eleventh century. The Duke granted that knight, whose surname was *De Magalhais*, land on the Lima River between Ponte da Barca and Ponte da Lima.[4] It is possible that a branch of the Magellan clan settled in Flanders, where a variant of the name, *Magelein*, is found in Ghent, a city with strong historic ties to Portugal.[5]

Ferdinand Magellan's parents were Rodrigo de Magalhães and Alda de Mesquita;[6] his paternal grandmother was a de Sousa, a noble family favored by the royal House of Avis. His father was sheriff of the port of Aveiro, an honorary position awarded for distinguished service to the crown. When they reached the age of puberty, Ferdinand and his brother Diogo (who took the de Sousa surname) were accepted as pages at the court of Queen Leonor in Lisbon, further evidence that the Magellans enjoyed the esteem of the royal family.[7] In Portugal, there were five grades of nobility below the royalty. The Magellans belonged to the fourth: "fidalgos entitled to a coat of arms and of noble lineage."[8]

The schooling of the children of Portugal's lesser nobility usually was limited to what was available from local churches, monasteries, and itinerant tutors. Magellan and his brother were more fortunate. Children educated at the royal courts of Renaissance Europe were taught reading and writing, religion, arithmetic, music and dancing, horsemanship, and martial skills. In Lisbon, court pages also were taught algebra, geometry, astronomy, and navigation. This emphasis on nautical studies had its origin with Philippa of Lancaster, the English princess who became queen of Portugal in 1387. Extraordinarily well-educated for her time, she had been tutored by Geoffrey Chaucer, who is said to have taught her the use of the astrolabe.[9] In an age when religious studies dominated education, she passed on to her children her deep respect for secular learning. Her son, Prince Henry, set Portugal on the path to becoming a great sea power.

At the court of Queen Leonor, pages were trained by the queen's brother, Manuel, the Duke of Beja. Cousin as well as brother-in-law to João II, the duke never enjoyed the king's affection or confidence. Manuel was related to the Braganza family, rivals of the House of Avis for the throne of Portugal, and the king distrusted him. After the premature death of the crown prince in 1491, Manuel became the legitimate heir to the throne, but João plotted to replace him in the royal succession with his illegitimate son, Jorge. The court split into two factions, one, including the queen, recognized Duke Manuel as the legitimate heir, while the other supported the king in his wish to be succeeded by Prince Jorge.[10] Since the Magellan family was loyal to King João, Magellan's relationship with Manuel was strained from the start. The antipathy that poisoned their later relations may well have stemmed from this source.

Nevertheless, it was a thrilling time for young Magellan to be at court.

Portugal

Scale 1 : 2,500,000

0   25   50   75

MILES

The king had enthusiastically resumed the policy of encouraging maritime
exploration initiated by Prince Henry. Each caravel that returned from an
exploratory voyage was an exciting source of new information promising
wealth and prestige for whomever might be chosen to participate in the

next expedition. The king's policy of keeping information about these voyages secret served mainly to stimulate speculation and gossip.[11]

In the rural north, Magellan had been accustomed to the respect commanded by members of his noble family. In Lisbon, supercilious peers regarded the youthful page as a country bumpkin. His resentment at their snobbery and the exciting stories of overseas discoveries heard at court combined to make young Magellan dream of winning honor and prestige with daring exploits in exotic, faraway lands.

Magellan remained in Lisbon after serving his apprenticeship as a court page. His name, along with those of his brother, Diogo de Sousa, and his friend (possibly cousin) Francisco Serrão, appear on the register of salaried palace employees.[12] Probably he was employed at India House (*Casa da India e da Guinea*), an annex of the royal palace. The agency for overseas trade and the jealously guarded repository for maps, globes, ships' logs, and reports of exploratory voyages, India House was home to the *Junta dos Matematicos* (the King's Science Council).[13]

Magellan felt keenly the excitement generated by the ships returning with reports of new discoveries and vast fortunes to be made overseas. He had ready access to the privileged information stored at India House, and he eagerly digested the new geographic concepts and navigational theories propounded by members of the Junta dos Matematicos – the same scholars who had interrogated Columbus when he sailed into Lisbon on his return from his first voyage. From the pilots, masters, and mates who sailed with the exploratory fleets, Magellan learned practical aspects of navigation not contained in the discourses of the savants of the Junta. By helping to outfit the fleets leaving for India each year, Magellan learned about rigging, caulking, repairing, and armaments, and about procuring and loading supplies for a long voyage. The more he learned, the more he hungered to sail with one of the great fleets.

Magellan's ambitions were rudely set back in 1495 when King João was stricken with uremia and died.[14] Duke Manuel, Magellan's nemesis and the legitimate heir, ascended the throne as Manuel I. The new king soon replaced many of his predecessor's counselors with his own supporters. While Magellan somehow managed to keep his modest position, the coveted commissions in the India fleets were reserved for royal favorites. With little chance of becoming a member of that select company, Magellan's prospects for sailing with an expedition bound for the Orient were anything but bright.

4

*I*ndian Ocean Campaigns

For a time after Manuel I ascended the throne in 1495, it appeared that Portuguese maritime exploration would languish. Many of the new king's counselors, from a faction out of favor during the reign of his predecessor, were more concerned with regaining confiscated lands and lost privileges than sponsoring expensive, risky sea voyages.[1,2] The new king was busy preparing for his wedding to Princess Isabel, the eldest daughter of Ferdinand of Aragon and Isabella of Castile—a union, Manuel hoped, that would produce an heir who could unite the kingdoms of the Iberian Peninsula.[3] This grandiose dream evaporated when Isabel died giving birth, and the child, Crown Prince Miguel, did not survive infancy. Yet despite these distractions, Manuel carried on the search for a sea route to India.

In July 1497, an expedition planned by João II before his death set sail from Lisbon with four ships and 170 men. Its leader was Vasco da Gama; its target, India. Taking his cue from Dias, Gama sailed far to the southwest in the Atlantic before turning east to double the Cape of Good Hope. The fleet sailed northward along the east coast of Africa, putting in at Malindi, where Gama was able to recruit an experienced Muslim pilot to guide them to India. Upon landing at Calicut on India's Malabar Coast, Gama took careful note of regional political structures, military forces, and the prices of merchandise (especially spices) in the busy markets. He also sought information concerning the Christian kingdoms that many in Portugal expected him to find there, probably because it was widely believed that the Apostle Thomas had preached and founded churches in India. The notion was fortified when Gama's men visited Indian temples and mistook stone carvings of Shakti, the Hindu mother goddess, for the Virgin Mary.[4,5]

In 1499, the return of two of Gama's ships, one laden with samples of spices, rare woods, and jewels, all purchased in Indian markets, caused a frenzy of excitement in Lisbon. The following year, a fleet of 13 ships carrying 1,200 to 1,500 men sailed for India under the command of Pedro Alvares Cabral.[6] En route, while standing to the southwest like Dias and Gama before him, Cabral raised the coast of Brazil and claimed it for Portugal. In 1503, Manuel dispatched three squadrons of three ships each to India, one of them commanded by Afonso de Albuquerque, who was to play a major role in the projection of Portuguese power into the Far East. It has been estimated that between 1501 and 1508, eighty-one ships carrying 7,000 men sailed in six convoys from Lisbon to India.[7] Together with the military occupation of its Moroccan conquests, these expeditions severely drained manpower from the small kingdom of Portugal.

The shortage of men for overseas military service brought the opportunity for which Magellan, laboring in frustration and obscurity at the palace, had been waiting. In 1505 he sailed for India with a fleet of 22 ships under the command of Francisco de Almeida, whom the king had named viceroy of India. In addition to the ships' crews, Almeida's fleet carried 1,500 soldiers, 200 artillerymen, and 400 supernumeraries, the latter a pool of unassigned gentlemen adventurers from which both military and civil needs could be filled. Among them were Magellan, his brother Diogo de Sousa, and his friend Francisco Serrão.[8]

Portuguese strategy in the Indian Ocean in the sixteenth century foreshadowed the amphibious tactics employed during the Pacific War of 1941–1945. Operating at the end of a 10,000-mile supply line and unable to commit substantial ground forces to their campaigns, the Portuguese used superior naval power to smash the combined fleets of the Egyptian-Venetian-Indian allies in the Arabian Sea, and seized strategic bases athwart the sea-lanes in East Africa and India. With their capture of Malacca in 1511, the Portuguese won control of the gateway to the Far East, shattering the centuries-old Arab monopoly of seaborne commerce in the Indian Ocean.

Magellan's name does not appear in the records until more than a year after Almeida's fleet arrived in East Africa. This probably was due more to the subordinate positions in which he served than to any lack of initiative or valor. Most of the reports addressed to the king dealt with the actions of senior commanders. Nevertheless, it was during this period that Magellan began to emerge from shadowy anonymity into history.[9]

Rounding the Cape of Good Hope on June 26, 1505, Almeida's fleet sailed northward along Africa's east coast, coming to anchor in the lee of the Primeiras Islands. From there, a ship with a detachment of soldiers was sent to reinforce the garrison at Mozambique, about 200 miles to the northeast. Almeida continued north with eight warships, the slower merchant vessels having separated earlier to sail directly to India. Arriving at the port of Kilwa on July 22, Almeida deposed a hostile sheik, replacing him with a rival who swore loyalty to the Portuguese king. The Portuguese then built a fort and assigned a military unit to defend it.[10]

From Kilwa the fleet proceeded to Mombasa, sacking and torching the city to punish another uncooperative sheik. Rejoined by several ships that had been detached from the fleet, Almeida then sailed across the Arabian Sea, stopping at the Angedive Islands (off India's Malabar Coast) where he built a fort. Arriving at Cananore on October 21, 1505, Almeida had himself formally installed as viceroy of India. He later transferred the seat of viceregal authority to Cochin because it was easier to defend, its cooperative rajah having permitted the construction of a Portuguese fort.

In the fall of 1505, loaded with spices and other merchandise, the annual flotilla left for Portugal, sailing from Cochin with the northeast monsoon. Observing the departure of the flotilla, the *Zamorin* (ruler) of Calicut and his Egyptian allies plotted a surprise attack on the remaining Portuguese warships. The Portuguese were advised of the plot by the Italian traveler Lodovico di Varthema, and a Portuguese squadron led by Lorenzo de Almeida, eldest son of the viceroy, intercepted and routed the attacking fleet off Cananore. In this action Francisco Serrão was cited for conspicuous bravery, and it may have been there that Magellan received the first of his numerous battle wounds.[11]

On December 26, 1506, Almeida dispatched a letter informing the king that he had ordered Captain Nuno Vaz Pereira to East Africa with supplies and reinforcements for the fortress at Sofala. The letter stated that ". . . among the servants of Your Highness [with Pereira] were . . . Fernão de Magalhães, Luis Mendes de Vasconcellos and Pero de Fonseca, who will serve as captains on the *bergantim* [based] at Kilwa."[12] Bergantims were large, oar-propelled, flat-bottomed galleys used for ferrying troops and supplies along the coast. Apparently Magellan had earned the respect of his commanding officer, and his assignment was deemed sufficiently important to report to the king.

Pereira left Cochin in November in the caravel *Espera*, calling at Malindi before proceeding to Kilwa, the base for the bergantim to which Magellan had been assigned. The actions of the Portuguese commander had irked the citizens of Kilwa, and rioting had broken out. Pereira soothed the ruffled feelings and replaced the inept commander. Late in January 1507, he sailed to Mozambique to meet with Albuquerque, who was en route to Aden with a squadron of warships to bottle up Egyptian naval forces in the

Red Sea. Pereira then sailed for Sofala on his primary mission to deliver troops and supplies to the beleaguered garrison at that ancient gold-shipping port.[13]

Leaving Vasco de Abreu in command of the Sofala garrison, Pereira sailed for India on September 19, 1507, on the ship *Sao Simao*. Among the young officers who accompanied him were Magellan and Serrão.[14] They arrived in Cochin in October, and Pereira was given command of the *Santo Espirito*, a caravel being built for the war fleet of Lorenzo de Almeida. By the time the *Santo Espirito* was ready, Dom Lorenzo's other ships had left Cochin, headed north in search of the Egyptian-Indian fleet. Instead of trying to catch up, Pereira steered south toward the Maldive Islands, probably intending to raid Arab shipping. Caught by a storm, the caravel was driven eastward to Ceylon (Sri Lanka). After a brief visit to that lush island, Pereira returned to India, joining the fleet the viceroy was assembling in Cananore.

There are no records of where Magellan was or what he was doing in 1508. It has been claimed that he returned to Portugal,[15] but that seems unlikely. There was barely enough time for the round trip; scarcely any for shore leave. Since he was with Pereira in India late in 1507 and again early in 1509, it seems reasonable to assume that his service in Pereira's command continued uninterrupted through that period.

While Pereira was making his inadvertent visit to Ceylon (presumably with Magellan aboard), Lorenzo de Almeida's ships were caught off a lee shore near Chaul (just south of modern Bombay) by a combined Egyptian-Indian fleet. The Venetian gunners on the Egyptian ships wrought havoc among the surprised Portuguese, who in two days of furious fighting lost 140 men, among them Dom Lorenzo. Unable to sustain further losses, the Portuguese fled.

Almeida was enraged by the loss of his son and the ignominious defeat of the Portuguese squadron. Vowing revenge, he set sail from Cananore on December 12, 1508, with twenty warships, among them Pereira's *Santo Espirito*. With the fleet were 1,300 Portuguese and 400 Malabar fighting men, the latter recruited in allied ports.[16] At Dabul (Dapoli), Almeida found some of the ships that had attacked his son's squadron. The viceroy ordered the bombardment of the fortress protecting the harbor, and when it was reduced to rubble, his troops assaulted the city with unparalleled ferocity. No one was spared; even women and children were put to the sword. The massacre was so terrible that it was memorialized in a curse widely used in the lands bordering the Indian Ocean: "May the wrath of the Franks (Portuguese) fall upon you as it did on Dabul."[17]

On February 2, 1509, near Diu on the Kathiawar Peninsula at the mouth of the Gulf of Cambay, Almeida's fleet sighted the Egyptian armada accompanied by Indian units from Cambay, Calicut, and Goa. Almeida gained a strategically advantageous position to windward of the enemy fleet and began to hammer their ships mercilessly with his artillery. On the second day of battle, when the Portuguese were able to close with the battered enemy ships, the *Santo Espirito* grappled with the Egyptian flagship. In the fierce hand-to-hand fighting that ensued, Captain Pereira was killed and Magellan was wounded.[18] The Turco-Egyptian admiral, Emir Husayn, escaped in a small boat, leaving the surviving ships of his fleet to flee or be captured. In a ghastly aftermath to the battle, Almeida ordered the torture of the Venetian gunners on the captured Egyptian ships. Their agony ended only when their broken bodies were strapped to the mouths of cannon and blown to pieces. The naval victory at Diu gave the Portuguese control of the sea routes between India and Europe, sounding the death knell for the Mameluke Empire in Egypt and for Venetian supremacy in the European spice trade.[19]

On March 8, 1509, Almeida returned to Cochin to find Albuquerque waiting smugly with an order from the king. Almeida was to surrender the viceroyalty and return immediately to Portugal; Albuquerque would become the new viceroy. Flushed with his victory at the Battle of Diu, and not disposed to hand his hard-won office to his bitter rival, Almeida had Albuquerque seized and placed in custody.[20] On April 21, a flotilla of four vessels dropped anchor in the port. Its commander, Diogo Lopes de Sequeira, carried orders from the king to reconnoiter Malacca, a strategically located stronghold on the narrow strait constricting the sea-lanes between India and the Far East. He also had orders to discover whatever he could about China.[21] Manuel realized that Malacca was the key to Portuguese control over the movement of spices from their sources to markets in India and Europe. Disturbed by reports that the Spaniards were seeking a westward route to the Spice Islands, he had repeatedly urged Almeida to get there first and, if possible, establish a base at Malacca. He had little appreciation of Almeida's problems with enemy naval forces along the Malabar Coast, and was impatient to secure Malacca and the Spice Islands.

In Cochin, Magellan was recovering from the wounds received in the Battle of Diu. On July 30, 1509, he signed a receipt for twenty sacks of wheat, partial payment for his military services.[22] At about the same time, Sequeira requisitioned a *taforea*, a supply ship capable of carrying horses and livestock, from Almeida's fleet. For the expedition to Malacca, its captain, Garcia de Sousa, had to recruit fighting men to supplement the crew. Among the seventy who signed on were Magellan and Serrão.[23]

On August 18, the flotilla left Cochin provided with rutters (sailing direc-

tions) and an Indian pilot. After erecting padrões at two locations in northern Sumatra where they were well received by the sultans, they anchored
off Malacca on September 11, 1509.[24]

The appearance of armed Portuguese ships sparked consternation
among the Arab merchants who conducted much of that port's thriving
business. From Muslim contacts in East Africa and India, they knew of the
efforts of the Portuguese to break the Arab-Venetian monopoly in the spice
trade, and of the ferocity with which these "Franks" attacked all who opposed them. The Portuguese were treated courteously, but with great caution. On the third day after their arrival, the sultan received a delegation
from Sequeira, accepting them as envoys of the king of Portugal. A peace
treaty was drafted, and permission was granted for the Portuguese to open
a *feitoria* (trading post) near the waterfront. Charmed by the courtesy and
apparent goodwill of the sultan, Sequeira sought permission to begin trading immediately so that he could load his ships in time to sail before the
approaching end of the southeast monsoon. The sultan readily assented.
In a warehouse some distance from the waterfront, he had a large quantity
of pepper that he would trade if Sequeira would provide a work party to
transport it to the pier.

In his eagerness to get the pepper, Sequeira ignored warnings from Chinese merchants that the sultan was planning treachery. The next morning,
using all the flotilla's longboats, he dispatched 100 men to the warehouse.
A friendly Malay girl he had met ashore warned Serrão of a possible ambush, but having been placed in charge of the work detail, Magellan's intrepid friend set out for the warehouse anyway.[25] The warnings proved
justified. Urged by Arab traders who had convinced him that the only good
Portuguese were dead ones, the sultan planned to trap the work party at
the warehouse and seize the lightly defended ships. As Sequeira's men
headed inland, a fleet of sampans converged on the ships, their grinning
occupants assuring the remaining crews that they had come to trade.

Captain de Sousa permitted only a few of the natives to board his taforea, but became alarmed when he saw many of them swarming aboard the
flagship. He sent Magellan over in a skiff to warn Sequeira of the danger.
Magellan found Sequeira in his cabin, stripped to the waist, blithely playing
chess with a Malay nobleman under the watchful eye of eight armed Malays who had crowded into the cabin, awaiting the signal to cut him down.
Only after Magellan told him that his ship was surrounded by potentially
hostile sampans did Sequeira sense the danger. He immediately cleared
the ship of visitors and sent the mate aloft to assess the situation ashore.
The mate, seeing signal smoke from the palace and noting that a mob had
moved between the shore party and its boats, bawled out that a trap was
being sprung.[26]

When they heard the mate's shouted warning, the men in the shore party saw that they had been cut off. Most of them fled toward the warehouse, but Serrão and some others tried to fight their way through the mob to the boats. They surely would have been killed had not Magellan and two other men from the taforea jumped into the skiff and raced to the beach, where they recaptured one of the longboats from the Malays and held a beach-head long enough for Serrão and the remnants of the embattled shore party to pile into the longboat. They were then obliged to fight through the hostile sampans to get back to their ships. Many in the shore party who had fled inland were captured. The rest, and many who tried to fight their way to the beach with Serrão, were killed. The exact number of casualties is unknown, but it would appear that more than half the shore party were killed or captured.[27]

The debacle shattered Sequeira's hopes for establishing a foothold at Malacca. Meeting in council aboard the flagship, most of the flotilla's captains wanted to try to rescue their captured shipmates and bombard the city in retaliation. Sequeira took a more cautious approach, offering ransom for the captives. He waited two days but received no response. Then, worried that the favorable monsoon winds would shift, Sequeira ordered the flotilla to sail for India.[28]

Shortly after leaving Malacca, the flotilla encountered a large, well-laden junk, and Captain Nuno Godin's ship gave chase. Portuguese adventurers in those times regarded the Indian Ocean as their private lake, and did not consider attacks on foreign merchantmen to be piracy. Once overhauled, the junk's crew fought furiously and repelled the boarding party. In a surprising turnabout, they swarmed aboard the attacking vessel.[29] Among the men-at-arms fighting desperately to save the Portuguese ship was Francisco Serrão. It is a matter of record that Magellan, accompanied in the skiff by Nuno de Castelo Branco and Martim Guedes, again came to his friend's rescue.[30] The loyalty between comrades who have shared the rigors of combat has been described as akin to love.[31] The bond thus formed between Francisco Serrão and Ferdinand Magellan would have consequences more far reaching than usually produced by the friendship of former comrades-in-arms, for theirs would threaten the foundations of the Portuguese maritime empire they had helped to build.

Undaunted by the nearly disastrous consequences of their first attempt to seize a junk, Sequeira's men tried again. This time their target was even more richly laden than the one that got away, and they succeeded in capturing it. The junk was taken in tow by the flagship, and a prize crew of twenty-eight under Jerónimo Teixeira went aboard, confining the Malay crew below deck. The desperate Malays holed the ship below the water-line, and it began to take on water. Fearing that it would sink and take the

flagship down with it, Sequeira ordered the tow rope cut, leaving Teixeira
and his men adrift on the foundering vessel. Their cries faded into the distance as the current carried the sinking junk back toward Malacca. Para-
lyzed by indecision, Sequeira was disposed to leave the prize crew to its
fate, but Magellan and Castelo Branco denounced that option as a disgrace. "Never could there be a better prize," Magellan argued, "than to save
the lives of our men on that junk!" Irritated, Sequeira ordered the two to
the rescue. Although it was a difficult and dangerous task, they took the
longboat and, aided by several shipmates from the taforea, succeeded. The
court chronicler who reported the story failed to say what happened to
the Malay crew.[32]

These incidents reveal much about Magellan's character, and illustrate
how bonds formed between members of small military units contrast with
the callous indifference of some in high command who, in the struggle for
power, lose their humanity.

Misfortune continued to plague Sequeira. One of his caravels was
wrecked in a storm, and the taforea was so badly damaged that it was
beached on a small island and dismantled. The remaining ships finally
made landfall at Travancore (a region on the Malabar Coast south of Cochin) in January 1510.[33]

Learning that Albuquerque had succeeded Almeida as viceroy, Sequeira

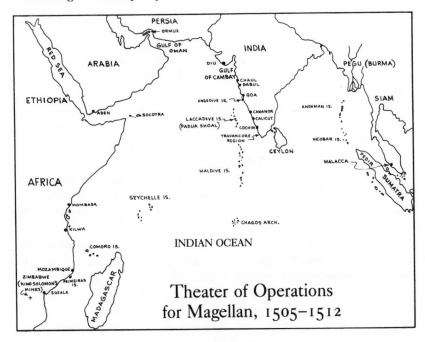

Theater of Operations
for Magellan, 1505–1512

sailed for Portugal, where he reported to King Manuel on the expedition to Malacca. Portraying himself as the hero of a tactical triumph, he omitted or disguised details that would have revealed his incompetence and coward-ice. Nevertheless, scraps of intelligence from Sequeira's report confirmed for the king the strategic position of Malacca with respect to trade routes between the Far East and the Indian Ocean. And the information obtained earlier in India from Varthema confirmed also that the Moluccas, islands he had visited east of Malacca, were the principal sources of cloves and nut-meg. The same intelligence also registered with Magellan and Serrão who, after landing at Travancore, embarked for Cochin.

On January 3–4, 1510, Albuquerque launched an assault on Calicut. It is not likely that Magellan and Serrão participated in that battle, for they had arrived in Travancore, 200 miles to the south, that same month. A story about Magellan having been wounded at Calicut, if not in error, may refer to the battle with Calicut naval forces that took place off Cananore in 1506.

Later in January Magellan left Cochin on a *nau* (cargo vessel) bound for Lisbon. Whether he was discouraged about his prospects in India with Al-buquerque as viceroy, or was war-weary and homesick, can only be conjec-tured. Whatever the reason, his homeward journey was short-lived.

The ship he boarded was one of three laden with spices and other mer-chandise accumulated in Cochin since the departure of Almeida. One ship left on schedule, but the other two (on one of which Magellan was a pas-senger) were delayed and never were able to overtake the first. On the sec-ond or third night out, the two ships, sailing together, ran aground on Padua Bank near the Laccadive Islands. As the weather was clear and calm, the grounding probably was caused by a pilot's error. The passengers and crew of both ships took to the boats and landed on a nearby islet. The fine weather made it possible to salvage most of the cargo of pepper and a good supply of fresh water and food, but since no one knew of their plight, it was clear that the longboats would have to sail to the mainland more than 100 miles to the east to summon help.[34]

Early in the sixteenth century, the traditions that encouraged selfless, disciplined behavior among mariners facing dire peril were not yet com-monplace. Assuming that rank and social standing gave them priority, the officers and the gentlemen passengers piled into the longboats. The mood of the seamen, who feared abandonment, grew ugly. They seized hold of the longboats and would not let them shove off from the beach.

Sensitive to the concerns of the seamen, Magellan called out, "Let the captains and gentlemen go, and I will remain with you sailors if they will give us their word of honor that upon arriving [on the mainland] they will send help for us!" The men quieted down and, having given their word, the officers and gentlemen prepared to depart. Magellan was in one of the boats discussing the unloading of the cargo when a seaman called out to him, "Oh, Mr. Magellan Sir, didn't you promise to stay with us?" He had indeed, Magellan assured the sailor. Leaping to the beach he cried, "See me here!"[35]

The two longboats sailed into Cananore eight days later, and a caravel was dispatched immediately to rescue the shipwrecked men and to recover the pepper. Given the tenor of those times, it may not be too cynical to wonder whether the rescue would have been so prompt, or even undertaken, were it not for the valuable cargo. A court chronicler who rarely had anything good to say about Magellan stated that the officers and gentlemen had indeed intended to abandon the sailors. Magellan, he said, stayed with them because he had a friend among them, ". . . a fellow of little account."[36] The caravel returned Magellan, the shipwrecked sailors, and the salvaged cargo to Cananore, whereupon Albuquerque immediately assigned the rescued mariners to a task force being prepared to attack Goa.[37] The city fell to the Portuguese on February 17, 1510, but unremitting pressure from enemy land forces forced them to evacuate it on May 30.

On October 10, 1510, in Cochin, Albuquerque convened a council of naval and merchant captains, businessmen, and government officials, hoping to get them to approve his plan to use merchant vessels to supplement his naval forces for a second assault on Goa. Magellan was among the 16 council members whose testimony has been preserved. Forthright in opposing Albuquerque's proposal, he demonstrated a keen appreciation of the seasonal monsoon in that part of the world. He pointed out to Albuquerque that headwinds would prevent the fleet from reaching Goa before November 8, and that if delayed, the merchant captains would have too little time before the change of the monsoon to repair their ships, load cargoes, and sail for home.[38]

Several other council members, Gonçalo de Sequeira in particular, were even more hostile to Albuquerque's plan. Although their opposition displeased him, their reasoning was too strong for the new viceroy to deny. He grudgingly allowed the merchant captains to decide for themselves whether accompany the war fleet to Goa. None did, and the council spokesmen who supported them earned the enmity of the viceroy. While there was no mention of Magellan in Albuquerque's correspondence with the king concerning these matters, it did contain a bitter denunciation of Gonçalo de Sequeira.

Toward the end of 1510, four ships from Lisbon commanded by Diogo Mendes de Vasconselos arrived in Cochin. With them was Giovanni da Empoli, representing the Gualterotti, a trading company in Flanders. Anticipating that the Portuguese would soon control Malacca, the company had sent Empoli to establish a trading post there at the earliest opportunity. Still convinced that he needed merchantmen for the assault on Goa, Albuquerque commandeered the four ships, and when Vasconselos and his captains protested, Albuquerque had them thrown into jail. In a letter to his father, Empoli complained bitterly of Albuquerque's high-handedness.[39]

Despite giving a good account of himself in the assault on Goa, Francisco Serrão also ran afoul of Albuquerque. In April 1510, he was given command of a caravel and ordered to Cochin for supplies. Once there, the sorry condition of his ship induced Serrão to have it repaired. Furious over the delay, Albuquerque accused him of dereliction of duty, had him arrested, and ". . . gave him good punishment."[40]

While Almeida's veterans showed little enthusiasm for the new viceroy, many remained in India to serve under him. Other than the report of his opposition at the Captains' Council in Cochin in 1510, there is little mention of Magellan in Albuquerque's records. With little to show for his years of military service but the scars of his wounds, and not wanting to return to his homeland impoverished, Magellan undertook a business venture designed to make him a handsome profit.

On October 2, 1510, before witnesses, Magellan signed a contract with Pedro Annes Abraldez, a merchant preparing to return to Portugal with the annual fleet. The terms of the contract stipulated that Magellan was to lend the merchant, at 10 percent interest per annum, the sum of 10 portugueses (gold coins each equivalent to 10 silver cruzados, one cruzado being was worth about $30 U.S.) to purchase pepper. So Magellan might realize a return on his investment commensurate with the enormous profit (nearly 500 percent) Abraldez expected from the sale of the pepper in Lisbon, the merchant agreed to pay him a premium of 100 cruzados plus a consignment of pepper worth 40 cruzados in Lisbon.[41] Thus, for his investment of 100 cruzados, Magellan expected a yield of 140 percent. Usury laws forbade interest charges of more than 10 percent per annum for cash loans, but premiums disguised as bonded guarantees backed by commodity shipments,[42] while not strictly legal, were commonplace among Portuguese businessmen in 1510. Today, Magellan's investment of 100 cruzados would be worth about $3,000 U.S. Unlike many Portuguese adventurers who enriched themselves from looting and piracy, he had little to show for his five years in the Orient.

In March 1511, Albuquerque sailed from Goa with a fleet that included Serrão's caravel. Magellan was with the fleet, although on what ship or in what capacity is not clear. Their destination was Aden, where Albuquerque intended to block shipping from entering the Red Sea, where cargoes were unloaded to be transported overland to Alexandria en route to Venice. Portugal, with its sea route around Africa, would then control the transport of spices to Europe.

The pilots predicted contrary winds, but Albuquerque ignored them and pressed on. He should have reconsidered, for after passing Padua Bank the fleet ran into the headwinds the pilots had warned of. Albuquerque then decided to attack Malacca instead, determined to punish the sultan whose treachery had prevented the Portuguese from reaching the Spice Islands.

After touching at northern Sumatra, taking unwary junks as prizes during its progress down the Strait of Malacca, the fleet of 19 warships hove-to in front of the port of Malacca on July 1, 1511. The sultan had 20,000 fighting men and 3,000 cannon. Against this formidable defense, Albuquerque had but 800 Portuguese assault troops and 600 Malabar archers, but the fortress fell after a seige lasting six weeks and a bloody battle. A contemporary Portuguese chronicler said of the battle, "Assuredly, from the time we began the conquest of India until now was no affair undertaken so arduous as this battle . . . nor one in which so much artillery was employed, or in which so many were engaged in the defense."[43] Magellan participated in the assault and final subjugation of Malacca, giving ". . . a very good account of himself."[44]

In November 1511, after sending missions to Burma and Thailand, Albuquerque dispatched a squadron of three ships under Antonio de Abreu in search of the Banda and Molucca islands that Varthema had identified as major sources of nutmeg and cloves. Francisco Serrão commanded one of them. A Spanish source claimed that Magellan commanded the third ship,[45] but this is not supported by Portuguese records.[46]

More likely he remained in Malacca, gathering intelligence about the archipelago to the east from local merchants, the crews of junks anchored in the harbor, and stevedors and warehousemen along the waterfront. He seems to have stayed in Malacca at least until the second half of 1512.[47] While there, Magellan acquired a young Malay slave to whom he gave the Christian name Enrique. A loyal and devoted servant until his master's death, Enrique was to play a significant role in Magellan's great enterprise.

For Francisco Serrão, leaving Malacca with Abreu's expedition in November 1511 was the beginning of an extraordinary adventure. Before returning to Cochin, Albuquerque had instructed Abreu and his captains not to molest commercial shipping or villages and towns encountered en route. Local authorities were to be treated with courtesy and respect, and their laws honored. A junk was purchased in Malacca to accompany the squadron and to carry trade goods. Its Indian captain would assist with the trade negotiations, and its Javanese pilot would guide them through the archipelago ahead. In addition to its Portuguese pilot, each of Abreu's ships carried a Malay pilot.[48]

Sailing southeast from Malacca, the expedition passed Billiton Island, then turned east, coasting the northern shores of Java, Bali, and Sumbawa. Continuing east through the Flores Sea, they entered the Banda Sea, then headed north to touch at Buru and Amboina. At Ceram, Serrão's ship, an Indian vessel captured at the Battle of Goa, began leaking badly. When it was determined that it could not be repaired, it was abandoned and burned.

With Serrão and his men crowded aboard the flagship, the squadron made its way to the island of Banda, where they procured another junk. While there, they found an abundance of nutmeg and mace for which they exchanged most of their trade goods, enough to fill their holds. With the monsoon about to shift, Abreu decided to return to Malacca with his precious cargo, but a storm dispersed the flotilla en route. Serrão's junk grounded on a reef in the Penju Islands 37 leagues west-southwest of Banda, stranding him with nine or ten of his crew on a small, uninhabited islet.[49] They kept a sharp lookout for pirates, and when they spotted a junk sailing toward them, hid in the bushes above the beach. While the crew of the junk investigated the wrecked vessel, Serrão and his men rowed quietly out to the junk and overpowered the few crewmen guarding it. When the junk's crew implored Serrão not to maroon them on the waterless islet, he promised not to if they would take him and his men to Amboina. There, merchants from Batochina (Halmahera) urged the Portuguese to go to the aid of the sultan of that island, who was at war with a rival. Serrão agreed, and led the sultan's army in a route of the enemy forces.

News of the incident spread quickly through the islands. In the Moluccas, two sultans, Boleyse (Abdul Hassan) of Ternate, and Almanzor (Al Mansur) of Tidore, were involved in a dispute. Although related, they were constantly at each other's throats. Boleyse invited Serrão to visit Ternate, an opportunity that he eagerly seized. Serrão and the six men who accompanied him were the first Portuguese to set foot in the fabled Spice Islands.[50] Demonstrating a talent for diplomacy as impressive as his military skill, Serrão resolved the dispute between the two sultans, although more to the satisfaction of his host than to Almanzor who, as part of the settlement, was required to give his daughter in marriage to Serrão. Pleased with his triumph, Boleyse made Serrão his grand vizier. The colorful Portuguese adventurer lived on Ternate in paradisiacal splendor until his death eight years later.

Junks sailing to Malacca brought Magellan letters from Serrão, telling him of the delights of the Moluccas and the unparalleled opportunities for trading in those islands. Excited by his friend's letters, Magellan sailed for Lisbon at the earliest opportunity, sometime between 1512 and 1513, probably intending to use the funds he expected to collect from Abraldez to purchase copper and other commodities for use as trade goods. In Portugal he would drift inexorably toward the shattering experience that led him to leave his native land forever and offer his services to the king of Spain.

5

*H*umiliation and Disgrace

 W*hen he arrived in Lisbon, Magellan learned that Abraldez* had died and that the merchant's father had fled to Galicia to escape his son's creditors.[1] Magellan had invested his entire fortune with Abraldez, and now its recovery hinged on the outcome of a lengthy and uncertain legal process. He had no funds to purchase the goods needed for starting a trading enterprise in the Moluccas, and prospects for recovering any part of his investment seemed remote until he learned that the Crown had not yet paid for a consignment of pepper purchased from Abraldez. Clutching at straws, Magellan petitioned Manuel for the funds owed him by Abraldez plus ten percent accrued interest and legal expenses incurred in filing claims against the estate. But the king and his ministers, never eager to authorize disbursements from the royal treasury, were in no hurry to consider his petition. Their attention was focused on a far more urgent matter.

Early in 1513, the town of Azamor (Azemmour) on Morocco's Atlantic coast refused to pay the annual tribute levied by Portugal since the conquest of the town during the reign of João II.[2] Muley Zayam, the Moroccan governor of Azamor, raised an army with which he hoped to defend the city from the anticipated Portuguese assault.

Determined to put down the rebellion and discourage further acts of defiance in his Moroccan territories, Manuel ordered the assembly of a punitive expeditionary force. With nearly 500 ships, 13,000 foot soldiers and 2,000 cavalry under the overall command of the king's nephew, the duke of Braganza, it was the largest military force ever to sail from Portugal. The fleet put to sea on August 13, 1513, with veteran navigator João de Lisboa as chief pilot.[3] Many able-bodied veterans of the Portuguese campaigns in

East Africa and India were called up to serve in that expeditionary force; Magellan and his brother, Diogo de Sousa, noblemen from a district that traditionally provided military forces when required by the Crown, were among them. They were assigned to a cavalry unit commanded by Captain Aires Telles.[4]

The expense of providing a suitable mount was an unwelcome burden for the financially strapped Magellan, who found a horse of no better quality than the impoverished knight Don Quixote's Rocinante. He was among the first to debark at Azamor, riding up to the walls of the city before the main body of troops had landed. In the ensuing skirmish, his horse was killed by a Moorish lance and he barely escaped with his life. Later, after the city had surrendered to the Portuguese, an army quartermaster offered him 3,700 reis to compensate for the loss of his horse, probably reflecting what the quartermaster thought the nag was worth. Since the usual rate for officers' horses lost in battle was 13,000 reis, Magellan was indignant. Going over the heads of his superiors, he wrote directly to the king, urging him to correct the injustice since ". . . [the horse] was killed in your service, in honorable combat, and at great danger to my person."[5]

Dom Manuel was never noted for generosity, even to those who served him well. He may have been offended by Magellan's letter, if indeed it was ever brought to his attention. That a minor court functionary should request the intervention of the king in such a trivial matter was presumptuous. To Manuel, busy with affairs of state, Magellan was a pest, a gadfly repeatedly bothering him with petty problems of personal finances.

The surprisingly quick surrender of Azamor during the first assault resulted from a lucky shot by a Portuguese gunner. When a cannonball struck and killed their general, Cid Mansour, the demoralized Moorish defenders capitulated. But the desert warriors outside the city were less easily discouraged, and their frequent raids maintained unrelenting pressure on the Portuguese. Whenever the raiders appeared, the cavalry would sortie from the city to drive them off. Having obtained a replacement mount, Magellan was one of the defenders who rode out daily to fight. In one skirmish, an enemy lance penetrated his knee, leaving him partially crippled; for the rest of his life he walked with a limp.[6]

More courtier than soldier, the duke of Braganza returned to Lisbon shortly after Azamor's fall, receiving much acclaim and gladly accepting the credit for its capture. Replacing him as commander at Azamor was João Soares, count de Meneses,[7] a veteran soldier who developed a strategy that finally stemmed the attacks by the desert raiders. Aware of Magellan's crippling wound and appreciative of his courage in battle, Soares appointed him quartermaster-major (*quadrilheiro-mor*), a post coveted by senior officers of the army because it involved the disposition of the spoils of war.

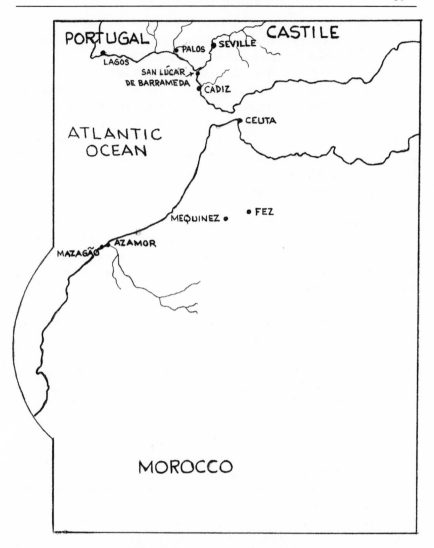

The Moroccan Campaign

The senior officers, especially those who had been close to the duke of Braganza, resented the appointment of a junior officer such as Magellan to the prized post. The count ignored their grumbling, probably confident that in Magellan he would have an honest quartermaster.

Toward the end of March 1514, a Moorish army made up of troops from Fez and Mequinez (Meknès) took the field, intent on driving the Portuguese from Azamor.[8] Learning of the impending attack, Soares dispatched

troops to intercept the enemy, and the opposing forces clashed early in
April. The first skirmish failed to slow the enemy advance, but a second
attack, supported by allied tribesmen, routed the Moorish army.

In their headlong flight, the Moors abandoned a huge herd of livestock
comprising 200,000 goats and 3,000 camels and horses.[9] It fell to Magellan
and the army's other quartermaster-major, Captain Álvaro Monteiro, to dis-
tribute the spoils fairly among the victors. Without proper corrals to
confine and separate the braying, milling mass of frightened animals, it
proved impossible to make an accurate count. To oblige the allies who had
helped route the Moorish army, and to diminish the size of the herd they
would have to drive to Azamor, Magellan and Monteiro allowed the tribesmen to take some of the goats, thus playing directly into the hands of jealous officers who begrudged them their posts. On returning to Azamor, the
two quartermasters were accused of improperly disposing of Crown property. Under cover of night, the charges read, Magellan and Monteiro had
delivered 400 goats to the enemy, pocketing the proceeds of the sale.[10]
These were serious charges, for in addition to the misappropriation of
Crown property, they included the treasonous act of aiding the enemy.

In May 1514, João Soares died, and he was succeeded as garrison commander by Pedro de Sousa, who, when he arrived at Azamor, probably was
unaware of the accusations against Magellan. With Soares out of the way,
the accusing officers stepped up their campaign of misinformation and rumor, bringing the matter to the attention of their new commandant, who
passed it on in a report to the king. Showing an incredible naiveté with respect to the Machiavellian realities of the royal court, Magellan scorned the
charges as unworthy of formal response. Instead, he left his post without
even bothering to ask the new commandant for permission, and departed
for Lisbon, where he requested an audience with the king.

Dom Manuel granted Magellan an audience, probably expecting him to
refute the rumors of corruption and treason that had been brought against
him. The king was dumbfounded when, rather than denying or even acknowledging the rumors, Magellan asked him for an increase in his *moradia*, a token allowance paid to members of the royal household.[11]
Contemptuous of the charges, and unable to believe that Manuel would
take them seriously, Magellan wanted evidence of his sovereign's trust in
his integrity, and recognition for his years of faithful service. He reminded
Manuel that noble blood ran in his veins, that he had rendered extensive
service to the Crown, and that on more than one occasion he had been
wounded in battle, most recently in Morocco.[12] The attending courtiers
sniggered at Magellan's limp and, by whispering that it was faked, aroused
the king's suspicions. Already resentful that this obnoxious fellow always

seemed to be hounding him for money, Manuel showed Magellan a letter from Sousa in Azamor, complaining that he had left his post without authorization and that serious charges were pending against him. The king refused Magellan's request and ordered him back to Morocco to face the charges.[13]

Outraged, Magellan returned to to Azamor. When an investigation revealed that the accusations were without substance, the charges were dismissed.[14]

This time armed with a proper travel authorization and a statement from Sousa clearing him of all wrongdoing, Magellan hastened back to Lisbon to petition the king once again to increase his *moradia*. His success in obtaining royal audiences must have stemmed from the historic obligation of the Crown to the rural nobility to which his family belonged, and the fact that he was a member of the royal household, because it is clear that the king had little use for him. To understand Magellan's obsession with the seemingly trivial matter of the *moradia*, it is necessary to realize that the requested increase, though a mere pittance in monetary value, would have represented a large advance in prestige.[15] To the knights and ladies of the royal court, the *moradia* was a quantifiable measure of the monarch's esteem, a clear indication of the recipient's stature at court. The word "stature" may be a key to Magellan's obsessiveness: A contemporary described him as short,[16] and in painted portraits he appears swarthy.[17] In Iberia, where the nobility were descended from Visigoths, many of the selectively bred bluebloods close to the throne were tall with fair complexions. Short stature and swarthiness were more common among undernourished, sunburnt laborers and peasants.

In Magellan, a craving for recognition was coupled with a combat veteran's disdain for the silken subtleties of courtly manners, in which directness was boorish and the simplest objectives were approached by devious routes. The king from whom he expected recognition took the devotion, suffering, and sacrifice of his subjects for granted, often failing to recognize even great deeds rendered in his service. Manuel had refused Vasco da Gama's request for a bonus for his soldiers and sailors after their destruction of the Calicut fleet,[18] and had rewarded Almeida for his naval victory at Diu by replacing him as viceroy. Unlike his predecessors who were warrior kings, Manuel was a creature of the court. His predilections are reflected in the ornate opulence of the architectural style that distinguished his reign.

The battle-scarred Magellan seems not to have made much effort to hide his disdain for this king who had never led his troops in battle, or for the sycophants who fawned over him. There is no evidence that Magellan ever sought allies at court who might have helped him press his pleas. Yet scorn for the king and his court does not fully explain his consistently self-defeating behavior in their presence. There was about Magellan a willful rejection of patterns of behavior he could not abide, much less master. This unwillingness to accommodate realities other than his own set the stage for his disgrace at the Portuguese court and later led to the disaster that ended his life and nearly destroyed all he had accomplished.

The months dragged on, and Magellan turned in frustration to a new line of importuning. While court chronicles do not state so clearly, he likely implored the king to allow him to take men, arms, and supplies to the Moluccas to help his friend Serrão establish a defensible, profitable Portuguese outpost. To Magellan it seemed a happy coincidence of his own best interests with the king's. His efforts to raise capital for the Moluccan trade had failed; all right then, he would join Serrão as an agent for the Crown.

In vain he tried to get the king and his counselors to recognize the enormous value to Portugal of his friend Serrão's achievements in the Moluccas. By 1515 Serrão, living in opulent splendor on Ternate, was considered a renegade for his defiance of an order from jealous superiors to report back to Malacca. In one of his letters to Magellan, Serrão grossly overestimated the distance to the Moluccas from Malacca.[19] Magellan may well have used this estimate to warn that the islands might lie on the Spanish side of the extension of the demarcation line agreed upon at Tordesillas. Despite their location, the discovery, occupation, and fortification of the Moluccas by Portugal could forestall any attempt by Spain to claim them. Nothing could have unsettled Dom Manuel more than the thought that the growing Portuguese dominance in the spice trade might be threatened by a legitimate Spanish claim to the Moluccas. The likelihood that Serrão's name and ancestry were Castilian (Serrano), did little to enhance the king's already strained confidence in him.

To make matters worse, Manuel received intelligence from Spain that King Ferdinand was preparing an expedition under Juan de Solís to explore westward along the coast of the *Castilla de Oro* (Central America) for 1700 leagues (100 degrees of longitude). The expedition's planners believed that this would bring them close to the coveted Moluccas and the western limit of the Spanish domain defined by the Treaty of Tordesillas.[20]

In speaking openly at court of Serrão's achievements in the Moluccas and of the uncertainty of the location of the treaty line extension, Magellan may have been trying to alert Manuel and his advisors to the need for action before Solís could claim the islands for Spain. But aside from being a rough-spoken pest whose welcome at court had worn thin, Magellan's insistence on publicly airing a matter sure to aggravate the king was ill received.

Because the king had questioned his honor, rejected his suggestions concerning the Moluccas, and denied recognition and honors to Serrão, whom he idolized, Magellan had ample reason to want to cause Manuel as much anxiety as possible. Whatever his motives, his actions were self-defeating. Perhaps the explanation given by the sixteenth-century Portuguese chronicler, João de Barros, is as good as any: "The demon that always in secret drives men to do ill made Magellan quarrel with the King."[21] Magellan is long dead, but history bears the indelible imprint of his internal demon.

It was against this background that Magellan, eager to present proof of his honorable conduct in Morocco and to request yet again a token increase in his *moradia*, sought another audience with the king. The hearing was a disaster; Dom Manuel refused to accept the proof of his innocence, and again refused to increase his allowance. For once sensing the depth of the king's displeasure with him, with uncharacteristic humility Magellan requested that he be permitted to serve his sovereign in any way that would please him. Manuel replied that the Crown had no further interest in his services. Stunned but still composed, Magellan then asked if he might go elsewhere to offer his services to a lord who would show him greater favor. The king responded icily that he might go where he pleased. When Magellan attempted to kiss the king's hand in one final act of courtesy, Manuel withdrew it and turned his back on the humiliated supplicant.[22]

Magellan limped away in utter disgrace, mortified by the gleeful tittering of the attendant courtiers.

P A I I I R T
$\mathcal{T}$he Enterprise

Portuguese sailors using a cross-staff to measure lunar distances and an astrolabe to determine the sun's altitude. When Magellan arrived in Seville to propose a westward expedition to the Spice Islands, Spanish authorities already knew that he was "very knowledgeable in matters concerning navigation."

Courtesy of the John Carter Brown Library at Brown University.

6

*C*onception

Т*here can be little doubt that when he pressed his unwelcome* demands on King Manuel late in 1515 or early in 1516,[1] Magellan was utterly convinced of the truth in his own arguments concerning Serrão and the Moluccas. Serrão was the first Portuguese, if not the first European, to have reached the Moluccas; although Varthema, a Bolognese, claimed to have visited the islands in 1506.[2] As military advisor to the Sultan of Ternate and son-in-law to the Sultan of Tidore, Serrão was in an excellent position to promote alliances and trade agreements ensuring Portuguese control over the export of spices from the Moluccas. But Manuel, a selfish and shortsighted monarch, was not one to set aside his prejudices easily.

Magellan viewed the world as through a tunnel, blotting out events peripheral to his goals, which once set he pursued with uncommon intensity. He was about forty years old in 1515, when 50 to 60 was considered aged, and had little to show for twenty-five years of service to the Crown, eight of them in military service overseas. With no estate, wife, or children, and only a crippled knee to remind him of his failed career, he saw his life slipping away without significant accomplishment. Desperate to give it meaning, he risked royal displeasure by repeatedly urging an unappreciative Manuel to take advantage of Serrão's presence in the Moluccas. For Manuel, preoccupied with the affairs of state, life was more complex. The subtle protocols practiced at court barely disguised the base scheming by which princes vied for power, and vassals for proximity to it. Across the border, the bold, crafty Ferdinand, King of Aragon and Regent of Castile, was scheming to displace Portugal from its dominant position in the spice trade.

Geographers and mapmakers in the Iberian kingdoms had begun to speculate about the extension of the Tordesillas Treaty line in the opposite hemisphere. Once the Portuguese conquered Malacca, mariners' estimates of its distance east of the meridian of Lisbon caused court geographers to suspect that the Moluccas lay close to the extended treaty line, but on which side? By broadcasting Serrão's overestimate of the distance to the Moluccas from Malacca, Magellan caused consternation at the Portuguese court. The prized Spice Islands might lie within the Spanish Hemisphere. Still more worrisome to Manuel was the knowledge that from neighboring Castile, Ferdinand was sending probes west into the Atlantic to search for an alternate route to the Moluccas.

As for Serrão, when his ship disappeared in the storm that struck Abreu's squadron in the Banda Sea, it was presumed to have gone down with all hands. Then, junks from the Moluccas brought letters from Serrão informing his superiors at Malacca of his situation, and requesting reinforcements, supplies, and materials for building a Portuguese stronghold. The jealousy of these superiors for Serrão's amazing luck was reflected in reports the king received from Albuquerque (now back at Cochin), which included their vitriolic comments. Instead of sending help, the jealous officers ordered Serrão to leave the islands and return to Malacca. As cited by Portuguese chroniclers who had access to them, Serrão's letters to the authorities in Malacca and to Magellan suggest nothing more than his earnest desire to promote Portuguese interests.[3]

Unlike his fretful king, Magellan was exhilarated by Serrão's letters. He also was fascinated by intelligence arriving in Lisbon from both Spanish and Portuguese voyages into the western Atlantic, and he shared the growing conviction among geographers and chartmakers that what the Spaniards were calling *tierra firme* across the ocean to the west was not a part of eastern Asia. In 1513 Balboa had discovered a sea on the south side of the Isthmus of Panama. Since then, geographers had been speculating whether there might be a terminus to the landmass in the western Atlantic that one could sail around, or if there were a *paso* (strait) leading into Balboa's sea.[4] Subtracting the sum of Marco Polo's estimate of the overland distance from Europe to China and mariners' estimates of the distance from Europe to the landmass across the Atlantic from Ptolemy's estimate of the earth's circumference brought most geographers to the conclusion that it would be just a short haul across Balboa's sea to China, and an even shorter one to *Cipangu* (Polo's term for Japan).[5]

These concepts, so disturbing to Dom Manuel, were exciting to Magellan. Eager to break free of the court intrigues and economic woes that had stifled his every effort to make something of his life, he yearned for an opportunity to link up again with Serrão and share with his old friend an adventurous life in the Moluccas. But Magellan's impatience with court protocol and his brash airing of the politically and diplomatically sensitive matter of Serrão's presence in the Moluccas made him seem to the king and his counselors like the proverbial bull in the china shop. Added to the cloud cast on Magellan's honor by the accusations against him in Morocco, these irritations apparently were sufficient to dispose Manuel to humiliate his irksome subject.

But Magellan could not suffer humiliation lightly, even from his king. Only recently had the notion arisen in Europe that kings ruled by divine right. Magellan's forebears served kings who earned the loyalty of their subjects on the battlefield, and loyalty was a reciprocal matter; in return for his services, a noble expected trust, courtesy, and support from his king. Magellan expected no less from Manuel, but got none of them, for Manuel was no warrior king; he was a pampered prince surrounded by obsequious courtiers. Notoriously stingy in rewarding those who had served him overseas, Manuel's largesse was usually directed to projects in which royal interest was promoted by self-serving courtiers whispering into his ear. After his humiliation at court, Magellan felt that he no longer owed allegiance to this ungrateful king, and that he had every right to offer his services to another monarch who would show him greater respect.

That he was thinking about doing just that is indicated by a letter Magellan wrote to Serrão. After both were dead, it was found among Serrão's personal effects on Ternate by Portuguese naval authorities. Magellan wrote: "God willing, I will soon be seeing you, whether by way of Portugal or Castile, for that is the way my affairs have been leaning: you must wait for me there, because we already know that it will be some time before we can expect things to get better for us."[6] Deeply wounded in his *amor proprio*, the very heart of his fierce Iberian pride, Magellan was searching for a way to repair his damaged honor.

There is little historical evidence regarding Magellan's activities in the interval between his disgrace at court and his arrival in Seville in October 1517. It is clear, however, that he did not waste his time sulking. Seeking out pilots, shipmasters, and scholars, he applied himself rigorously to the study of navigation, an art just beginning to evolve into a science. On his arrival in Spain, authorities in Seville obtained from certain parties in Lisbon references describing Magellan as "very knowledgeable in matters concerning navigation."[7] Yet before he sailed from Spain on his memorable voyage, his seafaring experience was limited. Magellan had been a seaborne soldier in the military campaigns of Almeida and Albuquerque in the Indian Ocean, and a passenger on long sea voyages between Portugal and

India. The only vessel he was known to have commanded was an oar-propelled bergantim in East Africa.

In Ponte de Lima on November 24, 1516, Diogo de Sousa received on his brother's behalf 80,751 reis (about 204 cruzados) from the Abraldez estate.[8] The order for the payment, authorized by the king in 1514, was dated June 5, 1516. Although this improved Magellan's strained finances and gave him the means to move about the country as he wished, it did not improve his opinion of the king. Dom Manuel had failed to order payment of the 10 percent interest accrued over the five years since the debt was due.

Magellan may have made the fateful decision to leave his homeland for Spain when he learned of the findings of the Spanish expedition into the southwest Atlantic that left San Lúcar on October 8, 1515, under the command of Juan Díaz de Solís. A Portuguese pilot of Spanish descent,[9] Solís sailed southward along the coast of Brazil, confirming the westerly trend of the coastline beyond Cape Frio that was first noted by Portuguese explorers. When the expedition reached Cape Santa María (near 35° S), Solís and his pilots estimated that they had passed beyond the Tordesillas Treaty line into Spanish territory. Beyond that cape the coastline turned sharply west. After following it some distance, Solís went ashore to explore the terrain beyond the beach, but the shore party had barely landed when it was attacked by a band of natives. Solís and his companions were slaughtered, roasted, and eaten in full view of their horrified shipmates. With its leader dead, the expedition was aborted. The survivors arrived in Seville in September 1516, with news of their leader's death and of a broad waterway south of Cape Santa María leading to the west.

Magellan had spent many long hours in the library and chartroom of India House, poring over the reports of the pilots of earlier Portuguese probes along that coast. When the information from the Solís expedition reached him, he realized that the Spaniards, aware that the coast south of Brazil was on their side of the treaty line, would intensify their exploration of that region. As for his knowledge of the Far East, in addition to what he had learned in Malacca and from Serrão's letters, Magellan may have seen accounts of the Abreu expedition into the Banda Sea and a chart of the Java Sea that Albuquerque had sent to the king. Francisco Rodrigues, a pilot with the Abreu expedition, had copied the chart from a Javanese source.

Magellan soon came to realize that this privileged information could be used to interest potential sponsors in an expedition to the Moluccas. With Serrão already there and disgusted with the Portuguese response to his achievements, Magellan could be sure of an enthusiastic welcome in Ternate no matter who his sponsor might be. He had no doubt that he could acquire sponsors in Spain, where interest in finding a westward route to the Orient was growing. Such a route, if as short as geographers expected, would make great sense for Spain, since all possible stopovers on the long eastern route were controlled by Portugal. Leading a Spanish expedition to the Moluccas might win for him the honors and wealth that had eluded him in the service of Portugal. That the success of such an expedition would be a disaster for the king who had humiliated him surely must have occurred to Magellan.

After leaving Lisbon, Magellan took up residence in Pôrto,[10] the principal port and commercial center of the region where he had lived as a child and where his brother and other relatives still resided.

From there, he scoured the kingdom for information on navigation in the western Atlantic and the seas south and east of Malacca. During this phase of Magellan's life it was said of him, ". . . he was always in the company of pilots, [and concerned with] nautical charts and [the determination of] longitude."[11] It is not stated who these pilots were, but there was an international company of pilots on the Iberian Peninsula at that time. Some were from Greece and the Aegean Islands, the Italian states, and the Balearic Islands; others were from Portugal, Castile, and their Atlantic islands. Because there was a great demand for their services in both Portugal and Castile, they moved freely back and forth between the two kingdoms. Columbus, a Genoese, and Vespucci, a Florentine, served both Portugal and Castile; Sebastian Cabot, a Venetian, served England before taking employment in Castile. Portuguese pilots commonly sailed with Castilian expeditions into the western Atlantic.

The maritime competition between the Iberian kingdoms put a premium on the services of pilots. Independent and mobile, the pilots were a loose fellowship bonded by their knowledge of the jealously guarded secrets of navigation. To the monarchs who hired them, pilots were little better than pirates. There may have been justification for this opinion since, like many mariners of that time, some pilots found piracy a convenient way to fill the gaps between periods of legitimate employment.[12]

One of the better-known pilots with whom Magellan may have had contact was João de Lisboa. A Portuguese of impeccable reputation, he had been chief pilot of the fleet with which Magellan had sailed to Morocco. Earlier, Lisboa had navigated along the coast of Brazil at least as far as the mouth of the Río de la Plata.[13] It has been proposed that he was the chief pilot of the 1513–14 expedition to Brazil financed by Cristóbal de Haro (who was to figure prominently in the Magellan expedition) and thought by some to have gone as far south as the Gulf of San Matías.[14]

Magellan's experiences on the high seas, his association with pilots, and his own studies of navigation and maritime geography gave him a healthy respect for the difficulties of long-distance voyaging. He was acutely aware that the pilots of his day, when navigating out of sight of land, had no means other than crude dead reckoning for determining how far east or west their ships had sailed from their point of departure. In contrast, the determination of latitude had been improved by the adoption of the astrolabe for measuring the height above the horizon of the sun or certain familiar stars. Taken from the deck of a rolling ship, such measurements were not always accurate, but in clear weather, simply by "eyeballing" the sun at noon or the pole star at night, an experienced pilot could get a rough idea of his latitude. The problem of determining longitude proved far-more intractable. On a long voyage, the accumulation of dead-reckoning errors usually produced enormous inaccuracies that a pilot would be unable to detect until he arrived at a known position.

Magellan's plan to promote Spanish interest in a westward voyage to the Moluccas was founded on his belief that these islands lay in the Spanish hemisphere, east of the extended line of demarcation. If he could convince Spanish authorities that he could reach the Moluccas by sailing west, and bring back to Spain proof of their position, he might have a reasonable chance of winning their support for his enterprise. But to establish the precise location of the Moluccas, an accurate method for determining longitude would be needed. Magellan's research into this problem led him to Rodriguo (Ruy) Faleiro.[15]

An eccentric, temperamental mathematician, astronomer, and student of the nautical sciences, Faleiro was a native of Covilha in the Serra da Estrela, a mountain range east of Coimbra in the province of Beira, Portugal. Since he bore the title of *bachiller*,[16] it is reasonable to assume that he had studied at a university (very likely Coimbra). His exalted opinion of himself may have been at least partially justified, for he was regarded even by his critics as possessing knowledge that could only have come from a "familiar demon."[17]

Faleiro could well have been that member of the royal *Junta do Astrolabio* (Astrolabe Council) known as Maestre Ruy or Rodrigo, whom King João II had consulted for applications of mathematics to navigational problems.[18] It is even possible that it was Faleiro who, on the island of Madeira, told Columbus of the existence of a New World.[19] In spite of his eccentricities, Faleiro was widely respected by his contemporaries for his theoretical contributions to navigational science.

At the time Magellan sought his advice, Faleiro was nursing a grudge against King Manuel. The grudge may have been prompted by the king's refusal to grant him the title of Judiciary Astrologer, or by Dom Manuel's bestowing of a newly created chair in astronomy at the University of Coimbra on an academic rival. Regardless, Faleiro considered it an outrageous affront to his honor.[20] Although both were proud, obsessed with personal honor, had a common interest in scientific navigation, and resented their king, Magellan and Faleiro were very different in temperament. One a stubborn, practical man of action, the other a brilliant but erratic theoretician, this odd couple became partners in the enterprise that led to one of mankind's greatest achievements.

Any discussion of Ruy Faleiro would be incomplete without mention of his brother, Francisco. The two were very close and had collaborated on new approaches to the solution of navigational problems. Francisco Faleiro is remembered in his own right for his publication of an important tract on the science of navigation.[21]

A father-and-son cartographic team also figured prominently in Magellan's search for geographic information during his last months in Portugal. Pedro and Jorge Reinel were the era's two most celebrated Portuguese cartographers. On their world maps made before 1519, the Molucca Islands were clearly located in the Spanish hemisphere.[22] It was probably these maps that first suggested to Magellan that Spain might have a legitimate right to those islands. A careful study of portulans—navigation manuals—made by the Reinels after 1519, however, indicated that later they came to believe that the Portuguese domain extended about five degrees east of the Moluccas, a figure very close to reality.[23]

In planning their enterprise, Magellan and Faleiro accepted the location for the Moluccas shown by the Reinels on their earlier world maps. At that time, the Reinels may not yet have divulged or even developed the data later shown in their portulans. Very likely these were gleaned from reports of the pilots of Haro ships operating in the Far East. There is little doubt that Pedro Reinel drew the planisphere Magellan took with him for his first audience with King Charles. Pedro's son, Jorge (who had set up shop in Seville), constructed a globe and a map for Magellan, who used them to illustrate his belief that the Moluccas lay in the Spanish hemisphere.[24]

Before Magellan wound up his affairs in Portugal, he contacted an international trading company with strong ties to the Fugger bank in Germany. Run by the powerful Haro family, the company had maintained its headquarters in Lisbon since 1503.[25] Natives of Burgos in northern Castile, the Haros were devout Catholics, but like many wealthy Burgalese were suspected of having Jewish ancestry. The senior partner, Cristóbal de Haro, managed the company affairs from Lisbon; his younger brother, Diego, ran the company office in Antwerp. Since the opening of the Lisbon office, Haro ships and financial resources had played a major role in the commercial development of the Portuguese overseas empire. As previously mentioned, an expedition sponsored and outfitted by the Haros and thought to have been commanded by João Lisboa had explored the coast of Brazil in 1513–14. Since commercial ships from Portugal were known to have visited Siam and Indochina years before the official missions dispatched by King Manuel in 1515–1517, it is reasonable to assume that Haro's were among them.[26]

As Magellan was preparing to leave for Spain, the Haros were attempting to recover from King Manuel enormous losses sustained from the actions of a Portuguese privateer, Estevão Yusarte,[27] who had attacked and robbed a fleet of 16 Haro ships in the Gulf of Guinea, sending seven of them to the bottom. The Haros sued the Portuguese Crown for 18,000 ducats. Dom Manuel ordered the apprehension and punishment of Yusarte but refused to compensate the Haros for their losses. The City of Antwerp, the governing council of the Netherlands, and the King of Spain all interceded on behalf of the Haros, but despite these pleas and the many incalculably valuable services to the Crown rendered by Haro enterprises, Manuel rejected all claims for damages. Stung by the king's miserliness, the Haros encouraged Magellan and Faleiro in their efforts to win Spanish sponsorship, and prepared to transfer their company headquarters to Spain.

It is unclear whether Magellan had previously dealt with the Haros or their agents. In Spain, he gave sworn testimony that he had known the Haros before his arrival in that country.[28] Possibly this relationship grew out of contacts with Haro ship captains and commercial representatives in Malacca in 1511–12.

While there is no direct evidence for it, subsequent events strongly suggest that before he left Portugal Magellan had been in close contact with Diogo Barbosa, an influential Portuguese expatriate in Seville who would become his father-in-law. The final recorded episode of Magellan's life as a Portuguese subject is notable because, like so many others in his adventurous career, it marked him as a man of honor. Before leaving for Spain, he effected certain "public instruments" renouncing his allegiance to the Portuguese Crown.[29] Winding up his affairs in the land of his birth and leaving behind his brother and sister, Magellan passed into Spain, accompanied by some pilots, relatives, and friends.[30] Faleiro followed some months later.

7

*B*irth

*F*illed with ambition and high hopes when he left his homeland, Magellan blundered into a hornets' nest of intrigue in Spain, where the nobility fiercely resented the Flemish counselors of the young Hapsburg archduke who had just inherited the thrones of Aragon and Castile.

The two kingdoms were united in 1497, when the husband of Queen Isabella of Castile succeeded to the throne of Aragon as Ferdinand II. After the premature deaths of their two eldest offspring, the mentally unstable third, Juana (Mad Joan), became heir to the thrones of both kingdoms. In 1496, Joan married Philip (The Fair), the Hapsburg Archduke of Burgundy, son of Maximilian I, the Holy Roman Emperor. Their eldest son, Charles, was raised in Flanders by his paternal aunt, the Archduchess Margaret of Austria, regent of the Burgundian Netherlands. Queen Isabella of Castile died in 1504. Having obtained her husband's promise to remain single after her death, Isabella stipulated in her will that Ferdinand would rule Castile as regent for their unbalanced daughter.[1] For Ferdinand, it was not an easy job. The proud nobles of largely rural Castile treasured the feudal rights inherited from their Visigoth, Vandal, and Swabian ancestors, while mercantile interests in Aragon's many cities and towns better appreciated the benefits of a central political authority. Because they feared that, as regent, the autocratic Ferdinand would usurp their feudal powers, the Castilian nobles enticed Archduke Philip of Burgundy to come to Castile with his wife, the mad but legitimate queen. As her consort, he was recognized as Philip I, King of Castile, but lasted only three months before dying suddenly in Burgos after eating a heavy dinner. It is likely that he was poisoned by an agent of his father-in-law.[2] Upon Philip's death, the regency of Castile reverted to King Ferdinand.

Queen Joan had adored her handsome husband and became unreasonably jealous when other women got near him. Devastated by his death, she went completely mad, keeping his embalmed body in her bed and traveling with it throughout her kingdom. She admitted no women, not even midwives, to the royal bedchamber and bore her fourth child unaided alongside Philip's corpse. Ferdinand, exasperated by her bizarre behavior, entrusted his deranged daughter to the care of a political ally, Juan Rodríguez Fonseca, and Mad Joan spent the rest of her life in protective custody. Fonseca, an intimate of the royal family, was Bishop of Burgos and Archbishop of Rosano (in Italy). Like many prelates of his time, he had used the Church to amass wealth and power. An astute businessman and a scheming power broker, he was also an able administrator who, as vice-president of the Supreme Council of the Indies, was a formidable figure at the Spanish court.

King Ferdinand developed a strong dislike for his grandson, Archduke Charles of Burgundy. To deny Charles his heritage, Ferdinand broke his pledge to the dying Isabella and married Germaine de Foix, a niece of Louis XII of France. She bore him a son, the legitimate heir to the throne of Aragon, and Ferdinand intended that the new prince would also succeed to the throne of Castile,[3] but the boy died in 1509. Ferdinand then named his grandson, Prince Ferdinand (Charles's younger brother), heir to the throne of Aragon and the regency of Castile. As the king lay dying in January 1516, Cardinal Francisco Ximenes de Cisneros, Archbishop of Toledo, convinced him that such a succession would be bitterly contested and tear the nation asunder. To prevent civil war, the dying king revised his will, naming Archduke Charles heir to the throne of Aragon; to Cardinal Ximenes he entrusted the regency of Castile.[4]

Ferdinand died on January 23, 1516, and Cardinal Ximenes duly assumed the regency. In defiance of the terms of his grandfather's will, however, Prince Ferdinand continued to assert his claims. Adding to the confusion, the dissident nobles of Castile redoubled their efforts to reclaim the feudal rights King Ferdinand had arrogated to the Crown. The resultant instability grew worse when Cardinal Adrian of Utrecht claimed the regency of Castile for Charles, the legitimate heir, who was eager to exercise his royal prerogatives.

The astute, capable Cardinal Ximenes proved equal to these challenges, defusing the threat of civil war by having Prince Ferdinand taken to Madrid and kept under tight surveillance. He then turned his attention to Prince Charles and coaxed him to be more conciliatory with the nobles, who still recognized Charles's mad mother as their legitimate queen and who suspected (rightfully) that Charles's Flemish counselors were planning to help themselves to Spain's royal treasury. The strategy worked, for the *corteses* (councils of nobles) in both Aragon and Castile reluctantly acknowledged the legitimacy of Charles's claims. During the interregnum, Ximenes was the acting head of state in both kingdoms, but disputes over the question of succession continued to strain the delicate bonds uniting them. To make matters worse, the cardinal had to raise a military force to quell a revolt in Navarre (a small kingdom in the Pyrenees that King Ferdinand had forcibly incorporated into Aragon) and mount a campaign in North Africa against Barbary pirates.

In Portugal at about that time, Magellan was starting to explore the possibilities for Spanish sponsorship of an expedition to the Moluccas. Almost certainly, as previously referenced, the initial contact with Spanish authorities was made for him by Diogo Barbosa, a Portuguese expatriate living in Seville, whose daughter Magellan later would marry.[5]

In 1491, for services rendered in the campaigns of Ferdinand and Isabella against the Moors, Diogo (later changed to the Spanish Diego) Barbosa was knighted Commander of the Order of Santiago, Castile's most prestigious military honor.[6] He took up residence in Seville, but in 1501 returned to Portugal, where he was given command of a ship in the India-bound fleet of João de Nova, which discovered the islands of Ascension and St. Helena.[7] In 1503, Barbosa returned via Portugal to Seville, where he became a respected member of that city's colony of distinguished Portuguese expatriates. The leader of this group was an uncle of King Manuel, Dom Álvaro de Braganza, to whom the Catholic Sovereigns (Ferdinand and Isabella) had awarded the presidency of the regional council and the stewardship of the fortress and arsenals of Seville,[8] probably for his support in the Moorish wars.

Dom Álvaro entrusted the management of these valuable properties to Barbosa, who had married a high-born Andalusian lady, María Caldera. They had many children; those whose names are known to history are Jaime, Isabel, Beatriz, and Guiomar. Also living with them was Duarte Barbosa, variously reported as Diego's son or nephew, who was to accompany Magellan on his great voyage.[9] In Spain in those times, "nephew" was a common euphemism for illegitimate son.

While Diego Barbosa was making the initial overtures to Spanish officials in Seville on behalf of Magellan and Faleiro, Archduke Charles was preparing to travel to Spain from Flanders to claim his heritage. In Brussels on March 14, 1516, Charles was proclaimed king of both Aragon and Castile. Although he had been urged by Cardinal Ximenes to come immediately, Charles's Flemish counselors delayed his departure as long as they could. Headed by Guillaume du Croy, Sieur de Chièvres, this group of avaricious courtiers had discovered that from Flanders the Spanish treasury could be raided with impunity. Before the new king set foot in Spain, they succeeded in transferring to private accounts over one million ducats.[10] Not until September 8, 1517, did Charles embark for Spain. After getting lost in a fog in the Bay of Biscay, the fleet carrying the new king and his retinue landed eleven days later at Villaviciosa, a fishing village in Asturias.[11] Magellan arrived in Seville on October 20, 1517.[12]

In Spain, the Supreme Council of the Indies advised the king and his court on matters concerning overseas and maritime affairs and moved with the court between the capitals of the Spanish kingdoms. Its operating arm, the *Casa de Contratacíon de las Indias*, was headquartered in Seville. When Magellan arrived, its principal officers were the canon Dr. Sancho de Matienzo, treasurer; Pedro Ochoa de Isásaga, paymaster; and Juan de Aranda, the factor (manager).[13] A merchant from Burgos, Aranda had been receptive to the overtures made by Barbosa for Magellan while the latter was still in Portugal. Sensing an investment opportunity, he wrote to the Haro company in Lisbon inquiring about the reputations of Magellan and Faleiro.[14] Satisfied by a favorable reply, Aranda notified Bishop Fonseca that the two Portuguese were headed for Spain with a proposal that should interest the Supreme Council.[15]

Fonseca then brought Aranda's notice to the attention of the regent, Cardinal Ximenes, who also served as president of the Supreme Council. By the time Magellan arrived in Seville, the highest authorities in Spain already had been alerted to the nature of the project he and Faleiro would propose.[16] Although a more auspicious beginning for Magellan's enterprise can scarcely be imagined, the accession to the throne of a young king eager to make his mark on history was to tip the scales even more in Magellan's favor.

When Charles belatedly landed on the coast of Asturias in September 1517, he brought with him a palace guard of German mercenaries. Learning of this, Cardinal Ximenes was horrified. The guards would seem to Spaniards like an invading army, compounding the resentment already aroused by the unconscionable raids on the Spanish treasury by Chièvres and his Flemish minions. The aged cardinal immediately set out overland to warn the new king, but never reached his goal. En route he was suddenly stricken ill; poison was suspected.[17] Taken to a sanctuary at Aranda del Duero, he died on November 8, 1517, unappreciated by the seventeen-year-old king to whom he had handed a united Spain. Charles began his reign committed to policies as alien to his Spanish subjects as the French language he spoke.

This young monarch to whom Magellan's fate was to become so inextricably linked was born February 24, 1500 in the city of Ghent in Flanders,[18] and was raised by his paternal aunt Margaret, Archduchess of Austria and Regent of the Netherlands. His grandfathers were Ferdinand II of Aragon and Maximilian I of the Holy Roman Empire. A solemn boy who took seriously the responsibilities to which he was born, the young prince was popular in Flanders. During the lavish ceremonies with which the royalty delighted the prosperous burghers of the Low Countries, Charles conducted himself with grace and dignity. Slight of stature yet surprisingly athletic, as he grew toward manhood Charles developed the pendulous lower lip and lantern jaw characteristic of the Hapsburg family.

The archduchess chose for her royal ward's tutor the dean of the University of Louvain, Adrian Dedel. A churchman and scholar, Dedel later became a cardinal and, eventually, Pope Adrian VI. Under his tutelage, Charles developed simple but profound religious convictions reflecting the medieval chivalric ideals of Burgundy,[19] strikingly similar to those passed down to Magellan from his eleventh-century Burgundian ancestors. Charles's other tutor was Guillaume du Croy, Sieur de Chièvres, hired by the boy's father to train him in the duties of a prince. A French-speaking Walloon with strong loyalties to France, Chièvres was Charles's chief political mentor. Unfortunately, he encouraged the young king to institute policies unpopular with many Spaniards. In the Spanish kingdoms political power was not the exclusive prerogative of the Crown; it was shared with a *cortes*. In Brussels in 1516, Chièvres, acting as the new king's ambassador, ignored the Spanish nobles and negotiated the Treaty of Noyon with France, agreeing to terms decidedly unfavorable to Spain.[20] His indifference to the sensibilities of the Spaniards continued when he nominated his nephew for the archbishopric of Toledo after the death of Ximenes in 1517. This brazen nepotism was resented so much that when Charles showed up in Zaragoza to preside over the Cortes of Aragon, the outraged nobles refused to recognize his claim to the throne unless he agreed to rule in partnership with his mother, Mad Joan, the legitimate queen. In this manner the shortsighted, self-serving counselors of the young king squandered the goodwill so carefully cultivated by Cardinal Ximenes. The situation became so tense that Charles's brother, Prince Ferdinand, had to be sent to Flanders for fear he would become the focus of a rebellion.[21]

Deep in Spain, surrounded by factions seething with discontent, it finally dawned on Chièvres and his Flemish associates that their very lives were at risk. Only by winning the confidence and esteem of his Spanish subjects could the safety of the king and his counselors be assured. Cristóbal de Haro, the wealthy merchant who had just moved his company's headquarters from Lisbon to Spain, had a prescription that promised a cure for the king's ailing popularity.

Bitter about King Manuel's refusal to compensate him for financial losses inflicted by the Portuguese privateer Estevão Yusarte, Haro saw in Magellan and Faleiro's project an opportunity to retaliate and, at the same time, earn a handsome profit for himself and his German bankers. He suspected that the project's potential for opening up new sources of revenue for the depleted royal treasury and for capturing the imagination of a disaffected public would appeal to the greedy Flemings around King Charles. In Bishop Fonseca, whose interest in the project had already been aroused by Aranda, Haro found a powerful ally close to the inner circle at King Charles's court. He assured Fonseca that if Charles could be persuaded to license the expedition, he (Haro) would be willing to finance it. Little did Magellan realize when he left Portugal that powerful figures close to the Spanish throne were already prepared to bring his proposal before King Charles.

When he arrived in Seville on October 20, 1517, Magellan received a warm welcome at the home of Diego Barbosa. Before the year was out, he married Beatriz Barbosa Caldera, one of the daughters of his gracious host,[22] which suggests that Magellan was no stranger to the Barbosa family. Whether or not they were distant relatives, as some have claimed, there existed between them bonds of friendship and trust. In view of the customs governing courtship among the Iberian nobility, the marriage probably was arranged before Magellan arrived in Seville.

Barbosa provided his daughter with a dowry of 600,000 maravedis (about $84,000 U.S.),[23] a substantial sum for Magellan, who never before in his troubled life had enjoyed the luxury of adequate personal finances. Magellan gave his bride the customary *arras* (a gift in consideration of her dowry),[24] and made provisions in a notarized will for the return of the dowry to his wife in the event of his death. Despite heavy financial pressures during the final stages of outfitting his fleet, Magellan scrupulously refrained from spending any part of his wife's dowry.[25] Little is known of the relationship between Magellan and Beatriz. They were together a little less than two years, during which time she bore a son and they conceived a second child.

Before Magellan left Portugal, he and Faleiro concluded an agreement that obliged each to keep their plans secret until both had arrived in Spain.[26] Should either wish to back out of the project, he would so advise the other within six hours. Any proposed modifications of the plan would be deposited with Diego Barbosa and Rui Lopes, another Portuguese expatriate in Seville.

When Magellan appeared in person at the Casa de Contratacíon, Aranda immediately took him in tow. The merchant had sensed an exciting investment opportunity in what he had learned from Barbosa, and had already "greased the skids" for Magellan and Faleiro by alerting Fonseca to their project. Later he would claim to have spent 1,500 ducats (about $60,000 U.S.) from his own pocket in bringing them to Spain. It is not clear whether Magellan had communicated directly with Aranda before he left Portugal. Once he arrived in Seville, however, negotiations proceeded so well that Aranda was inspired to write to Chancellor Sauvage, requesting permission to bring Magellan and Faleiro to court. But the cordial spirit of their negotiations was jolted by the arrival in Seville of Faleiro early in December 1517.[27]

Informed of the progress of the negotiations, Faleiro became furious with Magellan for having broken his pledge of secrecy and threatened to dissolve the partnership. His pique with Aranda was even greater for having drawn so much information from Magellan, and for writing to the chancellor about the project without the permission of its authors. Aranda kept his composure and gently suggested that Faleiro reserve judgment on the propriety of the letter until a reply was received from the chancellor. His attempts to dampen Faleiro's fury failed utterly. Only the timely intervention of Diego Barbosa and Rui Lopes saved the embryonic enterprise.[28] At their urging, the eccentric astronomer consented to a new partnership arrangement with Magellan, but his distrust of Aranda prevented any further negotiations with him in Seville.

With their major differences reconciled, the partners resolved to go together to Valladolid to seek a royal hearing. Magellan was agreeable to having Aranda travel with their party but, despite being forced by lack of funds to let Aranda pay his travel expenses, Faleiro refused to permit it. On January 20, 1518, the partners set out. Magellan was accompanied by two slaves—Enrique and a Sumatran girl about whom nothing is known; Rui Faleiro, by his brother, Francisco. It is not known whether Magellan's wife, Beatriz, accompanied them, but it is doubtful that she did.[29] They joined the well-guarded retinue of the duchess of Arcos and traveled at a leisurely pace toward Valladolid through Córdoba, Almadén, Toledo, Escalona, Cebreros, Ávila, and Arévalo. Aranda took a more direct route through Extremadura.[30]

Scarcely 10 miles beyond Seville, a mounted messenger caught up with Aranda, bearing two letters. One was a reply from the chancellor, instructing him to bring Magellan and Faleiro to court. The other, from the king, was for Magellan, inviting him to court ". . . because he wished to get to know him and grant him favors."[31] A courier was immediately dispatched to

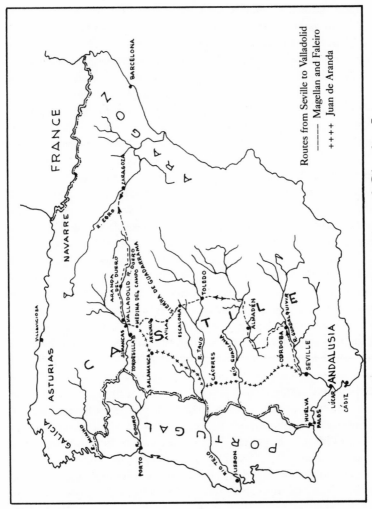

Spain At the Accession of Charles I

Routes from Seville to Valladolid
——— Magellan and Faleiro
++++ Juan de Aranda

deliver to Magellan and Faleiro the invitation from the king, the news from the chancellor, and Aranda's request that they meet him at Medina del Campo, about 25 miles south of Valladolid. The courier caught up with Magellan's party as they were crossing the Sierra de Guadarrama at Herradon de Pinares, west of Madrid.

Aranda was-waiting for them at Medina del Campo. At the inn where they stayed, he ". . . did them honor," which probably means that he picked up the tab for their wine, food, and lodging. Continuing their journey toward Valladolid, Faleiro and Aranda achieved an uneasy accord. It was strained again when, on reaching a village by a bridge crossing the Duero River, Aranda said to Faleiro: "Be not angry that I have written to the chancellor; rather because of it and for what I am about to do to inform His Highness about the information you brought to me from Portugal, you should be willing to give me a part of what God may grant you."[32] Pressing his demands further, Aranda suggested that a fifth of the profits from the proposed expedition would be fair compensation for his efforts on their behalf.

Both Faleiro brothers were outraged by this proposition and refused to consider it at all. Magellan also thought it excessive, but countered with an offer of a tenth. Aranda said that he'd be pleased to accept an eighth. Faleiro's mounting irritation exploded into a paroxysm of rage, as much because Magellan's counteroffer had been made without consulting him as from what he considered Aranda's brazen demands. At this point, Aranda had the good sense to back off. He left the partners to work out their differences and continued on alone to Valladolid.

The Magellan party stopped for three days at Simancas, where they held stormy discussions.[33] Believing that Aranda's services at court would be invaluable, Magellan urged his partner to accept Aranda's last offer. Francisco Faleiro remained adamantly opposed to giving him any share in their enterprise, but Rui, uncomfortable about having accepted cash advances and other favors, reluctantly agreed to the eighth that Aranda had proposed.[34] On February 16, 1518, the partners completed their journey to Valladolid.[35] Anxiously awaiting them was Aranda, who led them to his inn and treated them to another round of wining and dining. Although they enjoyed his expansive hospitality, the Faleiro brothers were still repelled by his eagerness to cut himself in for a share of their enterprise. The next day, Magellan joined them in finding other lodgings.

Several days later, Aranda sought out the partners again, boasting that he had not been idle since his arrival in Valladolid. He told them that he had already prepared the way with the chancellor and the council for their reception at court, and asked them to prepare a detailed estimate of the costs of their project. When they completed the estimate, Magellan and Faleiro took it to the inn where Aranda was waiting with a contract and a notary. The contract stipulated that, in return for his services with the chancellery, the king, and the justice system (no matter where the court might be located), Aranda would receive an eighth share of all profits from the enterprise.[36] In the presence of a notary they signed the contract, which was dated February 23, 1518.[37] Magellan's signature on this document appears for the first time in its Spanish form, *Hernando de Magallanes*, instead of the Portuguese *Fernão de Magalhães*.[38]

8

*R*oyal Support

King Charles had been in Valladolid since November 18, 1517, having arrived there only ten days after the death of Cardinal Ximenes at Aranda del Duero. His huge entourage of Flemish courtiers and German mercenaries[1] put a severe strain on the old Castilian capital. Soldiers, courtiers, merchants, tradesmen, office seekers, and petitioners of all kinds filled to overflowing every available lodging space. Thieves, beggars, prostitutes, spies, and assassins lurked in dark alleys and circulated among guests at inns and taverns, drawn to their prey like flies to a carcass. If Magellan and Faliero had arrived early in the city, it would not have been difficult for Portuguese agents to get to them before they could present their proposal to the young Spanish king.

Magellan's party had taken more time than necessary for the journey. The slow pace and the three days' delay at Simancas may have been designed to confound the Portuguese ambassador, Álvaro da Costa, who was already in Valladolid trying to arrange the betrothal of Doña Leonor, King Charles's sister, to Manuel.[2] Costa had orders to do whatever was necessary to foil Magellan and Faliero's plans. Magellan's own words reveal his concern about the Portuguese ambassador's presence and the problems he might cause: ". . . seeing that this was a matter of great importance, and that there was at the court of Your Highness the ambassador of the King of Portugal who could obstruct [our plans]."[3]

Charles, who had just turned eighteen at the time of his first audience with Magellan, relied principally on the advice of three Flemish counselors with whom he had been associated most of his life: Chièvres, whose pervasive influence had made him a virtual *alter rex;*[4] Chancellor Sauvage, despised by most Spaniards;[5] and Cardinal Adrian of Utrecht, who succeeded

79

Cardinal Ximenes as regent of Castile and president of the Supreme Council of the Indies. Because Cardinal Adrian took very little interest in the council's business, Bishop Fonseca, its vice-president, became the king's principal advisor on matters relating to maritime affairs and the administration of overseas colonies. An able, crafty politician in an inner circle dominated by foreigners, Fonseca best understood and represented the interests of the Spanish nation.

Upon being introduced at court, Magellan and Faleiro quickly realized that Bishop Fonseca was the official to convince that their project was worthy of the king's attention. Although he was generally skeptical of the exaggerated claims of mariners and conquistadors seeking support for their projects,[6] Fonseca was intrigued by what Aranda had told him of Magellan and Faleiro's proposal. Despite the impending betrothal of a Portuguese princess to King Charles, the potential advantages of the project to Spain were great enough to risk a breach with Portugal. Fonseca understood clearly that, should Magellan's expedition succeed in locating the Moluccas on the Spanish side of the extended demarcation line, it would deprive Portugal of its growing monopoly in the spice trade.[7] Such an outcome promised greater benefits for Spain than anything yet derived from Columbus's discoveries. Magellan, the spokesman for the partners, presented his arguments clearly and dispassionately.[8] He did not indulge in the inspired demagoguery that had often colored the statements of the great Genoese navigator, and to which Fonseca had objected when he thought them overblown.

It is hardly surprising that Fonseca appreciated Magellan's rational approach, for he, too, had developed an appreciation of the applications of astronomy to navigation.[9] At about the time he was dealing with Magellan, Fonseca received a letter from the island of Santo Domingo, in which the writer, a magistrate, expressed belief that parts of Brazil and the Portuguese stronghold of Malacca were in the hemisphere within which Spain could claim dominion over the newly discovered territories.[10]

Fonseca had supported Columbus in his initial attempt to reach Asia by sailing west, but became disillusioned at the admiral's insistence that he had achieved his goal when subsequent voyages made it increasingly apparent he had not. The intelligence brought back by the survivors of the Solís expedition, however, suggested that Columbus's goal might yet be attained, and Magellan and Faleiro seemed to offer a good way to find out, especially since Haro was willing to finance it.

Matters progressed with amazing speed. According to Magellan, Aranda took them ". . . to the Grand Chancellor, the Cardinal [Adrian] and the Bishop of Burgos [Fonseca] and then, with them, to His Highness." Faleiro

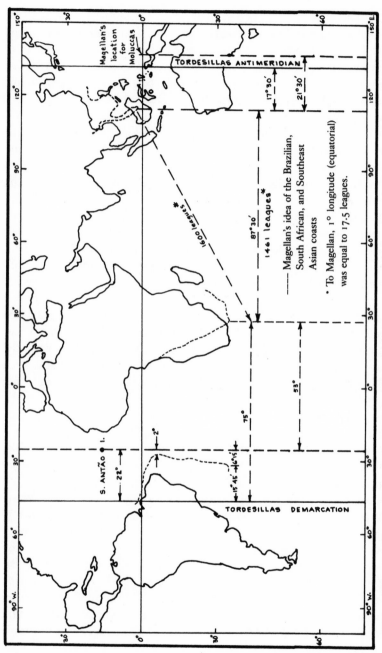

The World Envisioned by Magellan in His 1519 Memorandum to King Charles

Adapted from Rolando A. Laguarda Trías, 1975

Within the figure:

Magellan's location for Moluccas

TORDESILLAS ANTIMERIDIAN

17° 30′

21° 30′

1600 leagues *

87° 30′

1461 leagues *

—— Magellan's idea of the Brazilian, South African, and Southeast Asian coasts

* To Magellan, 1° longitude (equatorial) was equal to 17.5 leagues.

53°

75°

S. ANTÃO I.

22°

2°

16° 15′

15° 45′

TORDESILLAS DEMARCATION

merely stated that the negotiations began ". . . after having communicated and spoken with the Grand Chancellor and the [Supreme] Council [of the Indies]." There probably were two sets of interviews. The first, a matter of court protocol that might have been completed in a single day, introduced the partners and the nature of their project to the relevant authorities. There followed a series of substantive interviews in which the partners' ideas were probed in depth by Fonseca and his associates on the council,[11] culminating in one or more audiences with the king. All this took place between February 23 and March 22, 1518, when the partners received their commission from Charles.[12]

It had taken Columbus seven years to win the grudging support of the Catholic Sovereigns for his enterprise, but it took less than a month for Magellan to win the enthusiastic approval of their grandson, Charles I.

Behind the Supreme Council and the royal counselors to whom Magellan presented his arguments was the shadowy figure of Cristóbal de Haro. His ships had been sailing from Malacca since the Portuguese had seized it, and he was at least as well informed about the Far East as Magellan. Reports from his merchant captains provided him with valuable information about Indochina and China, and he suspected these places, and much of the huge archipelago to the south, lay on the Spanish side of the demarcation line.[13] Further, reports from the 1513–1514 expedition along the coast of Brazil convinced Haro that any southwest passage to Balboa's sea would be west of the demarcation.[14] If such a passage existed, Spain, not Portugal, would control its access. Augmenting Haro's influence at the Spanish court was the fact that he was the uncle of the wife of one of King Charles's personal secretaries, a young German, Maximilian Transylvanus. In a letter to his father, Cardinal Matthäus Lang, the archbishop of Salzburg, Transylvanus observed that Haro had assisted Magellan and Faleiro in presenting their arguments before the royal counselors.[15]

In January or early February 1517, Estavao Gomes, one of the Portuguese pilots who accompanied Magellan to Spain, had gone on his own to Valladolid to propose an expedition to the Malaccas with himself in command. Although his proposal was rejected, his impressive credentials won him an immediate appointment as a royal pilot. A decree signed by the king and issued on February 10, 1517, instructed the Casa de Contratación in Seville to hire him, and his name (in its Spanish form, *Esteban Gómez*) appeared on the agency's payroll on April 20 of the same year.[16] In 1519, Magellan selected Gomes to be pilot of his flagship, a choice he would have cause to regret.

When the partners presented their proposal to the king and his counselors, Faleiro's reputation lent considerable weight to his arguments. But it was Magellan who served as spokesman, for he ". . . spoke better than Faleiro about matters concerning the sea."[17] Although he was a short man, Magellan's magnificent black beard, soldierly bearing, and calm self-assurance gave him the appearance of a man who knew what he was about and who would not be bullied or suffer fools lightly.[18] His convictions were based on personal experience and close study of available documents and maps on the geography of the Far East and southwest Atlantic. He carried maps, globes, and Serrão's letters to illustrate his arguments.[19] His plain, heavily accented speech was in marked contrast to the flowery verbosity so common at court. Magellan was a different breed from the usual run of hopeful petitioners crowding the anterooms to the offices of King Charles's counselors. Among these were impoverished adventurers desperate to gain fame and fortune overseas, and professional seafarers such as Gomes, a pilot who yearned to command a royal fleet. What set Magellan apart from most of these petitioners was his quiet dignity. He avoided flamboyant overstatement as unbefitting a nobleman, and presented his ideas with a firm, understated authority, letting his carefully reasoned arguments stand on their merits.

Even so, the Flemings around the king were less than enthusiastic. An experienced diplomat, Cardinal Adrian listened to the complaints of the Portuguese ambassador and was concerned that Spanish support for the project might damage relations with Portugal. Fonseca overcame these doubts by pointing out to his fellow prelate that properly locating the meridian separating Spanish and Portuguese dominions in the Far East would prevent, not promote, conflict between Portugal and Spain. The extended line of demarcation, he emphasized to the cardinal, had not been properly identified by either papal bull or the Treaty of Tordesillas.[20] At first, the other Flemish counselors took little interest in Magellan's ideas. The Iberian zeal for maritime exploration seemed excessive to them. On the other hand, they were envious of the wealth from overseas enterprises that had poured into Haro's coffers in Lisbon and Antwerp. By arousing the greed for which these Flemings were notorious,[21] Cristóbal de Haro was able to convince them that huge profits could be realized from the project. Thus, the combined efforts of the powerful bishop and the wealthy merchant succeeded in stemming Flemish opposition to presenting the proposal to King Charles.

If official transcripts were made at these hearings, none has come to light. The writings of the missionary Bartolomé de las Casas provide the best source for what transpired, for he was at court when the hearings took place.[22] Magellan, he said, ". . . offered to show that the Moluccas and other islands [i.e. Banda] from which the Portuguese brought spices, fell or were located inside the demarcation or partition toward which the Catholic Sovereigns of Castile and King João of Portugal had started, [the one] from the east and [the other] from the west, but had not reached, and that they would discover a route to go to [these islands] outside the route used by the Portuguese, and this would be *by a certain strait of which they knew.*"

On one occasion, Las Casas was in the chambers of the Chancellor Sauvage when Bishop Fonseca brought Magellan and Faleiro to meet that official. Magellan had with him, said Las Casas, ". . . a well-painted globe showing all the earth, and he indicated on it the route he would take, except that the strait had been left blank on purpose, so that no one else would try to get there first;[23] and . . . the Bishop [Fonseca] took [the globe] and showed the Grand Chancellor the voyage that would be made; and I, speaking with Magellan, asked him which way he planned to go; he answered that he would go by way of Cape Santa María, which we call the Río de la Plata, and from there he'd continue along the coast; in this way he expected to find the strait. I asked him further: 'and if you do not find the strait, where would you be able to pass into the other sea?' He responded that if he did not find it, he would go by the route the Portuguese followed."

These comments by Las Casas, the even more limited observations of Transylvanus, and the secondhand information from Portuguese chroniclers provide the only records of the arguments used by Magellan. He and Faleiro were pressed for details about the proposed route, how they expected to determine longitude, the men, ships, and supplies required, how much it would cost, and their qualifications to lead such an expedition. The king must have been impressed, for he gave the project his swift approval. Aside from its obvious glamour, which could not have failed to excite the young king, the success of the project would be a diplomatic coup and an economic triumph. By stimulating a surge of national pride, it would strengthen the loyalty of his Spanish subjects to their new king.

The idea of an antimeridian (the extension of the demarcation line into the opposite hemisphere) had not occurred to the Vatican officials who drafted the papal bulls defining the maritime spheres of influence of Portugal and Castile, nor had it occurred to the diplomats of those two kingdoms when they drafted the Treaty of Tordesillas. The *Dudum Siquidem* (papal bull) of 1493 did not consider a special demarcation in the Orient. It decreed that Castile and Portugal were entitled to occupy lands in India not already possessed by the other.[24] Although he was convinced that the Moluccas lay within the Spanish hemisphere, Magellan probably had in mind this prior possession feature of *Dudum Siquidem* when he urged the authorities in Lisbon to send support to Serrão in the Moluccas. When

King Manuel ignored this sensible request, Magellan shared the disappointment and disgust felt by Haro and his fellow merchants in Lisbon. Since Serrão already had provided a secure beachhead from which Portuguese power in the Spice Islands could be quickly and easily projected, the failure of King Manuel to order the immediate establishment of a fortified trading post in the Moluccas seemed as counterproductive to Haro as it did to Magellan.

The antimeridian concept seems to have occurred first to merchants and then to diplomats in Portugal, triggering concern that China and the archipelago to the south, the principal source of nutmeg and cloves, might lie across the antimeridian in the hemisphere reserved for Spain by the Treaty of Tordesillas. After he transferred his allegiance to Spain, Magellan argued exactly that. Having no idea of the vast breadth of the Pacific Ocean, his confidence in this assertion was based on his acceptance of two erroneous suppositions: Ptolemy's underestimate of the Earth's circumference and Serrão's overestimate of the distance of the Moluccas east of Malacca. On the Reinel globe that he took to the Spanish court, the coast of Brazil south of Cabo Frio may have been left blank to ensure the continued confidentiality of information on the embayment beyond Cape Santa María brought back by the Solís expedition.[25] This opening to the west (actually the estuary of the La Plata River) may well have been where Magellan hoped to find a strait leading to the Great South Sea. There is no mention of such a strait in the written outline Magellan and Faleiro presented to King Charles.[26] They pledged themselves only to discover islands and continents rich in spices and other useful resources *within the domain reserved for Spain*. Neither were the Moluccas mentioned in their text (probably an attempt to avoid ruffling the sensibilities of the Portuguese—at least until the expedition demonstrated that these islands lay east of the antimeridian). When asked by Las Casas what route he would take if he failed to find a strait, Magellan replied that he ". . . would go by the route that the Portuguese followed."[27] Clearly he had no qualms about going eastward to the Moluccas. Since he had promised to avoid Portuguese territory en route, if it became necessary to sail eastward, he probably intended to do so well south of the track followed by Portuguese ships traveling to and from India.

When it became clear that the Crown would authorize the expedition, Haro volunteered to finance its outfitting. To him, the venture promised the opening of a vast trading area in the Far East under the protection of the powerful Spanish Crown. At Charles's request, Magellan and Faleiro submitted a written memorandum specifying the conditions under which they would agree to lead the expedition.[28] Emboldened by Haro's offer of financing, they gave the king two alternatives: one in which the Crown would bear all costs; another in which the partners would finance the voyage themselves (with Haro's backing). Much to the horror of Fonseca, who considered their conditions outrageous, Charles accepted them with only minor reservations. Because he wanted to maximize the benefits to the Crown, Charles agreed to finance the expedition from the royal treasury.[29]

FERDIN · MAGELLANVS · SVPERATIS
ANTARTICI   FRETI · ANGVS
TIIS ·   CLARISS ·

MAGELLAN, sixteenth-century portrait, artist unknown.

Courtesy of the Kuntshistorisches Museum, Vienna.

l'Infant Don Henri.

Duc de Viseu, G.ᵉ M.ᵉ de Chrⁱſt, prem. moteur des Découvertes.

PRINCE HENRY THE NAVIGATOR, patron of Portuguese exploration. From Joseph Francois Lafitau, Paris, 1733–1734.

Courtesy of the John Carter Brown Library at Brown University.

Trading junk returning to Okinawa from Malacca, early sixteenth century. On the Malacca waterfront, where such ships had until recently called, Magellan collected information about the Spice Islands.

Courtesy of S. Arasaki, Okinawa Prefectural Library.

Sixteenth-century Lisbon. Georgius Braun.

Courtesy of the Newberry Library. Edward E. Ayer Collection.

"May the wrath of the Franks fall upon you." Goa's flourishing trade in spices, precious stones, Arabian horses, and cotton lured the Portuguese, who massacred 8,000 while conquering the colony in 1511. Georgius Braun.

Courtesy of the Newberry Library. Edward E. Ayer Collection.

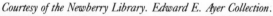

Portuguese carracks in the approaches to Lisbon. At the end of a 10,000-mile supply line, the Portuguese used superior naval power to increase their hold on the route to the east. With the capture of Malacca in 1511, the Portuguese controlled the gateway to the Far East. Gregorio Lopes.

Courtesy of the National Maritime Museum, London.

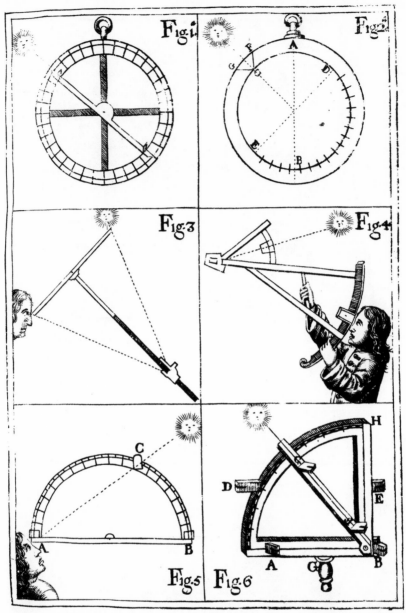

Top: the astrolabe, or "star taker"; center left: cross staff; center right: Davis Quadrant, developed subsequent to Magellan's voyage; bottom left: a nonreflective quadrant in use; bottom right: an early quadrant. Awkward to use on anything but a stable platform, and primitive at best, these instruments nonetheless opened the world to exploration.

Shipbuilding on the Central American coast, sixteenth century. Inspired by knowledge that their countrymen on the Pacific coast of the Isthmus of Panama were building ships to explore Balboa's Great South Sea, the officers of the *Trinidad* attempted a desperate Pacific crossing from the Moluccas.

MAGELLAN, twentieth-century portrait by Antonio Menendes, derived from sixteenth-century works.

Courtesy of the Museu de Marinha, Lisbon.

9
$\mathcal{T}$he Fleet

The capitulación *(articles of agreement) signed by King Charles* conceded most of the conditions stipulated by Magellan and Faleiro, going so far as to limit, for ten years, the licensing of other voyages of discovery to the Far East to persons approved by the partners. Among other items put forth in the *capitulación* were requests for the governorships of the new territories, and permission to ship to Spain 1,000 ducats worth of merchandise annually from the Moluccas, with tax exemptions. One condition that Charles found excessive was a stipulation that, should Magellan and Faleiro discover more than six islands, the pair be granted overlordship of two islands each, and be accorded the rights to rents and other commerce. (For a synopsis of the *capitulación*, see Appendix 5.) But the other extraordinary concessions, so rare for a king, and the speed with which negotiations were concluded underline the great importance Charles attached to the expedition. To avoid diplomatic difficulties with Portugal, documentary references to the objectives of the expedition were kept vague. A cryptic reference, ". . . to discover a westward route to the regions indicated *by searching for a strait* to the Mar del Sur,"[1] was the only indication of the proposed route.

King Ferdinand's ambitious grandson now sat on the throne of a united Spain. Son and heir of the reigning Holy Roman Emperor, Charles dreamed of ruling an empire greater than that of his namesake, Charlemagne. With Luther's challenges to the Roman Church disturbing the political equilibrium in central Europe, a Spanish overseas empire seemed a better prospect for fulfilling that dream, but the Portuguese were winning the race to the Orient. In Magellan's daring enterprise Charles saw an opportunity to beat the Portuguese to the Far East, making new discoveries and sowing the seeds of a worldwide empire. Fortified by Magellan's assurances that the Spice Islands, China, and Japan lay within the boundaries assigned to Castile by the Treaty of Tordesillas, Charles considered all of the Far East beyond Malacca a legitimate arena for Spanish exploitation.

In the Archive of the Indies in Seville is an anonymous document describing various Far Eastern locales. It contains what appears to be corrected and updated material from *O Livro de Odoardo Barbosa* (*The Book of Odoardo Barbosa*), a treatise written in India by a Portuguese who may have been Magellan's brother-in-law, Duarte Barbosa.[2] Since it was found in a bundle of documents containing rare fragments of manuscript in Magellan's own hand, it probably was presented to King Charles by Magellan before his fleet departed. Among the places discussed in the document are *Ofir* and *Tarsis*. In the Lisbon edition of *O Livro*, the equivalent passage deals with a locale called *Lequios*, an early Portuguese designation for the Ryukyu Islands (including Okinawa) and Formosa. Barbosa stated that Lequios was inhabited by rich, pale-skinned merchants who were well supplied with gold and silver ingots, silks, fine porcelains, and other precious goods. He added that he had been told that these merchants were honest folk, well dressed and better respected than the Chinese.[3] After the Portuguese seized Malacca, these merchants stopped sending their ships to that port,[4] no doubt moved by the reputation for savagery the Portuguese had earned in India.

The author of the document (likely Magellan) was clearly impressed by stories of the gold carried in the Lequian (Ryukyuan) ships, and he assumed that they had come from Tarshish and Ophir, the biblical sources of King Solomon's gold. Okinawan ships had been calling at Malacca two centuries before the Portuguese seized it, and their trade routes extended from Korea to Thailand and through much of the Malay Archipelago.[5] In Luzon, Okinawan merchants exchanged goods manufactured in China and Japan for gold. In Malacca, they bought spices and paid for them with Luzon gold. The spices were traded for the products and manufactures of Southeast Asia, China, and Japan, so that profits were earned on each leg of the circuit.

In Malacca in 1511 and 1512, Magellan learned about the wealthy Okinawan merchants who had traded there. Enrique, his Malay slave, interpreted as Magellan questioned mariners, longshoremen, port officials, merchants, and warehousemen along the waterfront. Translated from a medley of Malay dialects into Portuguese (which Enrique was just beginning to learn), much of the information was garbled, and Magellan may have confused references to Luzon, where the Okinawan merchants got their gold, with Lequios (Lu-chu, Ryukyu), their home islands. Europeans

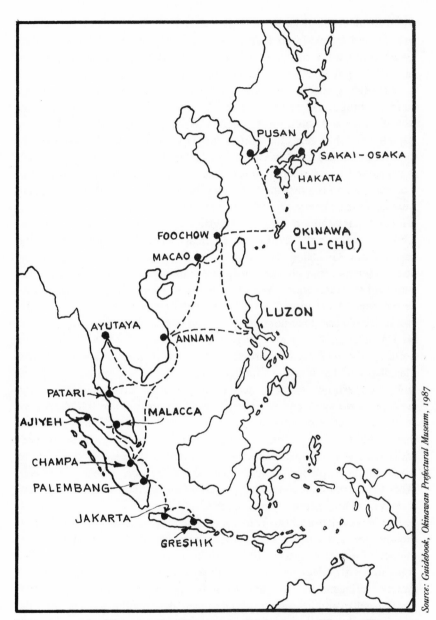

Source: Guidebook, Okinawan Prefectural Museum, 1987

Fourteenth-Sixteenth Century Okinawan Trade Routes

still had not reached Japan, and their extremely sketchy knowledge of it was derived from Marco Polo's secondhand information from the thirteenth century. On his globe of 1492, Martin Behaim put *Cipango* (Japan) east of *Mangi* (China), but in the latitudes occupied by the Philippines.[6]

In 1518, Magellan believed that these islands lay east of China within a band of latitude centered around 20° N, extending north for an indeterminate distance and south to the equator. As Polo had written that *Zipangu* (Japan) was rich in gold, and light-skinned merchants from *Lequios* had paid for their purchases in Malacca with gold ingots, it required no great leap of imagination for one steeped in scripture and fascinated by the prospect of locating the sources of King Solomon's gold to assume that what actually were Japan and the Ryukyu Islands were the biblical Tarshish and Ophir. It is ironic that, without realizing it, Magellan already had visited both places. The site of Tarshish, the Cretan colonial city of Tartessus, was on the banks of the Guadalquivir, not far from his home in Seville. Ophir was none other than the port of Sofala in Mozambique, where he had sailed with his first command, a bergantim based in Kilwa.[7] While we cannot be certain that Magellan enticed Charles with stories of gold in the islands east of China, the document in Seville and certain features of his memorable voyage suggest strongly that he did.

On the day he signed the articles of agreement, King Charles appointed Magellan and Faleiro joint commanders of the Moluccan fleet with the rank of captain general. The fleet would comprise five ships: two of 130 *toneles*, two of ninety, and one of sixty. Both commanders would receive an annual salary of 50,000 maravedis, and on April 17, 1518, the king ordered that an additional 8,000 maravedis per month be paid into their accounts while they were at sea.[8] Magellan was ecstatic; here was a sovereign to whom he could pledge his fealty without reservation or fear of betrayal. What he did not realize was that powerful figures close to the throne were already at work undermining his authority.

The first evidence of this is in a royal decree issued on March 22, 1518, the very day the articles of agreement were signed. Among other things, the decree names Juan de Cartagena to the post of *veedor general* (inspector general) for the fleet. A native of Burgos and a member of the Palace Guard, Cartagena was a confidant of Bishop Fonseca.[9] The bishop had used Magellan and Faleiro's proposal to increase his influence with the king and the royal council, drawing their attention to an area in which his expertise was desperately needed. While pleased with the power and prestige he had achieved, Fonseca was appalled that the king had given the command of a royal Spanish fleet to two Portuguese, granting them sweeping powers in the new lands they were expected to discover, and he immediately set out to dilute their authority. As a first step he arranged to have Cartagena appointed fleet inspector general, a political commissar whose principal function would be to guard against treachery by the foreign captains general.

The Portuguese ambassador, Álvaro da Costa, was dismayed to learn that King Charles had authorized the expedition. In a letter to King Manuel he described Magellan as ". . . a man of great spirit, very skilled in matters concerning the sea." The king should not be concerned about Faleiro, Costa wrote, ". . . for he is nearly out of his mind." On the other hand, Costa suggested, Magellan could still be useful, and it might be prudent to induce him to return to Portugal.[10] Costa's recommendation was discussed at a meeting of the Royal Council at Sintra,[11] but Manuel and a majority of the council were opposed to inviting Magellan back. Murder was discussed, and Vasco da Gama, the crusty old discoverer of the route to India, noted for neither compassion nor forgiveness, openly criticized the king for failing to have Magellan's head cut off when he had the chance.[12] Fearing that murdering Magellan might wreck his plans to marry Charles's sister, Manuel ignored Gama's advice. Instead, he ordered Costa to redouble his efforts in Spain to prevent Magellan from sailing.

With Magellan, Costa was unrelenting. He tried desperately to convince him that what he contemplated in the service of Spain would constitute treason against his homeland and bring disgrace not only on himself, but on his family in Portugal. Unmoved, Magellan replied that the Spanish fleet he would take to the Far East would not infringe on Portugal's legitimate territorial claims. Costa then tried another tack, urging Dom Jorge de Braganza, the patron of Magellan's father-in-law, to send the Barbosa family back to Portugal, uprooting them from their home in Seville.[13] On another front, he pressed Charles and his counselors to abandon their plans for the expedition, apparently succeeding with Cardinal Adrian, who had been skeptical from the beginning. A well-placed bribe to Chièvres probably secured the opposition of that greedy official, but nothing dampened the enthusiasm of the youthful king of Spain.[14]

Contrary to established procedure, the articles of agreement and the royal decrees relating to Magellan's enterprise had been drawn up and signed without prior consultation with the Casa de Contratación. Matters of this kind normally fell within the Casa's purview, and its officials made their pique clear in a bitter letter to the king. Thus reminded of the extreme touchiness of his Spanish subjects, Charles moved quickly to correct his oversight. In a long letter dated April 16, 1518, he informed the Casa of the negotiations with Magellan and Faleiro and of the articles of agreement, explaining that the extreme sensitivity of the matter required the attention of the highest court officials, precluding communication of the details until negotiations were concluded. The king assured the offended Casa officials that henceforth he would seek their advice and that of their senior pilots whom, in a rare display of royal flattery, he mentioned by name.[15] He further requested that the Casa recommend persons to serve as fleet fiscal officers, and a third party to see that "the said Portuguese . . . follow the prescribed route." Should both captains general perish during the course of the voyage, this third party would succeed them in command.[16] The letter, probably drafted by Fonseca, was no more than a royal sop meant to placate ruffled feelings at the Casa, the wily bishop's choice for the "third party," Cartagena, having already been appointed. With his protégé named inspector general, Fonseca insisted that the fleet fiscal officers should all be Castilians appointed directly by the Crown, assuring the young king that this was a reasonable precaution against possible malfeasance by the little-known foreigners to whom he had entrusted command of a royal Spanish fleet. What Fonseca really intended was that once the usefulness of the Portuguese joint commanders had been exhausted, the Castilian officers would depose them and place Cartagena in command of the fleet.

Magellan and Faleiro were back in Seville in May 1518, carrying orders from the king instructing the Casa to assist them in assembling a fleet. On May 7 each of the partners received from the treasurer of the Casa an advance of 30,000 maravedis for expenses,[17] but otherwise their reception at the Casa, although correct, was decidedly cool. It would not be possible, Magellan and Faleiro were told, to have the fleet ready by August 25, as Magellan had optimistically proposed; the king had been advised that December would be more realistic. Frustrated by the Casa's foot-dragging and fear that the king's confidence in them would be eroded by the efforts of Ambassador Costa and the Flemings, Magellan and Faleiro returned to court at Zaragoza at the end of May or beginning of June.[18] There, concern that Portuguese agents ". . . were out to kill Magellan and Faleiro . . ." caused them ". . . to walk in the shadows." Grateful to Fonseca for providing an armed guard to escort them to their inn when business at the palace kept them after sundown,[19] the two Portuguese were unaware that the bishop was maneuvering to control not only the financing of their enterprise, but ultimately its command.

In Zaragoza, the king honored both Magellan and Faleiro by dubbing them Knights of the Order of Santiago (St. James),[20] Spain's most prestigious military-religious society, sending a clear message to the Portuguese ambassador, the Flemish counselors, and the Casa in Seville: Any attempt to hinder Magellan and Faleiro would be considered an offense against the Crown. At the end of July or beginning of August 1518, the partners once more returned to Seville, this time with fresh orders from the king directing the Casa to proceed with the assembly and organization of the fleet.[21] Magellan's new knighthood apparently had the desired effect, or perhaps by now Casa officials were in tune with Fonseca. In a letter to the king dated August 16, 1518, they lauded the royal decision to authorize an exploratory voyage of such great promise.[22] While the letter expressed the Casa's satisfaction with the choice of Magellan as captain general, there was no mention of Faleiro. Perhaps his erratic behavior had become so apparent that he was discounted as a significant factor in the enterprise.

On July 20, 1518, responding to an urgent plea from the Casa for funds with which to carry out his orders, King Charles authorized the use of 6,000 ducats (about $240,000 U.S.) from a shipment of gold bullion from the Caribbean. The order stated that a Captain Nicolás de Artieta had already been dispatched to Vizcaya to purchase supplies, but that whenever possible, supplies should be ordered from Flanders.[23] The money was soon exhausted, and on August 16, the Casa informed the king that new shipments of gold bullion had arrived from the Caribbean and requested authorization to use some of it to cover the mounting costs of Magellan's fleet. The king replied on September 1, ordering the Casa to coin the bullion and use 5,000 ducats for the fleet. He added that future bullion shipments from the Indies should suffice to make up the full 16,000 ducats he had pledged to the enterprise.[24]

It fell to Juan de Aranda, the factor at the Casa, to select the ships specified in the articles of agreement. He traveled to Cádiz for this purpose and by October 1518 had purchased five naos (carracks) and moved them upriver to Seville. The approximate tonnage and cost of the five ships and cost of two ship's boats are listed in the table below.[25]

Ship	Tonnage	Price maravedis	U.S. $ 1990 gold price
San Antonio	120	330,000	35,310
Trinidad	110	270,000	28,890
Concepción	90	228,000	24,476
Victoria	85	300,000	32,100
Santiago	75	187,500	20,062
One *bergantín* (two-masted longboat)		49,584	5,305
Skiff for the *Trinidad*		3,970	425

Based on the records of the Casa, the costs of acquiring and outfitting Magellan's fleet can be summarized as follows:[26]

	maravedis	U.S. $
Ships and ships' boats	1,369,808	145,569
Materials, rigging and hardware	1,091,672	116,809
Labor (careening, caulkers, carpenters, sawyers)	254,055	27,184
Piloting charges (Cádiz to Seville)	1,054	113
Total	2,716,589	290,675

In addition, Aranda dunned the Casa 3,750 maravedis ($401) for personal expenses on his trip to Cádiz. Duarte Barbosa was sent to Bilbao to purchase armaments, which included swivel guns, light artillery, heavy mortars, and wall smashers (58 *versos*, 7 *falcones*, 3 *lombardas gruesas*, and 3 *pasamuros*), 70 crossbows, 50 muskets, 100 suits of armor (corselets, arm and shoulder guards, greaves, helmets, and breastplates), 360 dozen crossbow bolts, 1,000 lances, and 200 pikes. For the firearms there were 50 quintals of gunpowder and a considerable quantity of lead.[27] All this constituted a formidable arsenal for an exploratory voyage ostensibly undertaken with peaceful intent. Records provide few clues to the appearance of Magellan's ships; a discussion of the configuration, capacity and rigging of sixteenth-century Iberian *naos* is given in Appendix 1.

Magellan threw himself wholeheartedly into the task of preparing the fleet for sea, and the smallest details merited his attention and personal involvement.[28] He willingly pitched in when and wherever an extra hand would help get a job done properly and on schedule. An incident on the banks of the Guadalquivir in Seville, where the fleet was being fitted out, illustrates Magellan's close attention to that work and the frustrations he experienced.

Trinidad, the vessel he had chosen for his flagship, had been careened and recaulked. Early in the morning of October 22, 1518, she was to be refloated with the high tide, and Magellan wanted to enliven the event with ceremonial color. Protocol decreed that the royal standard of Castile should fly from the mainmast, and the banner of the ship's patron saint (in this case the Holy Trinity) atop the foremast. The waist of the ship was the proper place for displaying the banner of the ship's captain.[29]

By three o'clock on the morning of the twenty-second, Magellan was at work with Rodríguez de Mafra, one of his pilots, and a small crew, preparing to refloat the ship on the morning tide. At dawn, preoccupied with more serious matters, Magellan failed to notice that the royal standard and the ship's ensign were not flying at the mastheads. They had been sent to the flagmaker's shop for dyeing and had not yet been returned. However, four small banners bearing the Magellan coat of arms were draped on the capstans in the waist of the ship.[30]

A crowd of idlers had gathered on the riverbank to watch the proceedings, and among them circulated an agent of the Portuguese consul with orders to obstruct the operation if he could. Noting that the banners bearing Magellan's family crest were displayed on the ship while the royal standard of Castile was not, he managed to inflame the crowd by spreading word that the arms displayed were those of the king of Portugal, to which they bore a superficial resemblance.[31] The crowd grew ugly, hurling imprecations at the workers on the ship. A minor port official, puffed up with his own importance and spurred on by the crowd, strutted up to Magellan and demanded that he take down the offending banners. Magellan explained that they were not the royal arms of Portugal as the crowd believed, but those of the captain, a loyal vassal of King Charles. That said, he turned his back on the fellow and went back to work. The official, not at all satisfied, hustled off to get help.

Meanwhile, the crowd surged down to the water's edge where the ship lay on its props, the bolder among them intent on ripping down the offending banners. They were intercepted by Rodríguez de Mafra and some of the workmen, and a scuffle ensued in which Mafra was stabbed in the hand. At this point, Dr. Sancho de Matienzo, canon of the cathedral of Seville and treasurer of the Casa, arrived on the scene, annoyed that the ruckus was interfering with work ordered by the king. He reminded Magellan that, while he was within his rights to display his banners, by refusing to take them down he had played directly into the hands of the Portuguese agent. The old canon's logic was undeniable, and Magellan swallowed his pride, took the banners down, and stowed them out of sight.

Just as the unruly crowd was beginning to back off and Magellan and his crew were ready to resume work, the angry port official returned with the port captain. The two clambered onto the ship and confronted Magellan. "Where are the banners of the king of Portugal that you dared display on the capstans?" demanded the port captain. Having no wish to discuss the matter, Magellan turned his back on the two, prompting the enraged port captain to call to some nearby men-at-arms to arrest him. When Dr. Matienzo warned the port officials that they were interfering with the king's work and ordered them to leave, the men-at-arms drew their swords and threatened to cut off the cleric's head. The laborers on the *Trinidad* decided they'd had enough and fled, leaving the ship unattended as the tide flooded in.

Sensing the danger, the port officials released Magellan and stopped threatening Dr. Matienzo. Furious, Magellan walked away, intending to leave the port officials to fend for themselves, but the levelheaded canon urged him to stay, for without him there would be little chance to save the ship. Magellan relented and ordered the port officials to stay aboard to help, since many of the workmen had left. His loyal crew, having armed themselves, seized a few of the troublemakers from the mob and clamped them in stocks. Fearing similar treatment, the port officials departed in haste.

On October 24, still seething with indignation, Magellan wrote to King Charles complaining bitterly of the port officials. He was at least as much offended by their impropriety as by the inconvenience they caused, reminding the king that ". . . while others might serve [Your Highness] only with words," Magellan had pledged ". . . my estate, my person, and my life." He added, in a thinly veiled threat, "Keeping my word [to Your Highness], is worth far more to me than all the promises Portugal has been offering." Noting that he deserved better treatment, he asked that the offenders be punished. This letter in Magellan's own hand provides one of the best firsthand accounts of any episode of his globe-girdling enterprise.[32]

Charles replied promptly, expressing outrage over the incident. He promised an investigation, and ordered the chief magistrate of Seville to punish the guilty parties ". . . with all the rigor of justice." Given the peculiar methods employed in those days to inflict "justice" on wrongdoers, it is not pleasant to contemplate the fate of the harassers. The king also dispatched a letter to the political authorities in Seville, expressing his "astonishment" that the incident should have occurred in their jurisdiction, and that they had failed to cooperate with his captain general and the Casa. Another letter went to Dr. Matienzo, lauding his conduct and asking him to keep the king informed about the punishment of the guilty parties.[33]

As a further salve to his captain general's wounded ego, Charles elevated Magellan from *Caballero* (Knight) to the exalted rank of *Comendador* (Knight Commander) in the Order of Santiago.[34] This unmistakable sign of the king's esteem produced in Magellan an unshakable determination to honor his promises to the young sovereign.

10

$\mathcal{R}$ecruiting and Final Preparations

 By early April 1519, the ships of the Moluccan Fleet (as it had come to be known) had been reconditioned, armed, and outfitted for a long sea voyage. The partnership between Magellan and Faleiro was still in effect, with command of the fleet shared between them, but Magellan's capable involvement with every phase of the preparations had clearly established him as the leader. Constantly harassed by Portuguese agents, Magellan also confronted distrust, deviousness, and outright subterfuge from the Spanish officials who were supposed to be helping him. Despite these obstacles, he managed to keep the developing enterprise on track.

The scholarly, eccentric Faleiro was seldom mentioned in the official correspondence passing between the court and the Casa. While Magellan attended to outfitting the fleet, Faleiro busied himself with scientific matters such as overseeing the preparation of charts, globes, and navigational tables, and the manufacture of compasses, astrolabes, and other navigational instruments.[1] Of paramount importance was a thirty-chapter manual he had prepared containing astronomical tables, diagrams, and instructions for three methods of estimating longitude.[2] One, which Faleiro originated, depended on changes in compass variation observed as ships traveled east or west. Faleiro had charted these as a system of isogonal lines, but only for the North Atlantic.[3] Little realizing that it would be useless in uncharted seas with no record of previous observations, Magellan had high hopes for the system. The other two methods probably were adaptations of astronomical techniques described in ephemerides published between 1474 and 1506 by Regiomontanus (Johann Müller). One of these adaptations depended on lunar distances, the other on lunar-stellar conjunctions or lunar-solar opposition.[4] To calculate the longitude of a position, the time of an astronomical event observed from that position was compared with its predicted time on a reference meridian. The latter value was obtained from an *ephemeris*, a set of astronomical tables.

When Faleiro later was dropped from the roster, the only person in the fleet with the knowledge and skills to understand and apply his methods for estimating longitude was his replacement as fleet astronomer. On two of the three occasions during the voyage when conditions were suitable for testing the astronomical methods recommended by Faleiro, results were achieved that, for accuracy, would not be equalled for more than two hundred years.

It had long since become apparent to Magellan that while the funds promised by the Crown would purchase and outfit the ships for the fleet, there would not be enough left over for the trade goods he would need to make the expedition profitable; he brought this to the king's attention in a letter dated October 24, 1518.[5] Fonseca recommended that Cristóbal de Haro be invited to invest in the Moluccan Fleet. Since his arrival in Spain, Haro had already agreed to outfit an expedition to Darien to be led by Gil Gonzales Dávila and Andrés Niño. Although Charles issued his first invitation to Haro on March 10, 1519, the financier did not accept immediately. Only after another letter from Charles, dated April 6, urging him to go to Seville as soon as possible, did Haro begin to participate actively in Magellan's enterprise; he arrived in Seville in July, accompanied by Juan de Cartagena.[6] Charles made Haro manager of the Crown's mercantile interests in the enterprise and granted him the authority to establish a separate Casa de Contratación with exclusive control over the spice trade.[7] By shrewdly manipulating the young king, Fonseca and Haro had seized fiscal control of the enterprise before the first ship was acquired. Through their control of the proposed Casa for spices, Fonseca and Haro would have a choke-hold on the flow of these commodities into Spain, giving them leverage to force Magellan and Faleiro to share with them the generous benefits the king had conceded. As the royal authorization for a separate Casa for spices could scarcely have been concealed from the officials of the existing Casa, it must have taken all of Fonseca's considerable diplomatic skills to sell them on the idea.

Haro was quick to exploit his influence with the king.[8] On March 19, 1519, Charles instructed his chief magistrate in Hispaniola, Rodrigo de Figueroa, to look into the matter of one of Haro's caravels, which had sailed from Lisbon to Brazil six years earlier loaded with trade goods. Driven by contrary winds, it landed in Hispaniola, where its cargo disappeared. Haro suspected that it had been illegally confiscated. In a further extension of royal favor, Charles requested his sister Leonor, now queen of Portugal, to urge her husband, Manuel, to drop the punitive lawsuit initiated against Haro when he left Portugal for Spain. Haro's involvement with Magellan's enterprise was duly noted in a letter to Manuel from the Portuguese consul in Seville, Sebastião Álvares.[9] The financier from Burgos was not the only private investor to contribute funds to the Moluccan Fleet. Others included Alfonso Gutiérrez, Anton Fugger, and Juan de Cartagena.[10]

When Manuel learned that Haro was in Seville to lend his considerable financial resources and expertise to outfit Magellan's fleet, he awoke to the full magnitude of the threat to his jealously guarded spice monopoly. Furious, he ordered the seizure of Haro's assets in Portugal and its overseas territories, and forbade the *Casa da India* in Lisbon from contracting any further business with Haro's company.

Although Haro's support solved the enterprise's financial problems, the disruptive efforts of Manuel's agents in Spain continued to plague Magellan. Their job was made easier when Pedro de Isásaga, the cooperative comptroller (*contador*) of the Casa, was replaced by Juan López de Recalde, whose open hostility to the expedition points to the possibility that he had been bribed by Portuguese agents. His first move, designed to prevent the fleet from sailing, was to urge the Casa's pilots to refuse to sail on the grounds that Magellan was unjustifiably secretive about the details of the route he planned to take.[11] Recalde then set out to undercut the recruiting effort by refusing to pay the enlistment bonuses authorized earlier by the Casa's treasurer, Dr. Matienzo.[12] The delays were serious, and Magellan further suspected that false rumors about him might be reaching the king through Recalde and perhaps others at the Casa susceptible to the influence of Portuguese agents. Anxious to advise the king personally of the difficulties delaying the departure of the fleet, Magellan went to Barcelona, where Charles had been holding court since February, arriving toward the middle of April 1519.[13]

He apparently got Charles's attention, for on April 15, the king wrote to the Casa suggesting that ". . . certain pilots, under different pretexts, wish to renege on their obligation to sail with our squadron; I order you, with all the force of your laws, to insist on their obedience and compliance with their contracts; you will pay them their salaries regularly so that they will not have that excuse; I give you full power to treat as rebels those who persist in their refusal."[14]

In a letter of April 19, 1519, addressed to the captains, pilots, and seamen, the king ordered that ". . . during the voyage, each and every one of you must follow the advice and decisions of Magellan, so that you may go first and before all else to the Moluccas, or goods and lives will be lost."[15]

As an incentive for prospective crew members, the king issued a royal decree guaranteeing payment of rent for their lodgings and the security of their possessions during their absence with the fleet.[16]

In Barcelona, Magellan was called upon to testify in proceedings in which Juan de Aranda was accused by the Supreme Council of the Indies of improperly using his position at the Casa for personal gain.[17] Fonseca was incensed when he learned that Aranda, a subordinate, had extracted from Magellan and Faleiro a share of the profits expected from their enterprise. After the licentiate in charge of the investigation presented his findings to the council, Aranda was censured for using his office for private gain contrary to the king's interests. His contract with Magellan and Faleiro was cancelled and he was demoted from his position as factor at the Casa and denied the opportunity to recover the 1,500 ducats he had spent from his own purse on behalf of Magellan and Faleiro. His appeal of July 20, 1519, was rejected by the council.[18] It has been suggested that the charges against Aranda may have been initiated by Recalde, Haro, or Fonseca.[19,20] Haro and Fonseca would have had in common the desire to reduce the number of participants with shares in the enterprise; bad blood with Aranda could have motivated Recalde. In 1523, after Aranda resumed his post as factor at the Casa, one of his first acts was to fire Recalde.[21]

While at court, Magellan obtained from King Charles an order that during his absence his annual salary of 50,000 maravedis would be paid to his wife, Doña Beatriz. Should he die in the king's service, this allotment would continue throughout her life.[22] At Magellan's urging, the king also promised to confer the privileges of knighthood on the masters and pilots who sailed with the fleet.[23] Magellan returned to Seville with these concessions, arriving at the end of April after experiencing renewed pressure from two Portuguese diplomats, João Mendes and Nuno Ribeiro, who had accompanied the court when it moved to Barcelona in February.[24-26] Manuel had warned Charles that a Spanish fleet in the Moluccas would destroy the goodwill generated by his recent marriage to Charles's sister. Despairing of Charles's stubborn refusal to heed the warnings of his royal brother-in-law, Mendes and Ribeiro turned again to Magellan, who earlier in Seville had politely rejected their overtures when they urged him to return to Portugal. They fared no better in Barcelona.

Three Castilian noblemen were selected for positions of high command in the fleet: Cartagena, who earlier had been appointed inspector general, was named captain of one of the ships on March 30, and Luis de Mendoza, a native of Granada, was appointed fleet treasurer and captain of another ship. A third captaincy was awarded on April 6 to Gaspar de Quesada, a member of the personal staff of the archbishop of Seville. The ships to which the captains would be assigned were not specified.[27]

Cartagena's authority is evident from his generous compensation. As inspector general, his annual salary was 70,000 maravedis, and as captain of a ship he drew another 40,000. He was not required to relinquish his position in the elite Palace Guard, and his salary from that source would be paid into his account during his absence.[28] Although the amount of the latter stipend has not been reported, Cartagena's total compensation may have equalled or exceeded that of Magellan (50,000 maravedis annual salary plus 8,000 per month for sea duty).

On April 30, Antonio de Coca was designated fleet accountant with an annual salary of 50,000 maravedis. No records shed light on his place of birth or background,[29] though some have speculated that he was a bastard of the Fonseca family.[30] Whatever his antecedents, he must have enjoyed Fonseca's good graces to have been recommended to the king for such a prestigious appointment. Coca's rank entitled him to a staff of seven servants, among them a French chaplain, Bernard Calmette.[31]

On the same day Coca received his appointment, a royal order granted to Francisco Faleiro, Ruy's brother, an annual salary of 35,000 maravedis on the condition that he remain in Seville to help outfit ships for subsequent expeditions to the Moluccas.[32]

One of the most fateful appointments to Magellan's fleet was that of Gonzalo Gómez de Espinosa as master-at-arms (*alguacil mayor*). A native of Espinosa de los Monteros, high in the Cantabrian Mountains of Old Castile, he was between 30 and 33 years old at the time of his appointment in April 1519.[33] To avoid confusion with the pilot, Estevão Gomes (*Estéban Gómez* in Spanish documents), also an important figure in this story, it will be convenient to refer to Gonzalo Gómez as Espinosa. As fleet master-at-arms, his position would be roughly comparable to that of a warrant officer in charge of a marine detachment on an American or British naval ship. A tough, uncomplicated man, Espinosa seems always to have seen his duty clearly and never wavered in his performance of it. After Magellan's death and the subsequent massacre of the principal officers of the fleet, it was Espinosa who restored discipline among the demoralized crew, making possible the survival of some and the completion of the first circumnavigation of the Earth.

On July 20, 1519, Gerónimo Guerra of Burgos was assigned to the fleet. A letter from López Recalde to Fonseca stated that Guerra was ". . . a relative and employee of Cristóbal de Haro."[34] While his annual salary of 30,000 maravedis was to be charged against the expenses of the fleet, at the time of his appointment his duties were not specified. The royal order authorizing his enrollment merely stated that it ". . . will be useful for him to go in the fleet." When the fleet sailed, Guerra held the position of ship's clerk (*escribano*) on the *San Antonio*, the ship commanded by Juan de Cartagena.[35] Possibly his chief function was to spy for the inspector general.

Among the officers of the fleet, there was a distinction between the Crown-appointed high command and the professional mariners hired by the Casa. The former included the captains, inspector general, treasurer, accountant, and ship's clerks. Charged with fiscal, political, diplomatic, and judicial duties, they were paid annual salaries. The masters and mates were professional mariners, responsible for the operation and maintenance of their ships and the supervision and training of the crews. Hired by the Casa and paid a monthly wage, they were expected to know basic navigation. The pilots constituted a special category. Professional mariners hired by the Casa, they differed from the masters and mates in that they held royal commissions, were paid an annual salary, and were considered part of the high command.

A separate, catch-all category of personnel were the supernumeraries (*sobresalientes*), which included the master- and men-at-arms, unassigned gentlemen expected to bear arms when necessary, two interpreters (*lenguas*), servants (*criados*) and a slave (*esclavo*) of the high command, a surgeon (*cirujano*), two chaplains (*capellanes*), two barbers (*barberos*), a cooper (*tonelero*), two smiths (*herreros*), and four unassigned able seamen (*marineros*). Except for the surgeon, who was paid an annual salary, the wages of the supernumeraries were computed monthly.[36]

Archives in Seville indicate that the enrollment of masters, mates, and seamen for Magellan's fleet commenced in September 1518, but difficulties in hiring and keeping competent mariners prompted frequent juggling of available personnel between positions as the ships were fitted out for sea. Of those who eventually sailed as masters, Juan Sebastián del Cano and Juan de Elorriaga first signed on as mates, Antonio Salamón as an able seaman.[37] It is more difficult to track Juan Bautista, the Genoese who sailed as master of the *Trinidad*, because of homonyms and inconsistencies in the spelling of his name. Christian names with Spanish spellings were generally used, followed by the name of the town, district, or country where the individual was born or made his home (*natural* or *vecino*). For Juan Bautista (Giovanni Battista), this has been listed variously as Punzorol, Punçozol, Poncero, Punceron, Pinzerol, and Poncevera. The latter may be most nearly correct, since there is a Polcevera River just to the west of Genoa, near the town of Sestri, where he was born in 1468. When he first appeared on the rolls in September 1518, Bautista would have been about fifty, making him the oldest man in Magellan's fleet.[38]

As the spring of 1519 advanced toward summer, Magellan found it nearly impossible to recruit competent Spanish seamen.[39] The population of Castile had been slow to rebuild in the aftermath of the plague that swept Europe in the fourteenth century, and there was a shortage of laborers ashore. Next door in Portugal, the sea provided the best outlet for young men's energies, and many Portuguese seamen found berths on foreign ships. There was no shortage of Portuguese applicants when recruiting began for Magellan's fleet. In Castile, on the other hand, there were better opportunities ashore, especially in agriculture and in service occupations. With its poor wages and high risks, there was little to attract young Castilians to seafaring. To make matters worse, Magellan had to compete for crews with Dávila's expedition to Darien and with yet another squadron recruiting in Málaga for a voyage to the Levant (in the eastern Mediterranean).[40]

In the ports of Andalusia in those days, the customary way to recruit crews was for a crier to announce the inducements along the waterfront and in the town square. After 20 days of recruiting for Magellan's fleet, not a single Spaniard had enlisted,[41] so Magellan sent Espinosa to Málaga to seek recruits. Although he carried a letter of authorization from the Casa, town officials prevented Espinosa from making his announcements, ostensibly to avoid competition with recruiters promoting the voyage to the Levant. He returned to Seville with but one recruit. Magellan then sent Baltazar (Baldassare) Palla, the Genoese master of the *Santiago*, back to Málaga to try his luck; he did better, garnering six recruits.[42]

With 7,000 maravedis from Magellan's own purse, Juan Bautista twice was sent to Cádiz in search of recruits. Dr. Matienzo's letter of authorization did him no good; Recalde got to the town authorities first and Bautista was forbidden to recruit on grounds that the Dávila expedition had priority.[43] Juan Sebastián del Cano, now master of the *Concepción*, Duarte Barbosa, a supernumerary on the *Trinidad*, Juan Rodríguez Serrano, a pilot, and others, even the demoted Aranda, were dispatched throughout Spain to find willing seamen.

So few Spaniards enlisted that Magellan, over the furious objections of his detractors at the Casa, stubbornly continued to accept foreigners. As long as the ships' masters were satisfied with their competence, willing hands were enlisted regardless of nationality.[44] Among these were some Portuguese relatives of Magellan, including two pilots and an unspecified number of supernumeraries and servants. In addition there were 17 apprentice seamen (*grumetes*) and two stewards (*despenseros*), all Portuguese. The result was a stern letter to the Casa from the king dated June 17, 1519, stating that Magellan must understand that he could not take with him more than five of his countrymen. The remaining Portuguese were to be dismissed.[45]

Magellan filed a formal protest before a notary arguing that neither his
contract with the Crown nor his instructions limited his selection of personal staff from among his relatives. He warned Casa officials not to im-
pede the enrollment of these Portuguese, his relatives and servants, for if
he couldn't take them, he wouldn't go either–and the Casa would bear the
blame for the consequences.[46] Casa officials responded that the formal judicial action he had taken was not an appropriate means for settling their
differences. They had tried, the officials said, to reconcile his demands
with their instructions from the king. Then they filed a cross-complaint
charging Magellan not to take in the fleet more than the four or five Portuguese authorized by the king. Backing down slightly, they did agree to accept one of the Portuguese stewards.[47] Despite the dismissal of many of
the Portuguese, some who disguised their nationality were able to remain
aboard. Others, evidently shielded in some way by Magellan, were never
challenged.[48] Nevertheless, Magellan was forced to remove from the rolls
some of the more highly visible of his countrymen, among them the two
pilots, Pedro de Abreu and Miguel de Mesquita. Although licensed by the
Casa, they were not permitted to sail with the fleet.[49] Seeking evidence of
deliberate defiance of the king's orders by Magellan, Recalde took depositions from the recruiters about the practice of accepting foreigners, but
their testimony exonerated the captain general of subversion. The reluctance of Spanish seamen to sign on with the fleet, witnesses said, was due
to low wages and aversion to serving under a Portuguese commander.[50]
The wrangling between Magellan and the Recalde faction at the Casa continued until the fleet sailed from Seville, an ill will noted by the Portuguese
consul, Sebastião Álvares. He reported to King Manuel that Recalde and
his supporters ". . . could not stomach Magellan."[51]

The records of the Casa are imprecise with respect to fleet personnel.
When the crews learned that their ships were being supplied for a two-year
voyage into unknown seas, desertions increased rapidly. With new enlist-
ments, dismissals, and desertions each day, the crew rosters were in a constant state of flux. Estimates of the total number who sailed with the fleet
range from the 234 authorized in the articles of agreement to 400; two hundred and seventy is probably a realistic estimate.[52] Of the 105 foreigners
known to have sailed, there were 31 Portuguese, 29 Italians, 17 French,
and smaller numbers of Flemings, Greeks, Irish, English, Orientals, Ne-
groes, and a Moor. From Spain there were 165, including at least 29
Basques, many of whom did not speak Castilian. The fleet was a veritable
Tower of Babel, and the masters and mates would have their work cut out
for them to manage such a motley crew. A list of known personnel and
brief, biographical sketches of some whose actions are recounted in this
story has been included in Appendix 3.

By early summer of 1519, Magellan was painfully aware that the king's confidence in him was being undermined. Communications from Charles were no longer directed to him personally, but to the Casa. Failing to support his efforts to man the fleet with experienced mariners, the king's directives, passed along by the Recalde faction at the Casa, seemed designed to create a management mess for which Magellan could be blamed, giving the authorities an excuse to replace him as captain general. Bishop Fonseca now had men of his own choosing in command of three of Magellan's five ships: Cartagena on the *San Antonio*, Quesada on the *Concepción*, and Mendoza on the *Victoria*, each supported on his ship by confederates of high rank. On July 16, a letter from the king to the Casa directed Ruy Faleiro to remain in Seville to supervise the preparation of a second Moluccan fleet of which he would have full command.[53] With Faleiro, the Portuguese pilots, and many of the Portuguese crewmen gone, support for Magellan was much diminished should his command be challenged at sea.

Meanwhile, Charles was burdened with other concerns, some of which were of much greater significance to him than Magellan's enterprise. On June 19, 1519, following the death of his grandfather, he was elected Holy Roman Emperor. As he prepared to leave Spain for the imperial coronation in Aachen, he became increasingly preoccupied with politics in Germany, where Martin Luther's audacious challenges to the Church were creating political turmoil. He left the management of Spanish affairs to Cardinal Adrian, who would be named regent upon Charles's departure from Spain in May 1520.

The Flemish cardinal was chiefly concerned with the continuing opposition to Charles's reign from the proud, independent *hidalgos* of rural Castile. The flagrant rape of the Spanish treasury by Charles's Flemish advisors had produced in most of these noblemen a profound disgust.[54] Up to his neck in domestic difficulties, Adrian was content to leave overseas affairs, including Magellan's enterprise (about which he always had been skeptical), in the experienced hands of his fellow churchman, Bishop Fonseca. And so, just when Magellan was trying desperately to recruit competent crews for his ships, he was deprived of the protection of the king who had supported him so enthusiastically.

The removal of Ruy Faleiro as co-commander may have been precipitated by manifestations of the madness that afflicted him periodically in later years,[55] or by his intransigence in a dispute with Magellan over which of them would be entrusted with the royal standard.[56] It also has been suggested that, as the departure date approached, Faleiro began to doubt the applicability to the voyage of his system for determining longitude from compass variation. Perhaps the disruptive efforts of the Portuguese agents, the growing hostility of the Casa, and fear that his navigational system might fail and greatly damage his reputation added up to unbearable stress for Ruy Faleiro. In a person as irritable as he, it may have produced bizarre behavior casting doubt on his fitness to command.

Juan de Cartagena and Cristóbal de Haro arrived in Seville in mid-July with the recently appointed fleet treasurer, Luis de Mendoza.[57] The reassignment of Faleiro and the appointment of haughty, Castilian captains and other high-ranking officers–none with seafaring experience–to three of his five ships profoundly disturbed Magellan. He may have been relieved that he would not have to contend with Faleiro's temperamental outbursts during the long, dangerous voyage, but troubled by the prospect of losing his partner's scientific expertise; he insisted that Faleiro leave with him his astronomical tables and charts of magnetic variation, with instructions for using them to determine longitude.[58]

With so many impediments thrown into his path, Magellan may well have had second thoughts about the enterprise he'd begun with such high hopes, but he forged resolutely ahead. What the Holy Grail was for Gawain, this quest was for Magellan, and the Castilian dragons in his path failed to daunt him. The shimmering vision faded with the growing evidence that Charles had been persuaded to distrust his loyalty, but Magellan had passed the point of no return.

One wishes that Doña Beatriz had left some record of her husband's feelings during the last months before he sailed. That he suffered pangs of conscience for having forsaken the land of his birth to take service with its chief maritime rival is suggested by a letter Sebastião Álvares sent to Manuel.[59] Sensing Magellan's growing disillusionment, Álvares made one last attempt to change his mind about leading a Spanish fleet to the Moluccas. The letter, dated July 18, 1519, describes their last interview, portraying Magellan as conscience stricken but determined to fulfill his obligation to Charles. If the obvious irony in some of Magellan's statements seems to have escaped Álvares, it may have been due to his awareness of Manuel's vindictiveness to bearers of bad news. With that caution, here is a translation of Álvares's letter:[60]

Seeing that it was an opportune time to do what Your Highness had ordered, I went to Magellan's house, where I found him packing victuals, preserves, and other things. I told him that what he was doing seemed to me proof of his evil design. Because this would be the last time I would speak with him, I wanted him to remember how, as his friend and a good Portuguese, I had tried to dissuade him from the great error he was about to make. After asking his pardon, lest what I was about to say should offend him, I reminded him how many times I had spoken to him, and how he had always responded with courtesy, and that his replies had always given me hope that, in the end, he would not do such a great disservice to Your Highness. I had told him to desist, for this road he was taking had as many dangers as Saint Catherine's wheel.[61] Rather, he should take the road toward Coimbra and return to his native land in the good graces of Your Highness, from whom he would always receive favors.

In this interview, I wanted to alert him to all the dangers that I saw [ahead of him], and the errors he was making. He replied that honor gave him no other choice than to continue with what he had begun. I answered that to win honor improperly, and with such infamy, was neither wisdom nor honor, but rather lack of both. He could be sure that the foremost among the Castilian gentry of this city [Seville] held him to be an ill-bred scoundrel since, to the disservice of his true king and lord, he had undertaken such a venture. Worse, as he had been the one who had proposed, organized and set it going, he could be certain that he was held a traitor for opposing Your Highness's interests.

At this point he replied that he saw the error he had made, but that he hoped to safeguard Your Highness's interests and that, by this voyage, he would do you a real service. I replied that those who would believe such a thing did not understand what he proposed to do, since even if he should find what he expected without touching Your Highness's dominions, it would do them great harm. I reminded him that he had nourished a more sensible proposition when he told me that if Your Highness should order him to return to Portugal, he would do so without any further favors. Should this not be granted, there was always Serradossa, seven yards of sack cloth and gall-nut beads.[62] It seemed to me that he was sincere in how he felt about honor and conscience. So much was said that I am unable to write all of it.

At this point, he asked me if what I had told him had come from me, or whether Your Highness had ordered me to say it, and what reward you would grant him.[63] I replied that I was not a person of so much importance that Your Highness would entrust such a mission to me, but that it had come from me as it had on so many other occasions.

Here he wished to pay me a compliment, saying that if what I had begun with him should go forward without interference from others, then Your Highness would be well served, but that Nuno Ribeiro had told him one thing which meant nothing, and João Mendes another which could not be verified. Then he told me of the favors [that they said] Your Highness had promised.[64]

At this point, he began to show contrition, saying how deeply this matter had affected him, but that nothing had happened to give him reason to leave a king who had shown him so much favor. I replied that it would be more

certain and more truly honorable to do what he should and not to forfeit his
honor and the favors that Your Highness would grant him. If he weighed his
coming from Portugal because of the 100 reis, more or less, of moradia that
Your Highness had refused to give him (so as not to violate your laws),
against the arrival of two sets of orders [Cartagena's and the reassignment of
Faleiro] from King Charles at variance with his own, he would see whether
this insult would not outweigh it, and would do what his duty demanded
rather than stay [here in Seville] for what he had come to do.

  He was greatly astonished at how much I knew, and then he told me the
truth, how the courier had left (which I already knew). He added that he
could not foresee any reason to withdraw from the enterprise, unless the terms
of his contract were not fulfilled. Then he wanted to know what Your High-
ness might offer him. "What more do you wish to see than the orders?" I said
to him. "And didn't Ruy Faleiro say openly that he would not follow your
lantern and that he would navigate to the south or he would not sail with
the fleet?" He (Magellan) thought that he would go as captain general, while
I knew that there were other orders to the contrary, of which he would know
nothing until it was too late to salvage his honor. He should pay no heed to
the honeyed words of the Bishop of Burgos. Now was the time to make his
decision. He should give me a letter for Your Highness and I, out of friend-
ship for him, would take it to Your Highness and plead his cause. I had no
orders from Your Highness about this matter, and only spoke of what I had
told him many times before.[65] He ended by saying that he would have noth-
ing to tell me [make no decision] until he saw the response that the courier
would bring.[66] Our conversation ended there.

Álvares's letter continues at great length, and most of it need not be
quoted further, except for two paragraphs. One contains observations
about Faleiro: "On two occasions I spoke to Ruy Faleiro, but to all my
overtures he invariably responded that he would do nothing contrary to the
king who had granted him so many favors. He seemed to me to be a man
of unsound mind, his familiar spirit having taken away whatever sanity he
once may have possessed.[67] I believe that if Magellan can be won over, Faleiro will follow readily."

The other paragraph describes the route that Magellan had proposed to
take, and makes clear the ill will felt by Portuguese officialdom for Magellan and his enterprise:

The route which it is reported they are to take is direct to Cabo Frio, keeping
Brazil on their right until they pass the boundary line [the Tordesillas Treaty
line], and from there to sail west and northwest direct to Maluco. This land

of Maluco I have seen located on the globe and chart made here by Fernão [Jorge] de Reinel. These were not completed when his father [Pedro] arrived, [but] his father finished them and marked on them the lands of Maluco. On this [same] pattern are constructed all the charts being made by Diego Ribeiro. He [Reinel] makes all the compasses, quadrants and globes, but he does not sail with the fleet. He desires nothing more than to earn his living by his skill. From this Cabo Frio to the islands of Maluco by this route, no lands are shown on the charts they make. May God Almighty grant that they make a voyage like that of the Cortereals,[68] and that Your Highness be blessed with tranquillity and ever be envied, as he is by all princes.

The royal orders that Cartagena carried to Seville in July apparently certified his appointments as fleet inspector general and captain of the *San Antonio*. Later that same month, a separate order arrived specifying his position in the fleet heirarchy as *conjunta persona* with the captain general. The meaning of this term is unclear, perhaps deliberately so, but it certainly implies a status equal to that of Magellan. What is known of Charles's use of this term to designate Cartagena's status in the fleet comes from Magellan himself. In a note to the Casa, he wrote that there ". . . is to go [in the fleet] . . . the honorable Juan de Cartagena, as *conjunta persona*, as His Highness ordered in his letter." Magellan later added: ". . . His Highness so ordered according to the provisions and instructions received by Juan de Cartagena from His Highness."[69] This last comment suggests that the order was communicated to Magellan by Cartagena, not by the king or the Casa. It is reasonable to assume that the order had been drafted by Fonseca, signed by the king, and delivered to Magellan by Cartagena. The status that the king had granted Cartagena cannot have failed to make Magellan wonder whether, like Faleiro, he was to be replaced, or whether once at sea his command would be challenged. In Álvares's final report to Manuel about Magellan, he indicated that the latter was expecting a courier with a letter presumably from the court, clarifying Cartagena's status in the fleet relative to his own. It was becoming obvious to Magellan that, given the slightest excuse, the Castilian officers in the fleet's high command would attempt to replace him.

Because he suspected that he could keep his command only by maintaining his indispensability to the enterprise, Magellan nurtured the notion that he alone knew the location of a passage through the landmass in the western Atlantic, and stubbornly ignored the efforts of the Casa, the pilots, and the king to get him to reveal the route he planned to take. He also realized that, with their well-placed connections, the Castilian high command had him at a disadvantage in Spain. Once these pompous landlubbers were at sea, however, Magellan felt he could handle them. He therefore kept to himself his reservations about the ambiguity in the fleet's command structure, and carefully planned his moves.

His intimate involvement with getting the ships ready for sea had earned for him the respect of the professional officers and seamen, and he could count on the support of many of them. He cultivated a rapport with Espinosa, the tough, veteran master-at-arms, whom he felt he could trust.

With Castilian courtiers for captains on the *San Antonio*, *Concepción*, and *Victoria*, a captain for the *Santiago*, the smallest vessel of the fleet, had yet to be chosen. Magellan had originally hoped to name João Lopes Carvalho, one of the pilots who accompanied him from Portugal. When the Casa officials objected, unwilling to approve a Portuguese captain, Magellan suggested that he would transfer his own flag to the *Santiago* whenever its shallow draft would be useful for inshore exploration. The Casa still demurred. Finally, Juan Rodríguez Serrano, a veteran pilot and a Castilian acceptable to both Magellan and the Casa,[70] was named captain and pilot of the *Santiago*.

To replace Ruy Faleiro, Andrés de San Martín, a pilot employed by the Casa and highly regarded for his knowledge of astronomy and mathematics, was named fleet astrologer (astronomer), and there is evidence that San Martín's assignment was ordered by the king.[71] Commissioned by King Ferdinand in 1512, his reputation had earned for him what today would be called a high security clearance. With Amerigo Vespucci, pilot major of Castile, San Martín was the only Casa pilot entrusted with the secret rutters for navigating to the Indies. Other pilots, it was feared, would sell them to the highest bidder.

An incident shortly before the fleet's departure made the hostility of the court-appointed Castilian captains absolutely clear to Magellan. Luis de Mendoza, the fleet treasurer and captain of the *Victoria*, precipitated a nasty public row, challenging the captain general's choice of Diego Martín to be master of the *Victoria*.[72] Martín was a veteran seaman from Huelva, an Andalusian port near the Portuguese border. Initially assigned to recruiting, he had impressed Magellan. At Mendoza's insistence, the Casa had refused to pay Martín a master's wages, claiming that he was an informer planted by Magellan on Mendoza's ship and was not even qualified to be an able seaman. Magellan reported the incident to the king, and thought the matter resolved when Charles issued a stern rebuke to Mendoza, curtly ordering him to refrain from challenging Magellan and to obey him *en todo* (in all things). Later, the king included Martín among the fleet personnel granted insignia of chivalry.[73] But like many Castilian *hidalgos*, Mendoza had little respect for the young foreigner who had become King of Spain.

He remained intransigent, and the Casa still refused to approve the appointment of Martín as the *Victoria*'s master. Magellan finally succeeded in getting him a billet on the *Trinidad* as an able seaman.[74]

Meanwhile, the pilots continued their holdout for higher salaries, petitioning the king three times to augment their pay at sea by the 3,000 maravedis per month already granted the Portuguese pilot, Carvalho.[75] Charles responded by threatening to forfeit their salaries if they continued to hold out. Undaunted, they signed on only when he offered 30,000 maravedis annually plus 7,500 for expenses. In addition, Juan Rodríguez Serrano was granted an allotment of twelve bushels of wheat worth 1,920 maravedis.[76] Estevão Gomes was named pilot major of the armada and assigned to the flagship *Trinidad*.[77] Carvalho and Vasco Galego were named pilots for the *Concepción* and the *Victoria*, respectively. Juan Rodríguez de Mafra was assigned to the *San Antonio*, along with the astrologer, San Martín. Of the six pilots, San Martín, Serrano, and Mafra were Castilian; Gomes, Carvalho, and Galego, Portuguese.

Early in May of 1519, a young Venetian gentleman arrived in Seville by way of Málaga. Born Antonio Plegapheta in Vicenza, Italy, he is known to history as Antonio Pigafetta, author of a remarkable eyewitness account of the first voyage of circumnavigation. While his birth date is not known, Pigafetta is thought to have been about 27 or 28 when he signed on with Magellan's fleet. A member of the personal staff of Andrea Chiericati, papal ambassador to the court of King Charles, he had learned of the expedition in April, when the court was in Barcelona,[78] where he probably met Magellan. Eager for adventure, Pigafetta sought and received from his indulgent employer permission to sail with the fleet. Chiericati probably thought it a good idea to have an observer for the Vatican along, since one of the expedition's goals was to locate the boundary separating the Far Eastern territories of two of its client states. With the approval of both Magellan and the Casa, Pigafetta was accepted as a supernumerary on the *Trinidad*. Following the custom of using birth districts as surnames, he was enrolled as Antonio Lombardo. (Lombardy, then part of the Venetian state, is the Italian district in which Vicenza is located.)

Among the 64 other supernumeraries sailing with the fleet were three of Magellan's relatives: Duarte Barbosa (his wife's brother or cousin), Álvaro de Mesquita (probably a grandnephew of his mother), and Cristovão Rebêlo (thought by many to have been his natural son). In addition, Enrique, his Malay slave, was on the fleet payroll as an interpreter. All were to play important roles in the drama about to unfold.

By May, most of the billets had been filled. Through the Casa, King Charles issued a set of orders to the captains and pilots containing instructions concerning navigation. The fleet's route was indicated only in the most general terms, however, for Magellan had refused to divulge the location of the passage they were expected to find through or around the American landmass.

Although he had not discouraged the widespread belief that he knew of such a passage, he had little to go on other than a suspicion (derived from reports of the Solís expedition and possibly of a Haro-sponsored expedition to Brazil in 1513–14) that it might be found southwest of Cape Santa María (Punta del Este, Uruguay). Given the hostility to his command evident at the Casa and within his fleet, he was not about to reveal his uncertainty to anyone, not even the pilots. As he had indicated to the priest Las Casas in Barcelona, should he not find the passage, he was quite prepared to sail east to the Moluccas, keeping well south of the Portuguese sealanes.

Magellan's operational orders, grouped under 74 headings[79] and issued by Charles on May 8, are extraordinary for their minuteness of detail.[80] After the fleet cleared home waters, Magellan was to reveal to the captains and pilots the first expected landfall. Every evening, each ship would salute the flagship, giving the pilots the opportunity to get their instructions from the flag pilot. At night, the other ships would follow the lantern of the flagship. An elaborate system of signals was outlined to indicate course changes, sail adjustments, and hazards. Crews were to observe proper shipboard behavior at all times–no swearing or gambling would be tolerated, ". . . for from such often arises evil, scandal and, strife." Native peoples in the lands visited were to be treated with respect, with special care taken not to molest their women. Officers were to treat the crew with kindness and consideration, and were to taste the crew's rations every day, and so on, almost *ad infinitum*.

By August, the ships were fully armed and laded[81] with supplies and provisions for a two-year voyage (according to the Casa's books). Desertions were mounting with each additional day in port, and Magellan and the Casa officials (the more supportive of them, at least) waited anxiously for the courier to arrive from Barcelona with sailing orders. The royal orders were finally delivered to Dr. Matienzo, at that time serving as factor at the Casa.[82] The courier's services didn't come cheaply, amounting to 91 ducats (nearly $4,500) for the trip to Seville from Barcelona and return.[83]

In a moving ceremony in the church of Santa María de la Victoria de Triana, Matienzo delivered the royal standard to Magellan. The high command and officers of the armada swore solemn oaths of homage to the king and obedience to the laws of Castile. With equal solemnity, they swore to follow the courses indicated by Magellan and to obey him in all things.[84]

The church was decorated with the colorful linen and silk banners of each of the five ships, those of the *San Antonio* and the *Santiago* being the work of Francisco Villegas, a well-known painter from Seville.[85] On August 10, 1519, with a thunderous discharge of cannon, the ships of the Moluccan Fleet cast loose their moorings, raised their foresails, and glided down the Guadalquivir toward the port of San Lúcar de Barrameda.[86] Magellan and the captains remained behind to tidy up the inevitable administrative loose ends.

The fleet lingered more than a month at San Lúcar while much of the final business, including the recruiting of replacements for the Portuguese dismissed from the crew, was conducted through the local branch office of the Casa.[87] Last-minute purchases of supplies and the hiring of crew to fill vacant billets required Magellan to shuttle many times between Seville and San Lúcar in the small galleys used as water taxis. These frequent trips gave him precious last hours to spend with Beatriz, now pregnant with their second child, his infant son, and his wife's parents, who had welcomed him so warmly into their family.

During this last hectic month, Magellan sent a memorandum to Charles giving the locations of various places in the Far East (including the Moluccas) with respect to the antimeridian of the Tordesillas Treaty line. He did so, he wrote, ". . . because the King of Portugal may assert that they [the Moluccas] lie within his limit, and . . . no one understands it as I understand it."[88]

On August 14 he filed his will, naming his father-in-law and Dr. Matienzo as executors. The will reveals a deeply religious man, an aspect of his character that helps to explain the stubborn confidence that both awed and angered his shipmates. He named his children (the infant and the unborn child) as principal heirs to the many benefits assigned him by his contract with the Crown. His wife and sister were to be well cared for. There are modest sums for Cristovão Rebêlo and his Malay servant, Enrique, and the latter was to be freed. Magellan expected his enterprise to succeed, and that he would reap enormous material benefits from it. He also believed that, should he die in service to the Crown, his contract would be honored and the stipulated benefits paid to his heirs. Should the inheritance pass to his brother or sister in Portugal (both apparently unmarried), they were to reside in Castile, marry there, and use the Spanish form of their surname, *Magallanes*. Magellan was generous also to convents in Seville, Aranda del Duero, and Pôrto, and to a monastery in Barcelona, allocating to those humble appendages of the church part of his share in the profits from the enterprise. The full text of the will is given in Appendix 6.

PₐIVₚₜ

𝒯he Voyage

Tupinamba Indians fishing in Brazil. Of the Indians
Magellan's expedition met in Rio de Janeiro, Antonio Pigafetta
noted: "For a fishhook or a knife they would offer five or six
chickens; a pair of geese for a comb; for a small mirror or pair
of scissors, enough fish to feed ten people; for a bell or a ribbon,
a basket of [sweet] potatoes that taste like nuts or turnips. For
the king in a deck of playing cards such as we use in Italy, they
gave me six chickens, thinking that they had got the better
of me."

Courtesy of the John Carter Brown Library at Brown University.

11
$\mathscr{T}$he Atlantic

C*oncluding his business with the Casa and sending his final* memorandum to Charles, Magellan put his legal and spiritual affairs in order, bid farewell to his pregnant wife, infant son, and in-laws, and headed downriver to join the fleet at San Lúcar. One can picture him, seated in the stern of a small galley, gliding the 60 miles down the Guadalquivir, a lonely figure wrapped in a rough, woolen seaman's cloak against the clammy chill of a summer's night. The rhythmic creak and dip of the oars and the soft, gurgling rush of the water into the galley's wake intensified his loneliness, immersing him ever more deeply in troubled thoughts.

The rowers labored at their sweeps unaware of the powerful emotions surging in the breast of their silent passenger. Thinking of the family he was leaving behind, love, pride, and hope fortified his eagerness to sail. For Charles, who had given him this chance to win the honor, wealth, and glory that until now had eluded him, he felt a deep, abiding gratitude. But scheming courtiers were undercutting him in Spain just as they had in Portugal, and he suspected that their subterfuge would not end at the water's edge. He knew that the haughty Castilians of his high command were as contemptuous of him, a disgraced defector from Portugal, as they were of the youthful Flemish monarch who had appointed him. Once at sea, he must never relax his guard or let these Castilians anticipate him. By withholding details of the route he had planned, he would keep them off balance.

There was no turning back; the last bridges to his native land had been burned, and to fail his adopted king would leave him without honor, an object of scorn, or worse, pity. A glorious death in the performance of his duty would be far better. Yet he had dedicated his enterprise to the Holy Mother in the chapel of the monastery of Santa María de la Victoria in Triana, and his belief in her protective powers was deep and passionate. With her watching over him, how could he fail?

At San Lúcar, most of the remaining crew billets had been filled. Although there were still a few empty berths, the fleet was ready to sail. Waiting for a favorable wind to take them southwest into the Atlantic, the crew went ashore each day to hear mass. After the middle of September, the northeast trade wind began to blow steadily. Since Prince Henry's day, it had been used by Iberian mariners to sail to the Canary Islands and down the coast of Africa. Ready at last to make sail, Magellan led the crew ashore for confession at the Church of Nuestra Señora de Barrameda.

Before dawn on Wednesday, September 21, 1519, 40 days after their arrival at San Lúcar, the five ships hoisted sail and nosed into the Atlantic.[1] In the lead, flying the royal standard, was the flagship *Trinidad*. The first port of call was to be Santa Cruz, on the island of Tenerife in the Canaries, an obligatory stop for Spanish ships sailing to the New World. During daylight, the ships of the fleet adjusted course, speed, and set of sails by following the example of the flagship. At dusk, each ship was required to haul alongside the flagship, salute the captain general according to a prescribed formula, give a verbal report, and receive sailing orders. At night, navigational information was transmitted by an elaborate system of signals from an array of lanterns (the *farol*) on the poop of the flagship. Shoals, reefs, or land ahead were indicated by the firing of cannon or the display of additional strings of lanterns.[2]

The crews were organized into three divisions: the first under the mate, the second under the pilot, and the third under the master. There were three night watches: the first from nightfall to midnight, the second to about four hours after midnight, and the third until full daylight.[3]

At the start of the voyage, the operational command on each of Magellan's ships was as follows:

	Trinidad	
Rank	*Name*	*Nationality*
Captain general	Ferdinand Magellan	Portuguese
Pilot	Estevão Gomes	Portuguese
Master	Juan Bautista de Poncevera	Genoese
Mate	Francisco Albo	Greek
	San Antonio	
Captain	Juan de Cartagena	Castilian
Astrologer-pilot	Andrés de San Martín	Castilian

Pilot	Juan Rodríguez de Mafra	Castilian
Master	Juan de Elorriaga	Basque
Mate	Diego Hernández	Castilian

Concepción

Captain	Gaspar de Quesada	Castilian
Pilot	João Lopes Carvalho	Portuguese
Master	Juan Sebastián del Cano	Basque
Mate	Juan de Acurio	Basque

Victoria

Captain	Luis de Mendoza	Castilian
Pilot	Vasco Galego	Portuguese
Master	Antonio Salamón	Sicilian
Mate	Miguel de Rodas	Greek

Santiago

Captain and Pilot	Juan Rodríguez Serrano	Castilian
Master	Baltasar Palla (Genovés)	Genoese
Mate	Bartolomé Prieur	French

In the fleet were two opposing factions. Sure to support Magellan were the Portuguese mariners and supernumeraries assigned to the *Trinidad*, not a few of them relatives, friends, and servants. The Castilian high command on the *San Antonio*, *Concepción*, and *Victoria* were clearly aligned with Juan de Cartagena. Between these factions were the largely apolitical working officers (pilots, masters, mates) and crewmen, many of whom were neither Castilian nor Portuguese. Their interests were practical, focused on surviving the hazardous voyage. Should the Castilian captains rise against him, of the five ships, Magellan could count only on the *Trinidad* to remain loyal. The little *Santiago* could go either way; Juan Rodríguez Serrano, although Castilian, was a thoroughly professional officer likely to support the commander he deemed most competent to lead the fleet safely through the dangers ahead.

The trip to the Canary Islands from Andalusian ports usually took six days, and Magellan's fleet was no exception: Shaping a southwesterly course, the ships called at Santa Cruz on September 26, 1519, taking on water and wood and enlisting two able seamen and a supernumerary. The latter, Hernán López, replaced Lazaro Torres of the *Trinidad*, who remained behind.[4] After three days they moved to Monte Rojo (Punta Roja), another port on the same island, to take on a load of pitch. While they were there, a caravel from San Lúcar entered the harbor, looking for them.[5] On board was a courier with an urgent message for Magellan from Diego

Barbosa warning him that, before departure, several of the Castilian captains had boasted openly that they would remove him from command at
the earliest opportunity, if necessary by killing him.[6]

Magellan sent a reassuring reply to his father-in-law, writing that since
these captains had been chosen by the king, he would do all in his power
not to give them cause to revolt against him, but would work with them in
the service of the emperor to whom they had all pledged their lives. When

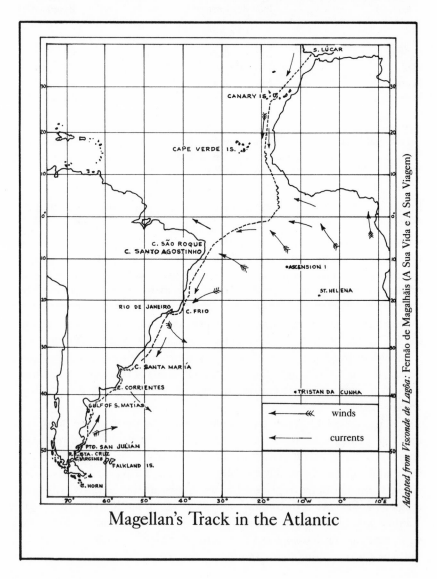

Magellan's Track in the Atlantic

Barbosa showed the letter to the officials at the Casa, they praised Magellan's equanimity and restraint.[7]

At midnight on October 3, the fleet weighed anchor and put to sea, proceeding cautiously under foresails only until well away from land. Holding to the southwest, by midday they were at latitude 27° N, 12 leagues (36 nautical miles) from Tenerife. At this point the *Trinidad* signaled a change of course to south by west, alternating between that heading and due south for the rest of the day. The course change was unexpected, as it had been agreed at Tenerife that the fleet would sail southwest to 24° N.[8] When the other ships approached the flagship for the evening salute, Magellan gave no explanation for the course change. They continued through the night and the next day on headings alternately south and south by west.

On October 5, sometime between dusk and midnight, the *San Antonio* hauled alongside the *Trinidad* and asked what course they were running. The pilot (Gomes) replied that it was south by west.[9] Cartagena then called out to Magellan to ask why the course agreed upon in Seville and confirmed at Tenerife had been altered, complaining that such changes ought not to be made summarily, but only after consultation with the captains, pilots, and masters. He further argued that the southerly course they were running risked too close an approach to Cape Blanco on the Guinea coast. Magellan responded testily that the other ships had only to follow his flag during the day, and his farol at night, and should not ask questions.[10] One account, hostile to Magellan, has him adding that while he knew Cartagena had been made *conjunta persona*, it had been done against his will and he did not intend to honor it.[11]

Suspecting the Recalde faction at the Casa of passing information to Portuguese agents, Magellan had filed a route plan indicating a course southwest from the Canaries to a point of departure for the Atlantic crossing west of the Cape Verde Islands. In reality he planned a route sometimes used by Portuguese pilots striking for Brazil, following the coast of Guinea south to about 6° N, where southeast winds would carry them to a landfall south of Cape São Roque.[12] Magellan knew this route could mire him in the doldrums for weeks, but he was willing to pay that price to avoid the Portuguese warships that might be lying in wait southwest of the Canaries. He also knew his chances of raising the coast of Brazil south of Cape São Roque would improve if he sailed far south before beginning the crossing. But he had no intention of revealing his plan to the Castilian captains; he kept them in the dark, expecting that frustration would goad them into actions he could anticipate and easily counter.

Enjoying fair winds, the fleet held a southerly course for fifteen days, passing between the coast of Africa and the Cape Verde Islands. At the latitude of Sierra Leone they ran into a series of tropical storms so furious the crews nearly had to cut away the masts.[13] At the height of these storms, ball-like electrostatic discharges appeared at the mastheads.[14] Thought to be manifestations of St. Elmo, the patron saint of mariners, these spectacular phenomena did much to calm the fears of the sailors. The storms subsided, and they entered the belt of equatorial calms, where for twenty days they were able to log only three leagues (nine nautical miles). Magellan prudently shortened rations, which led to grumbling among the crews. The sails hung limp in the still, stifling, tropic air. Aging swells, dying remnants of distant storms, randomly crisscrossed the sea surface. Torrential rains soaked everyone and everything, making it nearly impossible to keep anything dry. A steaming, suffocating miasma arose from belowdecks, carrying the stench of rotting food stores and the inevitable accumulation of filth in the bilges. As the ships gently rolled and pitched in the windless, sloppy sea, the creaking yards slammed back and forth with an annoying unpredictability that made everyone irritable and sleep all but impossible.

Cartagena and the Castilian high command were furious with Magellan for stubbornly withholding his reasons for the course change that had carried them into the doldrums. One day off the coast of Guinea, the *San Antonio* hailed the *Trinidad* for the customary evening salute, but instead of having the ship's master call out the prescribed *"Dios os salve, señor capitán general y maestre, e buena compañia!"* ("God save you, captain general sir, [ship's] master and good [ship's] company!"), Cartagena had a seaman call out the salute addressing Magellan merely as *"capitan."* At his captain general's command, Estevão Gomes informed Juan de Elorriaga, master of the *San Antonio*, that the salute must be rendered in the proper manner. Cartagena then interjected, shouting so all could hear, that his best seaman had given the salute but, if Magellan preferred, he would have it rendered by a cabin boy! For the next three days, Cartagena refused to let anyone on his ship render the evening salute.

During this interval, the master of the *Victoria*, Antonio Salamón, was caught *in flagrante delicto* in an act of sodomy with an apprentice seaman. When Magellan heard about it, he sent a messenger in a skiff to the other ships, requesting their captains and pilots to convene on the flagship for a court martial. After the trial, in which Salamón was found guilty, a lively discussion ensued among the assembled officers concerning the course they were sailing and the proper manner of rendering the evening salute. Emboldened by the presence of his fellow Castilians, Cartagena became increasingly insolent to Magellan, who at first ignored him. However, when his comments went far beyond the bounds of civility and clearly constituted insubordination, Magellan sprang from his seat, grasped him by the front of his shirt and hissed, *"Sed preso!"* ("You are under arrest!"). In panic, Cartagena appealed to his fellow officers to seize Magellan–open incitement to mutiny before witnesses. Not one Castilian made a move to defend his flustered compatriot.[15] Perhaps they were discouraged by the presence of armed guards prudently posted on the poop deck where they were assembled. Cartagena was pilloried ignominiously on the main deck, in the stocks normally reserved for the punishment of common seamen.[16]

The other captains, appalled that a Castilian nobleman should suffer such humiliation, implored Magellan to release him into the custody of one of them. Apparently satisfied that he had put down the challenge and anxious to get the matter behind him, Magellan agreed, handing Cartagena over to Luis de Mendoza, captain of the *Victoria*, after obtaining the latter's pledge to return the prisoner on request. Magellan chose the fleet accountant, Antonio de Coca,[17] to replace Cartagena as captain of the *San Antonio*.

After wallowing in the doldrums for three weeks, the sails rustled with a light intermittent breeze, and the ships began to move, ever so slightly at first, barely enough for steerage. Gradually the wind freshened and steadied as they entered the belt of southeast trade winds. Magellan ordered Gomes to shape a southwesterly course, and the fleet headed across the Atlantic with the wind on their port beam. They crossed the equator on November 20, somewhere between 15° and 20° west longitude.[18] The trades blew only intermittently at first, increasing in strength toward the end of the traverse, while the South Equatorial Current, of which Magellan and his pilots knew nothing, carried the fleet westward. After crossing the Line, Magellan chose a south-southwest heading,[19] probably expecting to raise the Brazilian coast south of Cape Santo Agostinho. Instead, the westward set of the current made the fleet's true course more nearly southwest by west, veering gradually to the west-southwest as the trade wind increased. By November 29 they were off the coast of Brazil between Cape São Roque and Cape Santo Agostinho. Had it not been for Magellan's prudence in sailing far to the south before attempting the crossing, the fleet's landfall might have been northwest of Cape São Roque where, for months, headwinds could have prevented his square-rigged naos from doubling the cape.

The approach to Brazil is noted in the first entry of a logbook kept by Francisco Albo, a Greek from Rhodes who began the voyage as mate on the *Trinidad*.[20] His log is the best surviving navigational record of the expedition, and many have wondered why he delayed the first entry until November 29. Perhaps Magellan promoted the diligent officer to acting pilot, and the log was begun on the day of his promotion.[21]

The fleet proceeded cautiously on alternate headings of southwest and southwest by south. On December 8, at latitude 19° 59' S, they raised land and found bottom at ten fathoms. As they coasted south-southwest, Albo noted that the mountains came down to the shore and ". . . had many reefs about them." After sailing past Cape Frio on December 11 and 12, the fleet steered due west and arrived at Guanabara Bay (the harbor of Rio de Janeiro) on the morning of December 13, 1519.[22] The spectacular harbor had been known to Portuguese navigators since 1502, and probably was the landfall Magellan intended when he headed south from the Canary Islands.

12

$\mathcal{B}$razil

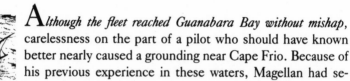A*lthough the fleet reached Guanabara Bay without mishap,* carelessness on the part of a pilot who should have known better nearly caused a grounding near Cape Frio. Because of his previous experience in these waters, Magellan had selected João Lopes Carvalho, the *Concepción's* pilot, to lead the fleet as it coasted southward from Cape Agostinho. In 1511, João de Braga, a Portuguese trader, had established a storage facility on an island in Guanabara Bay, and the next year the *Bertoa*, a Portuguese commercial vessel on which Carvalho was employed, loaded dyewood there. When the *Bertoa* left for Portugal, Carvalho stayed behind, remaining for four years (probably to maintain Braga's property) and taking a native mistress.[1]

Despite his previous experience in these waters, Carvalho was unaware of a strong inshore current in the Gulf of Macae between Cape São Tomé and Cape Frio. When a northeast wind strengthens the southwest set of the offshore Brazil Current, a current setting northeast is generated inside the gulf. Carvalho led the fleet too close to shore on the approach to Cape Frio, and the countercurrent caught the ships and swept them toward Cape São Tomé. Only the alertness of Pilot Major Gomes saved the fleet from disaster.[2] In a later century, a similar countercurrent west of Cape Frio is believed to have caused the wreck of the British frigate *Thetis* on Cape Frio Island.[3]

With his crews tired, hungry, and disgruntled from the long beat on short rations down the African coast, Magellan was anxious to replenish his fresh food, water, and firewood and to rest the men, even with the small risk of encountering a Portuguese ship. Carvalho had assured him that Guanabara Bay, with its friendly natives and abundant fruit, vegetables, fish, and

game, would be ideal for that purpose.[4] Magellan named the harbor Bahía
Santa Lucía in honor of the saint celebrated by the Church on the day the
fleet entered it, December 13, 1519. He was not the first to call it that, for
the name appeared in a Portuguese portulan thought to have been made by
Pedro Reinel in 1516, and again on a 1519 map attributed to Maggiolo.[5] In
1502, the harbor had been named Rio de Janeiro when it was visited by a
Portuguese flotilla commanded by Gonçalo Coelho. Along for the ride by
royal invitation was a flamboyant Florentine named Amerigo Vespucci.[6] By
an accident of history, the continental mass in the western Atlantic would
come to be known as America, derived from the given name of that public-
ity-seeking Italian voyager. The name [Rio de] Janeiro (written as *Sano Se-
neyro*) first appeared on a map produced in 1513 by a Turkish admiral, Piri
Re'is.[7]

Entering the beautiful harbor, the five ships passed the imposing, rocky
mass of *Pão de Açucar* (Sugar Loaf) on their port side, dropping anchor in
seven fathoms either off Flamingo Beach or in Botafogo Inlet at the foot of
Corcovado (Hunchback) Peak. A swarm of naked natives in canoes paddled
eagerly out to greet them. They probably were Tamojos, speakers of Tupi
(one of the Ge family of Amerindian languages).[8] Antonio Pigafetta, the
Trinidad's indefatigable supernumerary who became the expedition's principal chronicler, now had his first opportunity to indulge his interest in exotic places and people. Manners, customs, and beliefs held a particular
fascination for him, and with obvious delight and unabashed credulity he
recorded all that he saw and heard. Had he lived in a later century, he
might have been an anthropologist. He wrote that the arrival of the ships
coincided with the first rainfall after a long drought, and the awed natives
thought the mariners were benign supernatural beings bringing much-
needed rain. They were astonished to see the ships' boats set forth for
shore, and assumed that the motherships were giving birth. The boats nes-
tled alongside seemed to them like nursing infants.

When they realized that there were men aboard the ships with glittering
trinkets to trade, they swarmed on deck, offering parrots, chickens, fish,
and garden produce in exchange. "For a fishhook or a knife," wrote Pigafetta, "they would offer five or six chickens; a pair of geese for a comb; for a
small mirror or pair of scissors, enough fish to feed ten people; for a bell or
a ribbon, a basket of [sweet] potatoes that taste like nuts or turnips. For the
king in a deck of playing cards such as we use in Italy, they gave me six
chickens, thinking that they had got the better of me."[9]

Carvalho, who had lived among these natives, regaled Pigafetta with
tales of their cannibalism. The latter dutifully recorded a graphic account
of how the practice began:

They eat the flesh of their enemies, more in obedience to custom than because they find it savory. This custom, reciprocated between adversaries, was started by an old woman whose only son had been killed by the warriors of another tribe. After some time, one of them was captured and brought before the old woman. She, remembering her son when confronted by the prisoner, threw herself at him with wolf-like fury, biting him on one of his shoulders.

However, the captive succeeded in escaping and making his way back to his own people. He told how his captors had tried to devour him, showing as proof the marks left on his shoulder by the old woman's teeth. From that day on, the different tribes started to eat captives from other tribes, and thus the strange practice was initiated.

The bodies are not eaten all at once; each cannibal cuts himself a slice that he takes to his house where it is smoked so that it can be eaten later, in weekly rations, along with other delicacies. Thus, for a long time, he can relish the memory of his adversary.

"They are not Christians," wrote Pigafetta, "nor do they seem to worship anything." They lived ". . . in harmony with nature, more like beasts than anything else." Their communal houses, called *boii*, could accommodate one hundred persons. Inside, ". . . the noise they make is enormous." For sleeping, cotton hammocks (*amache*) were suspended above the longhouse floor by fastening the ends to tall stakes planted in the ground. The cooking fires were lit directly beneath the hammocks.

The men keep their hair shaved and pluck out their beards; they decorate themselves with the plumage of parrots, displaying around the anus large ornaments made with the longest feathers. They look most ridiculous. The color of these people is not completely black, but olive toned. Men and women are completely devoid of bodily hair. They walk about nude, with their nether regions uncovered.

The effect of the comely, stark naked, and exceedingly friendly women on Magellan's crew was electrifying. Homesickness forgotten, they enjoyed what a modern sailor might describe as "a fantastic liberty!" Carvalho cautioned them not to fool around with the married women. Wives, he said, were faithful to their husbands, and under no circumstances would betray them. The men jealously guarded their wives with bows and arrows, but for a hatchet or a knife would sell one or even two daughters.

Although he overlooked the lusty liaisons between his crew and the Tamojo girls, Magellan forbade the sailors to make slaves of them. To remind his men of their religious obligations, and to keep them from going completely native, he insisted on celebrating mass ashore on two occasions.[10] The Tamojos watched the solemn proceedings with wide-eyed wonder. Pigafetta commented that ". . . it would be an easy thing to convert these gentiles to the Christian faith."[11]

Magellan's prohibition against women aboard the ships proved impossible to enforce. "These young women," wrote Pigafetta, "swarmed aboard to offer themselves to the sailors, hoping to receive presents." One day in the company of Magellan, he witnessed an incident that he thought amusing. "One of the prettiest of the girls came aboard, undoubtedly for the same reason. Spying a nail about the size of a finger, and thinking she was unobserved, she picked it up and quickly inserted it into her private parts. Did she think she was hiding it, or did she think she was adorning herself? We were unable to determine which."[12]

While the stopover at Rio de Janeiro was for the most part a delight for Magellan's men, it was not without its grim moments. On December 20, the court martial that had found Antonio Salamón guilty of the crime of sodomy was reconvened ashore for sentencing. The 45-year-old master of the *Victoria* was condemned to death and executed on the same day.[13] Most likely it was the master-at-arms, Gonzalo Gómez de Espinosa, who had the unpleasant duty of carrying out the sentence. The spectacle of a public garroting may have been, for the natives of that subtropical paradise, their first exposure to the dark side of the Europeans who would soon change forever the world they knew. The victim of the crime, an apprentice seaman, suffered a punishment even more cruel: the taunts, brutal mockery, and ridicule of his shipmates.

The revels of the crew with the Tamojo women degenerated into an unabated orgy, and some of the officers, who should have tried to maintain a semblance of discipline, joined in. Among these was Magellan's kinsman by marriage, Duarte Barbosa, who absented himself from his ship for three days and nights. With the situation getting out of control, Magellan dispatched a squad of marines to arrest Barbosa and had him clapped in irons.[14] The next officer to incur Magellan's wrath was Antonio de Coca, whom he had promoted to captain of the *San Antonio* when Cartagena was stripped of his command. Coca had conspired with the *Victoria*'s captain, Luis de Mendoza, to release Cartagena from custody on his ship and bring him ashore,[15] ostensibly to join the revels but more likely as part of a plot to remove Magellan from command. Magellan was furious. He had both Cartagena and Coca arrested, deposed the latter from command of the *San Antonio*, and threatened to maroon Cartagena when the fleet put to sea. Once again permitting himself to be dissuaded by the other captains (probably because Cartagena was a favorite of Fonseca and had been appointed by the king), Magellan relented and confined the troublesome nobleman on the *Concepción* in the custody of its captain, Gaspar de Quesada. It would have been far better for Cartagena had Magellan left him at Rio de Janeiro.[16]

Needing a new captain for the *San Antonio*, Magellan selected his inexperienced kinsman Álvaro de Mesquita, a supernumerary on the *Trinidad*, over the well-qualified Gomes, who coveted the job. Although the pilot major was clearly his most experienced officer, Magellan knew that Gomes had petitioned the king for a fleet command, and he was not about to trust him with command of his largest ship. Denied the promotion he wanted, Gomes's smoldering resentment was fanned anew when Magellan transferred him to the *San Antonio* to serve as pilot for the novice captain, a move the frustrated Gomes undoubtedly regarded as a demotion from pilot major on the flagship.

Shortly after the fleet had anchored, Carvalho was greeted by the woman who had been his mistress during his previous sojourn in Brazil. With her was a seven-year-old boy whom she claimed was his son.[17] Carvalho cheerfully acknowledged the lad and took him aboard the *Concepción* as his cabin boy. Had it not been for Magellan's prohibition against women aboard the ships, the easygoing Carvalho might well have taken the lad's mother to warm his bunk during the cold subantarctic nights ahead.[18]

On December 17, the fleet astrologer, San Martín, who had transferred from the *San Antonio* to the *Victoria*, took his instruments ashore and tried to calculate the longitude by observing a conjunction of the moon with Jupiter. Disappointed with the results, he blamed errors in the astronomical tables Faleiro had provided.[19]

Impatient to begin the search for a westward passage, Magellan ordered Espinosa and his marines to roust the crews from their love nests ashore, clear the ships of native girls, and restore discipline to the fleet. Work parties cleaned, repaired, and reprovisioned the ships, and by Christmas Eve the fleet was ready for sea. Longboats towed the ships from their sheltered anchorage to the mouth of the bay, where the Feast of the Nativity was celebrated on board. On the night of December 26, the fleet stood well offshore under foresails only, the near grounding in the Gulf of Macae having given Magellan a healthy respect for the treacherous Brazilian coast. The next morning, carrying a fair wind from the north, the fleet headed west-southwest under full sail.[20]

On December 31, coastal mountains again appeared on the horizon. Behind a group of seven small islands the lookouts saw an opening to the west, but it turned out to be just a deep bay. Albo called it Los Reyes, a name he probably got from rutters aboard the *Trinidad*, and recorded its latitude as 25° 23' S. (It probably was the bay at 25° 28' S now known as Paranagua.)[21] Taking frequent soundings, especially at night, the fleet coasted southward, and by January 7, 1520, at 33° S, the low coastline to starboard had revealed no other openings to the west. San Martín recorded soundings of 85 fathoms, with fine, dark sand showing on the lead.[22] Maintaining a southwesterly course, they logged soundings indicating a shelving, sandy bottom, too shallow for night sailing, and on the afternoon of January 9, they anchored in 12 fathoms. The next day, an hour before sunset, they were at 35° S in soundings of 16 to 18 fathoms. Lowering mainsails, they proceeded cautiously during the night on a southwesterly heading. At dawn (January 11), no land being visible to starboard, they tacked westward against headwinds, searching for Cape Santa María and the waterway Solís had entered in January 1516. Emerging from a rain squall at midday, they saw on the horizon ahead what appeared to be several small islands. On closer approach, these turned out to be three hills on a low coast, the markers for Cape Santa María, first noted in 1511–12 by João de Lisboa,[23] the pilot who had guided the fleet with which Magellan sailed to Morocco in 1513.

13
$\mathcal{S}$torms and Mutiny

Having *identified Cape Santa María (Punta del Este on the* coast of Uruguay), Magellan was confident that they had crossed the demarcation line, and the land to the south and west could be legitimately claimed by Spain. Although San Martín had failed to get a longitude for Rio de Janeiro, Magellan's instincts were reinforced by the dead-reckoning of his pilots and what he already knew from reports of Portuguese voyages to Brazil.[1] No longer concerned that he might be detected by Portuguese ships, he could now explore every inlet promising a passage to the west.

After a daylight sighting of the cape on January 11, 1520, the fleet sailed past it during the night. Doubling back to the north the next day, they anchored in a shallow bay just west of the cape, and that night were struck by an easterly gale so strong the *Victoria* began to drag its anchor. Another anchor was deployed and held, but by then the lanterns on the *Trinidad* could no longer be seen. Worried, Captain Mendoza, who had been ordered never to lose sight of the flagship, sought the counsel of San Martín, Vasco Gomes Galego (his other pilot), and other professional mariners. They advised him to sit tight. It would be foolish, they told him, to risk losing their anchors to search for the flagship on such a stormy night.[2]

With the wind abating by the morning of January 13, the fleet reassembled and proceeded westward, following the shoreline. Sighting a prominent hill rising behind Cape Santa María,[3] Magellan is supposed to have cried out in Latin, *"Montem video!"* (I see a mountain!),[4] and from this exclamation, the city of Montevideo is said to have taken its name.

The ships proceeded cautiously west-northwest, "sounding lead in hand," for seven and a half leagues.[5] The *Santiago* and the *Victoria* led, their shallow drafts giving them an advantage in shoaling water. At sunset they anchored in five fathoms, well within the estuary of the Río de la Plata. The lead revealed a bottom of dark, firm sediment. Two days later, they had progressed 10 leagues (30 nautical miles) farther, and the water was "as fresh as the river flowing past Seville." With the bottom shelving to no more than three fathoms, the pilots protested that the fleet was in imminent danger of grounding. Setting out their anchors, they stayed six days, taking on fresh water.[6] Among other maintenance, one unpleasant chore probably undertaken in this interval was scrubbing the fouled water butts before refilling them.

It was becoming clear to Magellan that this could not be the entrance to a strait as he had hoped, but was the mouth of a great river system flowing from the continent. To be certain, he sent the *Santiago* upriver while the rest of the fleet explored the south shore of the estuary. It took Captain Serrano in the *Santiago* fifteen days for his reconnaissance. One account stated that the *Santiago* traveled upriver twenty-five leagues; another said fifty leagues.[7] Since a sketch made by Pigafetta shows both the Paraná and Uruguay rivers, the major tributaries of the La Plata,[8] it seems likely that Serrano took the *Santiago* twenty-five leagues up each of them. The total distance thus traveled (about 300 nautical miles) seems about right for fifteen days.

While the rest of the fleet was exploring the estuary, the crews saw many natives along the shore. They probably were Querandí (Chandri), members of a family of tribes populating the pampas at the time of first contact with Europeans.[9] Recalling the sad fate of Juan Díaz de Solís who, four years earlier, had been killed and eaten in this locale, Magellan would not allow his men ashore. Nevertheless, one day a giant Querandí paddled toward the ships in a canoe. Pulling up short, he shouted angrily at the Spaniards in a booming voice that reminded them of the bellowing of a bull.[10] It was all bluster, however, for the huge man made no attempt to board any of the ships, and before long paddled back to his companions on the shore. Wanting a closer look at the giant, Magellan dispatched a hundred armed men in three shallops to try to capture him, but by the time they reached the shore not a single native could be found. They had melted silently into the scrub forest on the riverbank.

On another evening, a solitary Querandí dressed in a skin like that of a goat paddled out to the flagship and climbed calmly aboard, showing not the slightest fear of the astonished Spaniards. Delighted, Magellan presented him with a jacket of red cloth. Shown a silver platter, the man was asked, by signs, whether such metal could be found in his country. Responding in kind, he indicated that it could, and in abundance. He left well fed and loaded with presents, but never returned.[11]

The fleet sustained two casualties while exploring the estuary: On January 25 Guillen Irés, an Irish apprentice seaman on the *Concepción*, fell overboard and drowned, and on February 3 in front of the present site of Montevideo, the body of Sebastián Olarte, an able seaman on the *San Antonio* who had been fatally kicked in a brawl with another mariner, was buried at sea.[12]

When the *Santiago* returned, the fleet headed south across the estuary, but hove-to off the opposite shore when a leak was discovered near the keel of the *San Antonio*. Anchored in seven fathoms, possibly off Punta Piedras, the fleet waited two days while the leak was repaired.[13]

The southward journey resumed at dawn on February 6. That night they anchored in eight fathoms, probably in Samborobón Bay, and were underway again at dawn, headed south by east. Off Cape San Antonio (36° 30' S) the wind slacked, preventing further progress. They anchored overnight to prevent drifting in the strong current, but the next morning were underway again, standing south past Punta Sur before altering course to the southwest. By February 9 they were off Cape Corrientes (near the modern beach resort of Mar del Plata), where beach sand carried seaward by a longshore current forms submerged banks. Beyond the cape, the coastline trends progressively toward the west.

Working southwest, the fleet lost sight of land on February 10, so Magellan altered course to the northwest the next morning. Shortly thereafter they were struck by a violent storm, accompanied by thunder and lightning, which lasted until midday, driving them toward the submerged sandbanks off Cape Corrientes. Perilously close to the cape at nightfall, the ships put out all anchors to avoid being driven aground. By the morning of February 13 the storm had abated, but as they maneuvered to gain sea room the *Victoria* took several hard bumps on her keel.[14] Standing well offshore to avoid the shoals, the fleet resumed its southward course the next day. On February 15, the weather closed in and the pilots were unable to shoot the sun until the nineteenth, when their latitude was 40° 17' S. Steering southwest by south, they reached 43° 26' on February 22.

The fleet was still out of sight of land on February 23 when Magellan ordered a course change to west-northwest. The next day, at 42° 54', they saw before them a large bay that they named San Matías in honor of St. Matthew, whose feast is celebrated on February 24. According to the diary of one of the pilots, they entered the bay intending to take on water and wood and also to see if there might be an "exit leading to the Moluccas,"[15] but finding neither an opening to the west nor a satisfactory anchorage, they departed that same night.

Holding course to the south, the ships reached 44° 21' and were well out to sea on February 28. They steered west-northwest until, at nightfall, they raised land again, probably Punta Delgada on the Valdez Peninsula just south of the Gulf of San Matías. As the fleet moved southward, the season advanced rapidly from summer to fall. The *pamperos*, violent winds roaring across the pampas from the southwest, brought cold blasts that gave these sailors from balmy Mediterranean regions their first taste of a subantarctic winter.

The increasing cold and the frequency of storms made it imperative that a sheltered anchorage be found where the fleet could lay in fresh supplies and undertake the maintenance and repairs needed to keep the ships sea-worthy. The memory of the beautiful harbor of Rio de Janeiro with its warm, flower-scented breezes and sultry maidens was a siren song heard by all in the fleet but its flint-hearted captain general. Officers and men alike implored him to return there for the winter, but Magellan knew he would be in direct violation of royal orders if he returned to Portuguese territory, where he would risk an encounter with hostile naval forces. He was also aware that, at Rio, discipline would be impossible to maintain, and should he lose control of the men, the Castilian captains would have cause to re-move him from command. He saw no option but to continue southward in search of a passage leading west, or failing that, a sheltered anchorage where the fleet could overwinter. In the spring, he could either continue south or sail east to the Moluccas, past the Cape of Good Hope. There would be no glorious winter in Rio for the shivering crew.

After sighting Punta Delgada, southwest headwinds forced the fleet to tack to keep from being driven back, away from the land. Heavy clouds and tumultuous seas made it impossible for the pilots to shoot the sun to verify their latitude. They missed the opening to Golfo Nuevo, a sheltered harbor on the south side of the Valdez Peninsula, where today there is an Argentine naval base, Puerto Madryn.[16] Heavy weather separated the ships for several days, but they were able to reassemble off a rugged coast at about 45° S. Discovering an anchorage in a small bay, they named it after the many penguins found there, along with some seals.[17] With no better word for penguins than "ducks," they called it *Bahía de los Patos*.

Six men in one of the ship's boats were sent to an islet at the entrance of the bay to search for wood and water. Not finding any, they killed a number of penguins and seals and loaded them into their boat, but as they were about to return to their ship, a great storm arose and they had to spend the night on the island. It was bitterly cold, and when they did not return the following morning, their shipmates feared they had frozen to death or had been eaten by the "wolves" (seals). By dawn the storm had subsided, and Magellan sent a shallop with a 30-man search party. The rescuers found the skiff pulled up on the rocky shore of the islet, but the men were nowhere in sight. When the searchers shouted for their stranded shipmates, a herd of more than 200 startled elephant seals lumbered to the shore from the rocks above. The sailors clubbed fifty of the frightened animals to death as they struggled toward the water. Among the rocks from which the herd had emerged were the six half-frozen sailors, who had survived the night by huddling amidst the steaming mass of seals. After the shallop returned with the rescued men and the carcasses, Magellan sent three boats ashore to hunt more seals, but the hunters could find only penguins. The seals would not come out of the water.[18]

As the yards on the *Trinidad* were hoisted to make sail, a sudden storm arose, and a violent gust caught the ship broadside, causing it to lurch suddenly. The anchor cables snapped and the ship skidded toward the rocky shore and certain destruction. In desperation the crew deployed the spare anchor; it held. All aboard confessed to one another, each commending the other to God, promising alms and a pilgrimage to the monastery of Nuestra Señora de la Victoria, where they swore to spend the rest of their days as lay brothers. The tempest lasted all day but subsided during the night. At dawn the entire fleet gave thanks to God for their salvation but, becalmed, were unable to leave the bay.

Fearing another storm, the crews took extra precautions in setting their anchors. It was fortunate that they did, because an even fiercer gale blew up at midnight and lasted three days. The storm was so furious that the forecastles of all five ships were blown away, and the sterncastles were badly damaged. During this ordeal, the terrified crews made pledges for pilgrimages to Santiago de Galicia and Nuestra Señora de Guadalupe y Monserrat. They prayed fervently for deliverance from the fury of the storm and the terrors of that godforsaken bay.[19]

When the storm subsided, the fleet sailed on, probing ever farther south for a protected anchorage. Eventually the five ships entered a narrow inlet that opened into a beautiful bay abounding with penguins and seals.[20] Hoping that at last they had found a harbor in which they could overwinter, Magellan dispatched a shore party to look for fresh water. While they were ashore, another terrible storm struck. Although the wind was fierce, the ships were sheltered from its full fury, and their anchors dug into the firm bottom and held. The storm lasted six days with winds so strong the men ashore could not make it back to their ship. Lighting fires at night to signal their shipmates, they subsisted on large mussels cast up by the waves,[21] returning only when the gale finally passed. As they had been unable to find a suitable source of fresh water, the fleet weighed anchors and stood out of the bay, which they named *Bahía de los Trabajos* (The Bay of Travail).[22]

Already well below the latitude of the Cape of Good Hope, Magellan still pressed southward. The consistent southwesterly trend of the coast-line reinforced his suspicion that, like Africa, this western landmass would terminate in a cape. Should he not find a strait, he might still be able to sail around the southern cape into Balboa's sea. He was determined to exhaust all possibilities in his search for a westward passage before considering his other alternative, sailing east to the Moluccas. If forced to that option, he would sail south of the regular Portuguese sea-lanes, but to resupply his ships with fresh food, water, and firewood he would have to risk a landing near the Cape of Good Hope. If they were detected by a Portuguese ship, King Manuel would be informed that Magellan's fleet had been seen along the Portuguese route to the Far East, a terrible embarrassment for King Charles. It was bad enough for Magellan that he had incurred the wrath of the Portuguese king; his honor would be shattered should Charles too be given cause to despise him.

Desperately, Magellan sought a haven where his battered ships could be repaired. On March 31, 1520, the day before Easter Sunday, they entered a bay at 49° 15' S that Magellan named in honor of St. Julian.[23] The en-trance, leading south-southwest between hundred-foot bluffs, narrows to a half-mile before opening out into a spacious inner harbor. The tidal range is substantial, between twenty and twenty-five feet, and tidal currents at the narrows reach velocities of six knots.[24] Magellan sent boat crews to scout for fresh water, wood, and wild foods. Their reports were favorable, and the fleet anchored in the inner harbor.

The journey along the Patagonian coast had been hard on ships and men. More than once they had barely missed being driven onto dangerous reefs, and they had been battered by storms so severe that even at anchor the ships suffered extensive damage. The men, cold and demoralized, yearned for a warmer clime, and the officers deeply resented that Magellan still refused them any details about the route that could take them to the Moluccas. Some were convinced he was a madman who would lead them all to a frozen death.

With the ships anchored, Magellan's thoughts turned to preserving wine and biscuit for sea rations when they set forth again in the spring. He or-dered reduced rations for everyone,[25] eliciting howls of outrage from officers and men alike, and deputations from each ship implored him to restore full rations. These would suffice, they argued, to return to Spain, where a new fleet could be outfitted to resume the search for a westward passage.

But Magellan faced ruin if the fleet returned to Spain without attaining any of its principal objectives. Someone else would lead the next expedition while he languished in jail for having deluded the king. At the very least he would be a laughingstock in Seville, bringing disgrace and dishonor to his family. Grimly determined to continue no matter what hardships lay ahead, he assured the men that they would not suffer from hunger and cold in this place. Fish and shellfish were abundant, and there would be game in the uplands back of the shore. They would not need the biscuit he was hoarding, and there was plenty of fresh water and firewood. Worksheds and barracks would be built ashore so that they could perform their chores and rest in warmth and comfort. By spring, Magellan told his men, the ships would be repaired and ready for the voyage to the Moluccas, an earthly paradise beside which the attractions of Rio would pale. They should not fear to push farther south. After all, didn't Norwegians and Icelanders routinely make long voyages at even higher latitudes? For himself, because he prized honor above all else, he would rather die than return to Spain before completing the task to which they had all pledged their lives. If necessary, he would sail as far south as 75° or polar ice. The men of Castile were renowned the world over for their toughness, courage, and resourcefulness. Would they now quail before a few snowflakes and go scurrying back to Spain like beaten dogs with their tails between their legs?[26]

Many of the crewmen may have been won over by Magellan's stirring exhortations, but the Castilian captains and administrative officers remained intractable in their opposition to this Portuguese captain general who withheld the details of their route. Already infuriated by Magellan's high-handedness, they had had their fill of this dangerous coast with its frequent storms and icy blasts. They spread the rumor among the ships' crews that, to get back in the good graces of King Manuel, Magellan had sworn to destroy the fleet by wrecking most of the ships and marooning the survivors. He would inform Manuel that there was no westward passage north of 50°, news that would bring unrestrained joy in Portugal and discourage Spaniards from organizing another expedition.[27]

Captain Quesada and Cartagena on the *Concepción*, Captain Mendoza of the *Victoria*, and some other officers from both ships, notably Juan Sebastián del Cano, master of the *Concepción*, met to discuss their situation. Suspicious of Magellan's motives, discouraged by the hazards and discomforts of the voyage, and dismayed at the prospect of overwintering on this cold, bleak coast, they agreed to present Magellan with a formal demand that he reveal exactly where he was taking the king's fleet and the route by which he planned to get there. Should Magellan preemptorily reject their demand as he had in the past, they were prepared to remove him from command.[28]

Early in the morning of Easter Sunday, April 1, 1520, Magellan summoned all hands but the deck watches ashore for religious services.[29] After the services, he invited the captains, pilots, and officers of the high command to dine with him aboard the *Trinidad*. Before returning to his ship, Cano sought out Juan de Elorriaga, master of the *San Antonio*, a Basque like himself, to inform him of the resolution made by the officers of the *Concepción* and the *Victoria*. Cano must have been uncertain of the support of his fellow Basque shipmaster, for he did not tell him that the conspirators were prepared to rise up against Magellan should he refuse to accede to their demands.[30]

Neither Quesada nor Mendoza went ashore for the services, and for the Easter banquet aboard the *Trinidad* the only one to show up was Álvaro de Mesquita, Magellan's kinsman and captain of the *San Antonio*.[31] Many of the absent officers may have feared that Magellan had been tipped off about the plot and would arrest them if they went aboard the *Trinidad*. Professional officers, including Serrano, San Martín, and the other pilots and shipmasters, probably stayed away to avoid trouble. Primarily concerned with navigation and keeping the battered ships afloat and their crews functioning, the pilots knew that their involvement in political squabbles could only diminish the chances that anyone would survive this voyage.

That night during the second watch, a boat from the *Concepción* carrying Quesada, Cartagena, and thirty armed men pulled silently alongside the *San Antonio*. With Mesquita, who had turned out to be an easygoing skipper, and most of the crew sound asleep, the ship was only lightly guarded. Whether the deck watch were dozing or just easily intimidated, no alarm was sounded when the armed party climbed aboard. Quesada and Cartagena went directly to Mesquita's cabin. Bursting in with drawn swords, they dragged him on deck, where the sleepy, bewildered crew had been assembled by the boarding party. Quesada reminded them of the unnecessary hardships Magellan was forcing them to endure and told them of their captain general's refusal to follow royal instructions.[33]

Under the new command, the men were told, they no longer would be maltreated. The captains, pilots, and other officers would be properly responsible for the fleet, for the issue of rations, and for the protection of royal property. The men of the *San Antonio* were asked to help restore properly constituted authority to the fleet.

Mesquita, having flatly refused to have anything to do with a revolt against Magellan, was shackled and placed under guard in the padlocked cabin of the ship's clerk, Gerónimo Guerra. Quesada then went to the crew's quarters, where he found the *Trinidad*'s chaplain, Pedro de Valderrama, hearing the confession of a seaman. On seeing Quesada, Valderrama said to him, *"Cum sancto, sancto eris; et cum perversis, perverteris."* He was quoting, from faulty memory, verse 27 of the Eighteenth Psalm, which properly reads: *"Et cum electo, electus eris, et cum perverso, perverteris."*[34] In the King James Bible this verse appears thus: "With the pure, thou wilt shew thyself pure; and with the froward [profane], thou wilt shew thyself froward." "Who said that?" demanded Quesada. "The prophet David," answered the priest. "These days, father, we don't know the prophet David," responded the mutinous captain.

The ship's master, Juan de Elorriaga, awakened by the ruckus, rushed on deck and, on learning that Captain Mesquita had been taken captive, angrily confronted Quesada. "I demand, in the name of God and King Charles, that you return to your ship! This is not the time to be going among the ships with armed men. I also demand that you release our captain!" Summoning the mate, Diego Hernández, Elorriaga ordered him to gather some men, issue arms, and free their captain. Enraged, Quesada cried out, "Must we be thwarted by this idiot?" Drawing his dagger, he hurled himself at the loyal shipmaster, stabbing him viciously six times, leaving him lying on the deck in agony, bleeding and mortally wounded. There was no further opposition from the crew.

Antonio de Coca, the fleet accountant, gathered up the weapons in the arms locker and from the few seamen who bore arms and locked them in his cabin. The ship's three Portuguese crewmen were seized and shackled. The mate, Hernández, was taken in irons to the *Concepción* and confined.[35]

With Elorriaga dying and Hernández imprisoned, the mutineers needed a professional officer to take charge of the *San Antonio's* crew. Quesada asked the pilot, Juan Rodríguez de Mafra, if he would do it, but Mafra refused and was shackled belowdeck. Cano was brought over from the *Concepción*, and his first act was to order the ship's guns prepared for firing. Next, Quesada ordered the ship's steward, Juan Ortiz de Gopeguy, to open the stores and issue the men whatever they wanted. When the steward protested, Quesada threatened him and forced him to comply.[36]

With the *San Antonio* secured, Cartagena returned to take command of the *Concepción*, while Quesada remained on the *San Antonio*. With Mendoza on the *Victoria*, three of the fleet's five ships were controlled by the mutinous faction. On the *Trinidad* and the *Santiago*, night yielded to dawn without anyone being aware of what had transpired.

Early on the morning of April 2, a crew from the *Trinidad* rowed a skiff over to the *San Antonio* to pick up four men for a shore party to scout for fresh water and firewood. As the skiff approached the *San Antonio*, the men in it were warned by a sailor that Quesada had boarded the ship with armed men, imprisoned Captain Mesquita and the pilot, and severely wounded Elorriaga. The men rowed quickly back to the *Trinidad* with the alarming news.[37] Magellan wasted little time determining the extent of the mutiny.

He sent the skiff back to hail the other ships, asking to whom they would be loyal. On the *San Antonio*, Quesada answered that he was now captain of this ship and that he owed his loyalty to King Charles. Similar responses came from Mendoza on the *Victoria* and Cartagena on the *Concepción*.[38]

On the little *Santiago*, moored alongside the *Trinidad* near the exit of the inner harbor, no one was aware of what had happened the previous night. When the *Trinidad*'s skiff hailed it, a puzzled Captain Serrano affirmed his allegiance to Magellan.[39] A professional mariner of long experience, Serrano had little interest in fleet politics, and Magellan's respect for him was fully reciprocated. Serrano soon realized what had happened, and could see that the mutineers held a clear advantage with their three ships and a preponderance of the fleet's firepower. Nevertheless, without hesitation, he aligned himself solidly with Magellan.

Later in the day, the longboat from the *San Antonio* arrived at the *Trinidad* with a message presenting a list of grievances, focusing on the mistreatment and hardships that the officers as well as the men had suffered under Magellan's command. To ensure that such mistreatment not continue, Quesada, Mendoza, and Cartagena had taken the drastic step of seizing the three ships, but if Magellan would promise to obey the king's orders by consulting them about the course to be sailed and all matters concerning the safety of the fleet and the well-being of the crews, they ". . . would acknowledge your leadership and kiss your feet and hands."[40]

Magellan sent the boat back with the message that the three captains should come to his ship to discuss the matter properly. If they did, he would hear them out and then, he assured them, he ". . . would do what was right." The longboat returned to the *Trinidad* with the captains' reply. "We don't dare board your ship," the message said, "for fear of mistreatment. Instead, we should all meet on the *San Antonio*, where we will do as you command." The tenor of their messages revealed to Magellan that, in spite of their advantage in ships, men, and firepower, his adversaries were irresolute and fearful of the consequences of what they had begun. Any further exchange of messages would only build their confidence and permit them to consolidate their position. Seizing the initiative, Magellan set his counterstroke in motion.

The tired, hungry crew of the longboat, waiting alongside for a reply, was invited aboard the *Trinidad* for a hearty meal and a cup of wine. At dusk, while they were eating, Magellan had their longboat secured out of sight from the ships of the mutineers. He then summoned his master-at-arms, the tough, reliable Espinosa, sending him with one of his marines to hand-deliver a message to Captain Mendoza. Two sailors rowed the skiff; Espinosa and the marine carried concealed daggers. Pulling hard against the last of the ebb, the oarsmen brought the skiff alongside the *Victoria*.

At first a nervous Mendoza refused to permit them aboard, but Espinosa taunted him, asking if the noble captain feared an unarmed messenger. His pride wounded, Mendoza told Espinosa to come aboard, and didn't object when he beckoned to the marine to follow him. Armored except for a helmet, Mendoza escorted them to his cabin, where Espinosa handed him Magellan's message. As he read it, Mendoza began to smile, as if what Magellan had proposed were preposterous. The smile expanded into scornful laughter as he handed the message back to Espinosa. It was his last laugh. Extending his left hand as if to reach for the letter, Espinosa grasped the scornful captain's hair, jerked his head back and, with his right hand, plunged his dagger into the exposed throat. As Mendoza slumped, the marine finished him with a savage dagger thrust that penetrated his brain, killing him instantly.[41]

Meanwhile fifteen heavily armed men led by Duarte Barbosa clambered into the *San Antonio*'s longboat. Under cover of darkness and with the tide now flooding, they drifted to the *Victoria* silent and unseen at the end of a long hawser paid out from the *Trinidad*.[42] On a signal from Espinosa (possibly a lantern swung from a port in Mendoza's cabin in the sterncastle), Barbosa and his men swarmed aboard, disarming the startled deck watch. The crew of the *Victoria* offered no opposition.

Magellan had chosen his target shrewdly. Of the three vessels controlled by the mutineers, the *Victoria* had the highest proportion of Portuguese and neutral foreigners in its crew.[43] The former would be loyal to Magellan and the latter anxious to stay out of factional squabbles, so Barbosa's boarding party anticipated little opposition, and got none. The Castilian who had just been killed had been an inept captain. Arrogant, overbearing, and appallingly ignorant of the most basic rules of seamanship, he had failed to earn the respect and loyalty of his crew.

Shouting "Long live the Emperor and death to traitors!" Espinosa, Barbosa, and their men raised Magellan's flag on the mainmast.[44] Later that night, when the tide turned again to ebb, the *Victoria*'s anchors were brought up to short stays, she was allowed to drift abreast of the *Trinidad*, and the anchors were reset. With the *Santiago* and the *Victoria* on either flank, Magellan now had three ships blocking the exit to the sea. The *San Antonio* and *Concepción* were trapped.

The tables had turned. Although the *San Antonio* was the most heavily armed ship in the fleet, the mutineers had overcome the crew and mortally wounded the master. It was doubtful that they could expect much cooperation from the resentful crew in a fight. The mutineers released Mesquita and begged him to plead with Magellan to have mercy on them, but Mesquita coldly refused, telling them it would be utterly useless. Their last remaining hope was to slip past the three ships guarding the harbor entrance.

Alerted by the thump of ground tackle, the creak of blocks, and the rustle of canvas, the watch on the *Trinidad* noted a flurry of activity on the *San Antonio*. Peering into the moonlit night, they saw that her yards were hoisted, her gun ports open, and her bow pointed seaward. She seemed poised to make a run for it, but from a perch on her bowsprit Mesquita shouted across the water to Magellan that they were going to anchor.[45] Expecting a battle in the morning, Magellan prepared for combat and took the precaution of doubling the watch for the rest of the night. Quesada apparently intended to run at dawn, giving Cano's gunners a chance to fire their broadsides in the morning light, but his plans were thwarted by the tide.

Some accounts say that Quesada, hoping for a quick start at dawn, had ordered two of the *San Antonio*'s three anchors raised. The third, which he had trusted to hold the ship, began to drag in the accelerating current.[46] Others contend that Magellan sent a lone seaman from the *Trinidad* to the *San Antonio* in a skiff. In one version of the story, he represented himself as a defector who hated serving under a Portuguese commander. In another, he was surreptitiously let aboard by friendly crewmen on the *San Antonio* resentful of the actions of the mutineers. With the ebb tide running, the seaman cut the anchor cable.[47] Whatever the cause, before daybreak the *San Antonio* was drifting helplessly toward Magellan's ships.

As the *San Antonio* came abreast of the *Trinidad*, Quesada could be seen on the quarterdeck, armored from head to foot and carrying a lance and a shield. Strutting like a peacock, he was bawling battle orders to which no one paid the slightest attention. The *Trinidad*'s gunners fired a few rounds of heavy shot into the *San Antonio*'s hull, one of which passed between the legs of the startled Rodríguez de Mafra, the loyal pilot chained belowdeck. Luckily, he was not injured.[48] When the *San Antonio* drifted near enough for grappling, an armed boarding party from the *Trinidad* leaped onto its deck, shouting, "For whom do you stand?" "For King Charles and for Magellan!" chorused the weary, bewildered crew of the *San Antonio*. Quesada and his henchmen were quickly rounded up and put in chains.[49]

Magellan immediately dispatched forty men in a longboat to the *Concepción*, where the fate of the *Victoria* and *San Antonio* had not gone unnoticed. Asked to whom they owed their loyalty, the crew responded that it was to Magellan. Would they be safe, they asked? Assured that they would be, they promptly surrendered their unresisting captain, the crestfallen Juan de Cartagena. He was taken to the *Trinidad* and shackled belowdeck with Quesada, Coca, Cano, and the other conspirators.[50]

Among the mutineers were the captains of three of the fleet's five ships, an experienced shipmaster for whom a replacement would be difficult to find, and most of the fleet's administrative officers. The three ships they seized had given them a firepower advantage of at least two to one over the *Trinidad* and the small, lightly armed *Santiago*. Had the mutineers been able to coordinate a sweep past Magellan's ships, they might have raked his two ships with broadsides and escaped with little damage. But the leaders of the mutiny knew nothing about naval tactics. As commanders they were indecisive, ineffective, and unable to win the loyalty of their crews. In Magellan they were up against a veteran of naval campaigns in Africa, India, and Malaya. A tough but fair commander who inspired many of his men and won the grudging admiration of most of the others, his reactions were quick, decisive, and ruthless. Using but few men and little equipment, his tactics were timed to take advantage of the cover of night and the strong tidal currents in the harbor. He gave the mutineers no opportunity to deploy their ships and their superior firepower against him.

Immediately following the surrender of the *San Antonio* and *Concepción*, Magellan ordered a court martial. The body of Mendoza was propped up and stood trial with the rest. With a vengeful Álvaro de Mesquita presiding, justice was swift and severe. Forty were found guilty and condemned to death.[51] The body of Mendoza was taken ashore, decapitated, and quartered. As befitting a nobleman condemned to death, Quesada also was to be decapitated, but no one wanted to be his executioner. Magellan offered to commute the death sentence of Quesada's squire, Luis Molino, if he would do it, and the inducement was enough to overcome the squire's reluctance. The sentence was carried out on April 7. Like that of Mendoza, Quesada's body was quartered, and the dismembered parts of the two captains were spitted on a pole as a warning against further rebellion.[52] Although Cartagena was found guilty of mutiny, a capital crime, Magellan could not bring himself to sentence him to death. As before, he was confined to quarters on one of the ships.

Because the fleet could ill afford the loss of so many men, the death sentences of the rest of those found guilty were commuted. Feet in chains, they were put to work at the pumps, cleaning the filthy bilges, and other hard, distasteful labor. Among them was the errant shipmaster, Juan Sebastián del Cano.

14

*W*inter in Patagonia

 With *the mutiny behind him and the grisly display ashore* reminding everyone of the futility of defying his orders, Magellan put the crews to work cleaning and repairing the ships. One of the first tasks was rummaging.[1] Provisions and trade goods were unloaded and stored in sheds erected ashore, and the reeking ballast was lugged out of the bilges and placed in the intertidal zone to clean it of accumulated filth. The ships were careened, rotted planks replaced, seams caulked, and hulls tarred below the waterline. A stone smithy was erected on a small islet in the inner harbor.[2]

After everything stowed in the ships had been taken ashore, an inventory revealed that unscrupulous chandlers in Seville had delivered but half the two-year supply of rations stipulated in the contract, disguising their subterfuge by issuing two invoices for each consignment laded. The remaining rations would suffice for only six months.[3] Worse yet, except for an abundance of mussels in the intertidal zone, there was not much wild food available locally. Although there were *ñandu* (Patagonian ostriches), *guanaco* (wild llama), rabbits and other large rodents in the area around Bahía San Julián,[4] Magellan's men did not know how to hunt them. Fresh water was neither abundant nor very good; the only surface water in the region was a chain of salt lakes in the uplands above the bay.[5]

Magellan realized that if they spent the entire winter in San Julián as he had intended, they'd have to rely on the ships' stores to survive. By spring there would be insuffient rations for an extended sea voyage. He therefore decided to resume the search for a westward passage as soon as possible, but first the ships had to be readied for winter sailing.

The cold at Bahía San Julián brought intense misery. Several men froze to death, and at least three suffered frostbitten hands.[6] A different kind of misery brought about the tragic death of an apprentice seaman, the victim of the crime for which the master of the *Victoria*, Antón Salamón, had been executed. Overwhelmed by shame and the ridicule of his shipmates, Antonio Baresa threw himself into the sea on April 27, 1520. His body was cast up on the beach on May 21.[7] Another casualty, a great loss to Magellan, was Juan de Elorriaga. Brutally stabbed when he opposed the mutiny aboard his ship, the loyal master of the *San Antonio* died on July 15.[8]

Barring a heavy overcast, a solar eclipse should have been visible at Bahía San Julián on April 17, 1520. Portuguese chronicles claim that San Martín used it to calculate the longitude of the bay, but it is doubtful that he did. Not visible in Europe, it probably was not listed in his ephemeris.[9] Whether or not San Martín was able to use the eclipse, Magellan was eager to test Faleiro's methods for determining longitude. He ordered his pilots to review the latter's thirty-chapter treatise and give him their opinion of its utility. All but one reported that they couldn't use any part of it; San Martín thought he might be able to apply the methods described in the fourth chapter (calculating longitude by observing conjunctions and oppositions of the moon and planets).[10]

Magellan was disappointed, for he had hoped to use Faleiro's magnetic-variation system to locate the Moluccas relative to the extended demarcation line. He was ahead of his time, for not until 1761 did John Harrison, an Englishman, develop a chronometer sufficiently accurate to use in determining longitude.[11]

Hoping to exploit the discontent of the crews laboring in the bitter cold, Cartagena and Bernard Calmette (the French chaplain of the *San Antonio*) tried to incite another mutiny,[12] but the Castilian nobleman had fallen so low in the esteem of the crews that the plot was promptly exposed. His tolerance exhausted by Cartagena's unceasing efforts to undermine his command, Magellan sentenced him and the mutinous priest to be marooned.

The *Santiago* was the first of the five ships to be reconditioned. Eager to find a strait or terminal cape leading to the west, or at least a harbor where the fleet's dwindling food stores could be replenished, Magellan dispatched the little ship to reconnoiter the coast to the south.[13] Leaving San Julián on or about May 1, 1520, Serrano and his crew ran into strong headwinds. Using short offshore and longer inshore tacks, they beat slowly to the south-southwest, keeping the coast in sight. On May 6, a lookout spotted an opening in the coast at 50° 08' S, about 60 nautical miles south-southwest of San Julián. A line of breakers indicated a bar at the entrance. Threading their way through the shoals, the *Santiago* entered a long, deep estuary abounding with seals and penguins. Serrano named it Santa Cruz, after the feast of the Holy Cross celebrated on that day.[14]

The Santa Cruz estuary is two nautical miles wide at its mouth. Inside, it gradually broadens to three, extending inland to the north-northwest fourteen nautical miles, where two good-sized rivers flow into it. Serrano and his crew anchored their ship and remained in the fine harbor nearly a fortnight, slaughtering seals and smoking the meat. They departed on May 22, intending to explore the coast to the southwest, but shortly after crossing the bar, the *Santiago* met with a violent squall that tore away its sails. Wallowing in heavy seas after the squall had passed, the little ship was struck on the stern by a mountainous wave that carried away her rudder.[15] As wind and waves drove the helpless vessel toward shore, Serrano rigged a spare sail to a spar and used it to steer the ship into the beach bow first. All but one of the crew of thirty-eight were able to leap from the bow onto the beach. Juan, Serrano's black slave, drowned when he mistimed his jump and a wave swept him into the sea. Within minutes, the *Santiago* was pounded to pieces in the surf.

For eight days the shipwrecked sailors remained on the beach where their ship had broken up, collecting timbers cast up by the waves. These they planned to haul to Santa Cruz to build a raft with which to cross the estuary to its northern shore. They had no food other than large barnacles found among the rocks,[16] and already weakened by cold and hunger, they discarded many of the heavy timbers en route to Santa Cruz. Arriving after four days of struggling over rough terrain, they had only enough timber for a two-man raft.[17] Fortunately for the weary, starving men, the estuary was teeming with easily caught fish.[18] After resting and feasting on fish to regain their strength, two strong young crewmen were chosen to try to reach San Julián to alert Magellan to their predicament.

After rafting across the estuary, the two sailors hiked inland for two days, heading north-northeast. Finding nothing to eat on the cold, dry pampas, they turned east toward the coast, where they found shellfish. Since the rough shoreline topography made beach travel impossible, they were forced inland again, taking with them what little shellfish they could carry. After eleven days of scrambling, half-frozen, across the rough, wintry terrain, they arrived at San Julián frostbitten, nearly naked, and so emaciated that the men who first spotted them did not recognize them.[19]

When Magellan learned of the fate of the *Santiago* and its crew, the weather was too stormy to risk sending a ship after them. He dispatched a rescue party of twenty men overland, loaded with bread and wine. Harking back to the example set by Diogo Lopes de Sequeira in the Indian Ocean, one wonders how many other commanders of the day would have bothered. It was bitterly cold, and for drinking water the travelers melted icicles over their campfires. When they reached Santa Cruz on June 26, the shipwreck victims said it had been thirty-five days since they had eaten bread.

While records do not indicate how the survivors and their rescuers got back to San Julián, they must have walked, reaching there about July 22, 1520.[20]

Upon their return, the crew of the *Santiago* was distributed among the four remaining ships. With two captains dead and a third sentenced to be marooned, Magellan had filled the vacancies with men he felt he could trust. Two of them were relatives: Mesquita, who resumed his interrupted command of the *San Antonio*, and Barbosa, the new captain of the *Victoria*. For captain of the *Concepción* he chose Serrano, whose loyalty had earned his gratitude, and for whose seafaring skills he had developed great respect.[21]

Early in June, about a month after the *Santiago* had departed on its ill-fated reconnaissance, a huge Patagonian appeared on the shore at San Julián.[22] In full view of the astonished Spaniards, he pranced about singing, dancing, and pouring handfuls of sand on his head. Magellan sent a seaman ashore to approach their visitor and imitate his movements, hoping that the fellow would interpret this as a gesture of peace. It worked. The tall Patagonian climbed into the skiff with the sailor, accompanying him to the islet where the forge had been built. There he was cordially greeted by Magellan and other curious onlookers from the ships, including that indefatigable amateur anthropologist, Antonio Pigafetta. When introduced to Magellan, the man made a sign, pointing upward with his index finger. Pigafetta interpreted this to mean that he thought that the strangers had come from the sky. His weapons consisted of a short, heavy bow with a string made of guanaco gut, and a bundle of arrows with stone points and feathered, cane shafts.

His face was painted red, with yellow about the eyes and heartshaped designs on the cheeks. Pigafetta observed that he ". . . was so tall that we reached only to his waist, and he was well proportioned." This probably was an exaggeration to impress audiences at the royal courts of Europe, which years later listened raptly to Pigafetta's tales. Another, perhaps more reliable, observer, "The Genoese Pilot" (probably the *Trinidad*'s Genoese master, Juan Bautista, or his compatriot, Leon Pancaldo), was more precise. He reported the height of these people to be from nine to ten palms (sixty-nine to seventy-seven inches or 175 to 195 centimeters), within the range reported for Tehuelches by nineteenth century travelers to Patagonia.[23] The Tehuelche described by Pigafetta was undoubtedly a big fellow, but he needn't have been a giant to have towered over Magellan, who was short, as were many of his men.

The native was clad in a cape made of skillfully stitched guanaco skins, and his feet were wrapped in skins of the same animal. Not being familiar with guanaco, Pigafetta's description of them is quaint: "That animal has a head and ears as large as those of a mule, a neck and body like those of a camel, the legs of a deer and the tail of a horse, like which it neighs, and that land has very many of them."[24] Their guest was fascinated with the articles of trade shown to him. Startled by the image staring from a large steel mirror, he sprang backward, knocking to the ground three or four sailors gathered around him. After being served a hearty meal, which he wolfed down with a speed that amazed his hosts, he was loaded with presents, including a mirror, comb, brass bells, and rosary beads.

The visitor was escorted back to shore by four armed men. Seeing him safe, a companion who had been watching from shore ran back into the brush and emerged with a file of eighteen men and women. The men carried only their weapons, while the women, wrote Pigafetta, ". . . were laden like asses." In spite of the cold, they were nearly naked. The women were not as tall as the men, but much fatter. Their enormous breasts, noted the observant Lombard, were a yard long. Both men and women wore paint on their faces and bodies, and like the first visitor, when these natives saw Magellan's men they began to sing and dance, pointing toward the sky. With them were four young guanacos, led with halters made of thongs. When hunting adults of that species, the natives used captured juveniles as decoys.

Six days later, a group of sailors were ashore cutting firewood when a Tehuelche even bigger than their previous visitor approached them. They brought him to their ship where he stayed happily for several days or perhaps a week. He was taught to say the words *Jesu, Pater Noster*, and *Ave María* and to recite simple prayers, which he did with gusto, in an exceedingly loud voice. His hosts baptized him with a Christian name, Juan. When he danced on the beach, his guanaco-hide foot coverings left enormous prints in the sand, sparking stories that led generations of Europeans to believe that the natives of Patagonia were a race of giants. Perhaps because the hide-wrapped feet of these robust people reminded Magellan of those of dogs, he called them *patagones*, possibly a contraction of *pata de cano* (dog paw). From this was derived the name Patagonia.[25]

When Juan left, Magellan presented him with a cap, shirt, jacket, trousers, comb, bells, and other trinkets, which pleased him greatly. The clothing, being much too small, emphasized his great size, making him look like an awkward giant. He reappeared the next day leading a full-grown guanaco which he presented to the captain general. Magellan again showered him with gifts, hoping that he might bring more of the animals, but Juan never returned.

Two weeks later, four more "giants" appeared on the shore, each painted with different designs. Desirous of taking some of these huge men to Spain as curiosities, Magellan ordered his men to capture a few. That this was done at all, and the manner in which it was done, foreshadowed the deceit and brutality so unconscionably employed by Europeans in their dealings with the peoples of the New World they claimed to have "discovered." Magellan's men resorted to a nasty trick, exploiting the Tehuelches' good-natured innocence. The two youngest and best proportioned of the four native men were loaded down gifts. When they could carry no more, the sailors offered each a set of fetters, knowing they were fascinated with objects of iron. With their hands full and their leather capes clutched about them to hold their gifts, they were unable to grasp the iron fetters. Magellan's men indicated by signs that they could carry the metal objects on their feet. Delighted with the novel idea, the innocent Patagonians permitted the shackles to be placed around their ankles. When they realized they had been tricked, they roared like bulls, invoking a god, *Setebos*, to rescue them.[26]

It took nine Spaniards to overpower the captives' two companions. Although their hands were tied behind them, one broke his bonds and ran away; the other was slightly wounded when struck on the head as he, too, tried to escape. The unhappy captives eventually quieted down, for they were not maltreated. One of them, obviously distraught, somehow indicated to his captors that he was upset over being separated from his wife. On learning of this, Magellan resolved to find the woman so that she might accompany her husband to Spain. He instructed Carvalho to take a squad of armed men, with the wounded native as a guide, to the natives' camp in search of the captive's wife. When Carvalho and his squad reached the camp, the natives had fled, but a light snowfall made it easy to follow their tracks.

At sundown on July 29, Carvalho and his men were about to give up their search when they were attacked by nine native warriors armed with bows and arrows. A seaman, Diego Sanchez Barrasa, was struck in the thigh by an arrow. It must have severed an artery, for he bled to death where he fell. The crossbows and light cannon the Spaniards had brought with them were of little use against the native warriors, who pranced about, never presenting a stationary target. The Spaniards defended themselves with shields and swords until the natives retired with their women, who had been hiding nearby.

In the camp abandoned by the natives, Carvalho's squad found a lot of half-cooked meat. Appropriating it, they set forth for San Julián. As it was cold and the meat was heavy, they stopped, lit a huge fire, and feasted for the rest of the night. In the morning they returned to their ships empty-handed.[27]

The two captured natives adapted quickly to shipboard life. "Each of the captives," wrote Pigafetta, "could wolf down a full basket of biscuit and drink a half bucket of water in one gulp. They also ate rats without even taking the trouble to skin them first." When Pigafetta questioned them about supernatural beings, they indicated that there were two principal demons, *Setebos* and *Chaleule*. Using signs, one of the captives told Pigafetta that he had seen these demons, and that they ". . . had horns on their head, long hair that reached their feet, and they belch fire from the mouth and anus."

On July 21, San Martín brought his instruments ashore to test Faleiro's system for using conjunctions of the moon with the planets to determine longitude.[28] His measurements resulted in the astonishingly accurate estimate of 61° west of Seville. Less than one degree in error, this was an accomplishment far beyond the capabilities of the other pilots. No ordinary pilot, San Martín was the only one in the fleet with the mathematical skills to use Faleiro's methods. To achieve such precision, he may have taken multiple readings of the measurements on which his calculations were based. Their tendency to cluster about a mean probably encouraged him to discard extreme values.

Among the papers confiscated from the *Trinidad* after its capture in the Moluccas in 1522 were maps sketched by the expedition's pilots, one of which gave the longitude for San Julián as 43°, and the other 46°. Neither indicated the prime meridian used. A Portuguese source stated that the data had been altered to favor Spanish territorial claims, but another explanation seems reasonable. Early in the sixteenth century there was little consistency in choosing a prime meridian, even on maps by the same cartographer. The meridians of Santo Antão and Boa Vista in the Cape Verde Islands were often used for this purpose. If Magellan's pilots had so used them, the 43° and 46° are roughly equivalent to San Martín's 61° west of Seville, and were probably derived from his calculations.[29]

On August 11, 1520, Cartagena and the priest, Calmette, were taken in a longboat to a small island, where they were marooned with their swords and a generous supply of wine and biscuit. When the last goodbyes were exchanged with shipmates who accompanied them in the longboat, there was a great outpouring of grief.[30]

Not until August 24 did the fleet depart from San Julián. On that day, San Martín measured the sun's altitude at noon and calculated the latitude to be 49° 18′ S, which is precisely correct.[31] Why Magellan waited for thirteen days after the abandonment of Cartagena and the priest before ordering the fleet to sail from San Julián is not clear. As winter was not yet over, bad weather might well have caused the delay.

The tragic events marking Magellan's stay at Bahía San Julián would not be the last in that grim port. In 1578, Thomas Doughty, the unruly captain of one of Sir Francis Drake's ships, was beheaded there in the shadow of what appeared to be a gibbet. Drake believed it to be the one on which, 58 years before, Magellan had impaled the dismembered body parts of his mutinous captains. Doughty also was found guilty of mutiny; given the choice of being marooned, tried in an admiralty court in England, or immediate execution, he chose the latter. The fate of the gibbet erected by Magellan is curious. The cooper on Drake's *Pelican* (later renamed *Golden Hinde*) cut it up and fashioned souvenir drinking cups from the wood.[32]

Magellan had learned from Serrano that the estuary at Santa Cruz offered a winter anchorage superior to that at San Julián. The abundance of fish, seals, and seabirds would make it possible for the men to sustain themselves by fishing and hunting, and by smoking the excess catch and storing it in barrels they could augment their dwindling food stores. Magellan also hoped to salvage timbers and other useful items from the wreck of the *Santiago*.

The fleet reached Santa Cruz in two days, although not without difficulty. Strong winds blowing from every quarter roiled the sea into a chaotic jumble of colliding, mountainous waves. After some anxious moments crossing the bar, the four ships anchored in the quiet, sheltered estuary on August 26, 1520.[33] Magellan dispatched a work party under the *Victoria*'s carpenter, Martín de Gárate, to the wreck of the *Santiago* to see if it could be rebuilt or what could be salvaged. The bad luck that had dogged the last journey of the *Santiago* extended to the man sent to rebuild it. Garate drowned while attempting to cross the estuary.[34] Magellan kept the men busy cutting firewood, hunting, fishing, and preserving their catches. On September 16, Jacomé de Mesina, a seaman from the *San Antonio*, died from an unreported cause.[35]

On the morning of October 11, although the sky was cloudless, the sun dimmed and turned dark red. Thinking it an ill omen, the superstitious crews became nervous and depressed. San Martín noted that the event occurred at 10:08 A.M. Although there was a solar eclipse visible from the northern hemisphere on that date, it is not likely that the penumbra would have been visible from their position deep in the southern hemisphere. More likely the cause was smoke from a distant grass fire set by natives to drive game into a trap.

Satisfied that the fleet's food supply had been replenished suffiently with smoked fish and game, Magellan was eager to resume the search for a passage to the west. On October 18 (spring in the southern hemisphere), the four ships weighed anchor and sailed from the productive estuary that, for nearly two months, had provided a snug harbor and abundant food.

15
$\mathcal{T}$he Strait

$\mathbf{M}$*agellan's four ships encountered strong southerly headwinds* as soon as they crossed the bar at Río Santa Cruz. Sailing on a close reach, the clumsy naos could make scant progress, but after two days the wind swung around to the north, and a following sea lifted the little ships by their sterns as they scudded before the breeze. Sheets of spray were thrown onto the wind-whipped sea as their blunt bows plunged, sending foam sliding into their wakes.

Sailing five leagues offshore on October 21, 1520, the lookouts spotted an opening in the coast, ". . . like a bay," said the entry in Albo's log. As they sailed abreast of it, they saw that it extended inland a considerable distance. Because that day commemorated the martyrdom of the Eleven Thousand Virgins of St. Ursula, Magellan named the cape at the northern extremity of the bay Cabo Vírgenes.[1]

Turning southwest to investigate, the fleet sailed past a long, sandy point extending southward from the cape, naming it Punta Vírgenes.[2] Today it is called Punta Dungeness. Albo correctly estimated its latitude at 52° and the distance to the opposite shore (Punta Catalina) at five leagues.[3] Fervently hoping that at last he had reached the entrance to a strait between the oceans, Magellan led the fleet into the bay. Carvalho, the *Concepción's* pilot, took a boat crew ashore to see what could be discerned from the summit of a small hill behind Punta Dungeness; when they returned, he reported that the bay appeared closed to the west.[4] Not satisfied, Magellan sent the *San Antonio* and *Concepción* ahead to explore the bay, giving them five days for the reconnaissance.[5] Both ships headed west, following the northern shore.

That night, while the *Trinidad* and *Victoria* were anchored behind Punta

Dungeness in Bahía Posesión, a violent northeast gale arose, causing their anchors to drag. To avoid being driving down on the opposite shore, the two ships sailed outside the bay to ride out the storm. When the gale subsided, they reentered and found better holding ground farther along the northern shore of the bay, possibly in the shallow cove now called Caleta Munición.[6] There was no sign of the *San Antonio* or the *Concepción* for two days, and Magellan began to worry that they had been wrecked in the storm. Smoke from a native campfire rising from the distant coastline made him wonder whether it was a signal from survivors. On the fourth of the five days allotted for the reconnaissance, the two ships were sighted, headed for the anchorage under full sail, banners and pennants flying and guns booming.[7]

When the storm struck, the *San Antonio* and *Concepción* were too far within the bay to beat out against the wind. The *San Antonio* had been sailing along the northern shore and, unable to anchor, was driven to the southwest. By dawn she was closing fast with the foaming surf over the shallow sands of Banco Orange. Clawing off the lee shore, she tacked northwest toward Cabo Orange, where the line of surf seemed to end.

When they finally passed the cape, a passage leading west opened before them. Relieved to have found sea room, the *San Antonio* entered it, scudding past the point of land now known as Punta Anegada. Before them stretched the First Narrows, a channel about two nautical miles wide leading southwest. With the wind astern the *San Antonio* boomed through the narrows into Bahía San Felipe, a broad lagoon about sixteen nautical miles wide, and found shelter from the storm in the lee of the northeastern shore.

The *Concepción* had also struggled to avoid being driven onto Banco Orange, and passed through the First Narrows sometime after the *San Antonio*. After the gale subsided, Serrano spent several days cautiously probing along the south shore of Bahía San Felipe. He found nothing of interest, only a few shallow inlets bordered by high banks.[8]

Meanwhile, the *San Antonio* continued westward and entered Second Narrows, a channel opening into Broad Reach, a wide gulf leading south. Because the water was still salty and deep, and the tidal current at least as strong on the flood as on the ebb, Mesquita and his pilot, Gomes, were convinced that the channel ahead would lead to the sea.[9] Satisfied that this was the strait Magellan had been seeking, Mesquita called a halt to further exploration and headed back, eager to bring the exciting news to his anxiously waiting kinsman. Returning through Bahía San Felipe, the *San Antonio* met the *Concepción*, and the two ships approached the rendezvous together, pennants flying, their crews cheering and firing salutes.[10]

Magellan was fervently hopeful, and ordered the fleet to get underway immediately. Sailing toward the First Narrows, they had traveled no more than a league when a lookout discerned what appeared to be a man-made structure about a mile inland. Hoping to find a village, Magellan sent a party of ten men ashore to investigate, but the men found only a native burial ground.[11] The superstitious sailors were only too glad to hurry back to their ship, for the place seemed doubly haunted: They had landed their skiff on a beach littered with great piles of bleached bones and the rotting carcass of a whale.[12]

On October 27, retracing the route explored earlier by the *San Antonio*, the fleet anchored in Paso Real, a sheltered roadstead between Isla Isabel and the Brunswick Peninsula.[13] Convening a council of his captains and pilots, Magellan solicited their opinions on the wisdom of pressing on with the exploration of the broad waterway stretching southward. All but Gomes were in favor of going forward. Convinced that this was the *paso* they had been seeking, the Portuguese pilot counseled returning to Spain, ". . . because there would still be the Great Gulf of China to cross." Should they be delayed by calms or storms, he warned, their supplies would not last and they would all perish. Magellan responded that, ". . . even though we may be forced to eat the leather chafing gear on the yards, we must go forward and discover what has been promised to the Emperor," adding, "God will help us and bring us good fortune."[14]

While Gomes was probably sincere in his counsel, he also knew that, should the fleet return to Spain, Magellan would be forced to defend his actions at San Julián. With Magellan so embroiled, Gomes would be the logical choice to lead a new expedition to the Moluccas. After all, had he not been pilot of the *San Antonio* when it was first to enter this vast inland waterway that surely must lead to the Great South Sea? But we really cannot know what was in the mind of this enigmatic pilot. One of the Portuguese who had accompanied Magellan to Spain, Gomes had earlier gone to Valladolid on his own to promote an expedition in search of a western route to the Orient. Refused, he had watched with envy as Magellan's enterprise won the king's approval.

Pigafetta wrote that Gomes ". . . hated the captain general exceedingly, because, before the fleet was fitted out, the Emperor had ordered that he be given some caravels with which to discover lands, but His Majesty did not give them to him because of the captain general."[15] It seems unlikely that Gomes, a professional mariner, would have confided this to Pigafetta, with whom he had little in common. More likely Pigafetta's sources for this statement were court gossip, shipboard scuttlebutt, or both, neither very reliable. Perhaps Gomes had been pleased enough with the appointment as Magellan's flag pilot, and valued his association with the expatriate Portuguese nobleman and his aristocratic family in Seville. However, when Cartagena's arrest left vacant the command of the *San Antonio*, the ambitious pilot probably anticipated promotion to its captaincy. When Magellan awarded it to Mesquita, Gomes was bitterly disappointed, the disappointment turning to outrage when he was transferred to the *San Antonio* to provide professional backup for the inexperienced Mesquita. Expecting a promotion, Gomes probably regarded the transfer as a demotion from flag pilot. Worse, he now had to serve under the landlubber who got the job he had coveted.

Following the captains' council, the fleet headed south into Broad Reach. The tidal currents, the saltiness of the water, and the great depth and width of the passage encouraged Magellan to believe that at last they had found a *paso* leading to the Great South Sea. As it was November 1, All Saints' Day, he named it, Canal de Todos los Santos (All Saints' Channel).[16] The eastern shore, where the fleet could see native campfires at night, he named *Tierra del Fuego* (Land of Fire). It is still known by that name and, until recently, it was still appropriate, as the flaring of gas from oil wells on Tierra del Fuego could be seen at night from the opposite shore and from ships passing through the strait. The wasteful practice of burning off recoverable gas from producing wells has since been discontinued.[17]

As Magellan's ships sailed southward in Broad Reach, a wall of snow-capped mountains spanned the horizon ahead. By the evening of All Saints' Day, they came to a point of land dividing the strait into three passages: two leading southward on either side of the point, and another leading east. They had reached Cape Valentín at the northern end of Dawson Island.[18]

Dawson is a beautiful island on which the Chilean navy maintains a modern refueling facility for ships that service the lighthouses and navigational markers in the strait. Highly esteemed by Chilean naval officers, there is superb trout fishing in nearby Río Fox, a delightful stream in a pastoral setting much like that of a well-managed estate in Scotland. But Dawson Island has a grim, dark history.

During the latter part of the nineteenth century, the Salesian Order of the Roman Catholic Church established Misión San Rafael on Bahía Harris on the island's east coast. Its intended purpose was to provide aid and comfort to the natives of the strait who were being driven from their lands by Chilean and European sheep ranchers and miners. Deprived of their accustomed fishing and hunting grounds, the dispossessed natives sometimes killed sheep for food. For this, the ranchers hunted them like animals.

Although the mission was started with the best of intentions, it soon be-

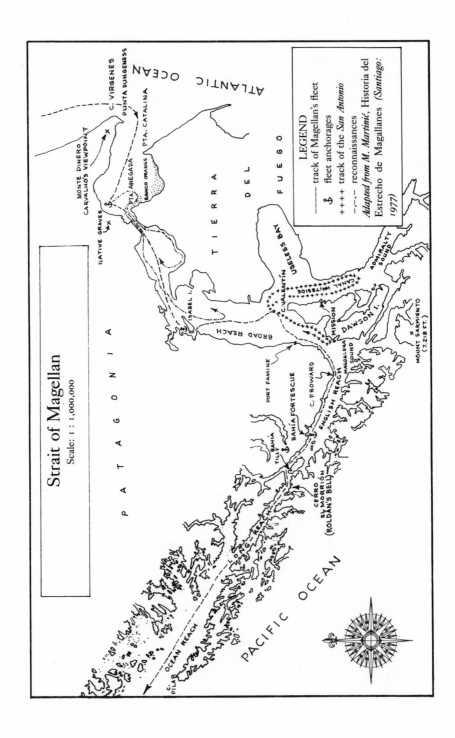

Strait of Magellan

Scale: 1 : 1,000,000

LEGEND

—— track of Magellan's fleet

⚓ fleet anchorages

++++ track of the *San Antonio*

—·—· reconnaissances

Adapted from M. Martinić, Historia del Estrecho de Magallanes (Santiago: 1977)

ATLANTIC OCEAN

C. VIRGENES
PUNTA DUNGENESS
PTA. CATALINA
MONTE DINERO
CARVALHO'S VIEWPOINT
NATIVE GRAVES
PTA. ANEGADA
BANCO ORANGE

TIERRA DEL FUEGO

USELESS BAY
C. VALENTÍN
CANAL WHITESIDE
ADMIRALTY SOUND
BROAD REACH
MISSION
DAWSON I.
MAGDALENA SOUND
MOUNT SARMIENTO (7,218 FT.)

ISABEL I.

PATAGONIA

PORT FAMINE
C. FROWARD
BAHÍA FORTESCUE
TILLY BAHÍA
CERRO EL MORRIÓN (ROLDAN'S BELL)
ENGLISH REACH
LONG REACH
OCEAN REACH
PILAR REACH

PACIFIC OCEAN

156

came little more than a concentration camp for natives from all over the region. In accordance with government policy, local authorities rounded them up and shipped them to Dawson Island. The resources of the church were unequal to the task, and hundreds of natives starved or died at the mission of infectious diseases. It became the last stop on the road to extinction for many unfortunate members of a doomed race.[19] The grim history of Dawson Island sadly was resumed for nearly two decades during the latter part of the twentieth century. Not far from the old mission (a naval base since 1950), the military government built a detention camp for political prisoners.

Confronted by the splitting of the channel at Cape Valentín, Magellan dispatched the *San Antonio* to explore the waterways leading east and south on the east side of the cape. After three days, Mesquita was to return to Cape Valentín, sail south along the western side of the cape, and wait for the other ships ". . . at the foot of some snow-covered summits" visible from Cape Valentín.[20] The meeting place would have been Cape San Antonio, in back of which mountains rise to well over 2,000 feet. Still snowcapped in the spring, their summits can be seen clearly from Cape Valentín.

Exploring the channels east of Dawson Island, Mesquita found Useless Bay, the opening to the east, a blind passage. Probing south into Canal Whiteside, he may well have sailed into Bahía Harris, later to become the site of the infamous mission. Farther south, Admiralty Sound, a long, mountain-rimmed fjord with a glacier on its south shore, leads southeast. If Mesquita entered it with the San Antonio, he would have found it to be a blind passage. He probably did not venture into the narrow Canal Gabriel leading northwest to Magdalena Sound.

With the other three ships, Magellan had sailed southward into Famine Reach, the passage between Dawson Island and the mainland. Beyond Cape San Antonio, the channel opens into a wide sound with two branches. One, Froward Reach, leads northwest; the other, Magdalena Sound, narrows to a channel leading south toward snowcapped peaks dominated by 7,218-foot Mount Sarmiento, its glaciers a dazzling white in the sun.

Reconnoitering the western shore of Famine Reach, Magellan may have investigated the bay inside Punta Santa Ana. On its shores in 1584, Spanish colonists would build a fortified town, Rey Don Felipe. When supply ships failed to arrive, many of the colonists starved to death. In 1587, the settlement was found abandoned by the English pirate, Thomas Cavendish. Learning of the colony's tragic fate from a survivor picked up earlier,

Cavendish named it Port Famine. The Spanish version of this name, *Puerto del Hambre*, has lasted to this day.

About ten nautical miles farther south, at Cape San Isidro, the shoreline turns southwest. At Cape Froward, thirteen nautical miles farther on, it takes another turn, toward the west-northwest, where heavily wooded mountains rise steeply from the shore on both sides of the channel. Sensing that this broad, straight waterway would lead him to the Great South Sea, Magellan could scarcely contain his excitement. Not wanting to wait for Mesquita, he sent Serrano with the *Concepción* to the designated rendezvous to lead the *San Antonio* into Froward Reach, where the *Trinidad* and *Victoria* would search for a suitable anchorage.

On the way to Cape San Antonio, Serrano may have made a brief reconnaissance of Magdalena Sound, but it is unlikely that he sailed past Punta Anxious into Magdalena Channel. The solid wall of snowcapped mountains to the south seemed a formidable barrier in that direction. Turning north, he reached the rendezvous point off Cape San Antonio on the western shore of Dawson Island. There was no sign of the *San Antonio*, nor could it be found in Canal Whiteside when Serrano sailed north to Cape Valentín in search of it. The *San Antonio*, the largest ship of Magellan's fleet, carrying the bulk of the fleet's provisions for the ocean voyage ahead, had disappeared.

After Mesquita completed the reconnaissance of the channels east of Dawson Island, he returned to Cape Valentín and headed south into Famine Reach. He anchored in one of the small bays near Cape San Antonio, perhaps the one now called Puerto San Antonio, directly in front of the snowcapped summits where Magellan had said he would meet them. The *San Antonio* commanded a clear view up and down the strait, but the other ships were nowhere to be seen.[21]

The intimidating landscape to the south, with glacier-covered mountains dominating the horizon, made it easy for Gomes, whose reputation as a pilot of vast experience was unassailable, to convince most of the officers of the *San Antonio* that Magellan was a madman who would lead them all to frozen deaths in these icy channels. With barely enough stores in their hold to last for the return voyage, he advised leaving for Spain at once. Mesquita firmly refused to consider the proposition. On November 8, 1520, Gomes and Gerónimo Guerra (whom Magellan had promoted from ship's clerk to fleet treasurer at San Julián) tried to get Mesquita to change his mind. When he again refused, a brawl erupted in which Mesquita stabbed Gomes in the leg and was himself stabbed in the hand. Mesquita was seized, chained, and tortured into signing a statement that Magellan had cruelly mistreated and murdered Castilian officers at Bahía San Julián.

Gomes, a Portuguese, wisely got Guerra, a Castilian, to assume the captaincy of the *San Antonio*. He then piloted the ship back through the strait, reaching the Atlantic on November 14, 1520.

Worried about the depleted food stores, Gomes headed straight for the Guinea Coast and Spain without stopping at Bahía San Julián to look for Cartagena and the priest, Calmette. The ship, on short rations for the entire trip, arrived in Seville on May 6, 1521, with 55 persons aboard. The Patagonian giant they had carried with them perished in the tropics.[22]

Mesquita, Gomes, Guerra, and the other officers were arrested as soon as they arrived in Seville. All but Mesquita were soon released in spite of the protestations of Magellan's father-in-law, who urged that he ". . . be set free and those that brought him, imprisoned." Depositions from the officers and crew of the *San Antonio* were taken by officials of the Casa. These were summarized in a letter to the emperor signed by Lopez Recalde and Dr. Matienzo. After disavowing the statement he had signed under torture, Mesquita presented the records of the investigation over which he had presided at San Julián, having kept them hidden while a prisoner on the *San Antonio*. Nevertheless, his story was not believed, and he remained in prison. The depositions of Gomes and his henchmen, unanimous in their condemnation of Magellan, were believed, and they were released from custody.

One of the wildest stories told by the deserters was that at San Julián Magellan had San Martín and a seaman, Hernando de Morales, tortured: San Martín for attempting to dispose of papers containing important navigational data, and Morales for malicious gossip. The story was that both were given three *tratos de cuerdo*,[23] a brutal punishment used by the Inquisition to extract confessions. With wrists lashed behind their backs, the victims were hoisted on a rope fastened to their bound wrists so that they were dangling in a "skin the cat" position. Then they were either bounced by means of a pulley or yanked by lanyards tied to their feet, dislocating the shoulder joints. As with most of the stories told by the deserters, this one was patently false. On the very day the fleet left San Julián, San Martín was busily making astronomical observations; Morales had died aboard the *San Antonio* during its return voyage to Spain.

When Bishop Fonseca was informed of the return of the *San Antonio* and of what had happened to Cartagena (possibly his natural son), he was so devastated he would not speak of it, but the shock soon gave way to anger. Mesquita, Gomes, Guerra, and several of the *San Antonio*'s other officers were summoned to court. Their stories were believed; Mesquita's was not. He was charged for the cost of his travel to court and sent back to prison. The others were honored and given a generous travel allowance. Mesquita remained in prison until 1522, when the survivors who returned with the *Victoria* corroborated his story. Thoroughly disgusted with Spanish justice, he returned to Portugal.

Fonseca's fury with Magellan was so great that he ordered the latter's wife and infant son taken into custody.[24] While they were not actually imprisoned, the family was put under guard to prevent their possible flight to Portugal.

The *Trinidad* and *Victoria* rounded Cape Froward and headed into that part of the strait now known as English Reach. Cape Froward, the southernmost point on the American mainland, forms an impressive headland, its bluffs rising steeply from the shore to more than a thousand feet. Behind the cape is 3,000-foot Mount Victoria; to the west-northwest, snow-capped mountains, heavily forested on their lower slopes, rise steeply from the channel on both sides.

While seeking a suitable anchorage along the mainland side of English Reach, Magellan investigated the bays and coves at the mouths of the rivers and streams draining the highlands behind the shore (Bahías Snug, Woods, Andrés, Cordes, and Fortescue). By far the best was Bahía Fortescue, twenty-eight miles west-northwest of Cape Froward. There are considerable heights on both sides of the entrance, and behind Wigwam, a small islet in the outer bay, the inner harbor (Caleta Gallant) provides shelter from winds from any quarter. A small river flows into the harbor near its junction with the outer bay.

Bahía Cordes, three nautical miles east-southeast of Bahía Fortescue, also offers shelter, a fine river, and a pleasant hinterland. However, dangerous shoals extending from its eastern shore make it impossible for all but ships' boats to enter the inner bay and severely restrict room for maneuvering in the outer bay. The smaller coves to the east-southeast provide little shelter and poor holding ground. Although it was a day's sail from where Magellan had parted company with the *Concepción*, and farther still from the rendezvous indicated to Mesquita, Magellan decided that Bahía Fortescue offered the best anchorage to prepare the fleet for the ocean voyage ahead. The *Trinidad* and the *Victoria* anchored in the outer bay toward the end of the first week in November. As it was teeming with small fish, Magellan's men named it the Bay of Sardines.[25]

The crews set about making the necessary repairs to their ships, cutting firewood, cleaning and filling the water barrels, and catching and smoking the abundant sardines. Bahía Fortescue proved a pleasant, well-watered harbor, verdant with spring foliage and a variety of succulent herbs. If only Magellan's men had known about antiscorbutics, the stalks of a rhubarb-like plant growing abundantly along the stream banks could have been dried and used as a life-saving supplement to their sea rations. The men enjoyed their brief respite in this sheltered, subantarctic oasis. When burned, one type of wood found there proved unforgettably fragrant.[26] Pigafetta was so enraptured by the beauty of that part of the strait that, recalling it years later, he wrote: "I believe that there is not a better strait in the world than that one."

As the *Trinidad* and *Victoria* were approaching Bahía Fortescue, it had been impossible to tell whether the waterway in which they were sailing continued beyond the mountains intercepting the horizon ahead.[27] Concerned that these mountains might obstruct their progress, Magellan sent an exploratory party ahead in a shallop to see whether the waterway continued to the sea. If they brought back good news, he promised, they would be suitably rewarded by the emperor.[28]

Of the shallop's crew for that historic reconnaissance, three names are known: Roldán de Argot, a Flemish gunner; Bocacio Alonso, an able seaman; and Hernando de Bustamente, a barber. Pigafetta wrote that the shallop ". . . returned on the third day, saying that they had seen the cape where the strait ended, and a great sea, that is, the Ocean." On learning this, commented Pigafetta, the captain general wept for joy and named it Cape Desire, ". . . because for a long time we had been desperate to see it."[29]

As Pigafetta told the story, the exploring party sailed the shallop all the way up the strait to the ocean before returning to give Magellan the good news, completing the round trip in three days. He was probably mistaken. The distance from Bahía Fortescue to Cape Pilar and return is over 200 nautical miles. Sailing during daylight, the shallop could have made little more than thirty nautical miles per day. A Spanish historian, writing early in the seventeenth century, hints at what may have been the truth of the matter: ". . . and Roldán's Bell, a large rock in the middle, at the beginning of the channel, was given this name because Roldán, an artilleryman, one of Magellan's companions, [climbed] it to reconnoiter."[30] This suggests a scenario somewhat different from Pigafetta's: The exploring party sailed the shallop northwest between Carlos III Island and the Brunswick Peninsula. Reaching the end of the island, they turned west into Crooked Reach. There, in front of the mouth of Canal Gerónimo, they experienced the fierce crosscurrents off the island's northern extremity, Cape Crosstide. To the west, at the tip of the Ulloa Peninsula on Santa Inez Island, a distinctively shaped rock, Cerro El Morrión (Helmet Hill), rises to 1,083 feet.[31]

The shallop tied up for the night in one of the two bays (Ridders or Butler) on either side of the helmet- or bell-shaped hill. The next morning,

Roldán climbed the hill and gazed up Long Reach. If it was a clear day, from the summit he had an unobstructed view into Ocean Reach, thirty-eight nautical miles to the northwest.[32] With no land on the horizon in that direction, Roldán thought he was looking at the place where the strait opened into the sea.

Satisfied that the channel ahead led to the ocean, Roldán scrambled down the hill to the waiting shallop. Heading back into English Reach, the crew may have tied up for the night in Bahía Mussel on the east side of Carlos III Island. There they may have feasted on the abundant shellfish for which the bay is named, toasting their success with the Spanish wine in their field rations. The next morning, an easy run of eleven nautical miles brought them back to Bahía Fortescue, where Magellan received them as heroes.[33]

By November 12, the *Concepción* had not yet returned with the *San Antonio*. Worried, Magellan set forth with the *Trinidad* and *Victoria* for the rendezvous off Dawson Island. En route, they encountered the *Concepción* heading toward them, and Serrano reported that they had found no trace of the *San Antonio*. The next six days were spent in a desperate search for the missing ship.[34] The most capacious of the fleet, the *San Antonio* carried provisions on which Magellan had counted for the sea voyage ahead. The *Victoria* was dispatched toward the Atlantic entrance to the strait, while the *Trinidad* and *Concepción* continued searching in the vicinity of Dawson Island.

The *Victoria* went all the way to Punta Dungeness, but found no trace of the missing ship. In accordance with royal instructions covering such emergencies, Captain Barbosa left messages at a prominent marker erected on the shore of the "first bay" (Posesion), and another on "a small island [perhaps Santa Marta] in the third." The royal instructions specified ". . . a stone cairn . . . five layers on the ground in the shape of a cross, and also a wooden cross with a message in a jug buried under it, with the date." One of the markers left by the *Victoria* was found fifteen years later by a crewman from the expedition of Simón de Alcazaba. Its discovery was described as follows: "We entered the strait [in the middle of January 1535], and to our right we found a cross, very tall, with letters that told when it had been erected, and we saw that it was from when Magellan passed by."[35]

On Magellan's orders, a cross was also planted ". . . on a small island at the foot of two snow-covered mountains in which the river has its origin." This could have been San Juan Island, off the west coast of Dawson Island between Cape San Antonio and Punta Valdes. San Juan Island can be seen clearly by ships sailing through Famine Reach. A small river, the Santa Ludgarda, drains into a bay behind the island. Two peaks rise to more than 2,000 feet on either side of the river.

While the *Victoria* searched the eastern part of the strait as far as the Atlantic entrance, the other two ships made a careful search of its central part and the waters east of Dawson Island. On November 18, the three ships assembled off Cape San Antonio. There had been no sign of the missing ship. Profoundly disturbed by its loss, Magellan asked San Martín to divine what had happened to it. The perceptive astrologer (now on the *Victoria*) had been well aware of the dwindling food supplies and of Gomes's dismay at Magellan's insistence on pushing forward. After consulting his star charts and casting a horoscope, San Martín gravely announced that Mesquita had been taken prisoner and that the *San Antonio* had sailed for Spain.[36]

Dismayed, but still determined to finish what he had begun, Magellan again headed up the strait with the three remaining ships. Taking advantage of the intelligence brought back by Roldán's scouting party, they sailed past "The River of Sardines" (Bahía Fortescue) and anchored at a site called by Magellan *Río del Isleo*. Since *isleo* denotes a small island or cluster of islets close to a larger one, Magellan's *Río del Isleo* could have been Bahía Mussel or Bahía Tilly on the eastern shore of Carlos III Island.[37] Noted earlier by Roldán's scouting party, both afford a sheltered anchorage and contain rocky islets. There, on November 21, Magellan ordered the captains, pilots, masters, and mates of his fleet to submit, in writing, their honest opinions on whether the voyage should continue. The text of this order was copied by San Martín into a notebook that was among the papers seized from the *Trinidad* by Portuguese authorities in the Moluccas. A Portuguese court historian who had access to these papers reported Magellan's words (as recorded by San Martín):[38]

> *I, Ferdinand Magellan, knight of the Order of Santiago and captain general of this fleet that His Majesty sent to discover the spiceries. . . . Know thou, Duarte Barbosa, captain of the ship Victoria, and its pilots, masters and mates, that I understand that all of you consider it a grave matter that I am determined to go forward, for it appears to you that there is little time for completing the voyage on which we have embarked. As I am a man who never scorns the opinion and counsel of anyone, all my decisions are put into practice and communicated generally to everyone so that no one need feel affronted; and because of what happened in Port San Julián concerning the deaths of Luis de Mendoza and Gaspar de Quesada and the marooning of Juan de Cartagena and the priest, Pero Sanchez de Reina [Bernard Calmette], you need not be afraid, for all that happened was done in the service of His Majesty and for the security of his fleet; and if you do not give me your advice and counsel, you will be in default of your obligation to the king-emperor, our sovereign, and to the oath of loyalty you swore to me; therefore, I command you, in his name and mine, and I pray and charge*

that whatever you may feel with respect to our voyage, whether to go for-
ward or to return, each of you will give me your opinion, with your reasons,
in writing, letting nothing prevent you from being entirely truthful. When I
have your opinions and reasons, I will give you mine, and my decision as to
what we must do.

It was dated November 21, 1521, in All Saints Channel, in front of the
Río del Isleo, by command of Captain General Ferdinand Magellan. The
order, dictated to León de Ezpeleta, clerk of the *Trinidad*, was notarized on
the following day by Martín Méndez, clerk of the *Victoria*.

San Martín, who had transferred from the *San Antonio* to the *Victoria*
after the mutiny at Fort San Julián, entered his reply at the foot of his copy
of Magellan's order:

Most magnificent lord, . . . while I doubt that neither this All Saints'
Channel nor the other two that trend east and east northeast, may be the
route for sailing to Maluco. . . . since we still do not know how far they
may reach, we should take advantage of the weather which favors us during
the height of summer. I believe that Your Grace should go forward while we
have the flower of summer in hand, to continue our explorations until the
middle of January . . . at which time Your Grace will judge whether it will
be appropriate to return to Spain, for from then on, the days will grow
shorter and the weather more severe than it is now. And should Your Grace
leave these straits in January, having in the meantime taken on water and
firewood, we will be well enough supplied to sail straight for Cadiz or San
Lucar from where we left. And, as for advancing farther toward the South
Pole than we are now, as Your Grace stated to the captains at Río Santa
Cruz, it does not seem to me that it would be feasible because of the terrible,
stormy weather. If we are now confronted by such labor and risk, what will
it be like farther [south] at 70 or 75 degrees to which Your Grace said he
would go in search of Maluco?[39]

All of Magellan's officers were so fearful of the captain general's wrath as
to agree the voyage should continue.[40] Magellan then swore, by the cross of
Santiago on his breast, that this also was his belief, ". . . because of the
good that had befallen the fleet." Therefore, they should follow him, for he
trusted that, since he had led them to the discovery of the strait they had
so desperately sought, God would see them through to the successful conclusion of their quest.[41] Formal sailing orders were delivered to the captains
of the *Victoria* and *Concepción* on November 24, and last-minute preparations were completed the next day. No longer much of a fleet, the little

squadron of three ships weighed anchor and left their anchorage at the Río del Isleo on the morning of November 26 to the accompaniment of cheers, artillery salutes, and the hoisting of banners and pennants.[42]

Sailing northwest by west, they passed some of the world's most spectacular scenery. Leaving English Reach, they breasted the crosscurrents at the mouth of Gerónimo Channel as they turned into Crooked Reach. On both sides, snowcapped mountains plunge steeply into a channel hundreds of fathoms deep. Santa Ines Island, with its gigantic glaciers reaching the waters of Icy and Whale fjords on either side of Mount Maxwell, was four to five miles to port. On the mainland to their starboard, mountain streams hurtled off high cliffs in waterfalls of dazzling beauty.

In later years, Spanish and Chilean mariners fastened iron rings into the sheer cliffs adjacent to such waterfalls. Because it was impossible to anchor in these deep channels, they would moor their ships to the rings while they filled their water casks at the falls. These sites are noted on Chilean hydrographic charts as *aguadas*.

Passing from Crooked Reach into Long Reach, the mariners saw the many rocky coves of unsurpassed beauty that line both sides of the channel. One such, on Jacques Island, must have been named by an English mariner. It appears on modern charts as *Bahía Pispot*.

As Magellan's three little ships sailed out of Long Reach into Ocean Reach, the character of the land to port turned more severe. On Desolation Island, the granitic rocks are nearly bare, with only stunted trees struggling to insert their roots into clefts, the scenery resembling that of Labrador. Branching off Córdova Fjord on this island is a little bay with an ominous name, Bahía Williwaw. When airmasses chilled by contact with snowfields and glaciers become unstable relative to the surrounding air, they rush suddenly down the mountain slopes with hurricane force. These are williwaws, and woe betide the sailor whose boat should be anchored in what he thinks is a sheltered cove, but which lies in the path of one of these monster winds. Even with bare poles, it will set his boat on beam ends. Fortunately for Magellan, he had clear sailing all along the strait.

To the southwest across the bare rocky mass of Desolation Island, Magellan's sailors sometimes thought they could hear the sound of booming surf. Their ears did not deceive them, but it would be nearly a hundred years before Schouten and Le Maire would prove that this indeed was the case.[43] As they progressed along Ocean Reach, they began to feel, faintly at first, but with increasing strength, the long Pacific swells rolling into the mouth of the strait.

On November 28, 1520, the *Victoria*'s crew sighted to port a cape on which was bestowed two names: *Fermoso* (Beautiful) and *Deseado* (Desired).

Today it is called Cape Pilar, and its latitude is 52° 42′ S, nearly the same as Cape Vírgenes (52° 20′ S) at the Atlantic entrance to the strait. Magellan's ships had spent 38 days in the 334-mile strait.

The *Victoria* sailed three times over the 250-mile stretch between Punta Dungeness and Cape Froward, the last two in search of the *San Antonio*.[44] The campfires seen at night and the burial ground were the only evidence of human habitation seen by Magellan and his men during their exploration of the strait.

With dangerous, rock-studded reefs on both sides, Magellan's squadron passed beyond Cape Pilar and out of the strait that now bears his name. They sailed into the great ocean spreading before them in such glorious weather that Magellan was inspired to name it *"Mar Pacífico."*[45]

16
${\mathcal{T}}$he Pacific

P*ast Cape Deseado (Pilar) no land could be seen to the west. In* that direction lay an unknown ocean glimpsed by Europeans only twice before.[1] Antonio Abreu had sailed eastward into the Banda Sea, arguably an arm of the Pacific, from the Indian Ocean in 1511. Primarily concerned with loading a cargo of spices, Abreu had little interest in the nomenclature of the waters in which he sailed. The honor for the "discovery" of the Pacific Ocean by a European has been credited to Balboa, who first glimpsed it from a peak in Darien (Panama) in 1513. A "discovery" implies that something heretofore unknown has been made known; Balboa realized that the sea to the south of the isthmus on which he stood was distinct from the ocean separating the New World from Europe, and so reported it. When Magellan boldly sailed out of the strait on November 28, he had no idea of the vastness of the ocean spreading before him. In 1520 less was known about the Pacific Ocean than we know today of interstellar space. Magellan knew only that on the equator, at an undetermined distance across this *Mar Pacífico*, lay the Moluccas. Of what lay between he knew nothing. His notion of the distance across the gulf before him was based on Ptolemy's twenty-eight percent underestimate of the Earth's circumference. Today, the probable error in the calculated distance (25.8 trillion miles) to Alpha Centauri, our nearest stellar neighbor, is about one percent.

Those who base decisions only on calculated risks will think, as did Gomes, that Magellan was a fool. In his *Essay on Criticism*, Alexander Pope wrote: ". . . fools rush in where angels fear to tread." Be that as it may, history would make dull reading if its movers and shakers had acted less foolishly. There was grandeur in Magellan's vision, however flawed his premises and selfish his motives.

The land to port fell away as the three little ships headed into the Pacific; to starboard it extended northward to the horizon. With the wind out of the northwest they worked north in search of a more favorable breeze and warmer weather, tacking into the long Pacific swells to keep a safe distance offshore.[2] As the squadron ploughed steadily northward, the wind gradually shifted to the west, then southwest, a common pattern for early summer in that part of the world. The northern margin of the globe-circling belt of prevailing westerlies intercepts the coast of Chile near the Taitao Peninsula at 46° 30′ S. From there to Cape Horn, the westerly winds are deflected to the south, producing the northwesterlies encountered by Magellan's ships as they emerged from the strait. Farther north, the counter-clockwise circulation around the South Pacific High shifts the winds along the coast to southwest, then south, finally steadying as the southeast trade wind.

Magellan knew well the wind systems of the South Atlantic and Indian oceans. Having hoped for a pattern similar to that of the South Atlantic for the sea into which he now sailed, he was gratified to note that the winds were shifting in accord with his expectations. Reassured of fair winds astern for what he believed would be a relatively short passage northwest to the Moluccas, he felt no great need to risk landing on the mainland to the east to replenish his provisions.

On December 2, Magellan's ships passed a point of land (probably Cabo Tres Montes at the tip of the Taitao Peninsula), where Pigafetta began noticing changes in the kinds of fish in the waters through which they were sailing. The subantarctic coastal species with which they had become familiar in the strait gave way to fish characteristic of warmer oceanic waters. He wrote:

In that Ocean Sea one sees a very amusing fish hunt. The [hunter] fish are of three sorts, and are one braza *[fathom] or more in length, and are called* dorado *[dolphin fish of the genus* Coryphaena*], albicore [sic], and bonito [tuna-like fishes]. Those fish follow the flying fish, called* colondrini, *which are one* palmo *[eight inches] or more in length and very good to eat. When the above three kinds of fish find any of those flying fish, the latter immediately leap from the water and fly as long as their wings are wet — more than a crossbow's flight [1,000 feet]. While they are flying, the others [swim] behind them under the water, following the shadow of the flying fish. The latter have no sooner fallen into the water than the others immediately seize and eat them. This spectacle is a fine thing to watch.[3]*

Pigafetta's interest in the Patagonian giant aboard the *Trinidad* led him to compile a list of ninety words, the first such of the Tehuelche language. His attempt to make a Christian out of the huge man failed at first. When Pigafetta showed him a cross and kissed it, the Tehuelche reacted in horror, crying out the name of the demon *Setebos*. He indicated that if Pigafetta should kiss the cross again, *Setebos* would enter his body and cause it to burst. Along with nineteen of the crew, the big fellow died of scurvy during the Pacific crossing. When he was dying, wrote Pigafetta, ". . . he asked for the cross, embraced it and kissed it many times, desiring to become a Christian before his death." They christened him Paulo.

Albo's log traces Magellan's path across the Pacific.[4] It has been said of this route: "He could hardly have shaped a better course if he had had modern sailing directions, not only avoiding dangerous, island-studded waters, but making the best use of prevailing winds and currents."[5]

Continuing northward along the Chilean coast until December 18, they sailed between the mainland and the Juan Fernandez Islands, which they failed to sight, missing their last opportunity to take on fresh water, fish, game, and edible wild plants. On reaching 33°–32° S on December 19, they altered course from north by west to northwest,[6] turning away from the huge landmass that had proved so difficult to get around. The squadron continued on that course until January 21–22, 1521, when a two-day headwind drove them slightly southward.[7] Resuming their northwesterly course, on January 24 they raised a small, uninhabited islet with a few trees on it, which they named San Pablo. Pigafetta gave its latitude as 15° S, Albo as 16° 15' S, the Genoese Pilot and the Portuguese chronicler, Barros, as 18° S. It probably was Puka Puka, 14° 50' S, 138° 48' W, in the Tuamotu Archipelago.[8] Soundings were taken but, as there was no bottom even close inshore, they were unable to land.

Proceeding successively northwest by west, west-northwest, west by north, and northwest, on February 4 the small fleet sighted a second uninhabited island, also wooded. Because there were many sharks around the island, they named it *Isla de los Tiburones*. For its latitude, Pigafetta recorded 9° S, Albo 10° 45' S, the Genoese Pilot and Barros 13° S. Again they were unable to land for lack of an anchorage. This island has been variously identified as Flint (11° 28' S), Vostok (10° 06' S) and Caroline (10° 00' S). The latter seems the best fit for the skimpy data, and it is the only one of the three with a lagoon, a likely habitat for sharks.[9]

The food remaining in the ships' stores had spoiled and the water had turned putrid. One wonders why they did not make an effort to land a longboat to search for water and fresh food. Two sources did report that the squadron spent two days at the Isla de los Tiburones,[10] but this does not jibe with Albo's log, which indicates that they sailed on after a brief inspection. Magellan and his pilots probably thought that they were already close to the archipelago southeast of Asia, and that a landing on either island was not worth the risk.

With fair skies and the trade wind steady astern, the squadron held to the northwest, crossing the equator on February 13, 1521 at about 160° W longitude.[11] Magellan probably planned to reprovision and refit his ships in the islands he expected to find on the equator east of the Moluccas. Then he could have sailed confidently to the Moluccas with his ships and crews fit for a possible encounter with Portuguese forces. By the time they reached the equator, however, the food shortage had become acute, and the dread scurvy had begun to take its toll.

Pigafetta described their condition: "We ate biscuit that was no longer biscuit, but powder of biscuits swarming with worms, for they had eaten the good. It stank strongly of rats' urine. We drank yellow water that had been putrid for many days." Magellan's strong words in the strait about continuing the voyage even if they had to eat the chafing gear had proved prophetic. Pigafetta continued: "We also ate certain ox hides that covered the tops of the yards to keep them from chafing the shrouds, and which had become exceedingly hard because of the sun, rain, and wind. We soaked them in the sea for four or five days, and then placed them briefly on hot ashes, and so ate them; often we ate sawdust. Rats were sold for a half ducat apiece, and even so, we could not always get them. But above all the other misfortunes, the worst was that the gums of the lower and upper teeth of some of our men swelled, so that they could not eat and they died of hunger." Twenty-five to thirty men fell sick, of whom nineteen died. Scurvy struck officers and crewmen alike, including the *Victoria*'s pilot, Vasco Galego; Antonio de Coca, who had sailed as fleet accountant and had served briefly as captain of the *San Antonio*; and Baltasar Genovés, who had sailed as master of the *Santiago*. Another ranking professional who succumbed to scurvy was the English master gunner of the fleet, Andrew of Bristol. The ship hit hardest by the disease seems to have been the *Victoria*.[12]

Although everyone suffered from hunger, scurvy proved selective in its victims. Like many others in the squadron, Magellan and Pigafetta remained remarkably healthy during the Pacific crossing. It is possible that the quince preserves packed by Magellan with his personal gear (a fact noted by the Portuguese consul in Seville) helped keep him in good health. Those who were squeamish about what they ate were the first to succumb. Others, like Pigafetta, who were willing to eat rats, stayed healthy. In the eighteenth century, when the necessity of antiscorbutics in seamen's rations first came to be understood, skippers such as Cook and Bligh had to resort to extraordinary strategies to get sailors to eat their sauerkraut.

With the health of his crews deteriorating rapidly, the need for fresh supplies had become desperate. Yet Magellan continued sailing alternately northwest and west northwest, passing along the echelon formed by the Line Islands and the Phoenix, Gilbert, and Marshall islands without sighting any of them. The wind shifted gradually from astern to the starboard quarter and strengthened as they entered the northeast trade wind belt. At 12° N on February 24, the squadron changed course to due west, sailing along that parallel and passing just north of Bikar and Bikini atolls in the Marshall Islands. On February 27, the course was shifted one point to the north, but reaching 13° N the next day, the squadron again headed due west.[13] Clearly, Magellan was striking for a landfall north of the Moluccas where, beyond the reach of the Portuguese, the health of his crews could be restored and his ships reconditioned. His target could have been Luzon, which faulty intelligence may have caused him to believe was *Lequios*, the Portuguese term for the Ryukyu Islands.

Magellan probably had heard in Malacca about the prosperous merchants of *Lequios* who had traded there until scared off by Arab stories of Portuguese barbarities. In Malacca these merchants had loaded their junks with spices, paying for them with gold acquired in Luzon in exchange for Chinese silk. As suggested earlier, Magellan may have confused *Luzon*, the source of the gold, with *Lequios*, the home islands of the merchants who brought it to Malacca. When asked about the location of the gold island, Magellan's sources on the Malacca waterfront may have given him sailing directions for Luzon, from which he deduced that it lay between 10° and 15° N. Believing he was headed for Lequios, Magellan probably hoped to coax its rulers into an alliance with Spain, a diplomatic coup that should earn for him the emperor's protection from Fonseca's certain wrath over the events at San Julián. If allied with Spain, the prosperous merchants of Lequios might also help ensure the profitability of the island seigniory stipulated in his contract with the crown.

By the time Magellan's crews had regained their health, the ships had been reconditioned, and an alliance with Lequios concluded, it would be late fall or winter, the season for the northeast monsoon in the China Sea. With a reinvigorated squadron and the wind at his back, Magellan could coast down to the Moluccas to join forces with his old friend, Francisco Serrão, who would be waiting for him.

The distorted ideas of Far Eastern geography at the time of Magellan's voyage are reflected in Pigafetta's account. Of their northwesterly course toward the equator, he wrote: "We passed, while on that course, a short distance from two exceedingly rich islands, one in twenty degrees of latitude of the Antarctic Pole, by name of *Cipanghu* [Polo's name for Japan], and the other in fifteen degrees by name of *Sumbdit Pradit.*" The latter name has mystified most scholars. It has been thought a possible corruption of the notation *Septem Cidades* on the Behaim Globe, but a recent toponymic study suggested that *Sumbdit* could be the product of repetitive mistranscriptions of *Cipanghu* (that Pigafetta understood to be two islands), and *Pradit*, a mistranscription of the Italian *pradetto* or the French *prédit* (aforementioned).[14]

Magellan probably did not know of Fernão Peres de Andrade's visit to Canton in 1517, or that Andrade's lieutenant, Jorge de Mascarenhas, while scouting the southern Ryukyus had landed on Iriomote Island that same year. On the other hand, if he had not learned from sources in Portugal of the earlier commercial expedition of Raphael Perestrello to Canton,[15] he might have learned of it from Cristóbal de Haro, whose trading ships provided intelligence about the latest developments in the Far East. While Magellan undoubtedly enjoyed Pigafetta's company on his flagship, he did not tell him much, if anything, of what he knew of the geography of the Far East. He probably would have been amused at the personable papal envoy's placement of Japan and part of China well within the southern hemisphere. One of Pigafetta's geographical conjectures, however, did prove correct. "If, upon leaving the strait," he wrote, "we had continued to sail west along the same parallel, we would have circled the world; and without encountering land, we would have returned, from Cape Deseado to the Cape of Eleven Thousand Virgins, both being located at 52° of south latitude."[16]

Magellan probably had expected to find eastern outliers of the archipelago containing the Moluccas not far from where he crossed the equator. His estimate of the distance of the Spice Islands east of the Cape of Good Hope was set forth in his memorandum to King Charles prior to the departure of the fleet, and this, coupled with his acceptance of Ptolemy's estimate of the earth's circumference, caused him to underestimate the width of the Pacific Ocean. Having failed to find the outlying islands he had expected on the equator, and with his men in such poor condition, Magellan dared not risk a direct route to the Moluccas, where Portuguese forces might be searching for him. That Magellan had an alternative target to the north is apparent from the information provided by Albo, Pigafetta, and the Genoese Pilot.[17]

On February 28, the squadron had reached 13° N and, sailing due west, sighted an island ahead on March 6. As the squadron approached it, an-

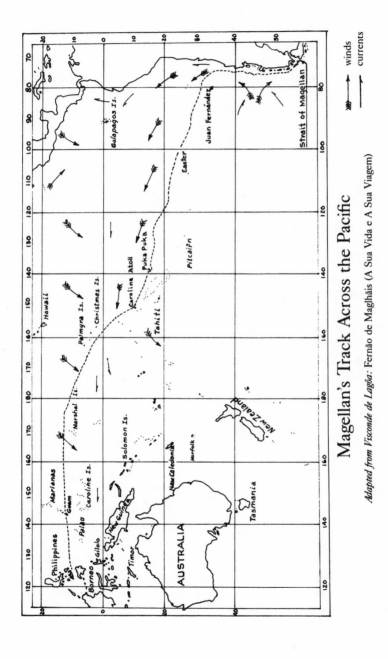

Magellan's Track Across the Pacific

Adapted from Visconde de Lagôa: Fernão de Maglhâis (A Sua Vida e A Sua Viagem)

173

other island, to the south of the first, rose above the horizon. On closer
approach, it became apparent that the more southerly island was the larger
of the two. There can be little doubt that these were Rota and Guam. The
former, with a peak rising to 1,614 feet, was the first to be sighted. Guam,
with a maximum elevation of 1,334 feet, appeared next.

As Magellan's ships sailed closer to investigate, a swarm of incredibly
swift, small sailing craft came out to inspect them. They were outrigger
canoes, cleverly rigged with lateen sails made of matting. Their maneuver-
ability and speed astonished the Spaniards. Pigafetta wrote: "They can
change stern and bow at will, and those boats resemble dolphins which
leap in the water from wave to wave."[18] Albo's description, although not
quite so colorful, was similar: ". . . and they moved so rapidly that they
seemed to be flying." These remarkable watercraft were the inspiration for
the name initially given to these islands by the Spaniards, *Islas de las Velas
Latinas* (Islands of the Lateen Sails).[19]

Magellan's ships no sooner had anchored off Guam and were about to
strike their sails, when a number of bold, curious natives clambered
aboard, not at all intimidated by the gaunt, starving Europeans. Innocent
of any notion of private property, they eagerly appropriated all the fascinating objects lying loose about the ships of these odd strangers. One not-so-
loose item that they gaily made off with was a longboat that had been
trailing on a painter from the stern of the *Trinidad*.[20]

The outraged Europeans chased the light-fingered visitors from their
ships. Now it was the islanders' turn to be outraged. In their society, hosts
were expected to lavish hospitality on their guests. Expecting these odd
strangers to be equally generous, they were insulted, and returned in force
with a fleet of war canoes. To frighten them away, Magellan ordered blank
shots fired from the *Trinidad*'s deck guns. Startled by the thunderous roar
of the cannon, the Guamanians fled. To avoid further thefts or an armed
attack under cover of night, the squadron sailed away to spend the night
well offshore.[21]

Infuriated by the theft of his longboat, Magellan resolved to get it back
and to teach the thieving scoundrels who stole it a lesson they would not
soon forget. The next day, he sent a well-armed landing force to the beach
where the stolen longboat had been taken. When the Spaniards landed,
warriors atop a ridge back of the beach hurled such a barrage of stones and
spears at them that ". . . it seemed as if it were hailing." Frightened by the
sound of the Spaniards' arquebuses, the defenders scattered.

The landing force then entered a small village nearby, where they
burned forty or fifty houses and many boats, killing seven villagers. Pigafetta described the effect of the crossbows used by the Spaniards: "When

we wounded any of those people with our crossbow bolts, which passed completely through their loins from one side to the other, they looking at it, pulled on the shaft now on this and now on that side, and drew it out with great astonishment, and so died. Others wounded in the breast did the same, which moved us to great compassion." Pigafetta also noted that, as the landing party prepared to go ashore, ". . . some of our sick men begged us, if we should kill any man or woman, to bring the entrails to them, as they would recover immediately."[22] The usually observant Lombard failed to note whether this was done. Although Magellan was a tough old soldier inured to the savagery of war, he was also proper. It is extremely doubtful that he would have condoned cannibalism, even for the benefit of those in his crews afflicted most horribly by scurvy.

The Guamanians having been punished and the stolen longboat retrieved, the landing force loaded their boats with coconuts and fruit taken from the village, and filled their water casks from a stream. After the battle, some of the islanders cautiously brought fresh foodstuffs to the ships to trade for the trinkets offered by the Spaniards. When asked by sign language where larger quantities of provisions might be obtained, they pointed to the west, indicating the direction of an island they called *Selan*.[23]

This first encounter with the natives of Guam caused Magellan to change the name of their islands from *Islas de las Velas Latinas* to *Islas de los Ladrones* (The Islands of Thieves). That unfortunate name stuck for nearly a century and a half. In 1662, at the urging of a missionary priest, Padre Diego Luis Sanvitores, the islands were renamed *Islas Marianas* in honor of Mariana of Austria, who had become queen regent of Spain on the death of her husband, Philip IV.[24]

The natives whom Magellan encountered on Guam were Chamorros, a Micronesian people whose blood lines since have been much diluted by more than four centuries of foreign occupation. They were light-skinned, tall, and robust and they impressed the Spaniards with their great physical strength. A report tells of a husky Chamorro who, standing between two Spaniards of good stature, playfully seized each by one foot, lifting them off the ground as easily as if they had been children. Another early account also emphasizes the playful, saucy nature of the Chamorros. A Spanish sailor, armed with a sword, had been posted to guard a ship in Umatac Harbor. Unseen, a Chamorro swam underwater close to where the sailor stood, and reaching out of the water snatched the sword from the sailor's hands and swam away with it. The mortified Spaniard cried out to some nearby soldiers to shoot the Chamorro with their arquebuses, but when he came up for air some distance away, the native held up his hands to show that they were empty. Seeing this, the soldiers did not shoot. After catching his breath, the Chamorro dove back underwater and swam away until well out of range. Resurfacing, he took the sword from between his legs where he had hidden it and waved it in the air, laughing and jeering at the frustrated guards.[25]

On March 9, 1521, Magellan's three ships sailed past the reef that surrounds much of Guam and pointed their prows west by south.[26] The reaction of the islanders was described by Pigafetta: "Those people, seeing us departing, followed us with more than a hundred boats, for more than a league. They approached the ships showing us fish, feigning that they would give them to us; but then threw stones at us and fled. And although our ships were under full sail, they passed between them and the [longboats trailed astern] very adroitly in those small boats of theirs. We saw some women in their boats who were crying and tearing out their hair, for love, I believe, of the seven whom we had killed."[27] Eventually, the triangular sails of the swift, flying proas faded into the distance with the taunts and laughter of their crews. With the trade wind on their starboard quarter, the squadron drove westward at a brisk seven to eight knots.[28] The lush, green mountains of Guam soon sank below the horizon, but memories of its handsome, insufferably impudent natives lingered long in the minds of its first European visitors. Although Magellan's crews were reinvigorated by the fresh water, fruit, and fish acquired from the natives, the fleet's only Englishman, Master Gunner Andrew of Bristol, was too wasted by scurvy to take nourishment. He died on the day of departure from Guam.[29]

On March 16, 1521, at 11° N, after sailing west by south for a week, the mountains of Samar rose above the horizon ahead.[30] Pigafetta wrote that Samar was 300 leagues from Guam, a fourteen percent underestimate. The actual distance is about 1,100 nautical miles (350 leagues). Having sighted land on the day of the Feast of Saint Lazarus, Magellan's name for the archipelago of which it was a part was *San Lázaro*. Today, we call those islands the Philippines.

The reefs along the coast of Samar prevented Magellan from attempting a landing, so the squadron sailed southward until it passed the reef-bound cape now known as Sungi Point. Directly ahead lay the island of Suluan in the entrance to Leyte Gulf. On October 25 and 26, 1944, over four centuries after Magellan sailed into it, Leyte Gulf would be the scene of a titanic naval conflict when three battle groups of Japanese warships were intercepted by surface and air units of the American Third and Seventh Fleets.[31]

Turning west into Leyte Gulf, the squadron sighted near Suluan Island a number of canoes, which fled at the approach of Magellan's ships.[32] About nine nautical miles to the west of Suluan lies another small island, Homonhon (called *Humunu* by Pigafetta, *Yunuguan* by Albo). Its northeastern shore forms a pleasant half-moon bay with a sandy beach. Since the island appeared uninhabited, the ships anchored there for the night. The next day, Magellan had two tents erected on the beach for the men afflicted with scurvy. The captain general went ashore daily to look after the sick, nursing them with great tenderness, giving them coconut milk to sip.[33] Two sources of fresh water were found on the little island, but that was not all. A work party returned to the ships with the news that they had found traces of gold in the bed of the stream where they had filled their water casks.[34] Because of this, the place was named *Aguada de Buenos Signos* (Good Signs Water Hole).

On Monday, March 18, a pirogue bearing nine persons approached, apparently from Suluan. Magellan cautioned that no one should move or speak without his permission. Because the visitors were obviously friendly and made gestures of welcome, they were invited aboard the flagship. Five came aboard; the other four went to fetch some companions who were fishing, returning with them shortly to join their friends on the *Trinidad*.

Magellan presented them with gifts of red cloth, combs, mirrors, bells, and ivory trinkets, making it clear that he wished to purchase fresh food. In return, the visitors offered him all that they carried in their pirogue: a jug of palm wine, fish, two kinds of bananas (which Pigafetta called figs), and two coconuts. Using gestures, they indicated that they would return in four days with rice, coconuts and, many other kinds of food.[35]

They were as good as their word, returning on Friday, March 22, with their pirogue loaded with coconuts, another jug of palm wine, sweet oranges, and a chicken, which they exchanged for caps, mirrors, combs, and other trinkets. The gold armbands and earrings worn by their chief probably reinforced Magellan's belief that the source of King Solomon's gold could not be far off.

Pigafetta happily indulged his fascination with native people and their ways, offering for posterity colorful descriptions of their appearance, behavior, and foodstuffs. He obviously enjoyed their palm wine, and provided an elaborate account of how it was made. Intrigued by coconuts, he described how a nourishing milk was made by pulping the meat and diluting it with water, resulting in a drink much like goats' milk. Two coconut palms, he averred, would support a family of ten.

His term for the natives was *Caphri* (Kaffirs), an Arabic term for unbelievers. They went mostly naked, observed Pigafetta, except for loin cloths made of the fiber of a certain bark. The chiefs were extensively tattooed, and wore cotton skirts embroidered with silk. The ear lobes of the people on a neighboring island, he was told, were so long one could pass an arm through the holes made in them.[36]

Albo recorded the longitude of Suluan-Homonhon as "189° from the meridian." If, by "meridian," he meant the line of demarcation (47° west of Greenwich), he was only two degrees in error. While Albo was a competent pilot, the estimation of longitude other than by dead reckoning was not in his repertory of skills, nor would it be for ordinary pilots for more than two hundred years. The only person in Magellan's fleet capable of making such a determination was the astrologer-pilot, San Martín. A Spanish scholar has recently proposed that San Martín carried his instruments ashore on Homonhon to determine the longitude by astronomical measurements, as he had done at San Julián.[37] By fixing the longitude of the eastern part of the San Lázaro Archipelago at 189° west of the Tordesillas Treaty line, San Martín gave Magellan unmistakable evidence that they had passed beyond the 180° extension of the line, into the Portuguese hemisphere. If this is so, it would have confirmed the suspicions planted in Magellan's mind by the great expanse of the ocean they had crossed.

Magellan had assured King Charles that the Moluccas lay in the Spanish Hemisphere, four degrees east of the extended Treaty line. He had driven his fleet to the edge of the Antarctic to discover the strait between the oceans, overcoming mutiny, the wreck of one of his ships, and the desertion of another. Crossing the broad Pacific Ocean without being able to re-provision his ships, he had lost nineteen men to scurvy and starvation. Finally, having reached the eastern edge of the archipelago southeast of China, which he suspected included the Moluccas, he found himself nine degrees west of the extended demarcation, in territory reserved by treaty for Portuguese exploitation. However, all was not lost. Unclaimed territory, discovered and occupied by either signatory in the hemisphere nominally assigned to the other, would be considered within the dominion of the occupying power. Under this treaty provision, if he could establish trading posts and conclude alliances with local rulers before the arrival of the Portuguese, Magellan could yet assure Spanish dominion over these islands.

With many of the sick crewmen having recovered their strength, the squadron got underway again on March 25. Sailing west from Homonhon soon brought Magellan's ships to the long eastern coastline of Leyte. Turning south, they sailed through Surigao Strait, passing between two pairs of small islands. The first pair can be identified as Cabigan and Hibuson; the second as Dinagat and Panaon. As they were proceeding cautiously through the strait, a storm arose, driving them west past the southern end of Panaon. On March 28, they hove to in front of Limasawa, a small island off the southernmost promontory of Leyte.

Here occurred an event that provided clear proof that Magellan's squadron, by traveling west across an uncharted ocean, had achieved the goal that had eluded Columbus. They had reached the eastern limit of the

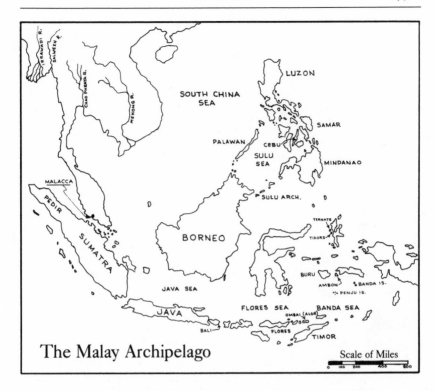

The Malay Archipelago

Scale of Miles

known world. A canoe bearing eight natives came out from Limasawa to inspect the ships. To his and everyone else's delight, Magellan's Malay slave, Enrique, understood the speech of their visitors.[38]

Magellan had acquired Enrique in Malacca in 1511. Pigafetta said that he was from Sumatra, but Philippine scholars have suggested that a native of Sumatra could not have understood the dialect spoken in the Central Philippines.[39] They deem it more likely that Enrique had been raised in the Central Philippines, was captured, then sold into slavery in Sumatra before being taken to Malacca. If so, Enrique was the first human to have completed a full circuit of the Earth.

17

*T*he Fatal Alliance

The *eight curious islanders whose language Enrique understood* were too timid to bring their canoe alongside the Spanish ships. To show goodwill, Magellan had a floating plank pushed gently toward them,[1] bearing gifts that the natives carried back to their island.

Two hours later, two barges (*barangay*) approached the ships. On the largest, seated regally under an awning of mats, was a person of obvious importance. His name was Colambu, ruler of a territory that, in addition to the islands of Limasawa and Suluan, included a district in Mindanao.[2] After a long conversation with Enrique, Colambu permitted some of his men to board the flagship, but did not accompany them. Magellan received the visitors courteously, loading them with gifts to take to their chief; in return, Colambu offered a bar of gold and a basket of ginger. So the islanders would not suspect how highly the Spaniards valued these commodities, Magellan politely declined the offering.

The next day, Good Friday, he sent Enrique ashore to negotiate for fresh food and to assure Colambu that the Spaniards had come in peace. When Enrique returned, Colambu came with him, boarding the flagship without hesitation. Again he offered gifts: two large fish and three porcelain jars filled with rice, which the captain general gratefully accepted.[3] Magellan gave Colambu a hat and a red-and-yellow robe of fine Turkish cloth; the men who accompanied him each received a knife and a mirror. Serving them refreshments, Magellan expressed his earnest desire for friendly relations, and in response Colambu insisted that Magellan become his blood brother by *casi casi*, in which the participants taste each other's blood.[4]

When the ceremony was completed, Magellan took Colambu and his retinue on a tour of the flagship, showing them samples of the trade goods stowed in the hold. Using compass and sea charts, he tried to explain that his ships had come from the opposite side of the world to arrive at these islands. He then ordered his gunners to fire some of the ship's artillery. It had the desired effect, for the roar of the cannon both awed and terrified his guests. Next, Magellan staged a mock combat to demonstrate the invulnerability of a man in full armor to attack by three men armed with swords and daggers. At this, reported Pigafetta, ". . . the king was rendered almost speechless."[5] Magellan boasted that one armored Spaniard would be worth a hundred of Colambu's warriors. When the wide-eyed island chieftan agreed, Magellan told him that he had two hundred men so armed on each of his ships. This was a gross exaggeration: He had less than half that number, and many of his men were still weak, a few dying. Unfortunately, Magellan was beginning to believe his own propaganda; self-delusion can ruin any career, and in a military leader it can be fatal.

Grateful for the hospitality and impressed by the power of Spanish arms, Colambu urged his host to allow some of his crew ashore, where they would be entertained and given a tour of the island. Magellan selected Pigafetta and a mariner whose name is not recorded. When they arrived on the island, the two were treated to a banquet. Pigafetta's companion got quite drunk from the palm wine dispensed liberally with the food, and so too, apparently, did Colambu. Early in the evening the latter left the entertainment of his guests to his eldest son and retired to his quarters to sleep it off. At dawn, bright-eyed and refreshed, Colambu arrived at his son's house to escort the Europeans back to the site of the previous night's banquet. Just as the party was about to resume, a boat from the *Trinidad* came to fetch the two weary revelers,[6] who returned to the ship accompanied by Colambu's brother, Siaui, and three others. A chief in his own right, Siaui ruled several districts in northern Mindanao.[7] Neither of the two chiefs lived on Limasawa. "When [the two brothers] wished to see one another," wrote Pigafetta, "they both went to hunt on the island where we were."[8]

Magellan invited Siaui and his three retainers to dine, and over the meal, the chief regaled his host with tales of the gold found in his district. As it had been by the gold jewelry worn by the Suluan chief, Magellan's notion that he was nearing the fabled source of King Solomon's gold was probably strengthened by these stories. In a summary culled from the reports of the expedition's survivors, a contemporary Spanish historian wrote that there was so much gold on an island near Mindanao that nuggets the size of hazel nuts and small fruit could be sifted from the beach sand.[9] Pigafetta told essentially the same story, adding: ". . . on the island of the king who came to the ship, there are gold mines."

The next day, March 31, 1521, would be Easter Sunday, and Magellan decided to conduct religious services ashore. By offering thanks to God for their deliverance from the perils of the hazardous voyage, and conducting a solemn Easter mass, he hoped to demonstrate to his island hosts the reverence with which Spaniards approached the most sacred of Christian holy days. Magellan sent the fleet chaplain, Pedro de Valderrama, ashore with some sailors to prepare a site, and Enrique went along to explain to the two chiefs that the Spaniards ". . . were going to land on the island, not to dine with them, but to perform a religious ceremony." Intrigued by the promise of a spectacle that they probably assumed would be followed by a feast, Colambu and Siaui consented, and had two slaughtered pigs delivered to the site.[10]

Magellan's notion of a solemn religious ceremony had a decidedly military slant. On Easter morning, noted Pigafetta, ". . . about fifty of us went ashore, not wearing full body armor, but carrying our weapons and dressed in our finest attire. At the moment our boats touched the beach, six bombards were fired as a sign of peace. We leapt onto the beach, where the two kings who had come to meet us embraced the captain general and placed him between them. We marched in formation to the place prepared for the mass, which wasn't very far from the beach. Before beginning the mass, the captain general sprinkled the two kings with perfumed water. When it was time for the offering, they went forward, as we did, to kiss the cross, but did not make the offering. When the body of Our Lord was raised, they showed their adoration with hands clasped, faithfully imitating what we were doing." At that moment, on a signal from Magellan, the gunners on the ships discharged all their artillery at once, producing a thunderous roar. "After the mass," wrote Pigafetta, "some of our men took communion. The captain general then ordered the performance of a sword dance, at which the kings were greatly pleased."

The sword dance to which Pigafetta referred is native to Toledo but performed in many parts of Spain. The dancers wear colorful linen shirts with baggy pantaloons in the Greek style and bandanas on their heads. Whirling this way and that, they slash their naked swords in wide arcs, coming breathtakingly close to the heads and bodies of the other dancers. In one step called "the throat cutter," several dancers thrust their swords at the throat of a dancer who, at the last moment, skillfully slips away between them.[11]

After the dance, Magellan presented the two chiefs with a tall cross adorned with a crown of thorns, requesting that it be erected on the highest point of the island. This cross, he told the chiefs, when seen by Spanish ships, would let them know that they would be received as friends.

Magellan then offered his ships and fighting men to help defeat their enemies. Colambu and Siaui, while acknowledging that they were at war with
two neighboring islands, declined because ". . . the season for fighting had
not yet arrived."[12]

While their reception at Limasawa could not have been more cordial,
and the crews had benefited enormously from the fresh fruit, fish, and
meat provided by their hosts, the Spaniards had not yet been able to replenish their supplies of less perishable foods. Other than ginger, neither
had they seen any evidence of spices. The people at Limasawa indicated
that such commodities could be obtained at *Seylani* (Leyte), *Zubu* (Cebu),
and *Calagan* (Mindanao), and Magellan decided to go to Cebu, the principal trading center of the region. Colambu promised to guide him there personally if he would wait two days and help harvest the rice crop on
Limasawa. Eager to get rice for his ships' depleted stores, and needing a
pilot to guide them through the reef-studded archipelago, Magellan agreed.

Seizing on this as a cause for celebration, Colambu and Siaui hosted another feast, serving vast quantities of palm wine along with roast pig and
other tropical delicacies. Natives and Spaniards alike spent all the next day
sleeping off its effects. Harvesting the rice took three more days. On April
4, seven days after arriving at Limasawa, Magellan's squadron set forth for
Cebu.[13]

With Colambu's *barangay* leading, the squadron sailed northwest, then
north through Canigao Channel, hugging the coast of Leyte to avoid Dana-
jon Bank and the reefs off Bohol Island. When they reached Baybay, a
small port on the west coast of Leyte, Magellan's guides told him that the
surrounding area was rich in gold and other valuable resources. From Baybay they headed west across the Camotes Sea. With plenty of sea room, a
fresh breeze, and all sails set, Magellan's ships overtook and passed the *barangay* that had been leading them. To allow it to catch up, they hove-to off
the Camotes Islands. Pigafetta reported that when Colambu ". . . caught
up with us, he was greatly astonished at the speed with which we sailed."[14]
From the Camotes, the squadron headed southwest. Soon, the mountains
of Cebu Island loomed in front of them. Off Bagacay Point, they entered
the narrow channel between Cebu Island and the small island of Mactan.

As they sailed down the channel, there came into view a densely populated shoreline with most of the houses on stilts. On April 7, 1521, with
banners and pennants flying, the squadron hove-to directly in front of the
bustling port of Cebu. Intent on making a grand impression, Magellan ordered the squadron's gunners to fire a salute using all their artillery. It had
the desired effect: Many of the town's terrified inhabitants fled into the
hills.[15]

The three ships nosed into the harbor and let go their anchors, and Magellan sent his young relative (possibly his natural son), Cristovão Rebêlo, ashore with Enrique to locate the authorities and assure them of his peaceful intentions. They found the local potentate, Rajah Humabon, surrounded by a crowd of retainers, all very much alarmed by the thunder of the artillery.[16] Enrique assured the rajah that the guns had been fired merely in salute. It was the custom, he said, for Spanish ships to so honor the rulers and citizens of the foreign ports they visited, and should be taken as a sign of peace. Relieved that his city was not under attack, Humabon asked Magellan's emissaries what brought their chief to Cebu. Enrique answered that his master, a captain of the greatest king in the world, had heard such good things about the ruler of Cebu that he had come to visit him, bringing greetings and an offer of friendship. His master also wished to purchase fresh food for his ships and to trade for the products of Cebu with the merchandise he had brought from Spain.[17] An emboldened Humabon replied that his custom was to require the payment of a port tariff by all visiting ships. In fact, he told them, only four days ago he had received such a payment from a Siamese junk that had called to take on a cargo of slaves and gold. Rebêlo haughtily drew himself up and, with Enrique interpreting, told Humabon that since his captain general served such a powerful monarch, he would not pay tribute to any prince. He had come with a message of peace, but if war was what the ruler of Cebu wanted, war he would have.

A Moslem merchant, apparently a resident agent for Siamese trading interests, whispered to Humabon that he had better be careful with these strangers: They were probably Portuguese, the "Franks" whose brutal conquest of Calicut and Malacca had spread terror and disrupted ancient trading patterns from India to the China Seas. Overhearing the merchant, Enrique told Humabon that his master served the Spanish king who also was emperor of all the Christians. The latter was even more powerful in men and ships than the king of the Portuguese. When the agent from Siam confirmed this, Humabon became thoroughly alarmed and announced that he would discuss the matter with his advisors and give his decision to the captain general the next day. He then treated Rebêlo and Enrique to an elaborate lunch.[18] After the two emissaries returned to the *Trinidad* and related all that had transpired, Colambu went ashore to tell his ally, Rajah Humabon, of his experiences with these strange visitors. The next day Enrique went ashore again to learn what the rajah had decided, this time with the fleet notary, Léon de Ezpeleta. Intimidated by the thunder of Magellan's guns and the stories of Portuguese savagery, Humabon came to the town square to greet them, not only announcing that he would waive the port tax for his distinguished visitors, but offering to pay tribute to their emperor. He was assured that it would not be necessary; the captain general sought only to trade among the islands, and hoped to make Cebu the center of his trading activities. Greatly relieved, Humabon agreed to work out a trading arrangement with the Spaniards. To insure their continued friendship, he suggested that Magellan become his blood brother.[19]

At ten o'clock on the morning of April 9, Colambu returned to the *Trinidad*, bringing with him the Moslem agent from Siam and a message from Humabon. While he was busy that morning arranging for the collection of the foodstuffs requested by the captain general, Humabon would send his nephew who, as husband of the rajah's eldest daughter, was the heir apparent, and some of his ministers to the flagship to conclude a treaty of peace.[20]

When the emissaries arrived that afternoon, Magellan received them with appropriate ceremony. The captain general, the young prince, and Colambu were seated on chairs covered with red velvet. The principal ministers were seated on leather-backed chairs, with the rest of the delegation seated around them on mats. With Enrique serving as interpreter, Magellan asked the prince whether it was the custom in his country to conduct treaty negotiations in public, and if so, whether they had been authorized by Humabon to negotiate in his name. Reassured by the prince on both counts, Magellan dropped to his knees and prayed that the proposed alliance would be pleasing to God in Heaven. The prayer seemed to trigger in him an extended outpouring of religious sentiment. The captain general's piety profoundly touched his guests, who remarked, wrote Pigafetta, ". . . that they had never heard anyone say such words, but that they took great pleasure in hearing them." Emboldened by their interest, Magellan urged his guests to accept the Christian faith.

When Magellan queried them about family relationships in their society, they said that ". . . when fathers and mothers grew old, they received no further honor, but their children commanded them." Shocked, Magellan told them that the Christian God ". . . had commanded us to honor our fathers and mothers, and that whoever did otherwise was condemned to eternal fire; that we are all descended from Adam and Eve, our first parents; that we have an immortal spirit; and many other things pertaining to the faith." Magellan, it seems, had begun a singular transformation: The silent, obsessive captain general was becoming an impassioned preacher, but not from unadulterated religious passion. In him, religious feelings were inextricably mixed with personal, political, and military goals. As Pigafetta told the story, after Magellan's sermon the islanders implored him to leave some men to instruct them in the Christian faith. He replied that though he couldn't spare even one man from his ships, those who sincerely wished to become Christians could be baptized by the fleet chaplain. But baptism, he warned them, must not be undertaken out of fear, the desire to please others, or the desire for personal gain. Magellan did not wish, wrote Pigafetta, ". . . to cause . . . displeasure to those who chose to live by their own law, but the Christians would be better regarded and treated than the others." Warming to his sermon, Magellan told the emissaries that, should they become Christians, their wives also would have to be baptized, for only then would it be permissible for their Christian husbands to sleep with them.[21] He promised a suit of Spanish armor to those of his guests who would adopt the Christian faith.

When the delegation assured him that Humabon would sign the peace treaty, and that they were all eager to be baptized, Magellan wept openly and embraced each of them. "Then he took the hands of the prince and the king of [Limasawa] between his own," continued Pigafetta, "and told them that by his faith in God, his loyalty to his sovereign the emperor, and by the [crusader's] habit he wore, he swore that perpetual peace would exist between the kings of Spain and Zebu."[22]

Before leaving, the delegation presented Magellan with several large baskets of rice and some live pigs, goats, and chickens, exclaiming that such poor gifts were not worthy of so great a personage. In return, Magellan gave the prince a bolt of finely woven white cloth and a cup made of gilded glass, at that time much prized in the islands.[23] He then dispatched Pigafetta and an unnamed companion ashore, bearing presents for Humabon, including a yellow-and-violet silken Turkish robe, a red hat, strings of glass beads, a silver dish, and two gilded glass drinking cups. They found Humabon in his palace, seated on a mat. Short, fat, tattooed, and naked ". . . except for a cotton cloth before his privies," he was eating turtle eggs and swilling them down with palm wine. The liquor was drawn through ". . . a slender reed," reported Pigafetta in what may have been, if not the first, one of the earliest descriptions by a European of the use of straws for drinking.

The two Europeans were invited to the house of the prince, where they were entertained with music, refreshments, and dancing. At the conclusion of this impromptu party, ". . . the prince had three quite naked girls dance for us," bragged Pigafetta. When he and his companion returned to their ship, Pigafetta told Magellan that they had been very well received.[24]

The next day, April 10, Magellan sent another delegation ashore to get Humabon's permission to bury two men who, weakened by scurvy, had just died. One was Juan de Aroche, a man-at-arms who had sailed from San Lúcar on the *San Antonio*; the name of the other is not known.[25] Humabon consented and provided a burial site in the square at the center of the town. The following day, funeral services were conducted with much of the town looking on, and the solemnity of the event left a deep impression on the people of Cebu. Several days later, Humabon declared his wish to become a Christian.[26]

While Magellan was experiencing heady success with his religious efforts, he was also busy establishing a commercial base in Cebu. The day of the funeral, a crew set up a *factoría* (trading post) in a building provided by Humabon, who promised protection for the enterprise and the four Spaniards assigned by Magellan to run it. The store opened for business on April 12, 1521.[27] Of the products put on display, items made of iron or bronze appealed the most to the curious townsfolk, who gladly gave gold in exchange. Rice, pigs, goats, and other foodstuffs were traded for trinkets and other small sundries. "They gave us ten gold pieces, each worth a ducat and a half (approximately $600 U.S.) for fourteen pounds of iron," wrote Pigafetta. Magellan forbade his sailors to trade for gold. If he had not, Pigafetta averred, ". . . every sailor would have given all that he possessed to obtain it, spoiling forever the trade in this metal."

Then began a series of events that, to Magellan, proved that the Holy Mother had heard his prayers and was watching over him, guiding his efforts. On Sunday, April 14, Humabon, his wife, son-in-law, his most important retainers, and his ally, Colambu, were baptized in a public ceremony in the central square of Cebu City. A large platform draped with bright tapestries and decorated with palm leaves had been erected for the occasion. Forty armed men, two of them clad from head to foot in gleaming steel armor, brought the royal standard ashore from the flagship. As soon as their boat touched the beach, the gunners on the ship let loose a deafening salute,[28] no doubt startling the huge crowd that had gathered.

Humabon greeted Magellan at the beach, warmly embracing him. Followed by the curious crowd, they proceeded to the town square where, in addition to the ceremonial platform, a tall, wooden cross had been erected. Standing before the cross, Magellan announced that all who wished to be baptized must burn the idols kept in their houses and replace them with crosses, and that they must come to this plaza every day, their hands clasped for prayer. He showed them how to kneel reverently, making the sign of the cross.[29] Magellan took Humabon's hand, and together they mounted the platform, seating themselves on two chairs covered with red and violet velvet. Magellan wore a robe of pure white, to demonstrate, he told the rajah, his love for those who were about to become Christians. The island's principal chiefs surrounded them, seated on cushions, with the lesser dignitaries on mats.

Magellan began the ceremony with a long, ponderous sermon in which he pointed out the many advantages Christianity would bring to Humabon's people. With Enrique interpreting, he told Humabon that he should thank God for inspiring him to become a Christian, for now he would more easily vanquish his enemies. Humabon replied that, while he wanted very much to become a Christian, some of his chiefs would not obey him, for they considered themselves to be his equals. Magellan replied that any chief who refused to obey Humabon would be killed and his possessions confiscated. Soon he would be going to Spain, but he would return with many ships and men. Then, if Humabon proved himself a loyal Christian, he would be made ruler of the entire archipelago.[30] Although one might wish for stronger evidence, Pigafetta's account of these events hints at the strategy evolving in Magellan's mind for asserting and maintaining control over his discoveries.

As there was no evidence that the Portuguese had reached these islands, prior discovery and alliances with local rulers, especially if they could be persuaded to accept Christianity, would provide a solid basis for claiming Spanish sovereignty. In the several weeks since he had arrived, Magellan had observed that the islands were occupied by diverse peoples ruled by independent rajahs. Because he would need to return to Spain for reinforcements, he would require a reliable native ally to provide a foothold from which—with the new fleet he would bring from Spain—he could gain control of the entire archipelago. With its rajah about to become a Christian, Cebu, the center of an extensive trade network extending all the way to Siam on the Asian mainland, was well suited for just such a foothold. The artillery salutes and elaborate religious ceremonies were not just manifestations of puffery by a self-annointed religious fanatic; they were calculated to overawe and intimidate the numerous, independent, potentially rebellious people of these islands.

On the baptismal platform, Magellan was resplendent in his robe of dazzling white, the intense black of his full beard standing out in stark contrast. He looked on as the fleet chaplain, Pedro de Valderrama, baptized Humabon, his heir apparent, and principal retainers and allies, including Colambu. All were given Christian names: Don Carlos (after Charles V) for Humabon, Don Fernando (after Charles's brother) for the heir apparent, Don Juan for Colambu, and Cristóbal for the Moslem trader from Siam, who diplomatically forsook the crescent for the cross.[31]

Later that day, the chaplain baptized Humabon's wife and forty other prominent women. The ranee was given the Christian name Doña Juana, in honor of the emperor's royal mother. Humabon's daughter was christened Doña Catalina, and Colambu's wife received the name Doña Isabel.

After Doña Juana was christened, Magellan presented her with a wooden image of the Holy Mother holding the infant Jesus.[32] Thirty-four years after the deaths of Magellan and most of his principal officers, a little wooden image of the Christ child, apparently of Flemish workmanship, was discovered by Juan Zamus, a sailor in the expedition of Miguel López Legazpi, the first to reach Cebu after Magellan. Found in a house whose occupants had fled when the Spaniards bombarded the city, the wooden image was recognized by the expedition's navigator-priest, Andrés de Urdaneta, who built a chapel for it. The icon has been preserved in the Augustinian church in Cebu City, where it is venerated as a sacred relic.[33]

By the end of that memorable Sunday, 800 men, women, and children had been baptized,[34] and the fervor would continue for eight days until nearly everyone on Cebu, and some from neighboring islands, had followed Humabon's example. All told, some 2,200 conversions resulted from Magellan's inspired preaching.[35] A fortuitous incident in which the captain general, filled with hubris, tried his hand at spiritual healing, probably did much to stimulate these wholesale conversions. The older brother of Humabon's heir apparent, ill and near death, had been too weak to present himself for baptism. On looking into the matter, Magellan discovered that the women attending the sick man, in a desperate attempt to cure their dying patient, had been making offerings to their customary idols. Scolding them for their pagan ways, Magellan promised that if they would burn their idols, and the patient would agree to be baptized, the power of Jesus Christ would cure him. Told that the patient had consented, Magellan led a solemn procession to the house of the sick man who, according to Pigafetta, ". . . could neither speak nor move." After the patient, his wife, and ten daughters had been baptized, Magellan asked him how he felt. The man responded immediately, saying that he felt fine. Magellan then gave him some almond milk to drink, and sent to his house a mattress, sheets, coverlet, and a pillow. Each day the patient was given almond milk, oil and water of roses, and some of Magellan's quince preserves. In less than five days, the man was walking.

Perhaps the miraculous cure had something to do with the quince preserves that had kept Magellan and the members of his mess healthy during the Pacific crossing, perhaps it was the psychological impact of the intense, powerful stranger, or perhaps the power of faith was indeed at work. In the Philippines, faith healing, given a spectacular start by Magellan, is still widely practiced.

While the captain general was preoccupied with religious matters, the sailors and some of the officers were up to their usual tricks with the local women. Cebu was proving to be an even better liberty port than Rio. Pigafetta remarked that ". . . [the men of Cebu] have as many wives as they wish, but one of them is the principal wife. Whenever any of our men went ashore, both by day and by night, everyone invited them to eat and drink . . . [and] the women loved us very much more than their own men. All of the women from the age of six years upward have their vaginas gradually opened because of the men's penises."[36] This outrageous treatment of female children was designed to prepare them to endure the barbarous custom of *palang*, which persists to this day in remote parts of the Philippines and Borneo.[37] Pigafetta described the practice as follows:

> *The males, large and small, have their penis pierced from one side to the other near the head, with a gold or tin bolt the thickness of a goose quill. In both ends of the same bolt, some have what resembles a spur with points on the ends; others like the head of a cart nail. I very often asked many, both old and young, to see their penis, because I could not credit it. In the middle of the bolt is a hole, through which they urinate. The bolt and spurs always hold firm.*

He then went on to describe what must have been, for the women, the painful process of accepting, during intercourse, what has been aptly described as this "load of phallic hardware."[38] It is easy to understand why the women of Cebu preferred Magellan's sailors to their husbands and usual lovers, and Magellan's men were more than willing to oblige them. Among the fleet's officers eager to come to the aid of the long-suffering women of Cebu was Duarte Barbosa, captain of the *Victoria*. At Rio, similar behavior by Barbosa, an otherwise reliable officer, had incensed the puritanical captain general.

Enraptured by his success with faith healing, and engrossed with winning converts to the cross, Magellan at first paid little heed to his men's debaucheries. While he and the chaplain were busy baptizing and preaching Christian values, the ships' crews demonstrated a wanton disregard for the doctrines of sexual restraint and the sanctity of marriage. The frequent, indiscriminate coupling with native women by Magellan's randy sailors outraged the men of Cebu, who particularly resented it when their wives and daughters were involved. Learning that Barbosa had left his ship for a love nest ashore, Magellan was furious. He removed Barbosa from command of the *Victoria*, replacing him with Cristovão Rebêlo.[39] Like Barbosa, Revêlo had sailed from Spain as a supernumerary on the *Trinidad*. During the voyage, he had impressed Magellan with his strong character, performing ably when sent ashore as the first of Magellan's ambassadors to Rajah Humabon. A Portuguese, Rebêlo was a native of Pôrto, and though his relationship to Magellan is obscure, Rebêlo is thought by at least one authority to have been his natural son.[40]

On the day of his baptism, Humabon told Magellan that several independent local chiefs would not submit to his authority. Determined to make Humabon the undisputed ruler of these islands, Magellan sent messages to the independent chieftains ordering them to acknowledge Humabon's authority. If they failed to do so, he warned, they would suffer death and the confiscation of their property. Several village chiefs flatly refused. Magellan sent a small force of sailors and marines in two ship's boats to punish one of the recalcitrant chiefs, burning his village, a town named Bulaya, and returning with a haul of confiscated livestock.[41]

Magellan then ordered the other defiant chiefs to deliver to Humabon a symbolic tribute consisting of a goat, a pig, a basket of rice, and a jug of honey. Should they fail to comply, their villages would suffer the same fate as Bulaya. Two of them delivered the tribute, but Lapulapu, a chieftain on Mactan Island, refused, sending word that if the Spaniards came to burn his village, he would be waiting for them.

Unwilling to tolerate the defiance of a petty chieftain, Magellan proposed to attack Lapulapu's village. Like Napoleon as he was about to invade Russia, and Robert E. Lee before Gettysburg, Magellan was dazzled by his earlier success. Feeling invulnerable, he boasted to Humabon that he would need only sixty men and would personally lead the attack. Humabon opposed the idea, as did Juan Serrano, Magellan's senior and most experienced captain, who told him that such a campaign would be foolhardy. The ships were in poor condition and too lightly manned to spare the sixty men. However, knowing that Magellan was not easily dissuaded once his mind was made up, Serrano added that if the captain general thought it necessary to attack the village, he should not go himself, but send someone in his place.

This was sound advice, and Magellan would have been wise to heed it. While the instructions King Charles had given him did not specifically forbid him to go ashore in areas controlled by hostile populations,[42] he was well aware of the disastrous consequences for the Solís expedition when, in the La Plata Estuary in 1516, its leader imprudently left his flagship to go ashore and was killed by Querandi. Magellan chose to ignore this lesson, Humabon's cautious advice, and the simple logic of his oldest, wisest captain. His confidence in the superiority of Spanish arms and the protection of the Holy Virgin made him certain he could intimidate and easily defeat the primitively armed defenders of a small village. Perhaps too, he was swayed by his knowledge of the military adventure in the Moluccas that secured an exalted status on the island of Ternate for his friend Serrão.

At midnight on April 26–27, 1521, Magellan set forth from Cebu for Lapulapu's village with sixty well-armed volunteers in three shallops on which were mounted light, portable swivel guns. In addition to swords and lances, the men carried harquebuses and crossbows. Although they wore armor, for ease in getting in and out of the boats they dispensed with their greaves (leg armor).

Lapulapu's village was shielded by a fringe of mangroves on the shore of a little bay at the northeastern end of Mactan Island, about nine nautical miles from Cebu City. Knowing Lapulapu for a formidable opponent, Humabon heartily disapproved of Magellan's plan. Nevertheless, as he didn't want his new ally to come to grief, he assembled a force of 1,000 warriors in thirty war canoes to back up the small Spanish assault force.

The attackers proceeded northeastward through the channel between Cebu and Mactan, and after rounding Bantolinao Point, entered the shallow bay fronting the village before dawn. Magellan intended to land his men quietly for a surprise attack, but he had been listening to divine voices instead of doing his homework. Uncharacteristically for one usually so painstakingly thorough, he had neglected to consider the tide. It was low, and a partially exposed reef extended 1,000 yards seaward of the beach. The shallops were unable to get close enough inshore to land their men or even to provide covering fire from their swivel guns. Undeterred, Magellan was determined to wade ashore with his men under cover of darkness and burn the village.

Humabon warned him to wait until daylight, because he knew the village would be surrounded by trenches with sharp bamboo stakes set to impale unwary night attackers. He urged Magellan to let him attack first with his 1,000 men, for he was familiar with Lapulapu's fortifications. Magellan's men could be held in reserve, ready to enter the fray when and where needed. Such tactical support, Humabon argued, would provide a tremendous morale boost for his warriors, and the attack would surely succeed.

Magellan was indignant. The whole object of this attack was to demonstrate the invincibility of Spanish arms. Not only did he reject Humabon's suggestion, he gave him express orders to keep his men in their canoes, offshore and out of the battle. From there they would see how Castilians fought.

At first light the shallops moved as close inshore as they could without grounding. Leaving the boat crews and swivel gunners with the shallops, Magellan leapt into the shallow water, closely followed by forty-eight fighting men, and waded ashore, setting a precedent for General MacArthur's landing on nearby Leyte over 400 years later. Unlike MacArthur, however, he had no cameramen along to record the event for posterity. Magellan and his men had to wade "two crossbow flights" (about 2,000 feet) before reaching the beach.

Accounts of the ensuing battle vary somewhat. Pigafetta, who fought alongside Magellan, gave the most dramatic version, but his story was written several years after the event with the object of titillating audiences in the courts of the crowned heads of Europe. Like Rustichello's rendering of Marco Polo's story, Pigafetta's account needs a grain of salt. In its essentials it probably is mostly true, but some details were very likely colored to make the story better for telling.

Other accounts were culled from testimony given by survivors of the ill-fated expedition (for the most part professional mariners) to official boards of inquiry, or in the courts where claims were filed against the Crown by heirs of those who died. Although some of these sources may have had reason to give biased testimony, the stories of most can be considered their best recollections of events.

Pigafetta stated that the landing on Mactan was vigorously opposed. "When we reached land," he wrote, "those men formed in three divisions to the number of more than one thousand five hundred persons. When they saw us, they charged down upon us with exceeding loud cries, two divisions on our flanks, and the other on our front." He described a furious fight at or near the beach, in which musket fire proved ineffective. After passing through the natives' wooden shields, the musket balls did not have enough energy left to do much damage.

They shot so many arrows at us and hurled so many bamboo spears (some tipped with iron) at the captain general, besides fire-hardened, pointed stakes, stones and dirt, that we could scarcely defend ourselves. Seeing that, the captain general sent some men to burn their houses in order to terrify them. When they saw their houses burning, they were roused to greater fury. Two of our men were killed near the houses, while we burned twenty or thirty houses. So many of them charged down upon us that they shot the captain through the right leg with a poisoned arrow. On that account, he ordered us to retire slowly, but the men took flight, except six or eight of us who remained with the captain.

We continued to retire for more than a crossbow flight from the shore, always fighting up to our knees in the water. The natives continued to pursue us, and picking up the same spear four or six times, hurled it at us again and again. Recognizing the captain, so many turned upon him that they knocked his helmet off his head twice, but he always stood firm like a good knight, together with some others.

Thus did we fight for more than an hour, refusing to retire further. An In-

dian hurled a bamboo spear into the captain's face, but the latter immedi-
ately killed him with his lance, which he left in the Indian's body. Then,
going for his sword, he could draw it out but halfway, because he had been
wounded in the arm by a bamboo spear. When the natives saw that, they
all hurled themselves upon him. One of them wounded him on the left leg
with a [bolo], which resembles a scimitar, only larger. That caused the cap-
tain to fall face downward, when immediately they rushed upon him with
iron and bamboo spears, and with their [bolos] until they killed our mirror,
our light, our comfort, and our true guide. When they wounded him, he
turned back many times to see whether we were all in the boats. Thereupon,
beholding him dead, we, wounded, retreated as best we could to the boats,
which already were pulling off. [43]

Another version of the story, recorded by Herrera,[44] was culled from the
official records to which he had access in Spain early in the seventeenth
century. These are thought to have included a Portuguese account describing the contents of San Martín's notebooks. Having remained on one of
the ships at anchor in the port of Cebu, San Martín did not participate in
the battle, but probably recorded what he was told by eyewitnesses. There
are other versions of the battle, some by participants. As with most mul-
tiple-witness accounts, there is noticeable variation in many details. The
essential elements of the story, however, are sufficiently similar to give it
credibility.

Juan Sebastián del Cano was not present at the Battle of Mactan. However, like San Martín, he had ready access to firsthand accounts from survivors. In his testimony about the voyage after returning to Spain as captain
of the *Victoria*—while he had ample cause to slant that part concerning his
role in the mutiny—Cano would have had little reason for misrepresenting
the events surrounding Magellan's death. His testimony was the basis for a
version of the Battle of Mactan proposed by a nineteenth-century Spanish
archivist, Rodrigo Agánduru Moriz, that helps to explain Magellan's extraordinarily rash behavior during the last hours of his life.[45] By synthesiz-
ing these other versions of Magellan's final battle with Pigafetta's firsthand
but suspiciously colorful account, the following scenario can be deduced:

The landing was unopposed. On attaining the beach, Magellan and his
men headed straight for the town. Finding it evacuated, they commenced
to burn some of the houses, a tactic to which Magellan seems to have been
addicted. While so engaged, they were attacked on each flank by two battalions of enraged natives. Magellan then divided his small force to counterattack on both flanks, but they were assaulted so furiously by such large
numbers of the enemy that they recombined to defend themselves. For

several hours, the harquebusiers and crossbowmen kept the enemy at a respectful distance. Eventually, the Spaniards ran out of powder, lead, and crossbow bolts. Perceiving this, the natives closed in, hurling stones, fire-hardened stakes, and iron-tipped bamboo lances and shooting poisoned arrows. Seeing that the situation was growing desperate, Magellan ordered a gradual retreat. Instead, most of the Spaniards, eager to reach the safety of the boats, fled pell-mell toward the beach, leaving Magellan with no more than eight defenders to cover the retreat. Outside the reef, beyond the range of their swivel guns, the men in the shallops were unable to provide covering fire.

Lapulapu's forces attacked with redoubled fury, aiming their spears and poisoned arrows at the unprotected legs of the retreating Spaniards. One of the poisoned arrows grazed Magellan's leg, and yet another mortally wounded Cristovão Rebêlo, who had been fighting valiantly alongside his father. When Magellan saw that the young man had been killed, he went berserk and hurled himself at the enemy, getting so far ahead of his defenders that they were unable to protect him. Surrounded by the enemy, he was pelted furiously with stones that knocked off his helmet. A defending warrior slashed his leg with a bolo and he fell helpless to the ground. Bamboo spears were thrust into his body wherever it was unprotected by armor. A spear through the throat was the *coup de grace*.

Without fire support from the swivel guns on the shallops, it is not likely that Magellan's small landing force could have reached the beach across a thousand feet of shallow coral, confronted as Pigafetta claimed by three battalions of the enemy. Nor is it likely that they could have broken through the enemy ranks to attack the village, which lay behind the mangroves fronting the beach. One has only to recall the awful casualties inflicted by determined Japanese defenders on U.S. assault forces on the tiny island of Betio in Tarawa Atoll in 1943, when low tide forced Navy landing craft to deposit the marines on a shallow reef well offshore. It seems more likely that Lapulapu expected to be attacked by a large force of Humabon's men supported by a smaller force of Spaniards. Not knowing where they would land, he assembled his defending forces in the interior of Mactan Island, holding them ready until the invaders entered into terrain suitable for counterattack.

When Humabon's war canoes failed to land a single warrior, Lapulapu could scarcely believe his good luck. Magellan's men had begun to burn the village when they were attacked on both flanks by Lapulapu's forces. If it had not been for the superior range of the Spaniards' crossbows, they would have been driven into the sea much more quickly. When they ran out of crossbow bolts, Magellan had no other recourse but to order his men to retreat. Thanks to his valiant holding action, most of his little force made it back to the boats. While Pigafetta may have doctored the details of Magellan's final hours to make a more colorful story, his praise for the uncommon valor of the fallen captain general was well deserved.

Seven Europeans, including Magellan, were killed in the Battle of Mactan, and another died of his wounds shortly after the battle. Fifteen of the enemy were reported killed.[46] Bearing the wounded survivors, the shallops returned to the ships at Cebu. When the men who had remained with the squadron learned that the captain general had been killed, ". . . great was the outpouring of grief by the crews, who [had come to] love and respect him and had been willing to endure much travail to go wherever he might lead them."[47]

Rajah Humabon cried like a baby when told of Magellan's death, but his confidence was shaken in his new allies and in the power of the religion he had just adopted. His disillusionment grew when he realized that the defeat by Lapulapu and outrage at the behavior of the ship's crews toward the island's women was causing his subjects to question his leadership.[48] At the urging of the ships' officers he sent a message to Lapulapu, requesting the return of Magellan's body, in return for which the Spaniards promised to give whatever merchandise from their *factoría* he might choose. The victorious chieftain refused, replying that he would not give up the body of such a man for anything, and that he intended to keep it as a memorial to his triumph.[49] There can be little doubt that Lapulapu also urged Humabon to get rid of his troublesome guests. Already disgusted with them, Humabon resolved to do just that.

With Magellan and Revêlo dead, the ships' crews had to choose a new squadron commander and a captain for the *Victoria*. For the latter position they elected Luis Affonso de Goes, a Portuguese supernumerary on the *Trinidad*. Duarte Barbosa was elected captain of the flagship, but they did not trust him with exclusive command of the squadron. Juan Serrano, the veteran pilot-captain of the *Concepción*, was elected co-commander.

One of the first decisions of the new high command was to close down the *factoría* and reload the trade goods in the ships. This completed, they asked for two pilots to guide them through the archipelago. Humabon was indignant;[50] their intent to abandon Cebu destroyed any traces of goodwill he may have retained for the Spaniards.

Enrique, Magellan's Malay slave and the expedition's interpreter, had fought alongside his master at Mactan and received a minor wound. Despondent over Magellan's death, he brooded aboard the *Trinidad*, nursing his injury. Magellan had stipulated in his will that upon his death Enrique would be freed from bondage and provided with funds for his support.

When Barbosa ordered him ashore to help recruit native pilots, Enrique declined, because, he said, of his wounds. Enraged at the slave's refusal, Barbosa swore that as brother to Magellan's wife, he would make sure that Enrique would never be manumitted, but remain her slave for life. Furthermore, he fumed, if Enrique didn't get out of his bunk and do as ordered, he would have him flogged. Seething with resentment and wounded pride, Enrique went to negotiate with Humabon. It would have been better for the expedition if he hadn't.

On May 1, Enrique returned to the *Trinidad* with an invitation from Humabon for the captains, principal officers, and ranking men of the squadron to attend a ceremonial banquet where they would be presented with fine jewels, a gift for the Christian Emperor. Barbosa was eager to go; Serrano advised caution, but was mocked by Barbosa for lack of courage. His Castilian pride stung, Serrano ordered a longboat made ready and was the first to leap into it. He was followed by Barbosa, the *Victoria*'s new captain, Affonso de Goes, the pilots San Martín and Carvalho, ships' clerks Ezpeleta and Heredía, the chaplain, Valderrama, master-at-arms Gómez de Espinosa, and Enrique. Sixteen others, including supernumeraries, able seamen, and a cooper, accompanied them. Pigafetta did not go; his face was swollen from a poisoned arrow that had grazed his forehead during the battle.[51]

When the shore party landed at the beach, they were warmly welcomed by Humabon, but as they were led to the banquet site, Espinosa and Carvalho noticed that the prince who had been miraculously cured by Magellan quietly took aside the priest, Valderrama, and escorted him to his house. Suspecting a trap, Espinosa and Carvalho hurried back to the longboat and rowed back to the *Trinidad*. They were telling the crew of their suspicions when they heard shouting and a great tumult ashore.

Realizing that their shipmates had been ambushed, Carvalho, now the senior officer, ordered the ships to move closer to shore and begin bombarding the town. As the gunners opened fire, Serrano, bound and bleeding, was dragged toward the beach. He called out to his comrades on the ships to cease fire, or he would be killed. Asked what had happened to the others, he shouted that their throats had all been cut, except for Enrique, who had been spared.

From this point, there is considerable divergence in the accounts of the survivors. Pigafetta, who obviously disliked Carvalho, said that Serrano had implored us ". . . to redeem him with some of the merchandise; but Johan Carvaio, his boon companion, would not allow the boat to go ashore [fearing treachery]." Instead, Carvalho ordered the ships to set sail, leaving Serrano on the beach, weeping. He ". . . asked us not to set sail so quickly, for they would kill him." Serrano, wrote Pigafetta, prayed that on Judgment Day, God would hold Carvalho accountable for his conduct.

A quite different version was provided by an anonymous Portuguese survivor of the voyage, probably Vasquito Galego, son of the deceased pilot of the *Victoria*, Vasco Galego. After the death of his father during the crossing of the Pacific, Vasquito apparently continued his father's log. The original manuscript is in the University of Leiden, in the Netherlands.

In this version of the story, Serrano's captors had demanded two lombards (artillery pieces) as ransom for their prisoner. When Carvalho sent these ashore in a skiff, the natives upped their demands. The crew of the skiff said that Carvalho would give whatever they asked for Serrano's freedom, but requested that he be released at a location where he could be picked up safely. When his captors refused to do this, Serrano called out that they were stalling and would try to capture the ships as soon as reinforcements arrived. He shouted to his shipmates that they had better leave quickly, for ". . . it were better for him to die than all should perish."[52] Less dramatic than Pigafetta's, this version may come closer to reality. During the voyage, Serrano had proved himself a loyal, capable, and brave officer. The picture painted by Pigafetta of the proud Castilian captain weeping, imploring Carvalho to save him when doing so would have put the ships and their crews in jeopardy, simply does not ring true. It seems more likely that, realizing that any rescuers attempting to reach him would be seized, Serrano told Carvalho to leave him and sail away.[53]

18

$\mathcal{T}$he Wanderers

After Estevão Gomes deserted with the San Antonio, *the fleet* lost two more pilots, Vasco Galego and Juan Rodríguez de Mafra, both from scurvy. Galego, a pilot on the *Victoria*, succumbed at sea on February 28, 1521, while the fleet was sailing westward north of the Marshall Islands.[1] Rodríguez de Mafra, who had transferred from the *San Antonio* to the *Concepción* after the mutiny at Port San Julián,[2] died on March 28, the day the fleet anchored off Limasawa. Andrés de San Martín, the astrologer-pilot, was aboard the *Victoria* at the time of Galego's death. When he and Juan Serrano, captain of the *Concepción*, were abandoned on Cebu, the fleet was left with but one of its original pilots, João Lopes Carvalho.

Three ship's masters had perished by the time the squadron fled from Cebu. Antón Salamón, master of the *Victoria*, had been executed in Brazil. Juan de Elorriaga of the *San Antonio* died from stab wounds inflicted during the mutiny at Port San Julián. Baltazar Palla (Genovés), who had taken over as master of the *Victoria* after the wreck of the *Santiago*, died on April 3, 1521, the day the fleet sailed from Limasawa.[3] After his death there remained but two masters among the survivors: Juan Bautista de Polcevera of the *Trinidad* and Juan Sebastián del Cano of the *Concepción*.

Of the mates (*contramaestres*) who had sailed from San Lúcar, Francisco Albo of the *Trinidad* had assumed the duties of pilot as the fleet approached the coast of Brazil. He was the *Victoria*'s pilot when it returned to Spain in 1522.[4] During the mutiny, Diego Hernández, the loyal mate of the *San Antonio*, was seized by mutineers and held captive. There is nothing in the records to indicate what happened to him after he testified at the inquiry conducted by Mesquita at Port San Julián. He probably replaced the

murdered Elorriaga as master of the *San Antonio*, and was aboard that ship
when Gomes seized it and sailed it back to Spain. Barthélemy Prieur of the
Santiago had transferred to the *Trinidad* after the former was wrecked in
Patagonia.[5] Miguel de Rodas of the *Victoria* served as that ship's master
after the death of Baltazar Palla. Juan de Acurio of the *Concepción* was transferred to the *Victoria* shortly after the flight from Cebu.

The records of the Casa de Contratación do not list the duty changes
among the personnel of Magellan's fleet during the voyage. The changes
indicated above are deduced from the times and places of death of ships'
officers and the availability of replacements. Altogether, twenty-six crew
members were abandoned to their fate at Cebu. Among them were three
captains: Serrano, Barbosa, and Goes. Also abandoned were the interpreter, Enrique, the chaplain, Valderrama, two ship's clerks, a cooper, a
caulker, and a gunner. The rest were supernumeraries and able seamen,
". . . the flower and cream of the fleet."[6]

With all its captains gone, the senior officer, Lopes Carvalho, a pilot,
took command. Taking stock of their situation, the survivors realized that
there were not enough men left to operate three ships.[7] Since the *Concepción* was in the worst condition, they decided to scuttle it. After distributing
its crew, usable gear, and cargo between the other two ships, it was burned
to the waterline off the southwest point of Bohol Island. Nothing remained
to remind the islanders of the inglorious defeat of Spanish arms.[8]

Lopes Carvalho was elected captain of the *Trinidad* and captain general
of the reduced, two-ship fleet. Gonzalo Gómez de Espinosa was entrusted
with the command of the *Victoria*. His former rank, master-at-arms, was
comparable to that of a modern marine warrant officer. That he should
have gotten the nod over Juan Sebastián del Cano, the experienced master
of the scuttled *Concepción*, is curious, for Cano clearly outranked Espinosa.
Apparently the crews had not forgotten nor forgiven Cano's part in the mutiny at Port San Julián. On the other hand, they placed a high value on
Espinosa's strong, steadfast character.[9] Juan Bautista de Polcevera, a Genoese, remained master of the *Trinidad*.

When the two ships set sail again about May 3 or 4, they took a southwesterly course, coasting along an island that Pigafetta called "Panilongon,
where black men like those in Etiopia [sic] live." Most authors have identified this as the small island southwest of Bohol presently named Panglao.
However, Albo stated that it was west of the southernmost point of Cebu.
If he was correct, Panilongon was the island of Negros, on which there is a
population of dark-skinned negritos.[10]

By this time, the supplies of non-perishable food on the two ships were
nearly exhausted. The crews had eaten most of the rice they had helped to

harvest at Limasawa, and were anxious to replenish their supply. As the two ships sailed southwest into the Sulu Sea, the highlands of the Zamboanga Peninsula of Mindanao, capped by the 2,844-foot Mount Silingan, hove into view. At 8° N, they anchored in a small bay with two tiny islands to the northeast.[11] This fits the area north of Duluguin Point on the west side of the Zamboanga Peninsula. The inhabitants, who proved friendly, called their region *Quipit*.

Their rajah, whose name was Calanao, did not hesitate to come aboard the *Trinidad*. He pledged everlasting friendship with the Spaniards and offered to supply all the foodstuffs they needed.[12] A grateful Carvalho gave him the shallop that had belonged to the *Concepción*, and when Calanao went ashore to arrange delivery of the promised foodstuffs, Pigafetta went along to sightsee. Traveling up a river in a barangay to the region's principal town, Pigafetta was given a supper of rice and salt fish washed down with the usual palm wine, and a bed for the night. The next day he walked about and observed many items made of gold. He was shown a valley in which, so his guide told him, raw gold was ". . . as abundant as the hairs of their heads." Since they had no iron for digging, the islanders didn't bother with the gold, and left it undisturbed. On the return journey downriver, Pigafetta saw three men hanging from a tree, evildoers and robbers, he was told. His hosts informed him that to the northwest lay ". . . a large island called Lozon, where six or eight junks belonging to the Lequian people go yearly."[13]

When the islanders delivered the promised foodstuffs to the ships, the Spaniards were dismayed to note that it was all perishable—there was no rice. Carvalho had traded the valuable shallop for food that would not keep. However, Calanao was able to provide sailing directions for Brunei, at the time a major port of call on the trade routes from China and the Ryukyus to Indochina, Malacca, and the islands of the Malay Archipelago. The Spaniards had first learned of the wealth of this bustling sultanate on the island of Borneo from the people of Cebu, and in Quipit there were merchants from Malacca and Java who asserted that Brunei was rich in gold and spices.[14] Intrigued, Carvalho decided to investigate, probably hoping to find there native pilots able to guide him to the Moluccas.

Sailing west-southwest across the Sulu Sea, the two ships arrived at Cagayan Sulu, due east of the northernmost point of Borneo. It was inhabited, wrote Pigafetta, by Muslims banished from Brunei, who regarded the Spaniards as gods[15] (an odd statement, since Muslims are monotheists). According to the account of "The Genoese Pilot," the inhabitants of Cagayan Sulu were hostile. Not only did they refuse to trade with the Spaniards, they fired arrows and blowgun darts at them.[16]

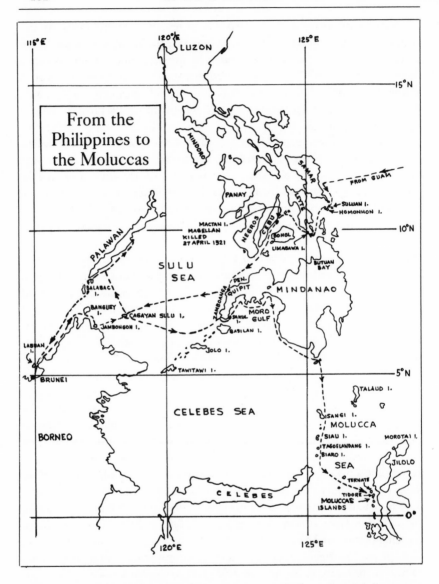

The encounter at Cagayan Sulu was not entirely unfruitful, however. From some source there, the Spaniards learned that food could be obtained at Palawan, a large, lush island to the northwest.[17] They set sail at once, intending to stay at that island, no matter what the cost, until they had reprovisioned their two ships.

About the end of May or the beginning of June, after raising the southern part of Palawan, the *Trinidad* and the *Victoria* sailed northeast along the island's east coast. At one place they saw a crowd of natives on the shore; a boat crew rowed toward the beach but pulled up short, fearful that the islanders might prove hostile hosts. At this point, Juan de Campos, who had been steward of the *Concepción*, offered to go ashore alone. He is reported to have said that some means must be found for procuring food, ". . . and that if the natives killed him, it would be of little consequence, for God would take pity on his soul."[18] Rowing ashore alone in a skiff, without the benefit of an interpreter he managed to convey to the natives that the Spaniards wanted to buy rice and would pay well for it. As soon as they understood, the island people set about gathering surplus rice, a task that took all night; the next morning, a substantial amount was delivered to the ships.

Their friendly hosts told them that a short distance to the north was a port where the Spaniards could obtain more food. The two ships set sail again and soon anchored off a town with a good harbor, probably at the site of the town now called Puerto Princesa.[19] There they were well received— Carvalho concluded a peace treaty with the local rajah—and were able to purchase goats, pigs, and a large quantity of rice. Pigafetta described the area as very healthful, and enjoyed himself wandering about observing the local customs, one of them cock fighting, still very popular in the Philippines.

While the ships were taking on supplies, there appeared a Christian negro named Bastiam (Sebastian) who knew a few words of Portuguese.[20] He claimed to know the route to Brunei and agreed to pilot the Spanish ships there. When the ships were ready to depart on June 21, however, he failed to show up. As luck would have it, just as the ships were getting underway, a junk entered the harbor. Desperate for guidance through the reef-studded archipelago, the Spaniards overpowered the junk and kidnapped three of its Muslim seamen, two of them pilots.

Retracing their route along the coast of Palawan, the *Trinidad* and *Victoria* sailed past the southern end of the island into Balabac Strait. Sailing west, they passed between the islands of Balabac and Banguey, and soon the highlands of North Borneo came into view. Heaving the lead continuously as they threaded their way through the numerous reefs, the two ships followed the coast to the southwest. On July 8 they were off the small island of Labuan at the northern entrance to Brunei Bay,[21] but were unable to enter against headwinds.

The next day the wind shifted and the *Trinidad* and *Victoria* sailed into the harbor. As they anchored in front of the port of Brunei, a fleet of pirogues swarmed out to greet them. Brunei was a busy, populous city. The buildings along the waterfront were built on pilings, and the harbor was teeming with water traffic. Junks lay at anchor, waiting their turn to load or unload cargoes at dockside. It was obvious to the Spaniards that this was no harbor full of savages to be intimidated and exploited; it was the bustling commercial center of a highly civilized kingdom or principality. Wisely, the Spaniards freed the two Muslim pilots and the seaman they had kidnapped at Palawan, sending them ashore with a message for the sultan announcing the arrival of two Spanish ships with greetings from the Holy Roman Emperor.[22]

The next day, the Spanish ships were welcomed by two pirogues and an ornately decorated prau with two gilded dragon's heads on its bow and stern, carrying musicians and drummers. A white-and-blue banner surmounted with peacock feathers flew from a staff at the bow. On board the prau were eight elderly emissaries from the sultan with presents for the Spaniards, including an assortment of foodstuffs and three jugs of arrack, a distilled rice wine that Pigafetta reported to be ". . . so strong it intoxicated many of our men."[23]

Six days later, three elaborately decorated praus with musicians playing gongs and drums circled the Spanish ships. After the serenade, the sultan's emissaries presented the Spaniards with more gifts and a permit to take on wood and water and to trade at their pleasure. Fearful that these strange visitors might be advance scouts for a Portuguese fleet, the sultan was anxious to know their country of origin and the object of their visit. The seizure and sack of Malacca had spread fear of the Portuguese throughout the China seas. The sultan feared that his city might become the next target of the terrible "Franks."

The Spaniards sought to allay the sultan's fears by assuring him that they were not Portuguese, but Spanish, representatives of an emperor who desired only peace. Accordingly, Gómez de Espinosa, Pigafetta, and five others were selected to carry Emperor Charles's greetings to the sultan. Although he had been elected squadron commander, Lopes Carvalho, a Portuguese, wisely did not accompany the delegation.

We ". . . entered their prau," wrote Pigafetta, "bearing a present to their king, which consisted of a green velvet robe made in the Turkish manner, a violet velvet chair, five yards of red cloth, a cap, a gilded drinking glass, a covered glass vase, three writing tablets and a gilded writing case. For the queen, three yards of yellow cloth, a pair of silvered shoes and a silver needle case full of needles." There were other presents for the lesser functionaries of the sultan's court.

After a ride of three or four miles in the prau, the delegation reached the city docks, where they were met by an escort with two huge elephants, on the backs of which were canopied howdahs draped with silk. The bedazzled Spaniards, who never before had traveled in such grand style, rode to the governor's house on the elephants. Preceding them were twelve bearers carrying their gifts for the sultan in large porcelain jars. When they reached the governor's house, they were treated to a sumptuous dinner, and that night they slept on cotton mattresses lined with taffeta, with sheets of fine Cambay cloth.

The next day at noon Pigafetta and his companions rode to the sultan's palace on the elephants. The streets along the way were guarded by men armed with swords, spears, and shields. Surrounding the palace was a masonry wall with fortress-like towers on which Pigafetta counted fifty-six bronze and six iron cannon.

Like most of the other buildings in Brunei, the palace was erected on stilts. Climbing a ladder, the Spaniards entered a large hall filled with Malay noblemen wearing silk sarongs embroidered with cloth of gold. Their fingers were heavy with jewelled rings, and the golden hafts of their daggers were studded with pearls and precious stones. The Spanish delegation was invited to be seated on a carpet next to the jars with the presents they had brought. At one end of the main hall was a smaller room elevated above the level at which they were seated. Adorned with silken wall hangings and brocaded curtains, it was an anteroom to the sultan's quarters. One of the curtains was drawn aside, and through a window at the back, the sultan, whose name was Siripada, could be seen with one of his young sons, chewing betel nut. Behind him were a number of women servants, all daughters of nobles.

The chief of protocol told the Spaniards that they must not speak directly with the sultan. "If we wished anything," wrote Pigafetta, "we were to tell it to [the chief of protocol], so that he could communicate it to [a person] of higher rank." He in turn would relay the message to an official stationed in the anteroom, ". . . and this man would communicate it by means of a speaking tube through a hole in the wall to one who was inside with the king."

Before they were allowed to communicate with the sultan, the Spaniards were instructed how to perform a peculiar ritual required by court protocol. Facing the sultan, they had to make obeisance by clasping their hands above their heads, raising first one foot and then the other, and then blow kisses toward the sultan. To Pigafetta, accustomed to the prostrations, genuflections, and ring kissing of Vatican protocol, this probably did not seem too unusual. One can readily imagine, however, the tough, crusty Gómez de Espinosa muttering under his breath at having to perform such a ridiculous maneuver in public. Perhaps the elephant rides made it worthwhile for him.

Once the proper obeisances were made, the gifts the Spaniards had brought were shown to the sultan. As each was displayed before him, the haughty ruler acknowledged it by only the slightest of nods. Each of the Spaniards was given a bolt of brocaded silk with a design worked in gold thread. Refreshments spiced with cloves and cinnamon were served. Then, the curtains shielding the sultan's quarters were closed; the interview had ended.

The Spanish delegation rode back to the governor's house on elephants, accompanied by seven porters bearing the sultan's gifts. When they arrived, nine more porters appeared, carrying large wooden trays with a feast of thirty-two courses with meats, poultry, fish, rice, and fruit, for which gold spoons were provided. Pigafetta reported that after each mouthful of food, they sipped distilled rice wine from small, porcelain cups the size of an egg. After spending the night in luxurious beds, they again mounted the elephants to ride to the waterfront where two praus waited to return them to their ships.[24]

For about three weeks the Spaniards were free to roam about Brunei exchanging trade goods for much-needed provisions. Two Greek sailors deserted and became Muslims.[25] Relations suddenly turned sour when three armed junks entered the harbor and anchored near the Spanish ships, blocking their exit. Suspecting that this might be part of a plot to seize his ships, armaments, and trade goods, Carvalho placed his crews on alert. His suspicions were further aroused when three crewmen, sent ashore to procure beeswax for caulking, failed to return.[26] One of the three was Carvalho's young son by his Tupi Indian mistress in Brazil.

On the morning of July 29, a fleet of more than 200 pirogues left the port of Brunei and headed straight for the Spanish ships. Fearful of being trapped, the Spaniards hoisted their anchors, losing one of them in their haste. They opened fire on the junks blocking their exit from the harbor, killing many Malay crewmen. Two of the junks ran aground trying to escape the devastating fire of the Spanish cannon; the Spaniards captured the other, took it in tow, and started to leave the harbor. Carvalho intended to stop at a nearby island said to be a source of myrobalan (a valuable plant product used in dyeing and tanning), but a squall arose that night, sinking the junk in tow.[27] The next day, the Spaniards returned to the scene of the battle and overpowered the crew of one of the grounded junks. In two days of fighting, the Spaniards suffered but one casualty.[28]

On the captured junk was a young prince, the son of a rajah on Luzon. He was serving as naval commander for the Sultan of Brunei and had just returned from a successful campaign against Laut, an island off the southeast point of Borneo. The object of the expedition had been to punish the island's rajah, who recently had switched his allegiance from Brunei to Java.[29] In addition to the ninety men on the junk with the prince were five noblewomen, one with a two-month-old child.[30] The Spaniards took sixteen hostages, including the prince and three young women of exceptional beauty,[31] whom they planned to exchange for the crewmen held in custody ashore and for such ransom as the prince might bring. The women were to be taken to Spain and presented to the queen.

The plan might have worked, but bringing the women aboard was a mistake that never would have occurred under Magellan's command. Carvalho was not self-disciplined, nor did he put the safety of those under his command ahead of his own selfish whims. He outraged his crews by taking the young women to his quarters to serve as his personal harem, thus destroying their value as virgins to be exchanged for the hostages (including his own son) or carried to Spain to present to the queen. To make matters worse, he made a private deal with the Luzon prince, releasing him in return for an unspecified amount of gold (which Carvalho kept for himself) and the prince's promise to secure the return of the hostages.[32]

"When the Moro king heard how we treated the junks," wrote Pigafetta, "he sent us a message by one of our men who was ashore, to the effect that the praus had not come to do us harm, but that they were going to attack the heathens [non-Muslims living in a nearby settlement hostile to the sultan]. As proof of that statement, the Moros showed [us] some heads of men who had been killed, which they declared to be the heads of heathens. We sent a message to the king, asking him please to allow two of our men who were in the city for the purposes of trade and the son of Johan Carvaio, who had been born in the country of Verzin [Brazil], to come to us, but the king refused."[33]

The Spaniards waited two days for the return of the hostages, then sent the sultan another message saying that they would wait for two more days. When that period expired without result, they upped anchors and sailed away, leaving to their fate Domingo Barruti, an able seaman who had been promoted to clerk on the *Trinidad*, Gonzalo Hernández, a smith listed as a supernumerary (who had begun the voyage on the *Concepción*), Carvalho's little Brazilian son, and the two Greeks who had deserted, Mateo Gorfo (Corfu) and Juan Griego, both able seamen.[34]

After leaving Brunei Bay, the two ships sailed northeast along the coast of Borneo, searching for a safe haven where they could lay up their ships for repairs. Without an experienced local pilot, this proved a difficult task. Between Labuan Island at the mouth of Brunei Bay and Balambangan Island off the northern tip of Borneo is a maze of dangerous islets and reefs, among them Vernon Bank, Mangalum Island, and Big Bonanza Shoal. On an islet called Bilabon by Pigafetta, one of the ships grounded ". . . because of the carelessness of its pilot, but by the help of God we freed it." A much worse disaster was narrowly averted when "a sailor of that ship incautiously snuffed a candle into a barrel of gunpowder, but he quickly snatched it out without any harm."[35] Later, the Spaniards intercepted four praus headed for Brunei. As they gave chase in the shallops, the praus fled for cover among some islands. Three got away, but the Spaniards succeeded in capturing one laden with coconuts.[36] Then the *Trinidad* ran aground on a shoal off Cape Sampanmangio. It took four hours to get her off according to The Genoese Pilot, who also noted the 24-hour tidal cycle.[37]

On August 15 on a small island off the north coast of Borneo, they found a protected anchorage with a beach suitable for careening. They named the island Nuestra Señora de Agosto; Pigafetta called it Cimbonbon. It could have been the island now called Jambongon, which corresponds reasonably well to the sounds produced by an Italian reading of Pigafetta's spelling, and to its given latitude of 7° N.[38] The *Trinidad* and *Victoria* remained there 42 days. All hands, officers and seamen alike, pitched in to probe, repair, and caulk the worm-ridden hulls of the two ships, all that remained of Magellan's once proud fleet.

On September 21, Carvalho was deposed as captain general. The crews of both ships were disgusted with his immorality, poor leadership, and deficient piloting, and overwhelmingly supported a motion by the two surviving shipmasters, Juan Bautista Polcevera and Juan Sebastián del Cano, to remove him from command. "Seeing that he hadn't carried out the King's instructions," wrote Bautista, "we agreed, Sebastián del Cano and I, with the approval of the crews, to depose him from the post of captain general; we named Alonso [Gonzalo] Gómez de Espinosa captain of the *Trinidad*, Sebastián del Cano captain of the *Victoria*, and they charged me with the command of the fleet."[39] Cano, who had exercised nominal command of the *Victoria* since the scuttling of the *Concepción*, was also elected fleet treasurer. Martín Méndez, who had been the *Victoria*'s clerk, was promoted to fleet accountant.[40]

Discipline in the fleet was at least partially restored by the stern but highly respected Gómez de Espinosa. Under the quiet, capable supervision of Juan Bautista, the survivors succeeded in repairing their leaking ships, but suffered two more casualties. On September 1, Filiberto Godin, a gunner on the *Victoria*, died of wounds received in the Battle of Mactan. On September 16, Pedro Muguertegui, an apprentice seaman originally assigned to the *Concepción*, perished from an unknown cause.[41]

The ever-curious Pigafetta took note of some of the more interesting fauna and flora on the island, once confusing one for the other. He described a wild boar hunt in which the Spaniards captured a good-sized tusker by pursuing it in a ship's boat as it swam from one island to another. He saw crocodiles on both land and sea, and described the local fish and shellfish. A fish that interested him had ". . . a head like a hog and two horns," and probably was a trunkfish. He described a huge clam, undoubtedly a *Tridachna*, which yielded 44 pounds of meat.

By far his most amusing observation concerned trees ". . . which produce leaves which are alive when they fall, and walk. Those leaves are quite like those of the mulberry, but are not so long. On both sides, near the stem, which is short and pointed, they have two feet. They have no blood, but if one touches them they run away. I kept one for nine days in a box. When I opened the box, that leaf went round and round it. I believe those live on nothing but air."[42] In reality, these animated "leaves" were insects camouflaged to avoid being eaten by predators. It is not fair to make fun of the gullibility of the gentleman from Vicenza, however; he was not a trained naturalist, and his observations of the plants and wildlife of the Malay Archipelago antedated those of Alfred Russel Wallace by more than 300 years.

The repairs were completed by September 27, and the two ships set sail once more in search of the fabled Moluccas.[43] While morale had improved with the change of leadership, the strict discipline and sense of mission formerly provided by Magellan had eroded. Behaving like pirates, the Spaniards treated native seaborne commerce as fair game. Sailing north, away from the reef-bound coast of northern Borneo, they hailed a large junk headed for Palawan from Brunei and signaled it to strike sails. When the junk failed to respond, they captured and looted it. On board the junk was Tuan Maamud, a rajah from Palawan, and his brother, Guantyl. In return for their freedom, the Spaniards demanded four hundred measures of rice, twenty swine, twenty goats, and one hundred fifty fowl, to be delivered within a week. The rajah readily complied, delivering more than had been demanded, throwing in for good measure coconuts, bananas, sugar cane, and several jugs of palm wine. The gratified Spaniards released the hostages, returned their weapons, and presented the rajah with several bolts of cloth, banners, and robes. When they set sail again on October 7, they were loaded with fresh foodstuffs.[44] "We parted . . . as friends," noted Pigafetta.

Sailing eastward through the Sulu Sea, they sighted Cagayan Sulu,[45] then headed east by south toward Jolo, where they had been told were rich pearl fisheries. But headwinds forced them north of east toward the Zamboanga Peninsula of Mindanao. On the way, they passed a number of small islands (probably the Pilas Group), where Pigafetta noted the sea gypsies who lived their entire lives on boats.[46] Their descendants still do.

With a favorable wind, the two ships sailed east through Basilan Strait, where they bartered with a passing prau, exchanging two elaborately wrought knives obtained from Rajah Maamud for seventeen pounds of cinnamon, the valuable spice derived from the bark of a tree that grows abundantly in that region. The two ships anchored at the island of Sakul, which lies off the southeastern end of the Zamboanga Peninsula, and remained there several days while the Spaniards sought information about the route to the Moluccas. With the side trip to Brunei having come to such a sorry end, the new high command had given up on Magellan's quest for information about Lequios, the islands he had believed to be the fabled Tarshish and Ophir. They now eagerly sought the route to the Moluccas, the expedition's primary target.

While they have been much castigated by historians for resorting to piracy on this leg of their journey, it should be remembered that the two ships were traversing seas in which piracy was a way of life. The thousands of islands and islets of the vast archipelago provided convenient bases from which pirates preyed on the rich sea traffic between China and India. With their captain general, all their captains, and most of their pilots dead, feeling vulnerable and lost, they depended on superior armament to overpower junks that otherwise might have done the same to them.

Leaving Sakul Island, the two ships sailed northeast in search, wrote Pigafetta, ". . . of a large city called Maingdanao . . . so that we might gather information concerning Maluco." In a flat calm they encountered a large native vessel, but with no wind the two Spanish ships were unable to close with it. Two ship's boats were sent in pursuit, and a bloody fight erupted when they caught up. Although the Malays, armed with scimitars and shields, defended themselves vigorously, seven were killed and the rest taken prisoner.[47] Among the captives were several chiefs from Mindanao, one of whom gave the Europeans their first solid information about the location of the Moluccas. This individual, the brother of a rajah, claimed that he had been at the house of Francisco Serrão in Ternate.[48]

This intelligence prompted the Europeans to change their course from northeast to southeast. Pigafetta provided a hopelessly scrambled itinerary of their progress east and south along the shores of the Moro Gulf. It is impossible to identify his place names with the current geographic nomenclature of that region. His fascination with the manners and customs of native peoples found vivid expression in his account of the cannibalism practiced by a tribe on Mindanao: ". . . near a river are found shaggy men who are exceedingly great fighters and archers. They use swords one *palmo* in length, and eat only raw human hearts with the juice of oranges or lemons."[49]

On October 27, the *Trinidad* and *Victoria* sailed eastward between

Tinaca Point, the southernmost promontory of Mindanao, and two small islands: Balut and Sarangani. In the latter was a small harbor where the two ships anchored. Among the curious local inhabitants who came to visit was an old man who claimed to know the way to the Moluccas; the Spaniards talked him and two friends into agreeing to guide them there, and promising to return the next day, he left the ship. When the old man failed to show up at sailing time, his two associates expressed their desire to leave, but Spaniards forced them to remain aboard and sailed away, followed by a fleet of pirogues filled with angry islanders. With a fresh wind astern, the two ships soon outdistanced their pursuers.[50]

Heading south through the Celebes Sea to Sangi Island, they sailed east between the latter and Karakelong Island, passing into the Molucca Sea. The wind dropped to a dead calm, and they were carried northward by the current. As they neared Sangi Island, one of the captive pilots and the brother of the rajah from Mindanao, the latter with his little son clinging to his back, leaped overboard and swam toward shore. The two adults made it, but the little boy slipped off his father's back and drowned.[51]

A headwind arose, making it difficult to tack past Sangi Island, but eventually the wind shifted and they were able to sail south by east. While passing Siau, Tagoelandang, and Biaro Islands to starboard,[52] the Spaniards suffered two more casualties. On the *Trinidad* on November 2, a gun blew up in the hands of the armorer, Pedro Sánchez, killing him. Two days later on the same ship, a gunpowder explosion killed Juan Bautista, a gunner[53] (not to be confused with Juan Bautista de Polcevera, the *Trinidad*'s master and, by his own account, now fleet commander).

After sailing past Biaro Island, the crews could see the mountains of Celebes off the starboard bow, whereupon the captive pilot ordered a course change to southeast. On November 6, 1521, they passed between Majoe and Tifore islands, where the Spaniards wanted to stop to take on water, but the pilot warned them that the inhabitants were ferocious and would attack them if they landed.[54] In the Moluccas, he said, the people were friendly, and the islands were not far away. He was correct. The tall peak of Ternate soon rose above the horizon; the principal target of Magellan's grand enterprise lay dead ahead.

19

ℳaluco

A*fter Ternate, the next peak to appear on the horizon was on* Tidore, the island immediately to its south. Two other islands then came into view. One of the native pilots informed the Spaniards that the island group before them was *Maluco*, the fabled Moluccas where clove trees grew in abundance,[1] along with nutmeg and ginger. Nearly 27 months had elapsed since Magellan's fleet had sailed from San Lúcar.[2] Of the five ships that set forth from Spain with 260 to 270 men, two ships with 107 men had survived to see the Spice Islands, more than halfway around the world from where they had started.[3]

Three hours before sunset on Friday, November 8, 1521, the *Trinidad* and *Victoria* sailed into the harbor of Tidore. Despite deliberately misleading information to the contrary obtained from Portuguese sources, they found good anchorage in twenty fathoms, conveniently close to shore. As the anchors were let go, both ships fired artillery salutes.

The longitudes reported by Albo for islands in the Moluccas were 190° 30' and 191° 45' *west* of the line of demarcation (more than 10° *west* of the extended line), clearly within the Portuguese hemisphere.[4] Albo must have determined these values by dead reckoning, using as a point of departure San Martín's astronomical fix at Homonhon. Pigafetta reported the longitude of the Moluccas as 19° *east* of the extended line of demarcation, in the Spanish hemisphere. This huge discrepancy suggests that one or the other of their records had been altered. It is conceivable that Pigafetta, with his connections at the Spanish court, could have been induced to fudge his records to support Spanish claims. Less likely to have done so was Albo, a Greek mariner who had scrupulously stayed out of fleet politics. An acting pilot for most of the voyage, he kept a meticulous record of his navigation. For him, professional pride was probably incentive enough to resist altering his records to suit the whims of Spanish diplomats. Albo's logbook, long buried in Spanish archives, did not come to light until the nineteenth century, when Martín Fernández de Navarrete included it in his collection of documents relating to Spanish voyages and discoveries in the 15th and 16th centuries.[5]

Notwithstanding testimony to the contrary given under oath by survivors of the voyage, Albo's log and a Portuguese extract from San Martín's notebooks indicate that when they sailed into the harbor of Tidore, the officers of the *Trinidad* and *Victoria* must have known that they had passed beyond the extended line of demarcation into Portuguese territory. But the knowledge did not deter them from seeking cordial relations with the rajah of Tidore and his allies, urging them to commit their island kingdoms to treaties of alliance with Spain.

On November 9, a prau bearing the rajah under a silken awning approached the Spanish ships. Eager to make a good impression, the Spaniards dispatched a delegation in one of the ship's boats to greet him. The rajah, Almanzor (Al Mansur), bade them welcome, telling them that some time ago he had dreamed that strange ships would come from far off; their arrival, he said, was a fulfillment of that prophetic dream. The Spaniards invited Almanzor and his entourage aboard the flagship, where they were honored and given presents. Almanzor then invited the Spaniards to go ashore as they pleased. He said, wrote Pigafetta, that we would be welcomed ". . . as if in our own houses."[6]

When they arrived, the Spaniards had expected to be greeted by Francisco Serrão, Magellan's former comrade-in-arms, who had been serving as military advisor to the rajah of Ternate. On inquiring about him, they learned that to promote peace, Serrão had forced Almanzor to give a daughter in marriage to Boleyse (Abdul Hussein), rajah of Ternate.

Almanzor resented Serrão's high-handed interference in his long-running dispute with his bitter rival on Ternate, and got even. Eight months before the arrival of the Spaniards, Serrão had come to Tidore to buy cloves. Inviting him to dine at the palace, Almanzor poisoned the flamboyant Portuguese adventurer, and Serrão died four days later, just as Magellan was approaching the Philippines.[7] By an odd coincidence, only seven weeks later Magellan too would die at the hands of a native prince who resented his interference in local politics. Ten days after Serrão died, Boleyse, his patron, was poisoned by his own daughter, wife of the rajah of Bachian (Batjan), with whom her father had quarreled. Boleyse died two days later.[8] Among the Moluccan princes, poisoning seems to have been as popular a political tactic as it was with the Borgias in Italy.

On Monday, November 11, two praus from Ternate approached the Spanish ships, their multiple tiers of oars dipping in cadence to the sound of gongs. On one was a son of Boleyse, a princely figure clad in a robe of red velvet, accompanied by Serrão's widow and her two sons. Fearful that entertaining the rival prince in the harbor of Tidore would offend Almanzor, the Spaniards sought the rajah's permission before inviting the prince aboard their ships, but the delay offended the prince, who ordered the praus to head back to Ternate. Anxious to repair the diplomatic damage, the Spaniards sent a boat after them with gifts for the prince. "He accepted them somewhat haughtily," wrote Pigafetta, "and departed at once."[9]

The encounter was not a total disaster, for on one of the praus was a Christian native who spoke Portuguese. He called himself Manuel, and said that he was a servant of Pedro de Lorosa, a Portuguese trader who had come to Ternate from Banda after the death of Serrão. Manuel accompanied the Spaniards back to their ships, where he explained that although the rajah of Tidore and the princes of Ternate were at odds, all of them were fed up with the Portuguese and would be willing to enter into an alliance with Spain. The Spaniards were delighted, and sent Manuel back to Ternate with a letter inviting Lorosa to visit them.

Like Magellan and Serrão, Lorosa had become disgusted with Portuguese officialdom. It had been sixteen years since his arrival in India, and the last ten had been spent in the islands east of Malacca, where he had been among the first Portuguese to arrive. It didn't take him long to respond to the invitation. On the afternoon of November 13, Lorosa visited the *Trinidad*, bringing the first news of Europe the crew had heard since the fleet sailed from the Canary Islands in October 1519.[10]

Lorosa told the Spaniards that a little less than a year before, a large Portuguese ship had arrived in Ternate from Malacca to take on a cargo of cloves. Its captain had told him that when King Manuel learned of the departure of Magellan's fleet from Spain, he dispatched two squadrons of Portuguese warships to intercept him. One sailed to the Cape of Good Hope to waylay Magellan there, should he choose to sail east to the Moluccas. The other headed for Cape Santa María at the mouth of the La Plata estuary, should Magellan go there in search of a westward passage.

When both squadrons failed to find Magellan, Manuel ordered Diogo Lopes de Sequeira, now commander of all Portuguese naval forces in India, to send six warships to intercept him in the Moluccas. With most of his warships already committed to a campaign against the Turks in the Red Sea, Sequeira was able to dispatch but one to the Moluccas; its commander, Francisco de Faria, unable or unwilling to take the big galleon through the dangerous reefs near Malacca against contrary winds, returned

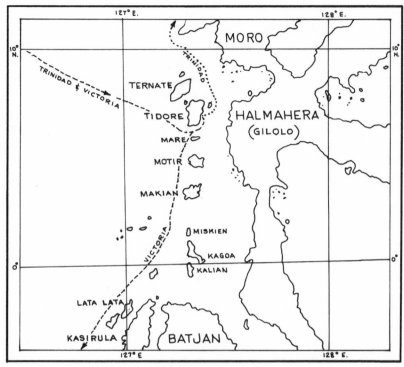

The Moluccas

to India.[11] Lacking warships to send, Sequeira learned that a small caravel and two junks were at Malacca preparing to sail for the Moluccas to purchase cloves, and he ordered their captains to be alert for intelligence. Even this feeble attempt to locate Magellan failed. While loading cloves on Batjan Island, the seven Portuguese who had sailed on the junks infuriated the local inhabitants by abusing their women. The outraged rajah had the Portuguese put to death, seized the two junks, and confiscated their cargoes. When the men on the caravel learned what had happened to their compatriots, they fled back to Malacca without a scrap of information about Magellan. A few days after they departed, the *Trinidad* and *Victoria* dropped anchor at Tidore.

Intrigued by Lorosa's news, and sensing his disillusionment with the manner in which the Portuguese were alienating the Moluccan rajahs, the Spaniards urged him to return with them to Spain. They assured him that his knowledge of the Moluccas and the spice trade would be invaluable in Spain, and that the Casa de Contratación would pay him well for his services. Lorosa readily agreed, promising to guide them to Banda, where they could load mace, a spice made from the inner layer surrounding nutmeg (the seed of a tree fruit), and then to Timor for a load of sandalwood.[12] "We plied him so well," noted Pigafetta, that Lorosa ". . . remained with us until three in the morning and told us many other things."

The next visitor to the Spanish ships was the elderly rajah of Gilolo (Halmahera), a friend and ally of the rajah of Tidore. Said to have been a great fighter in his youth, he was intensely curious about European weapons and how they were used; the Spaniards obliged him by staging a mock combat and by firing some of their artillery. The old geezer must have been impressed, for two days later on November 16, he returned and signed a treaty of alliance, pledging everlasting loyalty to the Spanish Crown. Within a month, similar treaties were signed with the rajah of Makian and the princes of Ternate.[13]

Meanwhile, the ever-curious Pigafetta enjoyed his trips ashore. He described the appearance, distribution and semiannual blossoming of clove trees and noted the details of the harvesting and processing of the cloves, which are dried flower buds from a tree of the myrtle family. The appearance, manners, customs, beliefs, and folklore of the people of Tidore and the neighboring islands fascinated him. The rajah of Tidore, he wrote, had a harem of 200 women, ". . . with a like number to serve them." No one was allowed to see them without the rajah's permission, and peeping Toms were put to death. His wives had provided Almanzor with eight sons and eighteen daughters. As a royal stud, however, he couldn't hold a candle to his aged ally on Gilolo, who had sired 600 children,[14] ". . . surpassing," it has been noted, "Augustus the Strong of Saxony, who boasted only 346 bastards."[15]

The behavior of European sailors toward native women was a persistent problem that all too often brought their expeditions to grief. Pigafetta noted that the men of Tidore ". . . are so jealous of their wives that they do not wish us to go ashore with our drawers exposed; for they assert that their women imagine that we are always in readiness."[16] Under the watchful eyes of Gonzalo Gómez de Espinosa, the former master-at-arms, now captain of the *Trinidad*, the Spaniards behaved themselves reasonably well on Tidore, and relations with their hosts remained cordial.

Although island boats came to the ships daily with bales of cloves, the Spaniards refused to trade for anything but food, preferring to negotiate directly with Almanzor for cloves. Their prudence paid off, for on November 24, the royal prau set forth from shore, gongs banging in cadence for the rowers as it steered toward the Spanish ships. After the din of the artillery salutes with which the Spaniards greeted the rajah had died down, Almanzor told them that many bales of cloves had been gathered and would soon be ready for loading.

Two days later, as the loading began, Almanzor returned to invite the Spaniards ashore for a feast. It was the custom on his island, he said, to so celebrate the loading of the first cloves. The Spaniards politely declined, remembering only too well what had happened on Cebu. They also had learned that three Portuguese employed by Franciso Serrão had been murdered at the spring where they had been filling their water casks.

The Spaniards told Almanzor that they would depart as soon as they finished loading the cloves. They would be honored, they said, if before their departure, he would visit them aboard their ships. He accepted the invitation at once, protesting that they must not leave so soon. On the verge of tears, he swore on the Holy Koran that he would always be faithful to the king of Spain, and begged them to stay. Still suspicious, but touched by his apparent sincerity, the Spaniards agreed to remain at Tidore another fortnight, and presented Almanzor with a royal standard and a banner bearing the royal seal to serve as symbols of his fealty to the Spanish sovereign. They also agreed to leave five men on Tidore to operate a trading post. Pigafetta wrote a rather tedious account of the daily trading and visits by officials from neighboring islands. As promised, Lorosa returned to the *Trinidad* with his wife and household goods, packed and ready for the long journey to Spain.

On December 9, new sails were bent to the yards, each new sail bearing a freshly painted cross of Santiago and the inscription: *Ésta es la enseña de nuestra buenaventura* (This is the sign of our good fortune). On December 17, as a parting gift, the Spaniards presented Almanzor with some harquebuses, several small cannon, and four barrels of gunpowder.[17] Noting that the two ships were very heavily laden, the observant rajah advised the Spaniards not to fire salutes as they departed; he feared the shock might spring open their strained seams. Unnoticed by the Spaniards, the ceremonial firing of artillery already had weakened the hull of the flagship.

Their holds crammed with cloves, the two ships were ready to sail on December 18. The *Victoria* got underway first and waited outside the harbor for the other ship, but the *Trinidad*'s anchor snagged, and as the crew struggled to free it, the strain opened a seam below the waterline. Water poured into the bilge at an alarming rate. Puzzled by the delay, the *Victoria* sailed back into the harbor to see what was wrong.

The *Trinidad* was partially unloaded and heeled over as far as possible in an attempt to slow the leak. The crew worked frantically all day at the pumps, but the water in the bilge continued to rise, ". . . rushing in as through a pipe," reported Pigafetta.[18] When Almanzor learned of the trouble, he sent a team of longhaired divers to help locate the leak; their hair was supposed to stream toward the leak as they approached it underwater. When it didn't work, the Spaniards realized that the ship would have to undergo extensive repairs.

It was already past mid-December and the monsoon was about to shift; the officers decided that the *Victoria* should take advantage of the last of the season's southeast winds to sail home by way of the Cape of Good Hope. The *Trinidad* would remain at Tidore until the necessary repairs were completed. By then, the northwest monsoon would have set in, blocking access to the Indian Ocean and the Cape route. Rather than wait many months for the monsoon to shift, the officers of the *Trinidad* conceived an audacious plan. When the repairs to their ship were completed, they would sail north in search of westerly winds to carry them to the west coast of the American landmass. Then they would follow the coast southward to the new Spanish settlement on the isthmus at Darien.[19]

Almanzor's reaction to the plight of the Spaniards couldn't have been more helpful. At first he expressed concern that no one would be going to Spain to carry news of him to the Emperor Charles. When told that the *Victoria* would soon leave for Spain ". . . in order not to lose the east winds . . .," he seemed relieved, and did all that he could to accommodate the stranded crew and help repair the *Trinidad*. He provided shelter for the sixty Europeans who would remain behind at Tidore, a warehouse for the cloves and other cargo, and 225 laborers to help the carpenters and caulkers repair the ship.[20]

Almanzor also dispatched two pilots to guide the *Victoria* as far as Timor, the point of departure from which Cano proposed to cross the Indian Ocean well south of Portuguese shipping lanes. What had happened to the *Trinidad* made him fearful of the consequences of overloading, so he ordered the *Victoria*'s cargo lightened. Sixty quintals of cloves were unloaded and taken to the warehouse provided by Almanzor. By the morning of December 21, 1521, the *Victoria* was ready to sail. Departure was delayed until midday to give the men staying behind with the *Trinidad* time to write last-minute letters to be carried to Spain. It is not clear when or how the final division of crews between the two ships was made; perhaps some were chosen by lot.

Forty-seven Europeans and thirteen Moluccans sailed with the *Victoria*. Among the Europeans were Francisco Albo, now its pilot, and Antonio Pigafetta, a supernumerary, both formerly of the *Trinidad*.[21] When the *Victoria* finally raised her anchors and stood out of the harbor, the men of the *Trinidad* followed as far as they could in their ship's boats. As wind filled the

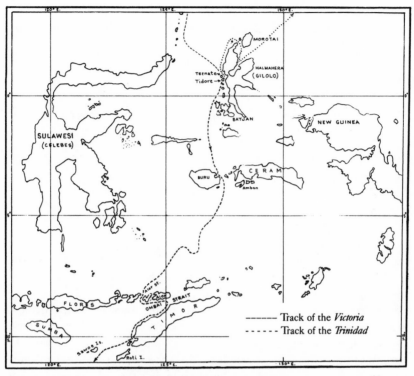

------- Track of the *Victoria*
- - - - - Track of the *Trinidad*

Departure from Tidore

Victoria's sails and she pulled slowly away, tears flowed and final farewells were shouted across the water. During their twenty-seven-month ordeal at sea and in strange lands with their alien, often hostile populations, the polyglot crews of the two remaining ships of Magellan's fleet had shared much together. There had been bitterness and suffering, but they had experienced the exaltation of knowing that in reaching the Moluccas by sailing west, they had done what no other men had done before. In the struggle to survive hostile surroundings, men in ships' crews and small military units often become linked by bonds of affection akin to love; the word "friendship" is inadequate to describe the depth of such affection. The last shouted farewells to the *Victoria* were made with the knowledge that they probably would never see one another again.

20

$\mathcal{T}$he Last Voyage of the *Trinidad*

 Although the workers provided by Almanzor were a great help, the *Trinidad*'s hull was in such poor condition it took nearly four months to complete the repairs. While the work proceeded, the rajah of Gilolo (the old warrior who had been so impressed by the martial skills of the Spaniards) paid them another visit, ostensibly to confirm his fealty to Emperor Charles but in fact to ask a favor: Would the Spaniards please loan him some artillery and several gunners to help him punish some rebels? To humor the old fellow, Espinosa obliged with two light cannon, a gunner, and two men-at-arms. The outcome of the punitive mission is not recorded, but apparently it was successful. The three soldiers returned to Tidore unharmed, and when the survivors of another Spanish expedition reached Gilolo in 1526, they were warmly welcomed.[1] On February 14, 1522, while the *Trinidad* was still undergoing repairs, João Lopes Carvalho, the pilot who served briefly as captain general, died.[2]

When the repairs were finally completed and reloading of the *Trinidad* had begun, the officers realized that the trade goods were taking up cargo space that might better be used for cloves. Accordingly, the bulk of these goods was left in storage at the trading post, around which the Spaniards erected an adobe wall cemented with mortar and reinforced inside and out with wooden beams. Artillery pieces salvaged from the *Santiago* and *Concepción* were set up to defend the walled compound. Juan de Campos, who had sailed from Spain as steward of the *Concepción*, and more recently served as clerk on the *Trinidad*, was put in charge, with Luis de Molino, Alonso de Cota, Diego Arias, and a Flemish gunner, Pedro, to assist him.[3]

Nearly five months after arriving at Tidore, the *Trinidad* was ready to sail. Gomez de Espinosa was captain; the master, Juan Bautista de Ponce-vera (assisted by León Pancaldo, a Genoese able seaman), assumed the piloting duties; and Diego Martín, whom Magellan had wanted as a master but was hired by the *Casa* as an able seaman, finally got his promotion when he filled Bautista's vacated position.[4]

The bold decision to cross the Pacific from west to east was inspired by the knowledge that in 1519, on the Pacific side of the Isthmus of Panama, Andres Niño and Gil González de Ávila had been building ships to explore Balboa's Great South Sea. Having crossed that sea in southern and near-equatorial latitudes, Espinosa and his pilots were aware of its immense width, but their ideas about its configuration in the northern hemisphere were derived from the guesswork of European mapmakers, who imagined that Asia was connected to the American landmass. The *Trinidad*'s officers reasoned that if they sailed far enough north, they would encounter west-erly winds like those of the North Atlantic, and these would carry them to the eastern shore. They estimated the mid-latitude width of the ocean to be 1,800 to 2,000 leagues (5,400 to 6,000 nautical miles).[5]

Unfortunately they knew nothing of the wind regime in the Philippine Sea, where between January and June the monsoon flowing out of the high-pressure system over Central Asia blows from the northeast. The westerly monsoon of the Moluccas, which commenced soon after the de-parture of the *Victoria*, would carry the *Trinidad* only as far as the Philippine Sea, and there it would run head on into the northeast monsoon.

With fifty-four men in her crew and about fifty tons of cloves and a small quantity of European trade goods in her hold, the *Trinidad* sailed from Ti-dore on April 6, 1522.[6] Her first stop was on the west coast of Gilolo, where the crew purchased fresh food. Sailing northward, they rounded the island's terminal cape and headed south through Morotai Strait to Kau Bay, where they stayed eight or nine days, buying pigs, goats, chickens, and co-conuts.[7]

On April 20, the *Trinidad* sailed from the bay and headed east by north. The light westerly winds astern soon yielded to the northeast monsoon, and intermittent headwinds steadied and became stronger as the northeast trade wind reinforced the monsoon. Realizing they had entered the trade-wind belt, the pilots ordered a change of course, setting the ship on a northerly tack. On May 3, the *Trinidad* spotted two small islands at 5° N latitude, probably Pulo Ana and Merir of the Sonsorol Group southwest of Palau. From this point, they alternated between easterly and northerly tacks. Sailing past the western Carolines, they sighted fourteen islands be-tween 10° and 20° N (probably in the Ulithi Group), where Espinosa noted ". . . small, naked folk . . . the color of the people of the Indies." The language of these islanders was unintelligible to the Spaniards, and they had no surplus food to trade.[8]

On June 11, after a month of battling northeast headwinds, the *Trinidad* sighted another island, one of the northern Marianas. When they dropped anchor there, the islanders swarmed aboard, just as they had at Guam sixteen months before. Having learned from bitter experience, this time the Spaniards took pains not to offend them. One of the islanders, who seemed knowledgeable, agreed to accompany them as a pilot.[9]

With the northern hemisphere moving into summer, the prevailing winds shifted from northeast to east, and above 20° N they continued to shift, first on, then aft of the starboard beam, as the ship held its northeasterly course. The Japan Current accelerated their progress, but the Asiatic mainland failed to materialize to port as the pilots had expected. They were east of Japan, and there were no more islands along their course. With their fresh food exhausted or rotted, the crew had nothing but rice to eat.

As they climbed into ever higher latitudes in search of westerly winds, the temperature dropped. Lacking suitable clothing the men suffered from the cold, and in addition to the inevitable scurvy, they began to succumb to an unfamiliar malady. Seeking its cause, the men cut open the cadaver of Juan Gonzalez, a caulker who had died after exhibiting symptoms of the disease, and found a parasite in his gut.[10]

East of Hokkaido (the northernmost of Japan's main islands), the *Trinidad* was struck by a severe storm, perhaps a typhoon passing to their south, that blew for five days with a fury so great that both the fore and after castles were carried away, the mainmast was broken in two places, and the sails were ripped to tatters. The storm subsided as suddenly as it had struck, but after it passed they were again confronted by headwinds.[11]

The men saw seals and tuna in abundance, but were too weakened by hunger, disease, and cold to try to catch them. From the courses steered and the pilots' estimate of 1,300 leagues run from the Moluccas, the *Trinidad* appears to have reached a point in the North Pacific 43° N and 165° E of Greenwich.[12] With the ship badly crippled by the storm and the men so weak they could barely work it, Espinosa and the pilots saw the futility of continuing to sail northeast into colder and stormier weather. Hoping that warmth and fresh food would restore the crew's health, the officers decided to return to the northern Marianas.

After sailing southwest for about twenty days, they sighted an island just after sunset, but not wishing to risk a landfall in the dark, they hove-to offshore during the night. In the morning they searched unsuccessfully for an opening in the reef, whereupon the native pilot made them understand there was a suitable anchorage at another island nearby. Finding it twenty leagues farther south, they experienced some difficulty with the reef but finally anchored safely in the lagoon. In the records of the Casa, the island first sighted is listed as "Mao," and its latitude as 20° N. It probably was Maug Island in the northern Marianas; the anchorage could have been at Agrihan. A contemporary Spanish historian placed it north of "Botaha" (Rota), which suggests Saipan,[13] but neither the description nor the latitude fit that large, well-watered island.

The Micronesian pilot went ashore and soon reappeared with two men carrying sugar cane and fresh fruit. Espinosa dispatched two of his healthiest crewmen to reconnoiter the island; they reported that it was small, contained no rivers or streams, and its human population numbered no more that forty. Dissatisfied, Espinosa went ashore to see for himself, discovering enough potable water among some rocks to fill fifteen water casks.[14] Since the island's resources were meager, the ship's officers decided to return to Gilolo. Unwilling to suffer further hardship, four crewmen fled from the ship with the native pilot; Espinosa was able to coax one of them back, but three remained behind. In September 1526, one of them, Gonzalo de Vigo, was found on Saipan by the Loaisa expedition. The other two had been killed by natives. Vigo sailed with his rescuers to Mindanao, making himself useful as an interpreter. On one occasion, he saved a shore party from ambush, and later accompanied the expedition to the Moluccas. In February 1534, when the expedition's survivors returned to Spain, Gonzalo de Vigo remained at Ternate.[15]

The voyage from the Marianas to Gilolo took six weeks, and the death rate among the scurvy-ridden crew was appalling. After two weeks, survivors were pitching overboard at least one body each day. By the time they reached Gilolo, the rate had increased to two a day. Of the fifty-four European crew members who sailed from Tidore on the *Trinidad*, thirty-three perished.[16] Casualties were highest in the lower ranks;[17] exhaustion and exposure to cold made the seamen more vulnerable than when they had sailed westward across the Pacific in fine weather with a following wind. Whether the scant rations were shared equally by officers and seamen is open to question. One would like to think so, but given the nature of hierarchies, it is unlikely.

After raising the island of Gilolo, the *Trinidad* approached from the northeast. Espinosa and the pilot probably intended to sail to Kau Bay, but were thwarted by a flat calm and a strong offshore current. Turning north through Morotai Strait, they managed to round the north cape of Gilolo and sail southward along the island's west coast. Off a place called Zamafo,[18] they encountered a boat manned by friendly inhabitants, some of whom they knew from their previous visit. The Spaniards learned that fifteen days after their departure from Tidore, a Portuguese fleet of seven ships, commanded by Antonio de Brito, had arrived at Ternate.

In Java, Brito had learned from junks arriving from Banda that two Spanish ships had been at Tidore. His suspicion that they were Magellan's was confirmed when Alonso de Cota was captured at Gorong Island, east of Banda. Cota, a Genoese, was one of the five crewmen from the *Trinidad* left to operate the *factoría* on Tidore, and had gone to Gorong to investigate trading opportunities.[19] When Brito arrived with his fleet at Ternate, his first order of business was to send a deputy to Almanzor to demand an explanation for the presence of a Spanish *factoría* on Tidore. Almanzor responded that he had dealt with the Spaniards only because they threatened him; renouncing his pact with Spain, he swore everlasting fealty to the king of Portugal. Several days later, Brito dispatched an armed contingent to Tidore to seize the Spanish *factoría*. Of the four remaining Spaniards, Juan de Campos and Diego Arias were captured; Pedro, the Flemish gunner, had died, and Luis Molino had gone to Moro (a part of Gilolo). The Portuguese demolished the *factoría* and confiscated its contents.[20]

The *Trinidad* had only one small anchor remaining and was in danger of dragging aground and breaking up. With his men so weak that only seven could keep their feet to work the ship, Espinosa resolved to request help from the Portuguese. He dispatched Bartolome Sanchez, the ship's clerk, to Ternate in a canoe manned by cooperative Gilolo islanders. Sanchez carried a letter to Brito from Espinosa explaining the plight of his men and imploring the Portuguese commander to send a caravel with provisions and anchors.[21]

When Sanchez arrived in Ternate, Brito first threw him in jail and then, knowing the Spaniards were too weak to go anywhere, settled down for a satisfying wait. After several days, he sent a shallop with Simón de Abreu, a naval officer, and Duarte Resende, who was to establish a Portuguese *factoría* on Ternate, to Gilolo with orders for Espinosa to surrender his ship. Following the shallop were Dom Garcia Manrique in a pinnace, and a caravel carrying a military contingent led by Gaspar Gallo; aboard the caravel was a prince of Ternate who boasted that he would consider it an honor should the Portuguese let him finish off the last of the Spaniards.[22]

When it appeared to Espinosa that Brito would not send help, he got enough of his crew on their feet to raise the small anchor, and moved the ship south to a better anchorage at a place called Benaconora.[23] When the Portuguese found them, they were repelled by the pestilential stench aboard the ship. Sick, emaciated men lay about the decks, many without the strength to move. The Portuguese took possession of the *Trinidad*,

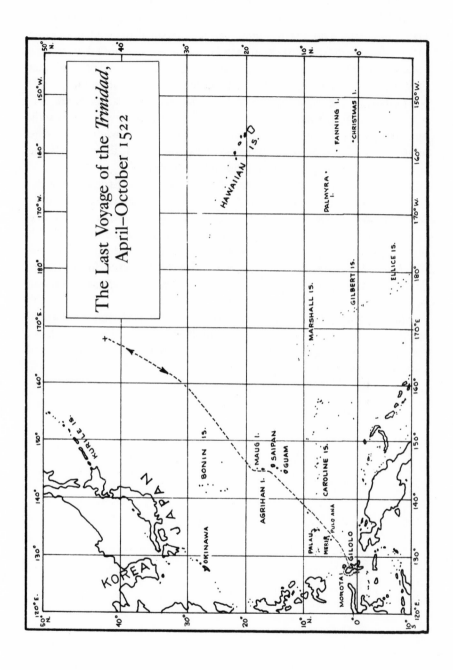

The Last Voyage of the *Trinidad*,
April–October 1522

confiscating its books, papers, charts, navigational equipment and light artillery and even stripping the crew of their personal belongings, leaving them only the tattered clothes on their backs. When Espinosa demanded a notarized list of everything taken from His Majesty's ship, he was told that they would ". . . give him the list when he was hanging from a yardarm!"[24]

The Portuguese took the *Trinidad* to Talangami, an islet between Ternate and Tidore. Espinosa and those of the ship's crew who could walk were put ashore on the islet and later taken to Ternate where they were imprisoned. The next day the *Trinidad* was moved to Ternate, and the crewmen too feeble to move were taken to a "hospital."[25]

At the Portuguese fort where they were incarcerated, Espinosa and the crew from the *Trinidad* found three of the men who had remained on Tidore to operate the *factoría*. The Portuguese sent a message to Luis Molino at Moro, offering safe conduct if he would come to Ternate to speak with his boss, Espinosa; when he showed up, Molino was seized and imprisoned with the others. They were all put to work constructing fortifications. The *Trinidad*'s anchor cable parted in a storm and the ship grounded and broke up; her timbers and cannon were salvaged for use at the fort. Of the twenty-one survivors of the last voyage of the *Trinidad*, only four would ever return to Spain. Pedro de Lorosa, the Portuguese trader who had cast his lot with the *Trinidad* rather than the *Victoria*, was declared a traitor and publicly beheaded.[26]

21

$\mathcal{T}$he World Encompassed

The Victoria *sailed from Tidore at midday, December 21,* 1521, guided by two pilots provided by Almanzor to lead them to Timor, the point of departure for the planned crossing of the Indian Ocean. At Mare, a small island near Tidore, they stopped briefly to take on firewood. As previously arranged by Almanzor, four canoes delivered the firewood alongside, taking less than an hour to load it aboard.[1] Heading south-southwest, the *Victoria* sailed past Motir and Makian. Albo located the former directly on the equator at a longitude of 191° 45'. Measured from the Tordesillas Treaty line west of the Azores, this placed the Moluccas west of the extended line of demarcation.[2]

Sailing southwest, the *Victoria* kept Batjan and Obi islands to port, then headed south with the Sula Islands to starboard. Guided by the Moluccan pilots, the ship sailed to an anchorage at Buru Island, where they purchased pigs, goats, domestic fowl, fresh fruit, and vegetables.[3] Leaving Buru, they passed through Manipa Strait with Ambon Island to port, and steered south-southwest into the Banda Sea. On New Year's Day their course was still southwest, with Ambon well astern. The pilots chose Alor Strait (between Pantar and Lomblen Islands) for the passage from the Flores into the Savu Sea.[4]

In the Savu Sea the *Victoria* was struck by a violent storm blowing from the southwest. Scudding before it, they fought to keep from being driven aground on the islands to the north. As usual, the crew prayed to the Holy Virgin for protection, vowing pilgrimages to her shrines. Although the ship was damaged by the storm, the *Victoria* found a safe anchorage at Ombai (Alor) Island, where they stayed fifteen days, repairing the ship, trading, and replenishing their stores of fresh food. For a pound of old iron, the Alor islanders were happy to give fifteen pounds of pepper or wax. Pigafetta wrote that the natives were naked savages who ate human flesh, a bit of local color that probably did not apply to the entire population. On Ombai, Cano hired an elderly pilot to help guide them to Timor.[5] Could he have been a cannibal?

Whatever his dietary predilections, the old fellow had his fun with Pigafetta, whose insatiable curiosity about the islands they were sailing past made him fair game for the tall tales with which old salts the world over like to regale gullible landlubbers. One beauty, duly recorded by Pigafetta, concerned a nearby island with a race of men only as tall as the length of a man's forearm. The ears of these diminutive folk, the old pilot averred, were so long they slept enfolded in them; one serving as a mattress pad, the other as a blanket.[6]

The *Victoria* left Ombai Island on January 25 and sailed south across Ombai Strait to the Island of Timor, where Pigafetta went ashore alone at a small village to negotiate for foodstuffs. The chief was willing to sell cattle, pigs, and goats, but demanded an exorbitant price. Desperate to augment their food stores before sailing into the Indian Ocean, the Spaniards kidnapped the headman of another village and ransomed him for six water buffaloes, ten pigs, and ten goats. For three weeks they coasted westward along the north shore of Timor, while the native pilots filled Pigafetta's ears with a potpourri of tall tales mixed with geographic, political, and economic facts and fancy concerning the Indonesian Archipelago and the coastal lands of Southeast Asia. The gentleman from Vicenza diligently recorded many of these stories, making little effort to discriminate fact from fancy. Typical of the latter was the story of a bird so large it could carry a buffalo or an elephant in its claws. Called *garuda* by Pigafetta's Malay-speaking informants, it probably was the roc (*rukh*) of the Sinbad legend.

When asked about Java, the most powerful kingdom in the archipelago, the pilots told Pigafetta about the practice of suttee, in which wives sacrificed themselves on the funeral pyres of their husbands. They also mentioned the Javanese variation of *palang*. On Limasawa, Pigafetta had seen young swains wearing golden spurs as phallic ornaments. On Java, they wore tiny bells instead, and he was told that the women delighted in hearing the little bells ringing inside of them.[7]

On Timor, Pigafetta noted the prevalence of "the evil of St. Job" (also called "the Portuguese disease"). He was referring to syphilis, but must have been mistaken, since that disease is not believed to have reached the islands of the Malay Archipelago until late in the sixteenth century.[8] What he saw was probably leprosy. By dampening the ardor of the *Victoria*'s sailors for the local women, its ugly symptoms probably spared the expedition further disastrous encounters with outraged islanders.

One night as the *Victoria* lay off the north shore of Timor, Martín de Ayamonte, an apprentice seaman, and Bartolomé de Saldaña, a cabin boy, deserted by swimming ashore.[9] This incident may have given rise to the stories of a brawl or mutiny on the *Victoria* at Timor.[10] Probably the two young crewmen were simply afraid they would not survive another trans-oceanic voyage.

Sailing westward along the north shore of the island, the *Victoria* encountered a Luzon junk taking on a cargo of sandalwood. The aromatic wood, which grows abundantly on Timor, was as much prized in the Orient as it was in Europe. Cano is said to have brought a sample of it to Spain in the *Victoria*.[11]

On February 8, the *Victoria* headed into the Indian Ocean from a port near the western end of Timor (Kupang, perhaps).[12] On February 10 she was still in the Savu Sea, drifting westward in a flat calm; at last, on February 13, with the islands of the Sawoe Group in view, a fresh wind arose and filled her sails. As the islands faded into the distance astern, the little ship nosed into the ocean called *Laut Kidol* (South Sea) by the Javanese.[13] "We took our course," Albo wrote in his diary, "to the Cape of Good Hope, and went WSW." Their course lay well south of Java, Sumatra, and the sailing routes commonly used by the Portuguese.

Sailing alternately south and west through the region dominated by the southeast trade wind, they entered the high-pressure cell over the South Indian Ocean and began to encounter headwinds, making progress to the west increasingly difficult. On March 18, while Albo was taking the sun's altitude, ". . . we saw a very high island, and we went towards it to anchor, and we could not fetch it; and we struck the sails and lay to until the next day, and the wind was west; and we made another tack to the north under storm sails; and this was on the 19th, and we could not take the sun; we were east and west with the island, and it is in 38° to the south, and it appears that it is uninhabited, and it has no trees at all, and it has a circumference of about six leagues."[14]

Since finding an anchorage seemed unlikely at this forbidding, apparently barren island (which we now know as Amsterdam), the *Victoria* continued on its course toward the Cape of Good Hope. To gain plenty of sea room for doubling the Cape (34° 21' S), Cano beat west-southwest to 42° 30' S against the prevailing westerlies.[15] Ill clad and poorly nourished, the crew suffered much from the cold. Since they had run out of salt for preserving food, the meat they had taken aboard at Timor had spoiled. There was little left for daily rations but rice and water, and to make matters worse, because the ship was leaking badly the crew had to put in long, exhausting hours at the pumps.

Beating westward between 38° and 40° S, by the middle of April the cold became intolerable. Faced with mutiny if he continued westward at these latitudes, Cano relented and headed toward Africa. On May 8, when it was too cloudy for Albo to take the sun's altitude, land appeared on the horizon. Cano and Albo had dared to hope that they had passed the Cape of Good Hope, but when they saw that ". . . the coast ran northeast and southwest and a quarter east and west," they realized that ". . . we were behind the Cape a matter of one hundred sixty leagues and opposite the Rio del Infante."[16]

With the wind from the west, they lay-to in sight of the coast for the rest of the day and the following night. The next day (May 9), wrote Albo, ". . . we made land and anchored, and the coast was very wild, and we remained thus until the next day; and the wind shifted to WSW, and upon that [the wind shifting onshore] we set sail, and we went along the coast to find some port for anchoring and taking refreshments for the people who were most suffering, which we did not find." It probably was at this time, although Pigafetta (who recorded the incident) did not mention the date, that some of the crew implored Cano to head for Mozambique, where they could throw themselves on the mercy of the Portuguese. However, wrote Pigafetta, ". . . the greater number of us, prizing honor more than life itself, decided on attempting at any risk, to return to Spain."[17] Failing to find a protected anchorage, the *Victoria* stood out to sea. With the wind from the west-southwest, they then beat west-northwest toward the Cape on alternating off- and onshore tacks.

By May 16 the *Victoria* had worked its way past Cape Agulhas and was 20 leagues east-southeast of the Cape of Good Hope when a violent squall struck the ship, springing the foremast and its yard. With the wind from the west, the ship remained hove-to all day while repairs were made.[18] On May 18 the weather was very rough, and the *Victoria* was still about twenty nautical miles southeast of the Cape of Good Hope. The following day, Cano finally succeeded in sailing past it. Pigafetta claimed that he cut it pretty close, coming within five leagues of the Cape, ". . . or else we should never have passed it." An analysis of the navigational details of the voyage, drawn largely from Albo's log, suggests otherwise: ". . . the Cape of Good Hope was finally doubled on [May] 19 without anyone seeing it."[19] Pigafetta stated that the Cape was doubled on May 6. Often careless with details and prone to exaggeration, he also stated: "We were nine weeks near that cape with our sails struck on account of the gales and because of fierce squalls." Although the *Victoria* was indeed plagued with headwinds and squalls as she neared the Cape, the African mainland was first sighted on May 8. According to her pilot, she doubled the Cape on May 19, 1522, less than two weeks later.

After rounding the Cape, Cano took the *Victoria* into Saldanha Bay (about seventy miles north of present-day Cape Town) for water and wood and to give his exhausted men a rest.[20] In the bay was a Portuguese ship bound for India. When hailed, Cano is reported to have told its captain, Pedro Cuaresma, who they were and from where they had come. Cuaresma must have been preoccupied with matters more pressing than the identity of this battered ship and its ragged, starving crew. Instead of capturing the Spanish intruder and sending it to the bottom, he merely saluted and went on his way.

After leaving Saldanha Bay on May 21, the *Victoria* was carried offshore by the strong Benguela Current into the belt of southeast trade winds. With the wind at last astern, Cano held a northwesterly course toward Cape Palmas. The long, nonstop transit of the Indian Ocean without re-provisioning had exhausted the ship's store of fresh food, and the resultant malnutrition led to another outbreak of scurvy. Four crew members perished as the *Victoria* beat westward around the Cape. Nine more died from June 1 to June 26, including Martín de Magallanes, a nephew of Magellan who had sailed from Spain as a supernumerary on the *Concepcion*.[21]

It is ironic that, while many of the *Victoria*'s crew were dying from a nutritional deficiency caused by the lack of green plants in their diet, below their feet, the cargo crammed in the hold consisted mainly of cloves, a dried plant material. More than two centuries would pass before enlightened ship captains, following the lead of Captain James Cook, would insist on including antiscorbutics in sailors' rations.

When the *Victoria* crossed the equator on June 7–8, Albo estimated the longitude at 3° 40 ' west of Cadiz (9° 57' west of Greenwich). This probably was 1°–2° east of the actual crossing. Scurvy continued to take its deadly toll: crewmen died on June 7, June 8, and June 9. Desperate for fresh provisions, Cano headed toward the coast of Guinea. As they sailed northward, the winds became light and variable, gradually shifting to the northeast, forcing Cano once again to tack. On June 21, he hove-to in front of Cape Roxo (near the border of modern Senegal and Guinea-Bissau)[22] and sent a boat crew ashore to search for food. While the *Victoria* waited for the boat to return, three more crewmen died. Pigafetta made the pious observation that ". . . on throwing [the bodies] into the sea, the Christians remained with the face turned to the sky, and the Indians with the face turned to the sea."[23] When the boat returned without having located any sources of fresh food, the *Victoria* set sail again, beating northward toward Cape Verde.

With many of the crew sick and dying, it became increasingly difficult to

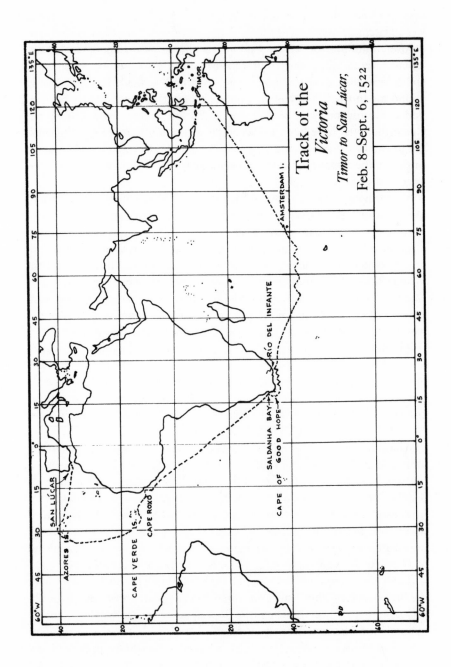

Track of the
Victoria
Timor to San Lúcar,
Feb. 8–Sept. 6, 1522

man the pumps. During the passage from the Cape of Good Hope, twenty-one men had perished from the combined effects of hunger, exhaustion, and disease. Confidence in Cano's leadership, never very high, waned rapidly. On July 1 the ship's officers agreed to put in at the Portuguese-held Cape Verde Islands, where by hiding their identity they hoped to purchase, in addition to fresh food, slaves for manning the pumps.

Bad weather prevented an easy passage, but on July 9 the *Victoria* anchored in the harbor of São Tiago, Cape Verde Islands.[24] Cano immediately sent a boat ashore carrying Martín Méndez, the ship's clerk, Martín de Judicibus, its sergeant-at-arms, and a Moluccan called Manuel, with instruction to tell the port authorities that the *Victoria* had been part of a convoy on its way back to Spain from "the Indies" (Spain's territories in the Western Atlantic). The *Victoria* had been struck by a storm as they were crossing the Line, badly damaging her foremast and separating the ship from the rest of the convoy. They were bringing their crippled ship to São Tiago for repairs and fresh provisions.

Méndez and his companions were received courteously by the port officials, who believed their story. Returning to the *Victoria*, they surprised everyone by announcing that, while the day was Wednesday by the ship's records, ashore they had been told it was Thursday. Albo and the other officers simply assumed they had made a mistake in record keeping, but Pigafetta was puzzled. He wrote: ". . . and I was more surprised than the others, since having always been in good health, I had every day, without interruption, written down the day that was current." Later, in Spain, he was advised that ". . . there was an error on our part, since as we had always sailed toward the west, following the course of the sun, and had returned to the same place, we must have gained twenty-four hours, as it is clear to anyone who reflects on it."[25]

Matters progressed smoothly for several days, during which two boatloads of food purchased ashore were delivered to the *Victoria*. On Sunday, June 13, a threatening sky in the evening caused Cano to fear that high winds might cause the anchors to drag, driving his ship deep into the harbor and making escape more difficult should their deception be discovered. He had good cause to be worried. The purchases ashore had been paid for with three quintals of cloves,[26] and if this should come to the attention of the port captain, he would know that the *Victoria* was carrying cargo obtained in Portuguese territories. Preparing for a quick getaway, Cano moved the *Victoria* outside the harbor.

On Monday, June 14, with his ship still underprovisioned for the journey to Spain, Cano sent thirteen men ashore in the longboat to purchase additional food while the *Victoria* waited outside the harbor. At midday, the longboat returned with a load of rice. Emboldened, Cano gambled by sending it back for more rice and, if possible, some slaves to man the pumps.[27] By sunset the longboat had not returned, and when it failed to appear the next morning, Cano moved the *Victoria* closer to the harbor to try to see what had happened. As he did so, the ship was hailed by a boatload of officials who ordered Cano to surrender. He was told that he and his men would be sent to Portugal on a ship due in from India, and a prize crew would take over the *Victoria*.[28]

Cano replied by demanding the return of his longboat and its crew. The officials said they would convey his message to the governor and return with an answer. While the *Victoria* waited outside, her crew could see armed men boarding four caravels inside the harbor. An apprentice seaman, Andrés Blanco, having died the day before, only twenty-two men remained on the *Victoria*, many of them sick. With his ship and crew in no condition to fight, Cano ordered all sails set and headed out to sea, abandoning the thirteen-man longboat crew.[29]

It is not entirely clear how the Portuguese authorities in São Tiago learned of the *Victoria*'s subterfuge, but one source states that the tip-off came when a boat crew from the *Victoria* went ashore to buy slaves and ". . . offered, sailor fashion, cloves for the slaves."[30] Pigafetta gave a somewhat different explanation: "We afterwards learned, sometime after our return, that our boat and men had been arrested because one of our men revealed the deception, and said that the captain general was dead, and that our ship was the only one remaining of Magellan's fleet."[31] Pigafetta did not name the culprit, but in the payroll records of the Casa de Contratacion there is a clue to his identity. The page containing the record for Simón de Burgos notes that he had been the cause of the imprisonment of the boat crew in the Cape Verde Islands.[32]

Burgos, a resident of the city of that name, was a rather unsavory character. When he enlisted in Magellan's fleet as a supernumerary assigned to the *Victoria*, he declared that he was Castilian, hiding his Portuguese birth. Upon his return to Spain, he tried to throw the blame for the boat crew's detention on Méndez and Judicibus, who had been in the first boat to go ashore. At the prison in São Tiago, he claimed, the Portuguese governor had said that he (Burgos) was not the informant.[33] From the notation on his payroll record, it would appear the Spanish authorities rejected his implausible story.

The *Victoria* sailed south and then west to get around the Cape Verde islands, and then headed north toward the Azores. The strength of the crew was restored somewhat by the food acquired at São Tiago, but with so few hands remaining to operate the ship, they had to labor incessantly at the pumps to keep it afloat. On August 4, the crew could discern on the horizon the 7,713-foot peak of Pico Island in the Azores. On August 6, the body of Etienne Villon, an able seaman from Brittany, was cast into the sea. The *Victoria* sailed past the islands on a northwest heading, but with variable winds her progress was painfully slow. On August 20 they reached 42° 31' N, in search of westerly winds to carry them to Spain. Headwinds and a strong current swept them back toward the Azores, and on August 29, San Miguel Island was still in sight. At last, during the final days of August, the wind began to blow out of the northwest.

On September 4, the *Victoria* was sailing east-southeast when the look-out spotted Cape St. Vincent at the southwest corner of Portugal. Two days later, on September 6, 1522, with twenty-one exhausted survivors on board, the *Victoria* lay-to off the mouth of the Guadalquivir. A boat came out to meet them with a pilot, Pedro Sordo (Deaf Peter), who guided the battered vessel across the bar into the harbor of San Lúcar.[34] In fourteen days less than three years, the stout little ship had completed the first circumnavigation of the earth.

The grim, determined Portuguese expatriate who had conceived the grand enterprise did not live to witness its history-making end. Magellan's ambition had been to forge a personal fief for himself and his heirs in the islands east of Malacca that he would claim for Spain. Through an icy strait at the bottom of the world he sailed into the vast, uncharted Pacific Ocean to the group of islands he named San Lázaro (later to be named the Philippines), and died trying to bind them securely to Spain.

If Magellan had dreamed of circumnavigating the planet, no mention was made of it in the plans he submitted to King Charles, nor is there any evidence that he divulged his plans for the return voyage to the captains and pilots of his fleet. Given his propensity for keeping his own counsel, it is not likely that he did. We do know, from his statement to Las Casas in 1518, that if he could not find a westerly route to the Moluccas he was prepared to sail east, around the Cape of Good Hope. Had he lived to make the return voyage, like Cano, Magellan probably would have chosen the Cape route. Considering the wind conditions and the risks, it was the only practical choice. If the idea of circumnavigation had occurred to him, he probably considered it but one of several ways to get the fleet home; never as an end in itself. His great enterprise brought only death to Magellan and grief to his family. The economic and political objectives at its heart were never fully realized. It was the circumnavigation, completed by a mutineer whom he had grudgingly pardoned, that caught the imagination of the world.

Long excoriated in his native Portugal and ignored in Spain, the land he had adopted, Magellan is now ranked with Columbus as one of the prime movers of the Age of Discovery. For its sheer magnitude and intellectually liberating consequences, his stupendous deed must be considered one of the outstanding events, perhaps the terminal one, of the European Renaissance. Like the strait at the bottom of South America, the resource-rich region surrounding it bears Magellan's name. Now an important political subdivision of the Chilean nation, it is graced by a center of higher learning, the Universidad de Magallanes. Astronomy, a science for which he had the deepest respect, honored the great discoverer by giving the name Magellanic Clouds to a prominent feature of the night sky in the southern hemisphere. In our time, a spacecraft named Magellan has crossed the interplanetary void to map the surface of Venus, a fitting tribute to the determined navigator who made possible the first manned circuit of the earth.

$\mathcal{E}$pilogue

W<i>hen the</i> Victoria <i>crossed the bar to the harbor at San Lúcar,</i> there were eighteen Europeans and three Moluccans aboard. A witness described the ship and its crew in the following terms: "On that ship, with more holes in it than a sieve, [were] 18 [Europeans], skinnier than an underfed old nag."[1] The eighteen who returned to Spain with the *Victoria*, the twelve captured in the Cape Verde islands, the fifteen recorded as fatalities, and the two who deserted on Timor add up to forty-seven, the number of Europeans reported to have sailed with her from Tidore.

The records are less clear concerning the Moluccans who sailed with them. Of the thirteen embarked at Tidore, there is evidence that one was taken prisoner in the Cape Verde islands and three arrived in Spain with the *Victoria*.[2] In a letter to the emperor, Cano reported that twenty-two crewmen had died en route from Tidore.[3] If the two Europeans who deserted on Timor are added to the fifteen reported to have perished, five Moluccans must also have died. That leaves four to be accounted for. Two pilots were provided by Almanzor to guide the *Victoria* as far as Timor. It does not seem unreasonable to assume that each took with him an assistant, and that all four men left the ship at Timor.

Cano wrote to the emperor from San Lúcar, giving him a summary of the voyage. He complained bitterly that a longboat with thirteen of his men had been seized by the Portuguese in the Cape Verde islands, and urged His Majesty to press for their immediate release. Since his men had labored so hard and suffered so much to bring the *Victoria* back to Spain, Cano begged His Majesty to grant them ". . . a fourth of the Crown's twentieth [share of the proceeds to be realized from the sale of the cargo], . . .

for we have discovered and encircled the entire world; going to the West, we have returned from the East."[4]

The next day, Cano managed to acquire a six-oared longboat to replace the one seized by the Portuguese in the Cape Verde Islands. Casa agents in San Lúcar provided bread, meat, fruit, and wine for the starving crew. Best of all, fifteen men were hired to tow the *Victoria* up the Guadalquivir. Arriving in Seville on Monday, September 8, the crew fired their artillery in one final salute.[5] As soon as the ship was tied up at the wharf, an armed guard was provided to protect the precious cargo and to keep curious visitors from boarding her.

On September 9, those of the crew able to walk fulfilled vows made during the ordeal of their homeward journey. Barefoot, in shirtsleeves, and carrying candles, the gaunt survivors of the circumnavigation filed in slow procession, first to the shrine of Nuestra Señora de la Victoria, then to the church of Santa Maria la Antigua.[6]

When he received Cano's letter, Charles V responded immediately, congratulating the captain and the crew of the *Victoria* on their remarkable achievement. Wanting to hear firsthand the story of their astounding voyage, the king ordered Cano to come at once to Valladolid, bringing with him the two most knowledgeable men in his crew. He assured Cano that steps already had been taken to secure the release of the thirteen men in Portuguese custody, and that he would grant to the crew the fourth of the Crown's twentieth as requested. A royal order to the Casa instructed them to provide Cano and his two companions with travel expenses and clothing suitable for an appearance at court. Cano was to bring the ship's papers and all diaries relating to the voyage.[7]

Cano chose the *Victoria*'s pilot, Francisco Albo, and its barber-surgeon, Hernando de Bustamente, to accompany him to court. When they arrived in Valladolid, the three were graciously received and honored. Later, however, they were interrogated by a judicial officer of the court, the Alcalde Santiago Díaz de Leguizamo, concerning the enmity between Magellan and Cartagena, the mutiny, its causes and grim consequences, and the circumstances that led to the death of Magellan.[8]

Cano provided a harsh indictment of his former chief, stating that the mutiny at Port San Julián had occurred because Magellan had refused to acknowledge Cartagena as co-commander, and consistently had failed to consider the advice of his other captains. He further stated that Magellan had punished the rebellious captains severely in order to replace them with his Portuguese relatives. While Cano had not been a witness to the battle at Mactan, he made it clear that he considered Magellan's death to have been the result of a rash, utterly needless commitment to a matter too trivial to have warranted the involvement of the captain-general.

Albo and Bustamente were competent professionals who had earned Magellan's respect by performing their duties faithfully and keeping clear of involvement in fleet politics. When interrogated by Leguizamo, they recounted the events of the voyage without rancor or prejudice. While they did not denigrate Magellan as Cano had done, neither did their statements substantially contradict those of the Basque shipmaster who had succeeded to the command of the *Victoria*.[9]

Pigafetta, most of the other members of the crew (including the Moluccans), and the thirteen men who had been detained in the Cape Verde islands were also received at court.[10] While the records do not indicate the sequence of court appearances of the *Victoria*'s survivors, it seems reasonable to assume that those of Cano, Albo, and Bustamente were first, with the others presented over several months. Pigafetta, a nobleman who had performed ably as the fleet's principal diplomatic emissary, felt slighted when Cano chose Bustamente as one of the two ". . . most well-informed of his crew . . ." to accompany him to court. Albo, the pilot, was an obvious choice, but the ship's barber? Concerning his own audience with the emperor, Pigafetta wrote: "Leaving Seville, I went to Valladolid, where I presented to His Sacred Majesty, Don Carlos, neither gold nor silver, but things more precious in the eyes of so great a sovereign. I presented to him, among other things, a book written by my hand of all the things that had occurred day by day in our voyage." The copy presented by Pigafetta to King Charles has been lost, but the surviving French and Italian editions of his manuscript reveal that he got even with Cano. His narrative, filled with details of the voyage, paid eloquent tribute to Magellan, whom he described as "so noble a captain," but nowhere does it contain any mention of the Basque shipmaster who brought the *Victoria* home.[11]

The Moluccan called Manuel demonstrated too keen an interest in the relative value of the various monetary units then in use in Spain, and in the market prices of pepper and other spices. Because it was feared that this knowledge would inflate the prices charged to Spanish traders for these commodities, he was not permitted to accompany his compatriots when they sailed with the Loaisa expedition to be repatriated in the Moluccas.[12]

Of the intelligence brought back to Spain by the *Victoria*, none fascinated King Charles more than the news of the treaties signed by the Moluccan potentates. Ruling over more territory as Holy Roman Emperor than any European monarch since Charlemagne, he had begun to dream of a worldwide empire. He dispatched other fleets to the Moluccas, but the long, hazardous route pioneered by Magellan proved a fearful obstacle to the supply and reinforcement of the few Spaniards who managed to reach those islands. Operating from established bases in India and Malacca, the Portuguese were in a far stronger position to enforce their claims to the

Spice Islands. After Charles married the sister of King João III of Portugal, the dispute over sovereignty in the Moluccas became a diplomatic embarrassment. In 1529, strapped for funds by the need to maintain massive military forces to hold his fragile European empire together, Charles sold all Spanish claims to the Moluccas to his brother-in-law in Portugal for 350,000 gold ducats.[13]

After the crew of the *Victoria* gave their accounts of the voyage to the court officials, Álvaro de Mesquita was released from prison. Brought back to Spain in chains after the seizure of his ship in the Strait of Magellan, he had languished in prison since the return of the *San Antonio* in March 1521. Gerónimo Guerra and Estevão Gomes, the officers who had engineered its defection, had charged him with acts of cruelty at Port San Julián, but it would appear that the testimony of the *Victoria*'s crew supported Mesquita's denial of those charges. In the euphoria produced by the successful circumnavigation, however, Charles chose to ignore the defection of the *San Antonio*. Gomes and Guerra were never charged with either mutiny or desertion, and their salaries, accumulated during the voyage, were paid in full. In 1523, King Charles authorized a search for a shorter western route to the Orient, and the next year Gomes was given command of a 50-ton caravel in which he sailed in search of a northwest passage. While he didn't find one, he explored the coast of North America from Florida to Nova Scotia.[14]

News of her husband's death may have reached Magellan's wife before the return of the *Victoria*. Carried along a junk-borne grapevine in advance of the arrival of the *Trinidad* and *Victoria* at Tidore, the story could have reached Malacca. From there, a Portuguese ship could have carried it to Lisbon, where her father had relatives, friends, and business associates. Because of the charges brought against her husband by Gomes and Guerra after the *San Antonio* returned to Spain in March 1521, Beatriz, whose second child had been stillborn in 1520 and whose infant son, Rodrigo, died in September 1521, was placed under house arrest to prevent her possible flight to Portugal. She died in March 1522, six months before the *Victoria* returned to Spain.[15]

Magellan's father-in-law, Diogo Barbosa, had been a minor investor in the Moluccan fleet, and after the *Victoria*'s return he and his son Jaime filed a joint claim for a share of the proceeds from the sale of its cargo. In 1525, the court rendered a judgment in their favor, but by then Diogo had died. Getting the judgment had been one thing, getting paid was another; Jaime never was able to collect a single maravedi of his father's investment.[16] Neither Magellan's brother, Diogo de Sousa, nor his sister, Isabel Magalhães da Silva, filed claims to any part of their brother's estate. Both died childless. In 1567, a Teresa de Magalhães, who claimed to be a sister of the discoverer, filed suit in Spain for the salary owed to Magellan. Her suit was denied on the grounds that his sister and brother were already deceased.[17]

On October 10, 1522, Charles V charged Cristobal de Haro with the responsibility for disposing of the *Victoria*'s entire cargo. Haro's agent, Diego Díaz, shipped most of it to Antwerp, where it was sold for 8,017,084 maravedis, 428,000 maravedis over the cost of the entire expedition;[18] the proceeds were immediately appropriated by the Spanish Crown. Even with powerful friends at court, it took Haro eighteen years just to recover his original investment.[19] This indifference to royal debts shows that, in money matters at least, the old notion that a king does not go back on his word did not apply to Charles V.

To conclude the extraordinary odyssey of the men of Magellan's fleet, we must now return to Ternate, where the survivors of the *Trinidad*'s ill-fated attempt to cross the Pacific to Panama were imprisoned. Antonio de Brito, the Portuguese commander to whom the Spaniards had surrendered, intended to follow his summary decapitation of Pedro de Lorosa, the *Trinidad*'s Portuguese passenger, by executing the ship's officers. However, suspecting that for diplomatic reasons the king would disapprove, he changed his mind. Seventeen of the prisoners were shipped to Malacca. Of these, four disappeared at sea while en route, including Juan de Campos, who had been in charge of the Spanish *factoría* on Tidore.[20]

To interrogate them further about the route taken by Magellan's fleet, Brito detained Bautista, the ship's pilot; Pancaldo, his assistant; and the ship's clerk, Sánchez. Master Antonio, a carpenter, and Antonio Bazazabal, a caulker, also were kept on Ternate to work on a vessel being constructed for a trade mission to Borneo. After stops at Banda and Java, the other prisoners finally reached Malacca, where they were placed in the custody of the Portuguese governor, Jorge de Albuquerque; during five months there four of the Spaniards died. Antón, Espinosa's black slave, was appropriated by Albuquerque and presented to his sister as a gift.[21]

Bautista, Pancaldo, and Sánchez remained in prison on Ternate. In a letter to the king, Brito wrote that he expected them to die of the fever decimating the Portuguese colony there. When they disappointed him by staying alive, he shipped them to Malacca, ". . . in order that they should die there, as there is much sickness." In a letter to the governor at Malacca, Brito advised, ". . . concerning the master, pilot and clerk, order their heads cut off and shipped to Portugal."[22]

From Malacca, the prisoners were sent first to Ceylon and then to Cochin on India's Malabar Coast. En route, the junk carrying Sánchez, Molina, and Cota disappeared and was presumed lost with all hands. Only eight of the *Trinidad*'s crew reached Cochin alive. Vasco da Gama was then viceroy, and he was not noted for compassion. At first imprisoned and threatened with torture and execution, the *Trinidad*'s survivors were set free, feeble and starving, to wander the streets of Cochin begging for subsistence. The viceroy forbade Portuguese ship captains to permit them to board homeward-bound vessels, but invited the hapless Spaniards to enlist in the armed force being assembled to fight the Arabs. With the help of a sympathetic representative of the queen of Portugal (the sister of Charles V), Espinosa succeeded in smuggling a letter out of Cochin to the emperor. Dated January 12, 1525, the letter told of the desperate situation of the crew of the *Trinidad*. Only six remained alive. "Now, Your Majesty," wrote Espinosa, "be advised that the viceroy ordered that I be seized as soon as he learned that I was in this city of Cochin, menacing me and telling me that my head would be cut off, and dishonoring me with many evil words, saying that he would hang the others." "We are being treated," he concluded, "worse than if we were in Barbary."[23] On December 19, 1525, Giovanni Caro, an Italian clergyman who had befriended the Spaniards, also wrote to Charles V on their behalf. The Portuguese were treating them more cruelly, he wrote, than infidels treat their Christian captives.[24] One of the Spaniards who died in Cochin was Diego Martín, who had taken over as master when Bautista and Espinosa jointly assumed fleet command after deposing Carvalho following the flight from Borneo.

One of the *Trinidad* survivors was luckier than the rest. In 1525, Juan Rodríguez, deaf and, at forty-eight, one of the oldest men of Magellan's fleet, managed to get on a ship leaving Cochin for Lisbon. The Venetian ambassador to Spain, in a dispatch from Toledo dated February 8, 1526, related that Rodríguez had been released from prison in Portugal.[25] The old salt truly must have loved the sea, for he requested, and received from the Casa, authorization to sail to the Indies in his own caravel.[26]

Juan Bautista and León Pancaldo were befriended by Genoese sailors on a Portuguese ship, and with their help succeeded in stowing away on the ship before it left Cochin. Discovered when the ship was at sea, they were taken off in irons at Mozambique and put aboard a ship bound for India. When the ship was unable to depart because of bad weather, the two were set free to struggle for subsistence ashore.

In letters from Mozambique dated October 20 and October 25, 1525, the two Genoese officers gave a summary account of the last voyage of the *Trinidad* and of their experiences since falling into the hands of the Portuguese. Their pitiable state is revealed in the following sentence from one of the letters: ". . . we live in fear of dying, for now there is much sickness in this land, yet while there are honorable men here virtuous enough to give us something to eat, we remain stranded, without clothing, without money; we implore your lordship to have compassion and mercy for us, our wives and our children, and to urge the emperor to demand that the King of Portugal send us with the first ships to arrive here." Juan Bautista did not live to see his home again. He died in Mozambique sometime during 1526.[27]

Pancaldo managed to stow away on a ship bound for Portugal. When he was discovered, the captain threatened to throw him to the sharks, but relented when Pancaldo told him that he had stowed away so that he could die among Christians. Taken to Lisbon, he was immediately thrown in jail. Released by royal order, he returned to Spain in 1527.[28]

Late in 1525, Enrique de Meneses, the viceroy who succeeded Gama after the latter's death, allowed the three *Trinidad* survivors remaining in Cochin to embark for Lisbon. Rather than an act of compassion, it may have been a political consequence of the marriage of the sister of Charles V to João III of Portugal. Nevertheless, when the three (Gómez de Espinosa, Ginés de Mafra, and the gunner, Hans Bergen) arrived in Lisbon on July 24, 1526, they were imprisoned. As soon as Charles V learned of this, he demanded that his royal brother-in-law release them. While the matter was being negotiated, Hans died, bequeathing everything he possessed to Gómez de Espinosa. After seven months in prison, Espinosa was released, and returned immediately to Spain, where he was honored by Charles V. Ginés de Mafra was detained because he had in his possession a box containing the papers of Magellan's astrologer-pilot, Andrés de San Martín. Portuguese authorities interrogated him and confiscated San Martín's precious papers. Mafra was freed twenty-seven days after the release of Espinosa.

Of the 54 men who sailed from Tidore with the *Trinidad* on April 6, 1522, only four lived to return to Spain: Gonzalo Gómez de Espinosa, León Pancaldo, Ginés de Mafra, and Juan Rodríguez. Altogether, of the 260 to 270 men who sailed from San Lúcar with Magellan in 1519, 35 eventually returned to Spain: 18 on the *Victoria*, 13 repatriated from the Cape Verde Islands, and four from the *Trinidad*. Gonzalo de Vigo, who deserted from the *Trinidad* in the Marianas, was picked up on Saipan by the Loaisa expedition but chose to remain at Ternate when the others returned to Spain. The *Victoria*, the only ship of Magellan's fleet to complete the voyage and the first vessel to circumnavigate the earth, made two subsequent voyages to Santo Domingo on the island of Hispaniola. Returning to Seville from the last of these voyages, she was lost with all hands.[29]

The human cost of Magellan's expedition was horrendous. Like most of his shipmates, Magellan forfeited his life in the effort. To his family in

Spain and to his relatives in Portugal, it brought grief and ruin. The expedition's principal objective, to bring back proof that the Moluccas lay on the Spanish side of the extended line of demarcation, was a scientific failure and a diplomatic disaster. The small profit realized from the sale of the *Victoria*'s cargo could never be construed as a reasonable return on investment. Yet, for all these worldly failures, Magellan's voyage represents a triumph of the human spirit. For this, and for its contribution to man's knowledge of the true size of his world and the extent of its oceans, his achievement stands unparalleled in history. In centuries to come, the memory of Magellan's magnificent exploration will surely continue to inspire men to expand their horizons into the unfathomed depths of space.

World map of 1472, based on Ptolemy's second-century geography. At the time of Magellan's birth little was known of what lay beyond familiar trade routes.

Courtesy Biblioteca Apostolica Vaticana.

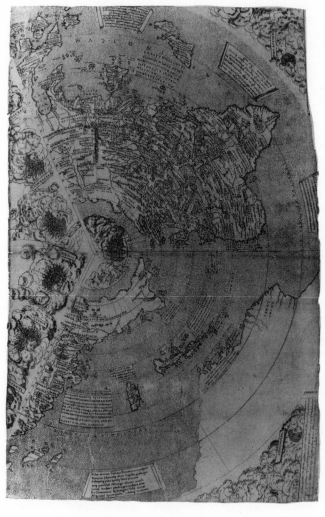

Giovanni Contarini, Florence, 1506. The reports of Spanish and English explorations to the west and Portuguese expeditions to the east are reflected here. The year before, Magellan had sailed for India as a member of Francisco Almeida's fleet.

Courtesy of the Seaver Center for Western Historical Research, Natural History Museum of Los Angeles County.

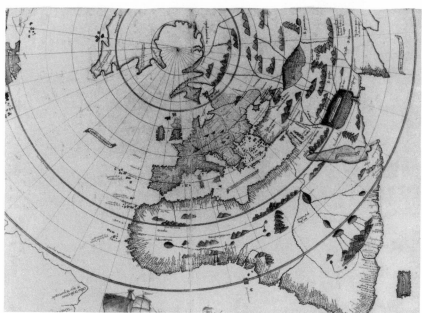

Vesconte de Maggiolo, Naples, 1511. Knowledge imparted by the steady stream of Portuguese convoys east around Africa to India's west coast is evident, but Western knowledge of the Far East, and of the vastness of the Pacific, is still clouded. When this chart was made, Magellan was likely in Malacca, gathering information from sources on the waterfront about the archipelago to the east.

Courtesy of the John Carter Brown Library at Brown University.

Juan Vespucci, Seville, 1526. Magellan's strait is acknowledged, and the Moluccas are shown clearly as Spanish territory. Juan Vespucci, a nephew of Amerigo, was a Spanish representative to the Badajoz-Elvas Commission of 1524, established to resolve Spanish and Portuguese claims in the East Indies.

Courtesy of the Hispanic Society of America.

"All the world discovered until now. It is divided into two parts according to the agreement between their Catholic Majesties of Spain and Don Juan of Portugal at Tordesillas in 1494." Diego Ribero, Seville, 1529. Information from the great voyages of da Gama, Dias, Columbus, and Magellan is included here. What is shown is relatively accurate; what is still unknown is simply left blank, keeping with cartographic practice at the time. The line of demarcation in the Pacific is west of the Moluccas, placing them under Spanish control. In an earlier map, Ribero (Ribeiro) placed the line east of the Moluccas. While he worked for Spain in 1529, Ribero had once served Portugal as a navigator for Vasco da Gama and Alberquerque on passages to India.

Courtesy of Biblioteca Apostolica Vaticana.

Battista Agnese, Venice, 1544. Magellan's circumnavigation, under the guidance of the twelve winds of antiquity, is commemorated. North America takes shape, but the form of the Asian landmass and the breadth of the Pacific remain uncertain.

Courtesy of the John Carter Brown Library at Brown University.

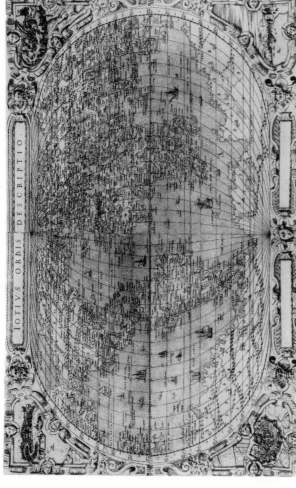

IOTIVS ORBIS DESCRIPTIO.

Gastaldi, Venice, 1562–1569. Finer details emerge as Spanish, Portuguese, English, French, and Dutch trade routes wrap the globe. A century would pass before Captain James Cook disproved the existence of Gastaldi's Terra Incognita, the great southern continent created by cartographers to counterbalance the known landmass of the northern hemisphere.

Courtesy of the John Carter Brown Library at Brown University.

Appendix 1 The Ships

Five ships for Magellan's fleet were purchased in Cádiz in 1518 by Juan de Aranda, factor of the *Casa de Contratación* in Seville. They were *naus* (carracks) of a design widely used for ocean commerce in the late fifteenth and early sixteenth centuries. Already well worn from years of hard service, they probably were products of shipyards on the Bay of Biscay, where oak forests on the nearby slopes of the Cantabrian Mountains provided a ready source of shipbuilding timber. Ship designs during this period were not committed to paper, but rather were kept in the heads of master builders who jealously guarded the secrets of their craft and taught them only to selected assistants. While the general configuration of ships of this type is known from the decorative artwork on contemporary maps, we can only guess at their actual dimensions, proportions, and details of construction.

The beamy, double-ended, carvel (flush-planked) hulls presented a tubby appearance. Although there was ample freeboard for ocean travel, the flat keels preserved the shallow draft of their riverine prototypes. The most noticeable features of the superstructure were the fore- and sterncastles; on Magellan's ships, the latter probably extended two decks above the main deck, the former, one. The poop deck, the exposed part of the quarterdeck, and the deck on top of the forecastle were protected by bulwarks.

On many sixteenth-century *naus,* there was a lower deck between the main deck and the bilge, and Magellan's ships probably were constructed around 1500 when this feature was just being introduced. While the two largest of his ships, the *Trinidad* and *San Antonio,* may have had a continous deck below the main deck, on the three smaller ships it probably took the form of partial decking around the inside of the hull, leaving a large opening over the bilge. The lower deck provided the main storage space for supplies and cargo. In heavy weather, openings in this deck substituted for the privy that projected outboard from the poop. After some time at sea, the stench from the bilge must have been overpowering.

With complements ranging from thirty-two on the *Santiago* to sixty or more on the *Trinidad* and the *San Antonio,* accommodations were scarce and cramped. In the sterncastle, the captain's cabin occupied the space between the poop deck and the quarterdeck. Accommodations for officers of high rank were located on the sheltered part of the main deck, under the quarterdeck. Aft of the officers quarters was the steerage, where the tiller extended from the rudder through an opening in the stern planking. Because the helmsman could not see to steer, an officer on the quarterdeck shouted commands to him through a hatch. With the ship running before a storm, the steerage area became thoroughly drenched by seas pouring through the tiller opening. But the helmsman was not the only mariner subjected to frequent soaking. Lower ranking officers, supernumeraries, the crew, and the cabin boys had to stow their gear and find sleeping space wherever they could in the exposed waist of the ship. A lucky few may

(continued on page 248)

245

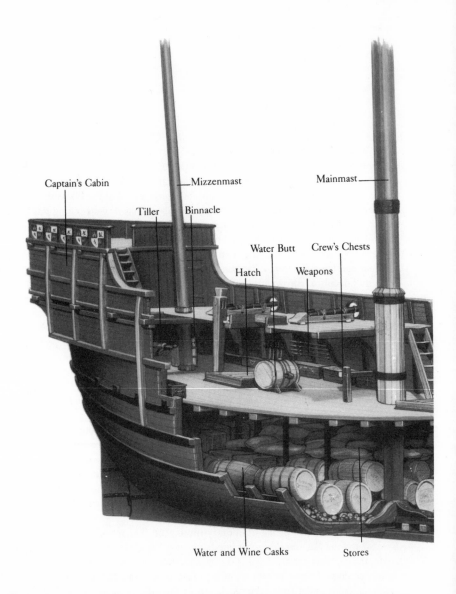

Captain's Cabin   Mizzenmast   Mainmast

Tiller   Binnacle

Water Butt   Crew's Chests

Hatch   Weapons

Water and Wine Casks   Stores

Already worn from nearly twenty years of service, the beamy, double-ended Victoria *nonetheless proved itself equal to the challenges of the first circumnavigation. Perhaps sixty feet long overall, with a beam of eighteen feet, the* Victoria *likely left Seville with a crew of some forty-five men. Only the highest ranking officers had the luxury of dry accommodations afforded by the ship's prominent fore- and sterncastles. For the rest, who stowed gear and found a place to sleep wherever they could, frequent soakings were commonplace. On the* Victoria *there may have been a partial deck along the inside of the hull below the main deck, leaving*

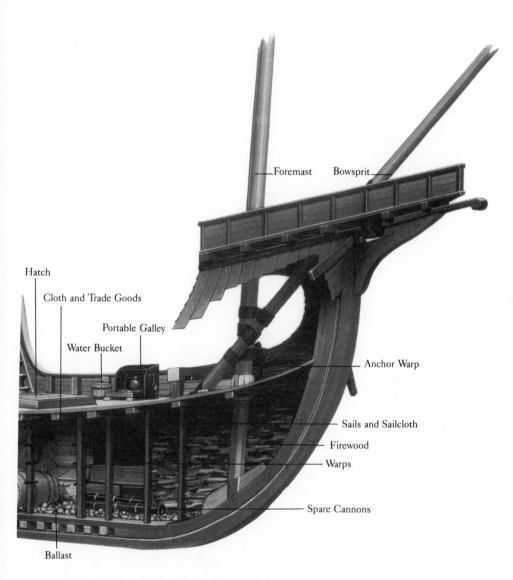

Foremast Bowsprit

Hatch

Cloth and Trade Goods

Portable Galley

Water Bucket

Anchor Warp

Sails and Sailcloth

Firewood

Warps

Spare Cannons

Ballast

a large opening over the bilge. The lower deck provided the main storage space for supplies and cargo, and in heavy weather served as a privy. Competing with provisions for space on the five ships was a cargo that included swivel guns, light artillery, heavy mortars, wall smashers, crossbows, muskets, suits of armor, crossbow bolts, lances, and pikes. For the firearms there was gunpowder and a considerable quantity of lead. Lionel Willis, © National Geographic.

have been able to find space in the storage areas below the main deck and in the fo'c's'le.

All five ships carried three masts: The mainmast was stepped on the keelson, and the foremast on the stem; the small mizzenmast was stepped into the main deck just forward of the sterncastle. The mainmast carried a small topmast, as did the foremast on larger ships. Magellan's *Trinidad* and *San Antonio* may well have done so, but it is not likely that the others did. Main, foremast, and topmasts carried square sails suspended from horizontal yards. The mizzen was lateen rigged with a triangular sail suspended from a long, diagonal yard. In addition to the three masts, a bowsprit angled upward, extending beyond the prow. It was lashed firmly to the foremast and stepped into the main deck. For running before the wind in light seas, a square spritsail suspended from a yard attached horizonally to the bowsprit could be deployed before the stem.

In a joint Portuguese-Spanish study of the Magellan voyage,[1] the relative proportions of the hulls, masts, and yards of his ships were calculated. While these calculations yielded hull dimensions smaller than appear likely for the numbers of men and the volume of supplies and cargo that the ships are known to have carried, the proportions of the masts and yards relative to the hull are consistent with those suggested by contemporary decorative drawings. Expressed as functions of the beam, these proportions are indicated in the following table:

Mainmast	=	$2\frac{1}{4}$ or $2\frac{1}{2} \times$ the beam (B)
Foremast	=	$\frac{1}{2}(5B-2)$
Mizzenmast	=	$2B$
Bowsprit	=	$\frac{1}{2}(5B-2)$
Main yard	=	$2B$
Fore yard	=	B
Spritsail yard	=	$\frac{1}{2}B$

In the records of the *Casa de Contratación*, the cargo capacity of Magellan's ships is given in *toneles*. This measure sometimes has been confused with the Biscayan *tonel*, the *tonel macho* or its equivalent, the *tonelada* of Seville. None of these is appropriate. The proper measure for ship capacity in Magellan's time is the *tonelada* described in the *Ordenanzas* of 1553. This *tonelada* was the volume occupied by a box with sides 9, 4, and 3 *palmos* long. Since one *palmo* was about 0.21 meters, the volume of the 1553 *tonelada* works out to about one cubic meter.

Although Spanish ships were said to have been of slightly deeper draft than comparable Portuguese vessels, the approximate hull dimensions of Magellan's two largest ships (*San Antonio* and *Trinidad*) were probably close to those estimated for a typical small (100–120 toneladas) Portuguese nau (circa 1497):[2] overall length about 20 meters; beam about 7 meters; depth (from the main deck to keel) about 4 meters. For the *Santiago*, Magellan's smallest ship, these dimensions were probably about 15–16 meters length overall, 5-plus meters in the beam and 3-plus meters depth (main deck to keel). The dimensions of the *Concepción* and the *Victoria* were probably between these.

There were two types of ships' boats: a longboat or shallop (*batel* or *chalupa*) and a launch (*lancha*); both were lapstraked and double-ended. The longboat, about 7 meters in overall length, carried two stubby masts that could be quickly stepped, and long spars with lateen sails. As it took a lot of space, the longboat usually was towed behind

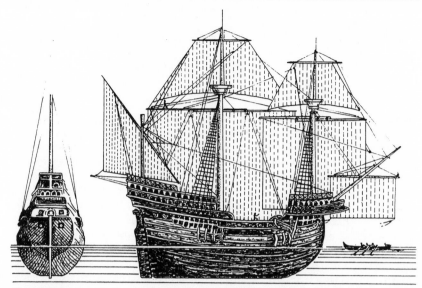

Sixteenth-century nao, similar to the Trinidad *and* San Antonio, *the largest ships of the Moluccan expedition. All five of Magellan's ships carried three masts from which squaresails were bent on horizontal yards; the two larger vessels may have had a topmast on main and foremast. All five ships were equipped with a sharply angled bowsprit rigged with a square spritsail. The mizzen was lateen rigged. A tiller extended from the rudder through an opening in the stern planking, and the helmsman, his vision blocked, steered by commands shouted down from the quarterdeck.* Illustration by the author adapted from *Junta de Investigacoes do Ultramar,* Coimbra, 1970.

the ship rather than stowed on deck. The launch, about 4 meters long, was normally stowed in the waist of the ship, on the main deck.

Notes

1. João da Gama Pimentel Barata, "A Armada de Ferñao de Magalhães" in *A Viagem de Fernão de Magahlães e a Questão das Molucas,* Actas do II Colóquio Luso-Espanhol de História Ultramarina, ed. by A. Teixeira da Mota (Lisbon: Junta de Investigações Cientfícas do Ultramar, 1973).
2. Jaime Martins Barata, *O Navio "São Gabriel" e as Naus Manuelinas* (Lisbon: Junta de Investigações Cientffícas do Ultramar, 1970).

Appendix 2 Shipboard Routine

The crew was divided into port and starboard watches that alternated duty shifts *(guardias)* of four hours, beginning at midnight. The afternoon watch was split (dogged) into two two-hour watches so an individual would not repeat a particular *guardia* on consecutive days. The first night watch (after sundown until midnight) was under the command of the captain. The second (when the navigational stars were brightest), from midnight to just before dawn, was the pilot's watch. The master's mate took the dawn watch. The morning and afternoon watches were the responsibility of the master and master's mate, respectively. Thus, the daytime work of sailing the ship – swabbing, pumping, maintenance, and repair – was under the direct supervision of officers who were professional mariners. Since reliable, spring-wound clocks had not yet been developed for use at sea, the timing of watch changes depended on sand clocks (half-hour glasses), turned eight times per watch. The Magellan expedition carried sixteen finely crafted Venetian *amopolletas* (sand clocks), costing 51 maravedis each.

The staple in crew rations was salted meat and for feast days salt fish or cheese. This was supplemented by rice, biscuit, salted flour, legumes, garlic, almonds, and raisins. For the hardworking seamen, the rations were more generous than those afforded laborers ashore, but on long voyages such as Magellan's, depletion and spoilage led to reduced rations and their inevitable consequence, scurvy and starvation. Magellan's ships carried no cooks; when weather was favorable for cooking, it was done over a sand bed in the fire-box *(fogon)* on the starboard side of the fo'castle. For the crew, cooking chores probably were assigned to apprentice seamen of the appropriate watch. The meals of the captain and other members of the high command probably were prepared by their personal cabin boys *(pajes)*.

On Spanish and Portuguese ships of those days, religious observances were an integral part of shipboard routine and played an important role in the maintenance of discipline and morale. Formal services were conducted daily by a chaplain, or if one were not available, by the captain. For each turning of the glass, day and night, some ritual was observed. Usually it took the form of a little ditty sung out by a cabin boy on that particular watch. Samuel Eliot Morison presented a number of these as they were recorded by Eugenio Salazar in 1573.[1] They reflect awe of the sea and the need for divine protection felt by those who sail on it. Touching in their simplicity and sincerity, some are profoundly religious in sentiment, others lighthearted and practical. An example of the latter was sung at the end of the captain's watch to rouse the men of the succeeding pilot's watch:

> *Al cuarto, al cuarto, señores de buena parte, al cuarto,*
> *Al cuarto en buena hora de la guardia del señor piloto,*
> *Que ya es la hora; leva, leva, leva!*

On deck, on deck, gentlemen of the starboard watch,
Hurry up on deck, Mr. Pilot's watch,
Right now; get up, get up, get up!

Note

1. Samuel Eliot Morison. *The European Discovery of America: The Southern Voyages* (New York: Oxford, 1974), Chapter VIII.

Appendix 3A Ships' Rosters

Trinidad

Name[1]	Origin	Initial Rank	Pay[2] (maravedis)	Remarks
Fernão de Magalhães *(Fernando de Magallanes)*	Portugal	Captain general	146,000/a	Died Mactan, 27/04/1521.[3]
Estevão Gomes *(Estéban Gómez)*	Portugal	Pilot major	30,000/a	Deserted, returned to Spain 6/03/1521.
Juan Morales	Castile	Surgeon	25,000/a	Died 25/09/1522.
Léon de Ezpeleta	Castile	Clerk	?	Died, Cebu, 1/05/1521.
Giovanni Battista di Polcevera *(Juan Bautista de Punzorol)*	Genoa	Master	3,000	Died, Mozambique, 1526.
Francisco Albo	Rhodes	Master's mate	2,000	Returned to Spain, 6/09/1522.
Antonio Luciano	Genoa	Carpenter	1,875	Died, Ternate, 1523.
Felipe de Troci	Genoa	Caulker	1,875	Died, 12/7/1520.
Andrew of Bristol *(Maestre Andrés)*	England	Master gunner	1,875	Died, 9/03/1521.
Gonzalo Gómez de Espinosa	Castile	Master-at-arms	1,800	Returned to Spain, 1527.
Jean Baptiste *(Juan Bautista)*	France	Gunner	1,500	Died, 4/11/1521.
Guillaume *(Guillermo)* Tanegui	France	Gunner	1,500	Died, Cebu, 1/05/1521.
Francisco Martín	Castile	Cooper	1,500	Died, Cebu, 1/05/1521.
Pedro de Valderrama	Castile	Chaplain	1,500	Died, Cebu, 1/05/1521.
Alberto Sánchez	Castile	Man-at-arms	1,200	Died, 29/08/1522.
Marcos de Bayas	Castile	Barber	1,200	Died, 24/08/1522.
Cristóbal Rodríguez	Castile	Steward	1,200	Died, Cebu, 1/05/1521.
Francisco de Espinosa	Castile	Able seaman	1,200	Died, Mactan, 27/04/1521.

Name[1]	Origin	Initial Rank	Pay[2] (maravedis)	Remarks
Ginés de Mafra	Castile	Able seaman	1,200	Returned to Spain, 1527.
Leone *(Léon)* Pancaldo	Genoa	Able seaman	1,200	Returned to Spain, 1527.
Giovanni *(Juan)* Genovés	Genoa	Able seaman	1,200	Died 2/1523.
Francisco Piora	Genoa	Able seaman	1,200	Deserted on Cebu; died 1/05/1521.
Martín Genovés	Genoa	Able seaman	1,200	Deserted, Marianas, 8/1522; reported killed by natives.
Antonio Hernández Colmenero	Castile	Able seaman	1,200	Returned to Spain, 6/09/1522.
Antonio Rodríguez	Castile	Able seaman	1,200	Died, Cebu, 1/05/1521.
Bartolomé Sánchez	Castile	Able seaman	1,200	Died, 6/02/1524.
Tomás Natin	Genoa	Able seaman	1,200	Fate not recorded.
Domingo de Barruti	Castile	Able seaman	1,200	Abandonded, Brunei, 7/1521.
Francisco Martín	Castile	Able seaman	1,200	Died, Cebu, 1/05/1521.
Juan Rodríguez	Castile	Able seaman	1,200	Died, 5/10/1522.
Diego Martín	Castile	Able seaman	1,200	Died, Cochin, 10/09/1524.
Domingo Álvares *(Domingo de Cubillana)*	Portugal	Apprentice seaman	800	Died *(Victoria)*, 7/06/1522.
Antón de Goa	Portugal	Appr. seaman	800	Died, Cebu, 1/05/1521.
Antón de Noya	Castile	Appr. seaman	800	Died, Mactan, 27/04/1521.
Francisco de Ayamonte	Castile	Appr. seaman	800	Died, Malacca, 11/1524.
João de Grijó *(Juan de Grijol)*	Portugal	Appr. seaman	800	Died 5/09/1522.
Luiz Peres *(Luis de Beas)*	Portugal	Appr. seaman	800	Died, Cochin, 5/1525.
Juan de San Andrés	Castile	Appr. seaman	800	Returned to Spain *(Victoria)* 6/09/1522.
Blás de Toledo *(Almunia)*	Aragón	Appr. seaman	800	Died 10/09/1522.
Antón Moreno *(Negro)*	?	Appr. seaman	800	Died, Malacca, 11/1524.

Name[1]	Origin	Initial Rank	Pay[2] (maravedis)	Remarks
Vasco Gomes Galego (Vasquito)[4]	Portugal	Appr. seaman	800	Returned to Spain (Victoria) 1522–1523.
Juan Gallego	Castile	Appr. seaman	800	Died 21/09/1522.
Gutiérrez de Bustillo	Castile	Cabin boy	500	Died 16/03/1521.
Giovanni Genovese (Juan Genovés)	Genoa	Cabin boy	500	Died, 19/10/1522.
Andrés de la Cruz	Castile	Cabin boy	500	Died, 18/10/1522.
Duarte Barbosa	Portugal	Supernumerary	1,500	Died, Cebu, 1/05/1521.
Álvaro de Mesquita (Mezquita)	Portugal	Supernumerary	1,500	Returned to Spain (San Antonio), 6/03/1521.
Enrique de Malaca	Central Philippines?	Interpreter	1,500	Remained in Cebu after 1/05/1521.
Cristovão Rebêlo (Cristóbal Ravelo)	Portugal	Supernumerary	1,200	Died, Mactan, 27/04/1521.
Luiz Afonso de Góis (Luis Alonso de Goes)	Portugal	Supernumerary	1,000	Died, Cebu, 1/05/1521.
Antonio Pigafetta	Lombardy	Supernumerary	1,000	Returned to Spain, 6/09/1522.
Juan Martínez	Castile	Supernumerary	1,000	Died 29/03/1521.
Gonçalo Rodrigues	Portugal	Supernumerary	1,000	Fate unknown.
Pedro Sánchez	Castile	Armorer	1,000	Died 2/11/1521.
Fernão Rodrigues	Portugal	Supernumerary	800	Died 29/03/1521.
Petit Jean (Juanito) Martin	France	Supernumerary	800	Died, Cebu, 1/05/1521.
Diego Sánchez Barrasa	Castile	Supernumerary	800	Died 29/07/1520.
Nuno Gonçalves	Portugal	Supernumerary	800	Died, Cebu, 1/05/1521.
Diego Arias	Castile	Supernumerary	800	Died 2/1523.
Pedro Gómez	Castile	Supernumerary	800	Died, Mactan, 27/04/1521.
Jorge "Morisco"	India (?)	Captain's page	500	Died 22/10/1522 (?).
Lázaro de Torres	Castile	Cabin boy	500	Left ship at Tenerife, 1519.

Name	Origin	*San Antonio* Initial Rank	Pay	Remarks
Juan de Cartagena	Castile	Captain and Inspector General	110,000/a	Marooned in Patagonia, 11/08/1520.
Antonio de Coca	Castile	Fleet accountant	50,000/a	Died *(Victoria)* 28/03/1521.
Gerónimo Guerra	Castile	Clerk	30,000/a	Returned to Spain 6/05/1521.
Andrés de San Martín	Castile	Astrologer-pilot	30,000/a	Died, Cebu, 1/05/1521.
Juan Rodríguez de Mafra	Castile	Pilot	30,000/a	Died 28/03/1521.
Juan de Elorriaga	Castile	Master	3,000	Died 15/07/1520.
Diego Hernández	Castile	Master's mate	2,000	Returned to Spain 6/05/1521.
Pedro de Sautua	Castile	Carpenter	1,875	Returned to Spain 6/05/1521.
Pedro de Bilbao	Castile	Caulker	1,875	Returned to Spain 6/05/1521.
Martín de Goytisolo	Castile	Caulker	1,875	Returned to Spain 6/05/1521.
Maestre Jaques	France	Master gunner	1,875	Returned to Spain 6/05/1521.
Roger Dupiet	Germany	Gunner	1,500	Returned to Spain 6/05/1521.
Jean Georges *(Jorge)*	France (?)	Gunner	1,500	Returned to Spain 6/05/1521.
Simón de Axio	Greece	Gunner	1,500	Returned to Spain 6/05/1521.
Juan de Oviedo	Castile	Cooper	1,500	Returned to Spain 6/05/1521.
Juan de Gopeguy	Castile	Steward	1,200	Returned to Spain 6/05/1521.
Pedro Olabarrieta	Castile	Barber	1,200	Returned to Spain 6/05/1521.
Sebastían de Olarte	Castile	Able seaman	1,200	Died at sea 3/02/1520.
Lope de Ugarte	Castile	Able seaman	1,200	Returned to Spain 6/05/1521.
Juanes de Segura	Castile	Able seaman	1,200	Returned to Spain 6/05/1521.
Jean de Francia	France	Able seaman	1,200	Returned to Spain 6/05/1521.
Giacomo de Mesina	Sicily	Able seaman	1,200	Returned to Spain 6/05/1521.

Name	Origin	Initial Rank	Pay	Remarks
Cristóbal García	Castile	Able seaman	1,200	Returned to Spain 6/05/1521.
Pero Hernández	Rivadesella?	Able seaman	1,200	Returned to Spain 6/05/1521.
Francisco de Morales	Castile	Able seaman	1,200	Returned to Spain 6/05/1521.
Antonio Rodríguez Calderero	Castile	Able seaman	1,200	Died, Cebu, 1/05/1521.
Francisco Marinero	Castile	Able seaman	1,200	Returned to Spain 6/05/1521.
Francisco Rodríguez	Castile	Able seaman	1,200	Returned to Spain 6/05/1521.
Pedro de Laredo	Castile	Able seaman	1,200	Returned to Spain 6/05/1521.
Luis de Vendaño	Castile	Appr. seaman	800	Returned to Spain 6/05/1521.
Martín de Aguirre	Castile	Appr. seaman	800	Returned to Spain 6/05/1521.
Colin Baseau	France	Appr. seaman	800	Returned to Spain 6/05/1521.
Lucas de Mesina	Sicily	Appr. seaman	800	Returned to Spain 6/05/1521.
Lorenzo Rodríguez	Castile	Appr. seaman	800	Returned to Spain 6/05/1521.
Miguel de Pravia	Castile	Appr. seaman	800	Returned to Spain 6/05/1521.
Juanes de Iruniranzu	Castile	Appr. seaman	800	Returned to Spain 6/05/1521.
Giovanni (Juan) Genovés	Genoa	Appr. seaman	800	Returned to Spain 6/05/1521.
Juan de Orue	Castile	Appr. seaman	800	Returned to Spain 6/05/1521.
Alonso del Puerto	Castile	Appr. seaman	800	Returned to Spain 6/05/1521.
Diego García	Castile	Cabin boy	500	Returned to Spain 6/05/1521.
Diego de Mafra	Castile	Cabin boy	500	Returned to Spain 6/05/1521.
Bernard Calmette (Calmeta, Pedro Sánchez de la Reina)	France	Chaplain	1,500	Marooned in Patagonia, 11/08/1520.
Juan de Chinchilla	Castile	Supernumerary	1,500	Returned to Spain 6/05/1521.
Antonio de Escobar	Castile	Supernumerary	1,500	Returned to Spain 6/05/1521.

Name	Origin	Initial Rank	Pay	Remarks
Francisco de Angulo	Castile	Supernumerary	1,500	Returned to Spain 6/05/1521.
Francisco de Molino	Castile	Servant	800	Returned to Spain 6/05/1521.
Roque Pelea	Castile	Servant	800	Returned to Spain 6/05/1521.
Rodrigo Nieto	Castile	Servant	800	Died, Mactan, 27/04/1521.
Alonso del Río	Castile	Servant	800	Returned to Spain 6/05/1521.
Pedro de Valpuesta	Castile	Servant	800	Died (Victoria) 22/06/1522.
Juan de Léon	Castile	Servant	800	Returned to Spain 6/05/1521.
Gutierre de Tuñón	Castile	Servant	800	Returned to Spain 6/05/1521.
Juan de Sagredo	Castile	Man-at-arms	1,000	Died, Malacca, 20/09/1525.
Juan de Minchaca	Castile	Crossbowman	1,200	Returned to Spain 6/05/1521.
Antonio Hernández	Castile	Interpreter	1,500	Returned to Spain 6/05/1521.
Juan Gómez de Espinosa[5]	Castile	Servant	800	Returned to Spain 6/05/1521.
Pedro de Urrea	Flanders	Servant	800	Returned to Spain 6/05/1521.

Concepción

Name	Origin	Initial Rank	Pay	Remarks
Gaspar de Quesada	Castile	Captain	48,000/a	Executed 7/04/1522.
João Lopes Carvalho	Portugal	Pilot	20,000/a 3,000/m at sea	Died, Tidore, 14/02/1522.
Sancho de Heredía	Castile	Clerk	?	Died, Cebu, 1/05/1521.
Juan Sebastián del Cano *(de Elcano)*	Castile	Master	3,000	Returned to Spain 6/09/1522.
Juan de Acurio	Castile	Master's mate	2,000	Returned to Spain 6/09/1522.
Antonio de Bazozábal	Castile	Caulker	1,875	Died, Ternate, 1523.
Domingo de Yarza	Castile	Carpenter	1,875	Died (Trinidad) 14/10/1522.

Name	Origin	Initial Rank	Pay	Remarks
Hans Bergen *(Vargue)*	Norway ?	Master gunner	1,875	Died, Lisbon, 1526.
Pierre de Bruxelles *(Pedro de Bruselas)*	Flanders	Gunner	1,500	Died, Malacca, 1522.
Roland d'Argot *(Roldán de Argote)*	Flanders	Gunner	1,500	Returned to Spain, 1522–1523.
Pedro Pérez	Castile	Cooper	1,500	Died, San Julián, 18/06/1520.
Juan de Campos	Castile	Steward	1,200	Lost at sea, 2/1523.
Francisco Rodrigues	Portugal	Able seaman	1,200	Returned to Spain, 6/09/1522.
Francisco Ruiz	Castile	Able seaman	1,200	Died *(Trinidad)* 5/10/1522.
Mateo de Corfu *(Gorfo)*	Greece	Able seaman	1,200	Deserted, Brunei, 6/1521.
Juan Rodríguez	Castile	Able seaman	1,200	Returned to Spain, 6/09/1522.
Sebastián García	Castile	Able seaman	1,200	Died *(Trinidad)* 22/10/1522.
Gómez Hernández	Castile	Able seaman	1,200	Returned to Spain, 1522–1523.
Lorenzo de Iruna	Castile	Able seaman	1,200	Died *(Victoria)* 13/5/1522.
Juan Rodríguez *(El Sordo)*	Castile	Able seaman	1,200	Returned to Spain in 1525.
Juan de Aguirre	Castile	Able seaman	1,200	Died *(Trinidad)* 13/09/1522.
Juan de Ortega	Castile	Able seaman	1,200	Died *(Victoria)* 20/05/1522.
Juan de Olivar	Aragón	Appr. seaman	800	Died before 5/1521.
William *(Guillén)* Irés	Ireland	Appr. seaman	800	Drowned, La Plata, 25/01/1520.
Cristovão da Costa	Portugal	Appr. seaman	800	Died *(Victoria)* 9/06/1522.
Gonzalo de Vigo	Castile	Appr. seaman	800	Deserted, Marianas, 1522.
Pedro de Muguertegui	Castile	Appr. seaman	800	Died *(Victoria)* 6/09/1521.
Martín de Insaurraga	Castile	Appr. seaman	800	Died *(Victoria)* 1/06/1522.
Joanes de Tuy *(Fernandes)*	Portugal	Appr. seaman	800	Died *(Trinidad)* 3/09/1522.
Rodrigo Macías	Castile	Appr. seaman	800	Died, Cebu, 1/05/1521.

Name	Origin	Initial Rank	Pay	Remarks
Juan Navarro	Navarre	Appr. seaman	800	Died, Moluccas, 2/1523.
Sean *(Juan)* Irés	Ireland	Cabin boy	500	Died *(Trinidad)* 20/10/1522.
Pedro de Chindarza	Castile	Cabin boy	500	Returned to Spain 1522–1523.
João da Silva	Azores	Supernumerary	1,500	Died, Cebu, 1/05/1521.
Martin de Magalhães	Portugal	Supernumerary	1,500	Died, *(Victoria)* 26/06/1522.
Hernando de Bustamente	Castile	Barber	1,200	Returned to Spain 6/09/1522.
Luis de Molino	Castile	Supernumerary	1,000	Lost at sea (junk) 1523–1524.
Martín de Judicibus	Genoa	Man-at-arms	1,000	Returned to Spain, 6/09/1522.
António Fernandes	Portugal	Servant	800	Died 16/08/1520.
Alonso Coto	Genoa	Servant	800	Lost at sea (junk) 6/02/1524.
Gonçalo Fernandes	Portugal	Blacksmith	800	Abandoned at Brunei in 1521.
Juan de la Torre	Castile	Supernumerary	500	Died, Mactan, 27/04/1521.
Braz Afonso *(Blas Alfonso)*[6]	Portugal?	Supernumerary	800	Died *(Trinidad)* 14/10/1521.
Joãzito Carvalho[7]	Brazil	Cabin boy		Abandoned at Brunei in 1521.

Victoria

Name	Origin	Initial Rank	Pay	Remarks
Luis de Mendoza	Castile	Captain and treasurer	60,000/a	Killed in mutiny, 2/04/1520.
Vasco Gomes Galego	Portugal	Pilot	30,000/a	Died at sea, 28/02/1521.
Martín Méndez	Castile	Clerk	?	Returned to Spain, 1522–1523.
Antón Salomone *(Salamón)*	Sicily	Master	3,000	Executed, Rio, 20/12/1519.
Miguel de Rodas	Rhodes	Master's mate	2,000	Returned to Spain 6/09/1522.
Simon de la Rochelle *(Rochela)*	France	Caulker	1,875	Died, Cebu, 1/05/1522.

Name[1]	Origin	Initial Rank	Pay	Remarks
Martín de Gárate (*Pérez*)	Castile	Carpenter	1,875	Died, Patagonia, 31/08/1520.
Jorge Alemán	Austria	Master gunner	1,875	Died, Patagonia, 29/09/1520.
Filbert Godin	France	Gunner	1,500	Died near Borneo, 1/09/1521.
Hans Alemán	Germany	Gunner	1,500	Returned to Spain, 6/09/1522.
Afonso Gonçalves (*Alonso González*)	Portugal	Steward	1,200	Deserted *Trinidad* 08/1522 in Marianas; killed by natives.
Michele (*Miguel*) Veneciano	Venice	Able seaman	1,200	Died at sea, 25/01/1521.
Diego Gallego	Castile	Able seaman	1,200	Returned to Spain 6/09/1522.
Lope Navarro	Navarre	Able seaman	1,200	Died at sea, 8/06/1522.
Níccolo (*Nicolás*) Genovés	Genoa	Able seaman	1,200	Died at sea, 6/02/1521.
Níccolo (*Nicolás*) de Napolés	Naples	Able seaman	1,200	Returned to Spain, 1522–1523.
Miguel Sánchez	Rhodes	Able seaman	1,200	Returned to Spain 6/09/1522.
Níccolo (*Nicolás*) de Capua	Naples	Able seaman	1,200	Died, Palawan, 30/07/1521.
Benito Genovés	Genoa	Able seaman	1,200	Died (*Trinidad*) 19/09/1522.
Felipe de Rodas	Rhodes	Able seaman	1,200	Returned to Spain, 1522–1523.
Étienne (*Estéban*) Villon	France	Able seaman	1,200	Died at sea, 6/08/1522.
Giovanni Greco (*Juan Griego*)	Naples	Able seaman	1,200	Deserted, Brunei, 1521.
Rodrigo Gallego	Castile	Appr. seaman	800	Died at sea, 18/01/1521.
Antonio Baresa	Genoa	Appr. seaman	800	Suicide, Patagonia, 27/04/1520.
Domingo Português	Portugal	Appr. seaman	800	Died at sea, 26/12/1520.
Juan de Arratía	Castile	Appr. seaman	800	Returned to Spain, 6/09/1522.
Ochote de Erandio	Castile	Appr. seaman	800	Died (Philippines) 21/03/1521.
Martín de Ayamonte	Castile	Appr. seaman	800	Deserted, Timor, 5/02/1522.

Name[1]	Origin	Initial Rank	Pay	Remarks
Pedro de Tolosa	Castile	Appr. seaman	800	Returned to Spain, 1522–1523.
Bernard Maury (*Mauri, Mahuri*)	France	Appr. seaman	800	Died at sea, 18/5/1522.
Sebastião Ortiz	Portugal	Appr. seaman	800	Died (*Trinidad*) 19/09/1522.
Juan de Zubileta	Castile	Cabin boy	500	Returned to Spain, 6/09/1522.
Francisco de Carvajal	Castile	Servant	800	Fate unknown.
Juan Martín	Castile	Servant	800	Returned to Spain, 1522–1523.
Simão de Burgos	Portugal	Servant	800	Returned to Spain, 1522–1523.
Bartolomé de Saldaña	Castile	Servant	800	Deserted, Timor, 5/02/1522.
Juan de Córdoba	Castile	Cooper	500	Fate unknown.
Juan Villalón	Castile	Supernumerary	800	Died (Philippines) 3/04/1521.
Diego Díaz	Castile	Supernumerary	800	To *Trinidad;* shipped out from Ternate; fate unknown.
Afonso de Moura (*Alonso de Mora*)	Portugal	Supernumerary	800	Died at sea, 23/12/1520.
Diego de Peralta	Navarre	Man-at-arms	1,000	Died at sea, 1/01/1521.
Gonzalo Rodríguez	Castile	Blacksmith	1,200	Died at sea, 4/01/1521.
Pedro García	Castile	Blacksmith	1,000	Died, Cebu, 1/05/1521.
Hernando de Aguilar[8]	?	Servant	800	Died, Cebu, 1/05/1521.
Fernão Lopes (*Hernán López*)[9]	Portugal	Supernumerary	800	Died at sea (*Trinidad*) 27/09/1522.

Santiago

Name	Origin	Initial Rank	Pay	Remarks
Juan Rodríguez Serrano	Castile	Captain and Pilot	30,000/a	Succeeded Magellan as captain general; died, Cebu, 1/05/1521.
Baldassare Palla (*Baltasar Genovés*)	Genoa	Master	3,000	Died (*Victoria*) 3/04/1521.

Name[1]	Origin	Initial Rank	Pay	Remarks
Barthélemy Prieur (Bartolomé Malo)	France	Master's mate	2,000	Died, Malacca, 11/1524.
António da Costa	?	Clerk	?	Fate unknown.[10]
Gaspar Dias (Díaz)	Azores	Supernumerary	?	Captain's servant and ship's steward; fate unknown.[10]
Juan García (Xinovés)	Genoa	Caulker	1,500	Died (Trinidad) 10/08/1522.
Richard Normand (Raxar de Normandía)	France	Carpenter	1,500	Returned to Spain, 1522–1523.
Laurent (Lorenzo) Corrat	France	Gunner	1,500	Fate unknown.[10]
Jean Massiat (Juan Macías)	France	Gunner	1,500	Died (Trinidad) 27/10/1522.
Antón Flamenco	Flanders	Able seaman	1,200	Fate unknown.[10]
Luis Martín (Martínez)	Castile	Able seaman	1,200	Fate unknown.[10]
Bartolomé García	Castile	Able seaman	1,200	Fate unknown.[10]
Agostino (Agustín)	Savona (Genoa)	Able seaman	1,200	Fate unknown.[10]
Bocacio Alonso	Castile	Able seaman	1,200	Returned to Spain, 1522–1523.
Pierre Gascon (Pedro Gastón)	France	Able seaman	1,200	Died (Victoria) 21/06/1522.
Doménico Battista[11] (Domingo Bautista)	Genoa	Able seaman	1,200	Died (Victoria) 14/06/1522.
Diego García de Trigueros	Castile	Able seaman	1,200	Died (Victoria) 21/06/1522.
Pedro Díaz	Castile	Appr. seaman	800	Died (Trinidad) 18/09/1522.
Alonso Hernández	Castile	Appr. seaman	800	Died (Trinidad) 6/10/1522.
Juan[12]	?	Appr. seaman	800	Drowned, Patagonia, 22/05/1520.
Jean Blaise (Juan Bretón)	France	Appr. seaman	800	Died (Trinidad) 17/09/1522.
Pedro Bello	Castile	Appr. seaman	800	Died (Trinidad) 14/09/1522.
Jerónimo García	Castile	Appr. seaman	800	Died (Trinidad) 3/10/1522.
Pierre Arnault (Pedro Arnaot)	France	Appr. seaman	800	Died (Trinidad) 15/09/1522.
Pedro García de Trigueros	Castile	Appr. seaman	800	Died (Trinidad) 29/10/1522.

Name[1]	Origin	Initial Rank	Pay	Remarks
Jean *(Juan)* Flamenco	Flanders	Cabin boy	500	Died *(Victoria)* 9/02/1521.
Francisco Ante[13]	Castile	Cabin boy	500	Died, Cebu, 1/05/1521.
Juan de Aroche	Castile	Sergeant-at-arms	1,000	Died *(Victoria)* 10/04/1521.
Martín de Barrena	Castile	Supernumerary	1,000	Died *(Victoria)* 9/04/1521.
Hernán Lorenzo	Castile	Supernumerary	800	Fate unknown.[10]
Maestre Pedro[14]	France?	Supernumerary	800	Returned to Spain 1522–1523.

Notes

1. Due to lack of records, this list of 241 names is incomplete. The number of men who sailed with the fleet probably was 260–270. Some were recruited in the Canary Islands.
2. Monthly, unless otherwise noted by an "a", which indicates per annum.
3. Dates presented in day/month/year sequence.
4. Son of *Victoria* pilot, Vasco Gomes Galego.
5. Probably related to the master-at-arms, Gonzalo Gómez de Espinosa, as they came from the same town.
6. Enrolled at Tenerife, Canary Islands.
7. Boarded at Rio de Janeiro.
8. His name is not on any of the enrollment lists, but appears in the list of those killed on Cebu as a servant (man-at-arms) of Captain Mendoza. He probably was hired at Tenerife in the Canaries.
9. Hired at Tenerife, he transferred to the *Trinidad* ". . . to make carbon black for repairing the ship."
10. After the *Santiago* was wrecked, these men may have transferred to the *San Antonio* and returned with it to Spain on 6/05/1521.
11. Son of Giovanni Battista Polcevera, master of the *Trinidad*.
12. Sometimes referred to as Juan Negro, he was the slave of the captain, Juan Rodríguez Serrano.
13. Serrano's stepson.
14. Hired for *Victoria* at Tenerife; not to be confused with Pedro de Bruselas *(Concepción)*, also known as Maestre Pedro.

Appendix 3B The Survivors

Arrived at San Lúcar on *Victoria*, September 6, 1522

Name[1]	Final Rank	Original Berth
Juan Sebastián del Cano	Captain	*Concepción*
Francisco Albo	Pilot	*Trinidad*
Miguel de Rodas	Master	*Victoria*
Juan de Acurio	Master's mate	*Concepción*
Martín de Judicibus	Master-at-arms	*Concepción*
Hernando de Bustamente	Barber	*Concepción*
Antonio de Pigafetta	Supernumerary	*Trinidad*
Juan Martín	Supernumerary	*Victoria*
Diego Gallego	Able seaman	*Victoria*
Antonio Hernández Colmenero	Able seaman	*Trinidad*
Níccolo Napolés	Able seaman	*Victoria*
Francisco Rodríguez	Able seaman	*Concepción*
Juan Rodríguez de Huelva	Able seaman	*Concepción*
Miguel Sánchez de Rodas	Able seaman	*Victoria*
Juan de Arratía	Apprentice seaman	*Victoria*
Juan de San Andrés	Apprentice seaman	*Trinidad*
Diego García[2]	Cabin boy	*San Antonio*
Juan de Zubileta	Cabin boy	*Victoria*

Three Moluccans, embarked at Tidore.

Victoria Crewmen Seized in Cape Verde Islands, Returned to Spain by 1523

Name[1]	Final Rank	Original Berth
Roland (Roldán) de Argot	Gunner	*Concepción*
Martín Méndez	Clerk	*Victoria*
Pedro de Tolosa	Steward	*Victoria*
Gómez Hernández	Able seaman	*Concepción*
Simón de Burgos	Supernumerary	*Victoria*
Pedro de Chindarza	Cabin boy	*Concepción*
Maestre Pedro	Supernumerary	*Santiago*
Juan Martínez	Supernumerary	*Trinidad*
Felipe de Rodas	Able seaman	*Victoria*
Bocacio Alonso	Able seaman	*Santiago*
Vasquito Galego	Apprentice seaman	*Trinidad*
Richard Normand	Carpenter	*Santiago*
Manuel (Moluccan)		

Trinidad Survivors Returned to Spain: 1525–1527

Name[1]	Final Rank	Original Berth
Juan Rodríguez (El Sordo)	Able seaman	*Concepción*
Leone (Léon) Pancaldo	Assistant Pilot	*Trinidad*
Gonzalo Gómez de Espinosa	Captain General	*Trinidad*
Ginés de Mafra	Master's mate	*Trinidad*

Notes

1. Total survivors: 34 Europeans, 4 Moluccans.
2. Some have assumed that this was the able seaman from Trigueros originally assigned to the *Santiago*, but Medina (*Descubrimiento*), p. CCCLXXXV) cited records showing that this Diego García died aboard the *Victoria*, near Cape Rojo on the coast of Africa, on June 21, 1522. The only other Diego García in the fleet was enrolled as a cabin boy on the *San Antonio*, and as there are no records of his death, it has been assumed that he returned to Spain with that ship. Perhaps, however, he was the cabin boy for San Martín, and accompanied the astrologer when he transferred to the *Victoria*.

Appendix 3C Biographical Sketches

These sketches have been selected and adapted from the 268 presented in José Toribio Medina's *El Descubrimiento del Océano Pacífico* . . . , Chapter XVI, *Los Compañeros de Magallanes*. Medina's principal sources on Magellan's crew were the records for the Magellan expedition in the Archives of the Indies in Seville. While these records were quite good for the professional officers and enlisted men of the fleet, they contained little or no information about the officers appointed by the court to positions of high command.

Because the outcome of the expedition was affected profoundly by the refusal of these courtiers to acknowledge Magellan's authority as captain general, this dearth of biographical data is unfortunate. On the other hand, the relative wealth of information about the expedition's ordinarily anonymous seamen and professional officers provides us with a happy contrast. Driven by the single-minded determination of their captain general, the skill and incredible stamina of these long-suffering mariners produced what well may be the grandest achievement in the history of seafaring, the first circumnavigation of the Earth.

Acurio, Juan de

This survivor of the first circumnavigation was born in Bermeo, Vizcaya, in Old Castile. Acurio was assigned to the *Concepción* as *contramaestre* (master's mate), and when that ship was scuttled following the massacre on Cebu, he transferred to the *Victoria* and returned with it to Spain, on September 6, 1522. Having been a witness to the treaties signed by the Moluccan chieftans, he was called to testify at the Conference of Badajoz-Elvas. There, in May 1524, Spanish and Portuguese diplomats tried unsuccessfully to resolve their nations' differences over the Moluccas. Acurio was paid for three years and twenty-eight days of service with the fleet, and was permitted to keep a fifty-five pound sack of cloves brought from the Moluccas. What became of him after Badajoz-Elvas is not known. Richer by far in experience, but little more in worldly goods than when he sailed from San Lúcar, he may well have gone back to sea.

Albo, Francisco (Alvo, Calvo)

A resident of Rhodes on the Greek island of that name off the coast of Anatolia (Turkey), his birthplace was listed as Axio. While no town by that name is shown on modern maps of Greece, there is an Axiós River emptying into the Gulf of Salonika near Thessaloniki. Albo's birthdate was not listed in the payroll records of the *Casa de Contratación*.

Initially assigned as master's mate on the *Trinidad*, when the fleet was approaching Cape Santo Agostinho on the coast of Brazil on November 29, 1519, Albo started a navigational log, probably because he had begun functioning as acting pilot or pilot's assistant. He maintained the log until September 4, 1522 when, as pilot of the *Victoria*, he recorded the sighting of Cape St. Vincent on the European mainland. This log (*Diario o Derrotero del Viaje de Magallanes* . . .) provides the best surviving record of the globe-girdling track of Magellan's fleet.

Payroll records show that Albo's service as master's mate ended on November 29, 1520, just after the fleet emerged from the strait. Magellan may have promoted him to pilot on that date, but it is not clear when Albo transferred to the *Victoria*. That ship's pilot, Vasco Galego, died in mid-Pacific, and its master, Antón Salamón had been executed in Brazil; its captain; Duarte Barbosa, was not a professional mariner. After Galego died, the only navigation officers aboard the *Victoria* were the astrologer-pilot, Andrés de San Martín, and the master's mate, Miguel de Rodas. Albo probably transferred from the *Trinidad* after San Martín was killed in the massacre at Cebu.

Upon his return to Spain with the *Victoria*, Albo accompanied Cano and Bustamente to Valladolid where, on October 18, 1522, he testified concerning the events of the voyage. At a formal hearing, his answers to the questions of a court judicial officer were notable for lack of personal bias.[1] A professional mariner to the core, Albo had been careful to avoid involvement in the political controversies surging through the fleet. By tending to his navigation and faithfully recording the positions of the fleet from the time he began keeping his log until the end of the voyage, Albo left for posterity a priceless record of the world's first circumnavigation.

Although a royal order dated February 13, 1523, granted to Albo an annual pension of 50,000 maravedis, there is nothing to indicate that he ever received any payments from it. Not among those present at the Conference of Badajoz-Elvas, it is not known what became of him. It has been suggested that, after testifying at Valladolid, Albo left Spain and entered the service of a Turkish admiral, Piri Re'is.[2] Since Albo's longitude estimates placed the Moluccas clearly within the Portuguese Hemisphere, the Spanish diplomats preparing for the Conference of Badajoz-Elvas may have tried to get him to alter some of the entries in his log book. If professional pride caused him to refuse such a request, he may have left Spain under a cloud. Returning to his home in Rhodes, he may have learned there about employment opportunities with the Turks.

Argot, Roldán de

A native of Bruges in Flanders, Roldán was assigned to the *Concepción* as a gunner. In the Strait of Magellan, he was a member of the boat crew sent ahead from the Bay of Sardines to determine whether the channel in which they had been sailing led to the ocean. After sailing up the channel for some distance, the crew waited with the shallop in an inlet while Roldán scaled a prominent hill and saw a straight, broadening channel leading northwest to a watery horizon that he took to be the ocean. Returning to the Bay of Sardines, he so informed Magellan who, according to Pigafetta, "wept for joy." As a reward for the good news they had brought, Magellan promised the boat crew an award of prize money (*albricias*) upon their return to Spain.

There has been some confusion over the location of the hill scaled by Roldán. Known as the *Campana de Roldán* (Roldán's Bell), subsequent navigators of the Strait of Magellan, including Captain Robert Fitzroy of the H.M.S. *Beagle*, have attempted to identify it. Mateo Martinić of the Universidad de Magallanes in Punta Arenas, Chile, has proposed an elevation on Santa Inez Island shown on Chilean maps as *Cerro El Morrión* (Helmet Hill). Its distance from the Bay of Sardines (Bahía Fortescue) is consistent with the time it took Roldán's shallop to make the round trip described in Piga-fetta's narrative. Looking northwest from its summit on a clear day, an observer's horizon lies beyond Paso Largo in the broad Paso del Mar, which opens into the Pacific Ocean.

Roldán was aboard the *Victoria* when it sailed from the Moluccas headed for Spain. Very ill when the ship reached the Cape Verde Islands, Roldán was sent ashore for treatment. From there he was sent to Lisbon with the shore party from the *Victoria* seized by the Portuguese in the harbor of São Tiago. By April 1523, Roldán was back in Spain and had established himself as a merchant in Seville.

Life as a merchant proved too tame for the adventuresome Fleming and on July 24, 1525, when the fleet of Jufré de Loaísa sailed from La Coruña to follow Magellan's route to the Moluccas, Roldán de Argot was enrolled as a gunner. He was not among the survivors of that ill-fated expedition. How he died is not known, but two incidents in which he was involved were reported. In January 1526, Loaísa's fleet was approach-ing Cape Vírgenes at the eastern entrance to the Strait of Magellan. North of the Cape, Cano, serving as pilot, mistook the mouth of the Río Gallego for the entrance to the Strait. Not recognizing the landmarks he had expected as his ship entered the estuary, Cano sent Roldán and seven others in a longboat to explore the waterway, a task strik-ingly similar to the one Magellan had given him six years before.

In February 1528, on Gilolo, Roldán was a member of a small force of Spaniards led by Andrés de Urdaneta that attacked a village held by the Portuguese. Roldán was hit in the face by a cannonball, making him, according to Urdaneta's report, "the ugliest man in the world."[3] That is the last notice of the world-roving Flemish gunner while he was still alive. In 1538, his name was mentioned during the course of an official interro-gation in Spain, but the language of the report implied that Roldán was deceased.

Barbosa, Duarte

Although it is clear the Duarte Barbosa was related to Magellan by marriage, it is not known precisely how. Barbosa has been variously described as Magellan's "brother-in-law," "cousin," and "relative." Close study of the available evidence led the Chilean archi-vist José Toribio Medina to opt for the brother-in-law relationship. The language of a 1540 suit to recover salaries owed by the Crown to Magellan and two cousins who sailed with him filed by Jaime Barbosa, son of Magellan's father-in-law Diogo Barbosa, suggests that Duarte may have been the eldest son of Diogo. As such, he would have been Magellan's brother-in-law.

It is possible that Duarte was the author of *O Livro de Odoardo Barbosa*, a detailed description of islands and lands from the Ryukyus to the Cape of Good Hope. Since the author had not traveled east of India's Malabar Coast, the Belgian historian, Jean Denucé, suggested that he may have gotten information about the lands east of Mala-bar from Magellan in Cochin in 1512–1513, during the latter's return to Portugal from Malacca.[4] While Albuquerque was viceroy, there were at least three Portuguese in India named Duarte Barbosa. The author of *O Livro* . . . shared at least one characteristic with Magellan's brother-in-law: the propensity for getting in trouble for neglecting his job. On one occasion, Albuquerque had him put in leg irons for that offense; during the course of his voyage, Magellan punished Duarte twice for the same reason.

In 1518, while the fleet was being fitted out for the voyage, Magellan sent Barbosa to

Bilbao to purchase armaments, and when the fleet left San Lúcar, Barbosa was listed on the rolls as a supernumerary on the *Trinidad*. In the harbor of Rio de Janeiro, Barbosa outraged Magellan by absenting himself from his duties for a protracted dalliance with some willing Tupi maidens, and the disgusted captain general had his brother-in-law apprehended and put in irons.

Barbosa redeemed himself at Port San Julián by leading the boarding party that recaptured the *Victoria* from the mutineers. Magellan rewarded him by making him captain of that ship, replacing Luis de Mendoza, killed during the mutiny. Later, in the Strait of Magellan, Barbosa took the *Victoria* all the way back to the Atlantic entrance in a fruitless search for the missing *San Antonio*.

On the Island of Cebu in the Philippines, Barbosa's libido again got the better of him, and he absented himself from his ship for three days of debauchery while Magellan and Chaplain Valderrama were baptizing thousands of islanders. When Magellan learned that Barbosa had deserted his ship and was setting a horrible example for the new converts, he was furious and removed his brother-in-law from the command of the *Victoria*, replacing him with another relative, Cristovão Rebêlo.

After Magellan and Rebêlo were killed on Mactan, Barbosa briefly shared the fleet command with Juan Serrano, but on May 1, 1522, five days after the death of Magellan, Duarte Barbosa's spotted career ended in the massacre at Cebu.

Bazozábal, Antón de

A Basque from Bermeo, Bazozábal was first assigned as a caulker on the *Concepción*, but later replaced Albo as master's mate on the *Trinidad*. A survivor of that ship's last voyage, he was imprisoned by the Portuguese on Ternate, where he is thought to have died in 1523. In July of that year, the Council of the Indies authorized payment of 20,000 maravedis of his back wages to his wife.

Bergen, Hans

In the records of the *Casa de Contratación*, Hans's name is badly garbled: the spelling used above was derived by Medina from one of several recorded by the *Casa's* scribes: "Ansbargen." If Medina's interpretation is correct and Bergen was Hans's home town, he was the only Norwegian to have sailed with Magellan, and the first of his nationality to have completed a circumnavigation of the Earth. The case for Hans's Norwegian nationality is strengthened by the names of his parents as they appear in the *Casa's* records: Borge and Elisabed.

Hired as a gunner, Hans shipped out on the *Concepción*. After it was scuttled off Bohol, he became master gunner on the *Trinidad*, filling the post left vacant by the death of Master Andrew. Along with the rest of his shipmates, Hans was imprisoned by the Portuguese on Ternate after the *Trinidad's* unsuccessful attempt to sail back across the Pacific Ocean. From Ternate he was sent to Malacca and then to Cochin, and after two terrible years in India in which most of his shipmates died, he was shipped to Portugal. Arriving in Lisbon on July 24, 1526, he was immediately jailed with his companions, Gómez de Espinosa and Ginés de Mafra.

After seven months in the Limonejo Prison, Hans died, willing all that he owned to his chief and companion in adversity, Gómez de Espinosa. Hans's estate, which consisted of back pay and a glass jug filled with nutmeg and cloves (shipped to Spain on the *Victoria*), was valued at 41,200 maravedis. To settle Espinosa's claim to the estate, the Crown authorized disbursement of half that amount from treasury funds, which Espinosa received on May 24 of the same year.

Burgos, Simón de

On enlisting with Magellan's fleet, this native-born Portuguese declared that he was Castilian, a native of Burgos. He had arrived in Castile in 1512, finding employment with a town official in Ciudad Rodrigo, but he was fired when he married against his employer's wishes. Leaving his wife, Catalina Alonso, at the house of a friend, Burgos went to Seville where, disguising his Portuguese nationality, he was accepted as a supernumerary on the personal staff of Luis de Mendoza, captain of the *Victoria*. He remained on the *Victoria* until seized by the Portuguese in São Tiago, Cape Verde Islands, on July 15, 1522. With the other members of a boat crew from *Victoria*, he was imprisoned in the Cape Verdes for five months and twenty-seven days before being shipped to Portugal.

Released by royal order, the men of the boat crew returned to Seville, where Burgos was accused of having alerted the port officials in São Tiago to the *Victoria*'s true identity. For misrepresenting himself as a Castilian when he enlisted, the *Casa* refused to pay him the wages accrued over the three hundred twenty-eight days of his service with the fleet, but provided him with 6,750 maravedis to travel to Valladolid, where he was interrogated further.[5]

Unable to clear himself and desperate to recover his withheld wages, Burgós next went to Ciudad Rodrigo in search of his wife, whom he hoped could be persuaded to support his claim that he was Castilian, not Portuguese. While he was unable to find the wife he had left with a friend, he did find witnesses willing to testify that he had resided with her in Ciudad Rodrigo. This testimony, however, was insufficient to disprove the charge that he was Portuguese and had enlisted under false pretenses. It is doubtful that Simón de Burgos ever recovered the wages owed to him for the voyage of nearly three years that had taken him completely around the world.

Bustamente, Hernando de

Born in 1493, Bustamente was a native of Mérida, in Extremadura. He was married to a lady named María Rodríguez, and had been an employee of the port of Contreras. Enrolled as a supernumerary, he was assigned to the *Concepción* as ship's barber, who also functioned as a medic, able to peform minor surgery. Bustamente was literate and considered a gentleman. In the Bay of Sardines (in the Strait of Magellan), he was one of the crew of the shallop sent ahead to see if the channel to the northwest led to the ocean.

When the *Concepción* was scuttled, Bustamente transferred to the *Victoria* and was one of the lucky survivors who, on September 6, 1522, completed the first circumnavigation of the Earth. As one of the two "best informed" of his crew, Cano selected Bustamente to accompany him to Valladolid for an audience with the Emperor, and on October 18, 1522, Bustamente testified before a court judicial officer concerning the events of the voyage. On May 23, 1524, at the Conference of Badajoz-Elvas, he testified in support of Spanish claims to the Moluccas.

When the second Spanish expedition to the Moluccas, commanded by Jufré de Loaísa, was organized in 1525, Bustamente invested eighty ducats (about 28,000 maravedis) in it. On April 5 of that year, he was appointed treasurer of the *Sancti Spiritus*, one of the seven ships of Loaísa's fleet. The expedition sailed from La Coruña with Juan Sebastián del Cano as chief pilot of the fleet and captain of the *Sancti Spiritus*. The passage through the strait was more difficult for Loaísa than for Magellan; Cano's ship was wrecked and two more ships deserted. Upon entering the Pacific on May 26, 1526, the four remaining ships were scattered by a terrible storm and were unable to reassemble. Only the *Santa María de la Victoria*, on which Bustamente was the accountant, reached the Moluccas. Four days after crossing the equator in mid-Pacific, Captain General Loaísa died and was succeeded by Cano, who perished a week later, on August 6, 1526.[6]

Cano's successor died after the *Santa María de la Victoria* left Guam, and Bustamente was one of two officers nominated to succeed him as captain general. Before the ballots could be counted, his rival, Martín Iñiguez de Zarquisano, threw them into the sea. The crew urged the two rivals to share command, but Zarqisano preempted Bustamente and assumed full command.

Later, in the Moluccas, Bustamente was charged with irregularities in his accounts, and imprisoned, and when released a year later, he resumed his duties as *contador.* After a vain five-year struggle to maintain their foothold in the Moluccas, the Spaniards surrendered to the Portuguese. Promised repatriation with the rest of his countrymen, Bustamente was taken to Malacca, where, after much difficulty getting the Portuguese authorities to permit him to embark for Europe, Bustamente finally boarded a ship bound for Lisbon. He did not live to see Spain again; he was poisoned while the ship was at sea.

Calmette, Bernard (Bernardo Calmeta)

A native of Lectoure in southern France, Calmette was chaplain of the *San Antonio*, a post in which he quickly became an ally of the captain of that ship and fleet inspector general, Juan de Cartagena. Although he had participated in the mutiny at Port San Julián, Cartagena was spared by Magellan and he was permitted considerable freedom. Chaplain Calmette took advantage of this and conspired with Cartagena to incite another mutiny. It was a fatal mistake; when Magellan learned of it, he sentenced both conspirators to abandonment on the desolate coast of Patagonia.

In the payroll records and casualty lists, the name of the priest marooned with Cartagena is given as Pero Sánchez, or Pero Sánchez de la Reina (or Viena). In the crew rosters and salary records for the servants of Cartagena and Coca, the name of the *San Antonio*'s chaplain is listed as Bernardo Calmeta. Two chaplains are known to have sailed with Magellan's fleet: Valderrama of the *Trinidad* and Calmette (Calmeta) of the *San Antonio*. In the records of the expedition, there is no mention of Bernardo Calmeta or Pero Sánchez after the fleet departed from Port San Julián. Nor does either name appear on the list of those who returned to Spain with the *San Antonio*. It appears that both names refer to the same person, the priest marooned in Patagonia. Since his French name may have been troublesome for his Spanish-speaking shipmates, Calmette may also have used the Spanish name that appears in some records.

Campos, Juan de

A native of Alcalá de Henares (near Madrid), Campos was enrolled as steward (*dispensero*) of the *Concepción*. After his ship was scuttled, he transferred to the *Trinidad*, on which he served as clerk.

At Palawan, when the crews of the *Trinidad* and the *Victoria* were reluctant to land for fear of a hostile reception, Campos volunteered to go ashore alone to try to procure food supplies. After the *Trinidad*'s skiff put him ashore, he walked inland for about three miles until he encountered some natives. Campos managed to win their confidence without the benefit of an interpreter, and by the next day a supply of foodstuffs had been collected, which was cheerfully delivered to the waiting ships.

The courage, tact, and skill shown by Campos in this episode won for him the admiration of Gómez de Espinosa, who later would replace Lopes Carvalho as captain general. When the *Trinidad* set forth on its ill-fated attempt to sail back across the Pacific, Espinosa placed Campos in charge of the Spanish *factoría* on Tidore. Twenty days after the departure of the *Trinidad*, Campos and his companions were overpowered by a Portuguese naval force recently established at Ternate.

Imprisoned on Ternate, Campos and his companions from the *factoriía* were later joined by Espinosa and the other survivors of the last voyage of the *Trinidad*. With their ship lying helpless off Gilolo, they had surrendered it to the Portuguese. Months later, the Portuguese shipped most of their Spanish captives to Cochin. The junk carrying Campos and three other Spanish prisoners never arrived in Cochin. Whether the four Spaniards were murdered, shipwrecked or captured by pirates to be sold into slavery, they never were heard from again.

Cano, Juan Sebastián del

There has been considerable controversy over the proper spelling of Cano's name. In addition to the spelling used above, the variants *Elcano*, *Delcano* and *Elkano* all have their adherents. Careful study of the flamboyant Basque navigator's signatures led Medina to the conclusion that he usually signed his name simply as *Cano*. The first two variants are fusions: one with the Spanish article alone, the other with the article and the preceding particle; the third variant, *Elkano,* is Basque.

Cano was born about 1487 in Guetaria a coastal town near San Sebastián, Guipúzcoa (one of the Basque provinces). A professional mariner, he rose through the ranks to become master of a 200-ton ship chartered by the king of Castile for service in the trade with North Africa and the Levant. Stranded in a North African port without funds to pay his sailors, Cano obtained a short-term loan from some Italians in the service of the duke of Savoy, but when the Crown funds he was expecting failed to arrive on time, Cano sold his ship to settle his debt to the Italians (whose urging that he had better do so *prèsto*, probably was anything but gentle). As the chartered ship was considered Crown property, its sale to foreigners constituted a violation of Castilian law, casting Cano's professional reputation under a cloud. Nevertheless, he was accepted for service with Magellan's fleet.

Cano was first entered on the fleet rolls in February 1519, as master's mate of the *Concepción*, drawing a monthly wage of 900 maravedis. For the month of April of that year, now master of the *Concepción*, he received 1,800 maravedis. Prior to the fleet's departure, he was advanced 18,000 maravedis against anticipated sea wages of 3,000 maravedis per month.[7]

Even before the fleet put to sea, captains Quesada of the *Concepción* and Mendoza of the *Victoria* had aligned themselves with Captain Cartagena of the *San Antonio* in a faction opposed to Magellan into which Cano unwisely allowed himself to be swept. On the eve of the mutiny at Port San Julián, he tried, unsuccessfully, to recruit to the rebel cause the other Basque shipmaster in the fleet, Juan de Elorriaga of the *San Antonio*. During the uprising, a boarding party from the *Concepción* led by Quesada seized the *San Antonio*, mortally wounding Elorriaga and taking captive the pilot and master's mate. Cano, summoned from the *Concepción* by the mutineers to operate the *San Antonio*, uncovered and primed the artillery, raising the anchors and maneuvering the ship into position to fire on the two ships still under Magellan's control.

After the uprising was quelled, Cano was one of the forty mutineers condemned to death. However, as the fleet could ill afford to lose the services of a veteran shipmaster, Magellan reduced his sentence. Through the long, bitter winter at Port San Julián, Cano, in chains, toiled at hard labor, but when the fleet set sail for the Río Santa Cruz on August 24, 1520, he was reinstated as master of the *Concepción*.

After his ship was scuttled at Bohol, Cano was named master of the *Victoria*. On September 21, 1521, Gómez de Espinosa, who had been captain of the *Victoria* since the massacre at Cebu, replaced Lopes Carvalho as captain general on the *Trinidad*. Cano replaced Espinosa as captain of the *Victoria* and was elected fleet treasurer. He was a signatory to the treaties concluded with the Moluccan chieftans in November and December of 1521. As captain of the *Victoria* during its historic journey from Tidore to Seville, Cano received much of the credit and most of the glory for the first circumnavigation.

Upon his arrival in Valladolid on October 18, 1522, Cano was received graciously by Charles V, who awarded him an annual pension of 500 ducats (175,000 maravedis) and pardoned him for his crime of selling a Castilian ship to foreigners. The emperor also honored him with an elaborate coat of arms with a globe bearing the motto: *"Primus circumdediste me"* (You were the first to encircle me). Like Albo and Bustamente, Cano was interrogated by an officer of the court regarding the events of the voyage. Unlike the dispassionate testimony of his two companions, Cano's was marred by a vicious diatribe critical of Magellan's leadership, accusing him of deliberate violations of royal orders. In March 1524, Cano was appointed to a royal commission assigned the task of formulating arguments to sustain Spanish claims to sovereignty over the Moluccas.

Despite the honors lavished on him by a grateful monarch, life ashore became increasingly uncomfortable for Juan Sebastián del Cano. Having sired children by two different women, his domestic situation was less than idyllic, and threats on his life caused him to petition the emperor for an armed guard. Who made these threats is not known, but it is possible that among the survivors of the historic voyage of the *Victoria* were some with old scores to settle.

Beset ashore with domestic and social difficulties, Cano yearned to go back to sea where life, though hard and frought with danger, was far less complicated. He seized the opportunity when offered the position of pilot major with the fleet of Jufré de Loaísa and the command of its second largest vessel, the *Sancti Spiritus*.

Aiming to follow Magellan's track to the Moluccas, Loaísa's seven-ship fleet sailed from La Coruña on July 24, 1525. Although he had sailed through the Strait of Magellan in 1520, Pilot Major Cano was unable at first to find it on his second attempt in 1526. Just as he located the entrance, gale winds arose and Cano sought shelter behind

Punta Dungeness, where he ran the *Sancti Spiritus* aground. The ship broke up on the beach, but most of the crew were saved and Cano transferred to the *Santa María de la Victoria*.

During a long, arduous passage of the fleet through the Strait, two ships deserted. Shortly after the remaining four ships sailed into the Pacific on May 26, 1526, they were scattered by a violent storm and were unable to reassemble. The *Santa María de la Victoria* headed alone across the Pacific. As had occurred aboard the three ships with which Magellan made the first crossing of that vast ocean, scurvy began to take its toll of the crew. Feeling the illness coming upon him as they crossed the equator on July 26, Cano dictated his will. Four days later, Loaísa died and Cano succeeded him as captain general, a position he held for less than a week. On August 6, 1526, another scurvy-ravaged body was committed to the deep–that of Juan Sebastián del Cano.[8]

Cartagena, Juan de

A native of Burgos in Old Castile, Cartagena's age at the time he was assigned to Magellan's fleet is not known, though he was married and had a daughter, Doña Catalina. On March 30, 1519, Cartagena, an officer of the Palace Guard, was named captain of the *San Antonio* and inspector general for the fleet. His annual salary for both posts totalled 100,000 maravedis. In addition, he continued to earn his salary as an officer of the Palace Guard while he served with the fleet.

From the moment of his arrival in Seville in July 1519, Cartagena displayed a haughty arrogance toward Magellan, whose authority he consistently failed to acknowledge. During the fleet's traverse of the Atlantic, irritated by Cartagena's public acts of insubordination, Magellan had him arrested, stripped him of the command of the *San Antonio*, and clapped him in stocks on the *Trinidad*. In deference to the pleas of the Castilian officers, Magellan released Cartagena to the custody of Captain Mendoza on the *Victoria*.

Contrary to Magellan's orders, Mendoza permitted Cartagena to go ashore while the fleet was anchored in the harbor of Rio de Janeiro. When Magellan learned of this, he transferred Cartagena to the custody of Captain Quesada on the *Concepción*. In Port San Julián, Quesada and Cartagena collaborated in the mutiny of 1–2 April, 1520. For his part in the mutiny, Quesada was beheaded. For his part, and for a later attempt to incite mutiny, Cartagena was marooned on the desolate coast of Patagonia.[9]

Coto, Alonso

Also known as Alonso Genovés, Cota, or Costa, Coto was a native of Genoa. Enrolled as a supernumerary and servant of the captain, he served on the *Concepción* as a man-at-arms. When that ship was scuttled, he transferred to the *Trinidad*. Coto was one of four crewmen assigned to run the *factoría* on Tidore, where twenty days after the *Trinidad*'s departure he was captured by the Portuguese and imprisoned on Ternate. Coto and a fellow prisoner were put on a junk bound for Malacca; the junk disappeared and neither of them was heard from again.

Elorriaga, Juan de

At the time he enrolled with Magellan's fleet, Elorriaga, a Basque, was living in Seville with his wife, Juana de la Haya. His name first appeared on the fleet payroll in December 1518, when he was listed as an unassigned master's mate. Assigned to the *San Antonio* in February 1519, by April of that year he had been promoted to the rank of master.

With the fleet becalmed off the coast of Guinea in November 1519, Magellan found it necessary to remind Cartagena of certain courtesies commonly observed in communications between the ships of a fleet at sea. It was Elorriaga, the master of the *San Antonio*, who informed his insubordinate captain of Magellan's demand that the customary protocol be observed.

Just before the Easter mutiny at Port San Julián, Cano tried to convince him that Magellan should be replaced as captain general, but Elorriaga refused to listen. During the mutiny, Elorriaga upbraided Captain Quesada of the *Concepción* for illegally boarding the *San Antonio* and seizing its captain. He demanded that Quesada immediately release Captain Mesquita and return to his own ship. Quesada responded by viciously stabbing Elorriaga, leaving him lying on the deck, bleeding. The mortally wounded shipmaster was able to testify at the court martial of the mutineers, but his condition gradually worsened. On July 15, 1520, the loyal, strictly proper Juan de Elorriaga died.

Galego, Vasco Gomes (Vasco Gómez Gallego)

A Portuguese by birth, it has been speculated that the Vasco Gallego who sailed with Magellan may have been the Vasco Galego de Carvalho who is said to have sailed with João de Lisboa to the Río de la Plata in 1506, but there is no reliable evidence for such an identity. He was, however, the same Vasco Gallego who, by an order from King Ferdinand dated July 12, 1514, was commissioned a royal pilot by the *Casa de Contratación* in Seville. A short time later, Galego sailed with the expedition of Andrés Niño to *Tierra Firme* (the mainland shore of the Caribbean).

In 1518, Galego was assigned to Magellan's fleet as pilot of the *Victoria*, with the understanding that his son, Vasquito, be permitted to sail with the fleet. The payroll records show that on July 31, 1519, Galego was advanced 30,000 maravedis (a year's salary) plus a cost-of-living allowance of 7,500 maravedis.[10]

Like most of the professional officers of the expedition (with the notable exception of Cano), Galego seems to have stayed aloof from fleet politics. He was on board the *Victoria* when it lined up with the rebels at Port San Julián, but was not involved in the mutiny. Falling ill (probably with scurvy) while the fleet was crossing the Pacific Ocean, he dictated his will to the ship's clerk, Sancho de Heredía and on February 28, 1521, when the fleet was sailing northwest of Bikini Atoll, Vasco Galego died. Surviving him were his widow, Margarita Hernández, and two sons.

Galego, Vasco Garcia (Vasco García Gallego, Vasquito)

The son of Vasco Gomes Galego and Catalina García of Bayona (in Galicia, near the Portuguese border), he was enrolled as an apprentice seaman on the *Trinidad* and later transferred to the *Victoria*, on which his father was pilot.[11] He was one of the shore party seized by the Portuguese in the Cape Verde Islands, imprisoned, and later returned to Spain. As the name for Vasquito's mother on the enrollment list is not the same as that given for Vasco Galego's wife, it seems fair to assume that he was Vasco's son by an earlier marriage. Vasquito is thought by some scholars to have been the author of the anonymous *roteiro*, written in Portuguese and preserved in the library of the

University of Leiden in the Netherlands.[12] It does not seem improbable that, after his father's death, Vasquito continued making entries into Vasco's logbook.

Gomes, Estevão (Estéban Gómez)[13]

A Portuguese, probably born in Pôrto about 1484, Gomes was one of the pilots who accompanied Magellan to Spain in October 1517. Having served on the ships of both Portugal and Spain, his name appears in its Portuguese or Spanish form depending on the language in which the account was written. Prior to his arrival in Spain, Gomes had made at least one voyage to India on Portuguese ships, though the most notable events of his career occurred while he was in the service of Spain.

After his arrival in Spain in the fall of 1517, it did not take Gomes long to establish his credentials. By a royal order dated February 10, 1518, he received his pilot's commission from the *Casa de Contratación* in Seville. While Magellan was busy marrying into the Barbosa family and rounding up support for his enterprise, Gomes was promoting his own proposal for finding a westward route to the Moluccas. It was rejected in favor of Magellan's more ambitious enterprise. On April 19, 1519, Gomes was named pilot major of Magellan's fleet.

His ambition was further frustrated in 1520, when Magellan passed him over twice for the captaincy of the *San Antonio*. After Cartagena had been deposed for insubordination, and his replacement (Coca) for incompetence, Magellan gave the command of the *San Antonio* to his nephew, Álvaro de Mesquita. Having coveted that command for himself, Gomes had further cause for indignation: he was transferred to the *San Antonio* to serve as pilot for the inexperienced Mesquita, and likely considered the transfer a demotion from his position as pilot major on the flagship.

In the Strait of Magellan on November 8, 1520, Gomes, assisted by Gerónimo Guerra, overpowered Mesquita and took charge of the *San Antonio*, which they sailed directly back to Spain, arriving in Seville on March 6, 1521. The stories concocted by the defectors did not satisfy the investigating authorities, and with four others from the *San Antonio*, Gomes and Guerra were imprisoned in Burgos. They were soon released, however, and not charged with mutiny. Mesquita, the inept but loyal captain of the *San Antonio*, languished in jail until the *Victoria* returned in September 1522 and the survivors corroborated his story.

In March 1523, Charles V ordered the Casa to help Gomes, still on the payroll as a pilot, recover personal effects from Diogo Barbosa, "so that he may serve us by making certain discoveries." Given command of a fifty-ton caravel, Gomes left La Coruña on August 3, 1524 to search for a northwest passage to Cathay. While he didn't find it, he explored the coast of North America from the Gulf of St. Lawrence to Florida. In Maine's Penobscot Bay he captured some Indians, then coasted southward before heading back to Spain. The ship docked in Seville early in June 1525. The Indians were presented to Charles V, who immediately set them free. What became of them is not recorded.

Gomes may have taken a turn at slaving, for there is evidence that in 1532, he "brought Indians from the Río Marañón." Whether it was the river of that name in Peru, or the Maranhão in Brazil is not clear. That same year, Charles V commended him for his services as pilot major with the Magellan expedition and on May 24, 1534, granted him a coat of arms.

In 1535, Gomes was a pilot with the Mendoza expedition to the Río de la Plata. The last notice of him is from 1537, when on January 15 he left Buenos Aires as pilot of one of two galleys that Mendoza sent up the Paraná River in search of a missing explorer, Juan de Ayolas. The galleys returned to Buenos Aires in October, but it is not known whether Gomes returned with them.

Gómez de Espinosa, Gonzalo

Magellan's great enterprise was plagued from the start by conniving Castilian officers determined to do away with their Portuguese captain general, and by a pilot major envious of his chief. Against the pride, jealousy, and treachery so prevalent in the fleet's high command, Gómez de Espinosa's steadfast loyalty, courage, and sound common sense stand in refreshing contrast.

This paragon of Spanish soldierly virtues was born about 1486 in Espinosa de los Monteros in the Cantabrian mountains of Old Castile. He married well, for his wife was the daughter of a well-educated man, the *bachiller* Sancho de Almaraz. By a royal order dated April 16, 1519, Espinosa was appointed *alguaçil mayor* (master-at-arms) for Magellan's fleet, at a monthly wage of 1,800 maravedis.

During the course of the Easter uprising at Port San Julián in 1520, Espinosa played a crucial role in recovering the *Victoria* from the mutineers. Off the coast of Borneo toward the end of July 1521, when the fleet had been reduced to the *Trinidad* and *Victoria*, he was elected captain general. The story of his globe-girdling odyssey has been told in the text. We now continue with what is known of his later life.

Released after four and a half years as a captive of the Portuguese in Ternate, Banda, Java, Malacca, Cochin, and Lisbon, Espinosa arrived in Valladolid in the middle of May 1527. On August 24 of that year, in recognition of his considerable services to the Crown, Charles V issued a royal order granting him an annual pension of 300 gold ducats (112,500 maravedis) to be paid from the newly-founded *Casa de Especería* (Bureau of Spiceries) in La Coruña. It proved an empty promise: Espinosa never received so much as a maravedi from it. In January, 1528, in Burgos, he filed a claim for the wages accumulated during his captivity. Based on his final rank as captain of the *Trinidad*, the sum due to him amounted to at least 600 ducats. The Treasurer of the Council of the Indies refused to authorize its payment, offering Espinosa a settlement of 200 ducats to withdraw his claim. He agreed to this, but was paid only 50 ducats. Payment of the remainder was made contingent on his participation in a new expedition being outfitted to sail to the Moluccas.

He did not go, for in July 1528, he was in Madrid, testifying on behalf of Jaime Barbosa, a brother-in-law of Magellan, who was suing the Crown for monies owed to Magellan's estate. In January 1528, Espinosa received 15,000 maravedis from the estate of Hans Bergen, the gunner who had died in prison in Lisbon. He received another 20,000 of the 41,200 maravedis remaining in Bergen's estate on May 24, 1531.

Owing to the deactivation of the Bureau of Spiceries in La Coruña, the pension granted to Espinosa had never been paid. To remedy this embarrassing oversight, on November 10, 1529, Charles V awarded him another life pension of 30,000 maravedis annually, this one to be paid out of the royal Treasury. He also gave him a job as inspector of ships leaving for the spiceries, with an annual salary of 43,000 maravedis. In 1537

Espinosa was living comfortably in the parish of San Nicolás in Seville; in 1543, at the age of sixty, he lived there still.

Gonçalves, Afonso (Alonso Gonzáles)

A native of Guarda in Portugal, Gonçalves was married to Catalina Yañez of Seville, the wet nurse for the infant son of Ferdinand and Beatriz Magellan. He was hired as steward (*dispensero*) of the *Victoria* at 1,200 maravedis per month. When he transferred to the *Trinidad* it was a fateful move, for when that star-crossed ship encountered an island in the northern Marianas after its unsuccessful attempt to return across the Pacific, Gonçalves was one of three crewmen who deserted and remained on the island. One of these crewmen was picked up on Saipan in 1524 by the Loaísa expedition. Gonçalves and the other crewman were killed by natives.[14]

Guerra, Gerónimo

All that is known of this enigmatic figure is that he was from Burgos and a relative and employee of Cristóbal de Haro. He was listed on the rolls of Magellan's fleet as the clerk of the *San Antonio*, with an annual salary of 30,000 maravedis. The wording of his appointment was so vague as to appear deliberate, and it is possible that he was planted with the fleet to safeguard the interests of the Crown and Cristóbal de Haro against possible malfeasance by the Portuguese captain general.

When Quesada seized control of the *San Antonio* during the mutiny at Port San Julián, it was in Guerra's cabin that Captain Mesquita was held prisoner. Yet after the mutiny was quelled, Guerra was a witness for the prosecution at the court martial of the mutineers. Magellan then named him fleet treasurer to replace Mendoza (who was killed during the mutiny). In the Strait of Magellan, Guerra teamed up with Gomes to seize control of the *San Antonio*. With Mesquita in irons, Guerra assumed nominal command of the ship. When the *San Antonio* returned to Spain, he was accused neither of mutiny nor desertion. Beyond that, nothing is known of his fate.

Hernández, Diego

At the time of his enlistment with Magellan's fleet, Hernández lived in Seville with his wife, Léonor Sánchez. He was hired as the master's mate of the *San Antonio* at a wage of 2,000 maravedis per month. During the mutiny, he was one of the loyal officers who demanded that the mutineers release Captain Mesquita, and he was seized by the mutineers, transferred to the *Concepción*, and confined. Released after the mutiny was quelled, he testified at the court martial of the mutineers at Port San Julián. While Hernández was probably aboard the *San Antonio* when it returned to Spain in May 1521, his name does not appear in the records of that event.

Irés Guillén (William)

One of three Galway Irishmen who sailed with Magellan, Guillén is listed in the payroll records only by his Christian name. He was hired as an apprentice seaman and assigned to the *Concepción*. On January 25, 1520, while the fleet was exploring the estuary of the Río de la Plata, he fell overboard and drowned.

Jorge ("Morisco")

A slave (probably from India) belonging to Magellan, Jorge accompanied his master on the *Trinidad* and was assigned a monthly wage of 500 maravedis and was granted an advance of 2,000 maravedis. After Magellan's death he remained aboard the *Trinidad*. In a touching display of affection for his mistress in Spain, when the *Victoria* sailed from Tidore, Jorge sent with it for Lady Beatriz a sprig of cloves carefully sewn into a packet made of palm leaves. One can imagine how it would have touched her heart had she lived to receive it. Jorge became a servant of Gómez de Espinosa when the latter transferred from the *Victoria* to the *Trinidad* to take command of the fleet. Espinosa reported that he died on October 22, 1522, a casualty of the last voyage of the *Trinidad*.

Judicibus, Martin de (Martín Genovés)

A native of Saona, near Genoa, he was enrolled as a supernumerary and assigned to the *Concepción* as a *merino* (sergeant of the guard) at a wage of 1,000 maravedis per month. When the *Concepción* was scuttled, he transferred to the *Victoria*, on which he returned to Spain. Since he did not appear at either of the two hearings at which *Victoria* survivors were called to testify, it is likely he had already returned to his home in Italy. Before he left Spain, he told his story to Peter Martyr and Maximilian Transylvanus. Referring to his investigation of the events of the Magellan expedition, Martyr wrote: "I have questioned a young Genoese, Martín de Indico [a translator's error, read Judicibus] who helped in every way."

Lopes Carvalho, João de

A Portuguese (the time and place of his birth are unknown), he was one of the pilots who accompanied Magellan when he left Portugal for Seville. Having satisfied the examiners of the *Casa de Contratación* with his credentials and knowledge of navigation, on April 27, 1518, he was commissioned a royal pilot with an annual salary of 20,000 maravedis, which was increased to 3,000 maravedis per month while at sea after he was assigned to the *Concepción*.

Because Carvalho had been in Brazil from 1511 to 1516, Magellan was led to believe that he would be able to guide the fleet safely along that coast. His confidence in Carvalho's ability was shaken when, after letting him lead the way in the *Concepción*, he sailed dangerously close to shore in the Gulf of Macaé. The fleet was saved from running aground by the alertness of Pilot Major Estevão Gomes on the *Trinidad*.

After the fleet arrived in the harbor of Rio de Janeiro, Carvalho discovered that during his previous stay there he had sired a son by a native woman. He gladly acknowledged the seven-year-old lad as his son and took him aboard the *Concepción* to serve as his page.

After the massacre at Cebu, Carvalho became the senior officer of the fleet. Fearful that his undermanned ships would be overwhelmed, he gave the order to sail away, abandoning the wounded Serrano on the beach. At Brunei, when it appeared that his ships were in danger, Carvalho once again ordered them to leave in haste, abandoning a shore party that included his young Brazilian son. When he subsequently kidapped and abused several high-born native women from a captured junk, the outraged crews of the *Trinidad* and the *Victoria* stripped Carvalho of his command and elected Gómez de Espinosa in his place.

Carvalho was aboard the *Trinidad* at Tidore when the *Victoria* sailed for Spain on December 21, 1521. Taken ill, he dictated a will in which he acknowledged a debt to Magellan of 25,808 maravedis, naming Ginés de Mafra as executor, and on February 14, 1522, while the *Trinidad* was still at Tidore undergoing repairs, João Lopes Carvalho died.

Lopes Carvalho, Joãozito[15]

The son of João Lopes Carvalho and a Tupi Indian woman. Several days after the fleet had entered the harbor of Rio de Janeiro, the little boy's mother appeared and presented him to his father. Carvalho acknowledged the seven-year-old lad as his son and took him aboard the *Concepción* to serve as his page. When the *Concepción* was burned off Bohol, Joãozito transferred to the *Victoria*. At Brunei, with two other members of a shore party, he was abandoned when, under his father's orders, the fleet departed in haste. What became of Joãozito is not known, but he can be considered to be the first Brazilian to have crossed the Pacific Ocean.

Luciano, Antonio (Maestre Antonio)

A native of Baragine, near Genoa, he was hired in 1519 as a carpenter and assigned to the *Trinidad* at a monthly wage of 1,875 maravedis; before sailing, he received an advance of 7,500 maravedis. He remained with the *Trinidad* until it was surrendered to the Portuguese in the Moluccas. When other prisoners from the *Trinidad* were sent to Malacca, Luciano and Bazozábal, a caulker, were detained on Ternate to work on the construction of a ship, and they were reported to have died there in 1523.

Mafra, Ginés de

Born about 1493 in Jérez de la Frontera, he was a resident of Palos. One of the first to enlist with Magellan's fleet, Mafra was assigned to the *Trinidad* as an able seaman, and he remained with that ship until imprisoned by the Portuguese on Ternate. At the time his ship was seized, he was probably serving as master's mate. Shipped by the Portuguese to Cochin in India, he remained there for two years, without resources. With Gómez de Espinosa and Hans Bergen, he was finally allowed to embark for Lisbon, arriving there in July 1526. Immediately upon arrival, Mafra and his companions were confined in the Limonejo prison, where Hans Bergen died. Espinosa was released in December 1526, but because Mafra had in his posession a box with books and papers from the *Trinidad*, he was detained and his papers confiscated. Among them were the precious navigational notes of Andrés de San Martín.

Mafra was released from prison in January 1527 and made his way back to Spain. After an audience with the emperor, he hurried to his home in Palos where, to his dismay, he found that his wife, thinking him dead, had remarried and sold his house and all his possessions. He complained of this in a letter to the emperor, who ordered the appropriate officials in Palos to investigate the matter and to resolve it.

Whether the sticky domestic dilemma was ever resolved is not known, but by 1531, Mafra had had his fill of life ashore and went back to sea. On November 20, 1536 in Guatemala, Pedro de Alvarado wrote a letter to Charles V, informing him that he had outfitted a small fleet for an exploratory voyage on the *Mar del Sur*. With this fleet went ". . . Ginés de Mafra as pilot major, who is one of the best men of this *Mar del Sur* that we know, because he [sailed] with Magellan." While Alvarado did not specify the destination of the fleet, probably it was Peru. At that time, reports of great riches being discovered there were causing much excitement in Guatemala.

On October 25, 1542, from the port of Navidad in New Spain (Mexico), Mafra again sailed westward into the Pacific, this time as a pilot with the fleet of Ruy López de Villalobos. As with many other hardy Spanish mariners of his day, that vast ocean proved a fatal lure: It swallowed him up. We do not know where, when, or how Ginés de Mafra died.

Magalhães, Martin de

A native of Lisbon and a fidalgo in the household of the king of Portugal, his parents were António Martins and Catarina de Magalhães, the latter a cousin to Magellan. One of the twelve Portuguese authorized to sail with the fleet, Martin de Magalhães was enrolled as a supernumerary on the *Concepción*, with a salary of 1,500 maravedis per month, with an advance of 6,000 maravedis before sailing. He remained with the *Concepción* until it was scuttled, then transferred to the *Victoria*. He very nearly completed the circumnavigation, but on July 26, 1522, as the *Victoria* approached the Azores Islands to begin the final leg of its historic journey, Martin de Magalhães died, leaving a will stipulating that 100 ducats from his estate be paid to Magellan's heirs to retire a debt owed to his deceased relative. The 10,000 maravedis he owed to Bocacio Alonso was to be paid from his back wages.

In 1543, a claim was filed with the Council of the Indies for payment of the wages owed to Martin de Magalhães. The claimant was Ana de Oquintal, the widow of his father. Since her name does not correspond with the Catarina de Magalhães listed in the enrollment records as Martin's mother, she probably was his stepmother. On September 18, 1545, over the objections of the Royal Treasurer, the council ordered that she be paid 41,884 maravedis, the wages owed to her stepson. As late as 1548, still not satisfied, Ana had filed suit to recover the 100 ducats withheld from Martin's estate for payment of his debt to Magellan's heirs.

Malaca, Enrique de

Listed in the enrollment records merely as Enrique, the name Malaca is not necessarily indicative of his birthplace. As a youth of about fourteen, he was acquired by Magellan as a slave after the Portuguese sack of Malacca. Pigafetta said that he was from Sumatra, but Philippine linguists have suggested that the dialect spoken by the natives of Cebu and Limasawa would not have been intelligible to someone from Malacca or Sumatra. Since Enrique understood this dialect (Visayan), he may have been raised in the Central Philippines, sold into slavery in Sumatra, and eventually taken to Malacca where Magellan found him. That a strong bond of affection had developed between master and slave is evident from the terms of Magellan's will and from Pigafetta's account of Enrique's grief over his master's death. In addition to his affection for his slave and longtime companion, Magellan also placed a high value on Enrique's linguistic talents, enrolling him with the fleet as an interpreter (supernumerary) on the *Trinidad* at 1,500 maravedis per month, which was near the top of the scale for supernumeraries. Chaplain Valderrama, Duarte Barbosa, and Álvaro de Mesquita (the latter two men-at-arms who later became captains) were paid at the same rate. Among the supernumeraries on the *Trinidad*, Enrique's rate of pay was exceeded only by that of the ship's surgeon and the master-at-arms. Before sailing, Enrique received an advance of 6,000 maravedis.

At Mactan, Enrique was wounded fighting alongside his master. In the official casualty records of the expedition, he was listed as a victim of the massacre at Cebu. This does not seem to have been the case, however. Enraged by the insults of Duarte Barbosa while he was grieving over Magellan's death, Enrique is suspected of having gotten even by plotting with the disillusioned Humabon the murder of Barbosa, the other ranking officers of the fleet, and the capture of the ships. All but the last of these objectives were achieved at the fatal banquet on Cebu: The fate of Enrique is not known. If, as linguistic authorities have suggested, he had spent his childhood in the Central Philippines, he should rate the distinction of having been the first person to circumnavigate the globe.

Martín, Diego

A resident of Huelva in Andalusia, Martín was married and had two sons who sailed with the fleet as able seamen: Francisco on the *Trinidad* and Luis on the *Santiago*. Impressed with his experience and character, Magellan first assigned Diego Martín to recruiting duties, and then tried to get him certified as master of the *Victoria*. This the officials of the *Casa de Contratación* refused to do, on the grounds that he was a troublemaker, ". . . not even qualified to be an able seaman." In reality, they were uncomfortable with Martín's cozy relationship with Magellan, of whom they were deeply suspicious. Magellan finally succeeded in getting him a berth on the *Trinidad* as an able seaman.

Martín remained with the *Trinidad* until it was seized by the Portuguese in the Moluccas, at which time he was its acting master. Taken prisoner by the Portuguese, he was sent from Ternate to Cochin, in India, where he died on September 10, 1524. One of his sons, Francisco, was killed at the massacre at Cebu; the fate of the other son is not known. As he was not among the expedition's survivors, Luis probably perished during the voyage, but his death was not recorded.

Méndez, Martín

Born about 1493, and a native of Seville, Méndez was assigned to the *Victoria* as ship's clerk. At Port San Julián he served as recorder at the court martial of the mutineers. On September 21, 1521, when the *Trinidad* and the *Victoria* were off the coast of Borneo, Gómez de Espinosa replaced Lopes Carvalho as captain general, and Méndez was elected fleet accountant. In the Moluccas, he was the official recorder of the treaties signed with the Moluccan chieftans. When the *Victoria* stopped at the Cape Verde Islands on its return to Spain, Méndez and two others were the first to go ashore to negotiate for fresh food. Successful on this first attempt, he returned later with twelve others in the *Victoria's* longboat for more food supplies. Méndez and his companions were seized by the Portuguese port authorities and imprisoned. On February 13, 1523, after they had been released and returned to Spain, Charles V granted Méndez a lifetime annual pension of 75,000 maravedis and a coat of arms.

Considering his reputation for reliability and his key role in recording the Moluccan treaties, it is odd that there are no records of formal testimony by Méndez concerning the events of the voyage. Nor was he invited to testify at the Conference of Badajoz-Elvas, where Spanish and Portuguese diplomats attempted to resolve the dispute over sovereignty in the Moluccas. Perhaps, like Albo, he was regarded as too honest, and the Spanish diplomats may have feared that he might reveal that the longitudes calculated by the Greek pilot favored the Portuguese claims.

In 1525, at a salary of 60,000 maravedis annually, Méndez was put in charge of purchasing supplies for an expedition being outfitted to follow the track of Magellan. For reasons that are not clear, the captain general, Sebastian Cabot, objected to having Méndez sail with the expedition. When royal pressure was applied on Méndez' behalf, Cabot reluctantly agreed to take him. Although he sailed as an unassigned supernumerary, Méndez was listed as third in line to become captain general should Cabot die during the voyage. Méndez invested 30,000 maravedis of his salary in the expedition and, in addition to trade goods, brought with him many fine articles of personal clothing.

On Santa Catarina Island off the coast of Brazil, Méndez became ill and unable to walk, and Cabot abandoned him on the island with two other members of the expedition, Francisco Rojas and Miguel de Rodas (the latter also a veteran of the Magellan expedition). Marooned on the island, Rojas became deranged and dangerous. In October 1527, Méndez and Rodas tried to escape from the island in a canoe paddled by some natives, but the canoe capsized in a storm. The bodies of some of the Indian paddlers eventually washed up on a beach. Near the bodies were found a shield and a bottle of lemon water that had belonged to Méndez. He and his companion were presumed dead.

Mendoza, Luis de

As with most members of the high command of Magellan's fleet, very little is known of Mendoza's background except that he was a native of Granada. By royal order he was appointed treasurer of the fleet and captain of the *Victoria* at an annual salary of 60,000 maravedis, with an advance of 30,000 maravedis plus 10,000 for expenses. As soon as he arrived in Seville to take up his duties with the fleet, Mendoza became involved in an ugly, public row with Magellan. When Magellan complained of this in a letter to the king, Charles issued a sharp reprimand to Mendoza, demanding that he obey Magellan ". . . in all things."

After Magellan had stripped Juan de Cartagena of the command of the *San Antonio*, he entrusted the custody of the insubordinate officer to Mendoza on the *Victoria*. It was a misplaced trust. In defiance of Magellan's orders, Mendoza allowed his prisoner to go ashore at Rio de Janeiro. There, the unrepentant Cartagena promptly tried to stir up a revolt.

On April 1, 1520, at Port San Julián, Mendoza aligned his ship with those of the mutineers and demanded that Magellan divulge the route by which he planned to sail to the Moluccas. The next morning, Magellan sent Gómez de Espinosa to the *Victoria* with a message for its captain. Armored, but without a helmet, Mendoza took the message, read it, laughed, and scornfully handed it back. At this display of arrogance, Espinosa plunged his dagger into Mendoza's unprotected throat. The marine who had accompanied Espinosa followed through with a dagger blow to the head that split Mendoza's skull, killing him instantly. At the court martial of the mutineers at Port San Julián, Mendoza's corpse, propped up in a chair, was formally tried and convicted of mutiny. His body was quartered and the parts hung from a gibbet.

Mesquita (Mezquita), Álvaro de

Born in Estremoz, Portugal, to Fernão and Ines Gonçalves de Mesquita, Álvaro was related to Magellan through the latter's mother. With his brother Martin and his son Francisco, Álvaro accompanied his ambitious relative when he left Portugal for Seville. They all enlisted with Magellan's fleet, but when the king objected to the large number of Portuguese on the rolls, Martin Mesquita was one of those dismissed. Álvaro was accepted as a supernumerary on the *Trinidad*, and Francisco was enrolled as Magellan's page.

At Rio de Janeiro, Mesquita replaced Antonio de Coca as captain of the *San Antonio*. Coca had failed to win Magellan's trust after replacing Cartagena as captain. During the revolt at Port San Julián, the *San Antonio* was boarded by an armed contingent from the *Concepción* while Mesquita was asleep in his cabin, where he was quickly overpowered and confined, unable to prevent the takeover of his ship. Restored to his command after the mutiny was quelled, Mesquita presided over the court martial of the mutineers. In the Strait of Magellan when the *San Antonio* was sailing apart from the rest of the fleet, Gomes and Guerra, the disgruntled pilot and ship's clerk, urged Mesquita to leave Magellan and take the ship back to Spain. When Mesquita refused, a violent struggle ensued in which Mesquita was stabbed in the hand and Gomes in the leg. Gomes and Guerra prevailed, took control of the *San Antonio* and sailed it directly back to Spain. It arrived in Seville on March 6, 1521, with Mesquita in irons.

A board of inquiry apparently believed the story told by the defectors, for Mesquita was jailed despite the vigorous protestations of Magellan's father-in-law. Gomes and Guerra, after being held in prison briefly during the investigation, were set free. When the *Victoria* returned in September 1522, the members of its crew corroborated Mesquita's story and he was released from prison. Thoroughly disgusted with Spanish justice, he returned to Portugal. His son, Francisco, who had remained with the *Trinidad*, was killed in the massacre at Cebu.

Napolés, Nicolás de

Born in Naples about 1483, Nicolás had emigrated to Castile before 1506. One of the older men enrolled with Magellan's fleet, he was assigned to the *Victoria* as an able seaman. In testimony given years after the voyage, he claimed to have been a frequent visitor to Magellan's house in Seville, where he had held the infant Rodrigo in his arms. He also claimed to have been one of the volunteers who fought alongside Magellan at the Battle of Mactan.

In 1537, Napolés testified on behalf of a former shipmate's widow who, even at that late date, was still trying to collect her deceased husband's wages and the proceeds from the cloves he had sent from Tidore on the *Victoria*. Napolés declared that he had been present at the death of Juan Rodríguez, the widow's husband. As Rodríguez died aboard the *Trinidad* on October 5, 1522, and Napolés returned to Spain with the *Victoria* in September of that year, this cannot have been true. He probably concocted the story to help the widow recover from the royal treasury assets from her husband's estate.

In testimony regarding the death of Magellan, Napolés stated: ". . . because this witness was then at his side, I saw him killed." While this story and the one about holding the infant Rodrigo in his arms could have been true, they also may have been an old sailor's yarns that got better with each telling. It has been suggested that the inconsistencies in the testimony of Nicolás Napolés may have arisen from the presence on the *Trinidad* of another seaman with the same name. The enrollment records do not show such a homonym. The Nicolás Napolés who returned to Spain with the *Victoria* and subsequently resided in Seville, probably was the same person who testified for the widow in 1537.

Palla, Baldassare (Baltasar Genovés)

This veteran mariner was born about 1484 in Porto Moris, near Genoa. Magellan first assigned him to recruiting and then as master of the *Santiago*. After that ship was wrecked in Patagonia, Palla was made master of the *Victoria*, a position left vacant by the execution of Antón Salamón. On August 6, 1520, Magellan promoted Palla to the rank of pilot. One of those who survived the crossing of the Pacific but failed to recover from the the effects of scurvy, Palla died on April 3, 1521, while the fleet was anchored off Limasawa Island in the Philippines.

Pancaldo, Leone (Léon Pancaldo, Pancado)[16]

A native of the district of Saona in Genoa, Pancaldo was born about 1481. His father, Manfino, like Columbus's father, was a carder of wool. He was acquainted with Diego Colón, Columbus' son, whose power of attorney he held in Genoa in 1514, while the younger Colón was in Hispaniola. Like many Genoese seamen of his time, Pancaldo had worked on both Portuguese and Spanish ships.

When he enlisted for service with Magellan's fleet, Pancaldo was assigned to the *Trinidad* as an able seaman with a monthly wage of 1,200 maravedis. The payroll records indicate that he had a wife, Salvaja, who lived in Genoa, and that he received an advance of 48,000 maravedis before sailing from Seville.

Pancaldo remained with the *Trinidad* until its surrender to the Portuguese in the Moluccas. After the flight from Brunei, when Espinosa replaced Carvalho in command of the fleet, Juan Bautista, the Genoese master of the *Trinidad*, assumed the duties of pilot; his countryman, Léon Pancaldo, assisted him. Their plausible, but ill-timed attempt to navigate from the Moluccas to Panama across the North Pacific is recounted in Chapter Twenty. When that effort failed, they brought the *Trinidad* back to the Moluccas, where it was seized by the Portuguese and they were imprisoned. The story of their efforts to escape from Portuguese captivity is told in the Epilog.

In Mozambique, Pancaldo stowed away on a ship bound for Lisbon, where he was imprisoned immediately on arrival. His jailers confiscated papers, written in Italian, that he had brought with him. They are believed to have been records of the navigation of the *Trinidad*.[17]

After Charles V arranged for Pancaldo's release from prison, efforts were made in Portugal and France to enlist his services. He did go to Paris to discuss the French offer, but was dissuaded from accepting it by a Portuguese agent at the French court. The king of Portugal then invited him to visit the Portuguese court. In a letter dated October 3, 1531, Pancaldo turned down the invitation, because he was too old and ". . . did not wish to put his feet in the sea again."

While he did spend several years at home with his wife in Genoa, the call of the sea proved irresistible to the old sailor. In September 1537, Pancaldo sailed from Cádiz as captain of the *Santa María,* an old cargo ship belonging to a consortium of Genoese merchants. It was loaded with merchandise for the Spaniards in Peru, who were looting the Inca Empire of its silver and gold.

Pancaldo had intended to take the *Santa María* through the Strait of Magellan and then sail north to Peru. Unable to negotiate the tortuous strait with the old, heavily laden *Santa María,* he turned back and headed for the Río de la Plata, where he hoped to find buyers for his cargo in the settlement started by Pedro de Mendoza. Entering the La Plata estuary, Pancaldo took his ship some distance upriver. Failing to find any Spanish settlers, he sailed back into the estuary. One clear day, from mid-channel, the lookout spotted a sail and other signs of human activity on the south shore. It was the the newly founded settlement of Santa María del Buen Aire (Buenos Aires). In their eagerness to reach it, the crew of the *Santa María* ran it aground. While the ship was a total loss, the crew salvaged the cargo, sails, anchors and other equipment.

In Buenos Aires, Pancaldo and his associates found a ready market for their merchandise. As the settlers had no cash, the associates accepted promissory notes in payment. Whether it was for lack of a ship or that he was waiting for payment on his promissory notes, Pancaldo remained in Buenos Aires and died there in August 1540.

Pigafetta, Antonio (Antonio Lombardo)

The principal chronicler of Magellan's voyage, his name has been spelled in a variety of ways; the one above is the most common. In a letter to the Marquis of Mantua written in 1523, he signed himself *Plegapheta.* A native of the Italian city of Vicenza in the district of Lombardy, he was entered on the rolls of the Magellan expedition as Antonio Lombardo. His age was not given but he is thought to have been about thirty years old in 1519. His family in Vicenza was prominent and politically influential, and as a youth he was accepted into the service of Andrea Chiericati, a member of the College of Prothonotaries Apostolic in the Vatican, and an intimate of Pope Leo X.

In 1518, the Pope named Chiericati as ambassador to the Court of Charles I, King of Spain. In December of that year, with Pigafetta in his entourage, Chiericati left Rome for Zaragoza. There, Pigafetta learned about the preparations underway in Seville to send a Spanish fleet to the Moluccas. The idea of going along to see something of the world appealed strongly to the young Lombard, and because of the expedition's diplomatically sensitive nature, he had little difficulty convincing Ambassador Chiericati that it would be a good idea to send him along as a Vatican observer. Armed with letters of introduction to the *Casa de Contratación,* Pigafetta set out for Seville, arriving early in May 1519. He was enrolled as a supernumerary and assigned to the *Trinidad* with a monthly salary of 1,000 maravedis. Before departure, he received four months pay in advance.

Pigafetta kept a richly detailed diary in which he made entries each day of the entire voyage. Despite the uncritical credulity with which he recorded even the most outrageous stories told to him by natives of the lands he visited, copies of Pigafetta's journal provide us with the most complete record of the Magellan expedition.

During the voyage, Pigafetta developed a boundless admiration and genuine affection for the expedition's gruff, secretive captain general. At Mactan, he fought alongside Magellan and witnessed his death at the hands of Lapulapu's warriors. The face wound that Pigafetta received in the fighting saved his life. Inflamed and sore after the battle, it prevented him, usually an enthusiastic party-goer, from attending the fatal banqet at Cebu at which many of the fleet's officers, seamen, and supernumeraries were slain.

Pigafetta transferred from the *Trinidad* to the *Victoria* before the latter left Tidore for Spain. The indefatigable Lombard, starved and emaciated but still enjoying his customary good health, returned to Seville with the *Victoria* on September 8, 1522, debarking with his possessions wrapped in a Brazilian hammock.

Snubbed by Cano when the *Victoria*'s captain was invited by Charles V (now Holy Roman Emperor), to bring with him to court the two most knowledgeable men of his crew, Pigafetta made his own way to Valladolid. There, he presented the emperor with a day-by-day record of the voyage, copied from his diary. He was received coolly by the monarch and was afforded none of the honors lavished on Cano and his selected lieutenants. On November 10, 1522, Pigafetta was paid his accumulated wages and a sum representing the value of his *quintalada* (allotted share of the *Victoria*'s cargo).

Undaunted by his cool reception in Spain, he went to Portugal to tell his story to King João III, and then to France, where he was graciously received by the queen mother, Marie Louise of Savoy. Among the novelties "from the other hemisphere" that he presented to her was another copy of his account of the voyage. From France he went to Italy, At the request of the Duke of Mantua, he began to prepare the story of his voyage for publication. While working on the manuscript at his home in Vicenza, Pigafetta was invited to Rome so that Pope Clement VII might hear from the author's own lips the marvelous story of the voyage. Early in 1524, he arrived in Rome where, as a member of the pope's household, he completed work on his manuscript. Later that year, the Venetian senate granted him a copyright for its exclusive publication under the title of *Notizie del Mondo Novo*, but by then his enthusiasm had been diverted to other matters, and he failed to publish it.

En route to Rome from Vicenza, Pigafetta had encountered Philippe Villiers de l'Isle-Adam, grand master of the Order of Rhodes, a military-religious order of crusader knights dedicated to the defense of the outposts of Christendom threatened by the Turks. Entranced by the romance of its holy mission and by the martial spirit and religious fervor of its grand master, Pigafetta gave up his soft job at the Vatican, joined the Order of Rhodes as a knight-errant, and dedicated his manuscript to his new hero, Philippe Villiers.[18] Nothing certain is known of his fate, but Pigafetta is generally thought to have died fighting the Turks.

Polcevera, Giovanni Battista di (Juan Bautista de Punzorol)

Born in 1468 in Sestri, near the mouth of the Polcevera River west of Genoa, this veteran shipmaster generally is referred to in Spanish documents as Juan Bautista. The difficulty that the Spanish scribes at the *Casa de Contratación* had with foreign place names accounts for such misspellings of his birthplace as: Punzorol, Poncerón, Pinzerol, Poncero, and Poncevera.

An experienced Genoese mariner who had served on Portuguese ships, Polcevera signed on with the Magellan expedition in September 1518. On two occasions, Magellan sent him to Cádiz to recruit sailors, providing from his own pocket. 7,000 maravedis for travel expenses. These recruiting efforts were frustrated by a hostile official of the *Casa de Contratación*, who forbade Polcevera to advertise for seamen in competition with recruiters for the fleet of Andrés Niño. Demonstrating his confidence in the veteran Genoese mariner, Magellan installed him as master of the flagship *Trinidad*, a position that he held until he was elevated to pilot when Gómez de Espinosa took command of the fleet following its flight from Brunei.

The story of Polcevera's monumental, but unsuccessful effort to navigate the *Trinidad* from the Moluccas to Panama across the North Pacific, his struggle to survive Portuguese captivity, and his unfortunate death in Mozambique has been told in the epilogue and, in this appendix, in the biographical sketch of his shipmate and compatriot, Léon Pancaldo.

Quesada, Gaspar de

One of the members of the high command of Magellan's fleet appointed by the crown, there is no biographical information of any kind about him in the records of the *Casa de Contratación*. In a letter to King Manuel, Sebastião Álvares, the Portuguese consul in Seville, wrote that Quesada ". . . was a servant of the Archbishop [of Seville]." In appointing him captain of the *Concepión*, King Charles merely stated that he had been ". . . informed about his reputation and abilities."

Rebêlo, Cristovão (Cristóbal Ravelo)

A native of Porto, Portugal, his parents were listed as Duarte and Catalina Rodríguez Ravelo (Spanish spelling). Because Magellan had named Rebêlo in his will, Medina and other writers have suggested that he may have been Magellan's natural son. Enrolled with the expedition as a supernumerary with a monthly wage of 1,200 maravedis, he was assigned to the *Trinidad* as a servant of the captain general. Before the departure of the fleet from Seville, he received an advance of 3,200 maravedis.

Rebêlo replaced Duarte Barbosa as captain of the *Victoria* after Magellan deposed the latter at Cebu for behavior unbefitting an officer and gentleman. Rebêlo held that rank for only a few days, for he was killed on April 27, 1521, while fighting at Magellan's side at Mactan.

Rodas, Miguel de

A native of Rhodes, there is some confusion about his date of birth. In a declaration made on May 23, 1524, Rodas stated that he was forty-eight years old; in another declaration made on the same date, he stated that he was thirty-two, but this disparity could have a rational explanation. The age given by Rodas in his first statement may have been thirty-eight and erroneously recorded as forty-eight. The thirty-two years mentioned in the second declaration may have referred to his age at the time of his enlistment with Magellan's fleet five years earlier. If such were the case, the year of his birth would have been 1486 or 1487.

An experienced mariner, Rodas was hired as master's mate on the *Victoria* at a monthly wage of 2,000 maravedis, and he received four months' pay in advance before the fleet sailed. He became the ship's master in 1519, following the conviction and execution of its former master, Antón Salamón. He held that position until September 8, 1522, when the *Victoria* returned to Seville. When he debarked, among his possessions were two sacks of cloves and a navigational chart.

Honored with the other survivors of the circumnavigation, Rodas was granted a lifetime annual pension of 50,000 maravedis by the emperor. Like so many of Charles's grand gestures, it proved to be an empty one, and three years after it had been granted, Rodas still had not received a maravedi of it. In May 1523, he attended the Conference of Badajoz-Elvas, providing testimony supporting Spain's claim to the Moluccas.

In 1525, Rodas was named pilot major of a fleet being readied to sail to the Moluccas under the command of Sebastian Cabot. The latter, who disliked Rodas intensely, objected vigorously to this appointment, but was overridden by Charles V. After the fleet sailed, Cabot made life miserable for Rodas, and on February 14, 1527, he marooned him on an island off the coast of Brazil in the company of Martín Méndez, a former shipmate on the Magellan expedition, and a dangerous character named Francisco de Rojas. Desperate to escape from Rojas, who had gone mad, Rodas and Méndez tried to reach the mainland in a canoe, with some natives. The canoe may have capsized in a storm, as some effects that had belonged to Rodas and Méndez were found washed up on a beach with the body of a native.

Rodríguez, Juan

Known to his shipmates as "El Sordo" (The Deaf One), Rodríguez was a resident of Seville. Born about 1477, he was hired as an able seaman and assigned to the *Concepción* at a monthly wage of 1,200 maravedis, and before sailing he received an advance of four months' wages.

When his ship was scuttled off Bohol in the Philippines, Rodríguez transferred to the *Trinidad*. When that ship was surrendered to the Portuguese in the Moluccas, Rodríguez and the rest of its crew were imprisoned at the Portuguese fortress on Ternate. From there he was sent to Banda in a small junk on which he served as pilot, then to Malacca, and from there to Cochin. In Cochin, he had better luck than his fellow prisoners, for he succeeded in getting permission to board a Portuguese ship bound for Lisbon, arriving there in 1525.

He was the first of the *Trinidad* survivors to return to Spain. By 1526, he was the proud owner of a caravel that sailed with a convoy to the West Indies. On July 1, 1527, he testified on behalf of Cristóbal de Haro in support of the latter's claims against the Crown. In 1537, Rodríguez was living in Seville, still trying to recover from the Crown the proceeds from the sale of a sack of cloves that he had shipped from Tidore in the *Victoria*, intended for his wife.

Rodríguez Mafra, Juan

A native of the Andalusian port of Palos, Mafra was born about 1470 and had sailed with Columbus to Hispaniola and Paria (the coast of Venezuela) on his second and third voyages. In 1499, with Diego de Lepe, whom he claimed was his brother, he explored the northeast coast of South America from Cape Santo Agostinho on the bulge of Brazil to Paria. With Rodrigo de Bastidas, he visited the Caribbean coast of Panama in 1500–1502. In 1512, he was commissioned a royal pilot by order of King Ferdinand, and in 1518, King Charles renewed his commission and ordered him to report for duty with Magellan's fleet.

Magellan first assigned him to recruiting. Later, while working with Magellan to refloat the *Trinidad* after it had been careened and caulked before the expedition left Spain, Mafra was stabbed in the hand during the fracas that broke out over the display of a banner bearing Magellan's coat of arms.

When the fleet sailed from Spain, Mafra was pilot of the *San Antonio*. In Port San

Julián, a party of mutineers led by Quesada boarded the *San Antonio*, and when he refused to cooperate with them, Mafra was seized and confined below decks in chains. The next morning, the *Trinidad* fired on the *San Antonio* as it tried to escape the trap that Magellan had set for it. A cannon ball ripped through the planking where Mafra sat in chains, passing between his legs without even scratching him.

In the shakeup of personnel in the aftermath of the mutiny, Mafra was transferred to the *Concepción*, on which he served as its pilot until he died as the fleet was approaching Cebu on March 28, 1521. After the return of the *Victoria* to Spain, an order was issued to pay his widow, Catalina Rodríguez, 20,000 maravedis, the salary accrued by her husband at the time of his death.

Rodríguez Serrano, Juan

Usually referred to by his second surname, it has often been assumed that he was Portuguese;[19] one writer claimed that he was a brother of Magellan's friend and correspondent, Francisco Serrão.[20] Such assumptions are at variance with statements by Pigafetta and Brito (the Portuguese commander at Ternate) that Serrano was Castilian. Medina cited Lopes Castanheda (a prominent Portuguese court chronicler whose work was first published in 1551) for giving as Serrano's birthplace the town of Fregenal (de la Sierra) in Extremadura, western Castile.

Whether Portuguese or Castilian by birth, Serrano had served on Spanish ships since his youth. Married to Juana Durango of Seville, he made his home in that city. In 1499–1500, with some caravels commanded by Alonso Vélez de Guevara, Serrano crossed the Atlantic to Cape Santo Agostinho on the coast of Brazil. In 1514, by order of King Ferdinand, Serrano was commissioned as a royal pilot with an annual salary of 30,000 maravedis plus an allotment of wheat. That same year, he sailed as pilot major of the fleet that carried Pedro Arias de Ávila to Darién.

In 1518, King Charles renewed Serrano's commission as a royal pilot, and he was directed to report to Magellan's fleet and assigned to the *Santiago* as captain and pilot. Before sailing, he received a year's salary (30,000 maravedis) in advance plus 7,500 maravedis and two twelve-bushel sacks of wheat as a cost-of-living allowance. His stepson, Francisco, sailed with him on the *Santiago* as his page; a black slave named Juan also accompanied him.

Serrano's steadfast loyalty to Magellan, his significant contributions during the voyage, first as captain of the *Santiago* and then of the *Concepción*, his election to fleet command after the death of Magellan, and his capture during the treachery at Cebu, have all been related in the preceding text. Whether he was killed on the beach at Cebu, or survived his wounds to be sold into slavery in China, as has been suggested, is not known. All that we know is that the faithful captain was left, bound and bleeding, in the hands of his captors on the beach at Cebu.

In 1525 and again in 1526, Serrano's widow, Juana Durango, received partial payments of the salary owed to her husband. As late as 1531, however, she was still having trouble collecting the remainder and the royal pension that had been promised to her.

Salomone, Antonio (Antón Salamón)

A native of Trapani in Sicily, born about 1473, he was an experienced mariner and was hired by the *Casa de Contratación* in September 1518. First assigned by Magellan to recruiting duty, he later was named master of the *Victoria*. While the fleet was becalmed off the coast of Guinea, he was caught in an act of sodomy with an apprentice seaman. Tried, convicted, and sentenced to death, Salomone was executed in the harbor of Rio de Janeiro on December 20, 1519.

San Martín, Andrés de

For San Martín, as for the other officers of Magellan's high command, the official records of the expedition are devoid of biographical information. While one historian wrote that San Martín was Portuguese and another that he was French, there seems little reason to doubt Pigafetta's assertion that "our astrologer" was from Seville. Nothing is known of his life prior to 1512, when he was commissioned as a royal pilot by order of King Ferdinand. The royal order included the instruction (singular for a pilot) that he ". . . be prepared to serve us at sea as well as on land."

A skilled astrologer, he possessed a far greater knowledge of astronomical measurements and their applications to navigation than other professional pilots of his day. Under the impression that these special skills qualified him for promotion to a higher rank, he applied for the position of pilot major of Castile when it was left vacant by the death of Amerigo Vespucci in 1512. In 1518, after news reached Spain of the death of Vespucci's successor, Juan Díaz de Solís, San Martín again applied for the post. For the second time his hopes were dashed: King Charles again chose a foreigner, Sebastian Cabot, for the coveted position. The king did, however, raise San Martín's salary by 10,000 maravedis.

With pilots Serrano, Mafra, Carvalho, and Galego, King Charles ordered San Martín to report for duty with Magellan's fleet. On July 31, 1519, he received an advance of 30,000 maravedis plus 7,500 maravedis for cost-of-living expenses. Assigned to the *San Antonio*, he functioned as astrologer and astronomer-pilot for the fleet. At Rio de Janeiro, San Martín transferred from the *San Antonio* to the *Victoria* and remained with that ship until his death. In the Strait of Magellan, he was the only pilot who encouraged Magellan to continue with his explorations through the summer, but warned about sailing farther south. He was one of the Spaniards presumed slaughtered by their hosts at the fatal banquet on Cebu on May 1, 1521.

Of the pilots who sailed with Magellan's fleet, San Martín was the most accomplished in the art of celestial navigation. The longitudes that he calculated from land-based, lunar-stellar observations at Port San Julián in Patagonia and Homonhon Island in the Philippines were surprisingly accurate, and beyond the capabilities of other pilot-mariners of his day. They probably were the points of departure for the dead-reckoning estimates of longitude in Albo's log.

Those of San Martín's navigational notes seized by the Portuguese when the *Trinidad* surrendered in the Moluccas seem to have been the basis for sixteenth-century Portuguese accounts of Magellan's voyage. Other papers that had belonged to San Martín were taken in Lisbon from Ginés de Mafra, but later were transferred to Spain, probably during the period of union with Portugal (1580–1640). These were consulted in Spanish archives in the seventeenth-century by Antonio de Herrera, for his chronicle of Spanish discoveries.[21]

Saldaña, Bartolomé de

A native of Palos sponsored by Luis de Mendoza, Saldaña was enrolled as a supernumerary on the *Victoria*. On the night of February 5, 1521, when the *Victoria* was anchored off Timor, Saldaña and an apprentice seaman, Martín de Ayamonte, deserted by swimming ashore. They were eventually captured by the Portuguese and taken to Malacca.

Sánchez, Bartolomé

The birthplace of Sánchez was listed as Huelva, but at the time of his enlistment with Magellan's fleet, he lived in Seville with his wife, Juana Rodríguez. He was hired as an able seaman and assigned to the *Trinidad* at a monthly wage of 1,200 maravedis; before departure, he received an advance of 4,800 maravedis.

A literate man, Sánchez replaced Léon de Ezpeleta as clerk of the *Trinidad* after the latter was killed at Cebu on May 1, 1521. When the *Trinidad* returned to the Moluccas after its unsuccessful attempt to sail across the North Pacific to Panama, Espinosa dispatched Sánchez to Ternate with a letter to the Portuguese commander, requesting help. He was imprisoned by the Portuguese, and an armed force was sent to seize the *Trinidad* and the surviving members of its crew.

When most of the *Trinidad* survivors were sent to Malacca, Sánchez was among those detained. In a letter to the king of Portugal, the Portuguese commander at Ternate described Sánchez as a ". . . good seaman and pilot." Later, with Alonso Coto, Sánchez was put aboard a junk headed for Malacca. Since the two never arrived at Malacca, they were presumed lost at sea. The junk may have been wrecked or captured by the pirates who infested those waters.

Silva, João de

One of the Portuguese authorized to sail with Magellan's fleet, Silva was a native of Graciosa in the Azores Islands and a cousin of Magellan's wife. He sailed as a supernumerary on the *Concepción*.

In April 1521, Magellan was planning to leave Silva on Cebu, in charge of a trading post. While Silva did remain there, it was not in the manner Magellan had anticipated. On May 1 of that year, he was one of the twenty-six from Magellan's fleet who attended Humabon's fatal banquet, and he was probably killed or sold into slavery.

Tolosa, Pedro de (Perucho Vizcaino)

A native of Tolosa in the Basque province of Guipúzcoa, Tolosa was enrolled at the last minute to replace an enlistee who had failed to report for duty. He was assigned to the *Victoria* as an apprentice seaman, and remained on that lucky ship for the entire voyage. When it returned to Spain on September 6, 1522, he was its steward.

Valderrama, Pedro de

A native of Ecija in Andalusia, Valderrama, a chaplain, was assigned to the *Trinidad*. Classified as a supernumerary, his monthly wage was 1,500 maravedis, and before sailing, he received an advance of 1,970 maravedis. Oddly, it was not Calmette, the chaplain of the *San Antonio*, but Father Valderrama who heard the confession of Juan de Elorriaga after the latter was mortally wounded on the *San Antonio* during the mutiny.

For Father Valderrama, the high point of the voyage, and probably of his life, must have come shortly after the fleet arrived at Cebu. There, aided by Magellan, he presided over the conversion and baptism of thousands of pagan Filipinos. After Magellan's death, Father Valderrama was a guest at Humabon's fatal banquet, where, before the massacre began, Espinosa and Carvalho saw him being escorted away from the banquet site by the prince who had been miraculously cured by Magellan. How he fared after the slaughter started is not known.

It was forty-four years before another Spanish expedition would reach Cebu. By then, even if he had survived the massacre, Father Valderrama probably would have been dead. When the expedition of Miguel López de Legazpi reached Cebu on April 27, 1565, evidence of the pioneering missionary activities of Magellan and Valderrama was found by a Basque seaman in a hut hastily vacated by its occupants as the Spaniards came ashore. In a little box was a wooden statue of the Christ Child, and that it was an object of veneration was evident from the fresh flowers carefully placed around it.[22]

Vigo, Gonzalo de

From Vigo, a town in Galicia in northwestern Castile, Gonzalo de Vigo was hired as an apprentice seaman for the *Concepción* at a monthy wage of 800 maravedis, with an advance of 3,200 maravedis before departure. When his ship was scuttled off Bohol, Vigo transferred to the *Trinidad*. While that ship was returning to the Moluccas after its unsuccessful attempt to cross the Pacific Ocean to Panama, Vigo and two other seamen, fearful of the scurvy that was devastating the crew, deserted at a small island in the northern Marianas.

The other two seamen were killed by natives, but Vigo survived and made his way to Saipan. There, on September 4, 1526, he was discovered by the crew of the *Santa María de la Victoria*, the flagship of the Loaísa expedition that had made its way alone across the Pacific. Pardoned for his desertion from the *Trinidad*, Vigo stayed with the expedition, performing admirable service as an interpreter on Mindanao and in the Moluccas. In 1536, when the Spaniards were sent home from Ternate by the Portuguese, Vigo did not accompany them. Whether he had died or stayed behind to live in the islands is not clear.

Yarza, Domingo de (Iraza, Ycaza, Icaza, Aroca)

A native of Deva in the Basque province of Guipúzcoa, Yarza was hired as the carpenter of the *Concepción* at a monthly wage of 1,875 maravedis, and before sailing, he received an advance of 7,500 maravedis. When the *Concepción* was burned off Bohol in May 1521, Yarza transferred to the *Trinidad*, and he was among the many who perished during its return from its unsuccessful attempt to reach Panama. Espinosa recorded the date of his death as October 14, 1522.

Zubileta, Juan de

A native of Baracaldo in Vizcaya, he was enrolled at the age of fourteen as a page (cabin boy) on the *Victoria*. His monthly wage was 500 maravedis, and he was advanced 2,000 maravedis before departure. Zubileta was one of eighteen Europeans on the *Victoria* when it returned to Spain on September 6, 1522.

Notes

1. Albo's deposition was reproduced in its entirety by Medina in his *Colección* . . . , pp. 305–308.
2. Morison, p. 470.
3. Mairin Mitchell, *Friar Andrés de Urdaneta, O.S.A.* (London: MacDonald & Evans, 1964) p. 45.
4. Denucé, pp. 24–25; Lagôa I, pp. 280–281; Parr, pp. 379–380.
5. Lagôa I, p. 289.
6. Mitchell, *Friar Andrés de Urdaneta, O.S.A.*, p. 27.
7. Lourdes Díaz-Trechuelo, "La organización del viaje Magellánico . . ." in A. Teixeira da Mota (ed.)., p. 310.
8. Medina, following Navarrete, gave the date of Cano's death as August 4, 1526. The source for this was an account written from memory by Urdaneta in 1537. Mairin Mitchell (note 3 above) stated that August 6 is the correct date, as it is the one given in Urdaneta's original diary, taken from him in Portugal in 1536. Returned to Spain during the reign of Philip II, the latter is now preserved in the royal archives in Madrid.
9. Denucé, p. 275. Medina stated that they were marooned on August 11, 1520, "*tres*" (three) days before the fleet left Port San Julián. *Tres* could have been intended to read *trece* (thirteen). Denucé gave the date of departure of the fleet as 24 August.
10. Díaz-Trechuelo, in Mota, p. 295.
11. Lagôa I, p. 277.
12. Morison, p. 322. The Leiden manuscript as printed at Coimbra (Portugal) in 1937 as *Um Roteiro Inédito*, M. de Jong, ed.
13. The details of Gomes's life included in this sketch were derived from J.T. Medina, *El Portugués Esteban Gómez al Servicio de España* (Santiago, Chile: Imprenta Ezeviriana, 1908).
14. Lagôa I, p. 284.
15. Ibid., p. 307.
16. The biographical details in this sketch were drawn from J.T. Medina, *Algunas Noticias de Léon Pancaldo . . . Estudio Histórico* (Santiago, Chile: Imprenta Elzeviriana, 1908).
17. Some scholars have proposed that the anonymous *Roteiro da viagem de Fernam de Magalhães*, an archival find published in Lisbon in 1826, may have been derived from Pancaldo's confiscated notebooks. Medina, who published a Spanish translation of the *Roteiro* in Volume II of his *Colección* . . . , did not think so. The matter is unresolved.
18. Denucé, p. 11, cited Marino Sanuto, *Diarii* . . . (Venice: 1882–1884).
19. Lagôa I, pp. 307–309.
20. Parr, p. 63.
21. Denucé, p. 25.
22. Mitchell, *Friar Andrés de Urdaneta, O.S.A.*, p. 126. The image found by Juan Zamus, the Basque seaman, was of Flemish workmanship. Although it did not match precisely Pigafetta's description of the image presented to the queen of Cebu, it would be difficult to imagine a source other than the Magellan expedition. It is still venerated in the Augustinian church in Cebu City.

Appendix 4 Magellan Genealogy

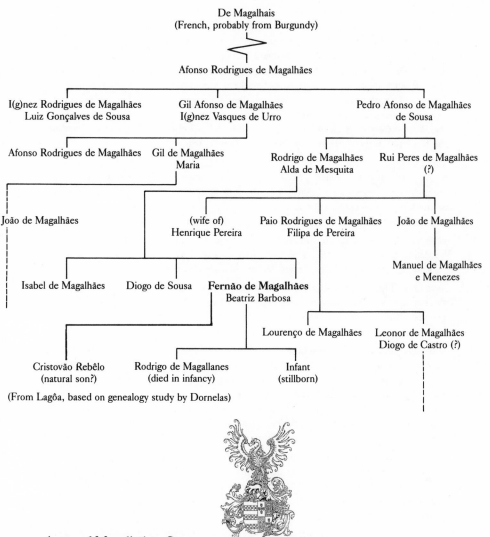

De Magalhais
(French, probably from Burgundy)

Afonso Rodrigues de Magalhães

I(g)nez Rodrigues de Magalhães
Luiz Gonçalves de Sousa

Gil Afonso de Magalhães
I(g)nez Vasques de Urro

Pedro Afonso de Magalhães
de Sousa

Afonso Rodrigues de Magalhães

Gil de Magalhães
Maria

Rodrigo de Magalhães
Alda de Mesquita

Rui Peres de Magalhães
(?)

João de Magalhães

(wife of)
Henrique Pereira

Paio Rodrigues de Magalhães
Filipa de Pereira

João de Magalhães

Manuel de Magalhães
e Menezes

Isabel de Magalhães

Diogo de Sousa

Fernão de Magalhães
Beatriz Barbosa

Lourenço de Magalhães

Leonor de Magalhães
Diogo de Castro (?)

Cristovão Rebêlo
(natural son?)

Rodrigo de Magallanes
(died in infancy)

Infant
(stillborn)

(From Lagôa, based on genealogy study by Dornelas)

Arms of Magalhãis e Sousa

In his *Fernão de Magalhãis* . . . , Visconde de Lagôa accepted the conclusion of the Portuguese genealogist, Sr. Afonso Dornelas, that the coat of arms used by the great discoverer included those of Sousa de Arronches, as represented above.

Appendix 5 Memoranda to King Charles

In a series of audiences in Valladolid in 1518, Magellan and Faleiro presented their proposal to the royal court. Favorably impressed by their arguments, King Charles and his counselors invited the partners to prepare a document specifying the conditions under which they would agree to lead the proposed expedition. Emboldened by the king's obvious enthusiasm for the venture and by the prospect of financial support from Cristóbal de Haro, the two partners submitted their audacious demands in a memorandum to King Charles. The memorandum and the king's itemized responses are preserved in the *Arquivo General de las Indias* in Seville. The following English version is based on the fine French translation by the Belgian historian, Jean Denucé:

ARTICLE 1: For the first ten years, the king will not license anyone to equip vessels to sail to the newly discovered lands; Magellan and Faleiro claimed that they'd be able to accomplish all the necessary discoveries, whatever number of ships might be authorized by the king to follow the same route. If more ships should be needed than they could command between them, the partners would select the additional captains.

RESPONSE: Charles avoided commenting fully on the subject of this prerogative; he wanted to know immediately what route the two explorers proposed to take, because, he said, it is not impossible to reach the same discoveries by different routes.

ARTICLE 2: The king must assign to the partners a twentieth of the profits obtained in the new lands, as well as rents and rights, less expenses; the title of admiral and the governorship of the new territories would be conferred on the partners and their legitimate heirs.

RESPONSE: The king observed here that the extent of the discoveries would have to be more or less determined; as for the title of admiral, certain privileges and related matters would have to be examined; the governorship of the new territories would be granted to the partners and their heirs, but the king would retain the supreme power. He would not accord them judicial powers in these territories because, by doing so, he would violate the laws of the kingdom; experience had shown that judicial powers in the hands of an admiral sometimes led to troublesome consequences for the Crown.

ARTICLE 3: Magellan and Faleiro asked that they be permitted, each year, to ship merchandise worth 1,000 ducats (cost of manufacture) with the fleets leaving for the new colonies; these articles would be sold or exchanged as the partners saw fit; on reentering Spain, they would be subject only to a levy of one twentieth, and all other taxes would be excluded.

RESPONSE: Charles considered the 1,000 ducats worth of exempted goods an "advance" that would enable the officers of the Indian fleets to realize the profits they hoped for, but he did not want the exempted goods to be confused with the customary merchandise sent on these ships. The spices belonging to the partners would be exempt from import and certain other taxes; as for the other rights, he would await the return of the fleet to see how much the import tax should be; he noted that the one twentieth tax requested in this clause was at variance with Article 5, in which the partners offered to a pay a fifth.

ARTICLE 4: Should the partners discover more than six islands, the king would grant two of their own choosing to them, their heirs, and successors; they would be entitled to overlordship, rents, and all the commerce of these islands, except ten percent for the king.

RESPONSE: Charles found this condition excessive and reduced the partners' share to a fifteenth of the profits from the two islands chosen and a twenty-fifth of the profits realized from the products of all the others.

ARTICLE 5: The partners would be taxed on a fifth of the proceeds from the products of the first expedition, less outfitting costs; they would receive an additional hundred quintals of the king's merchandise on each ship returning to Spain.

RESPONSE: The king remarked that, to be consistent with Article 3, he would not grant the twentieth in question; on the other hand, since he had authorized them to import 1,000 ducats worth of merchandise, it would not be reasonable to grant them an extra hundred quintals of his own goods.

ARTICLE 6: If ships of His Majesty or of third parties should discover lands or islands during the first ten of the ensuing years, Magellan and Faleiro would have a twentieth of all the proceeds and profits, since they will have been the promoters of these discoveries.

RESPONSE: Charles observed that the two captains must first specify the field of their discoveries; in sum, this stipulation is at variance with the first.

ARTICLE 7: Should His Majesty wish, under the conditions stated above, to equip the fleet at his own expense, Magellan and Faleiro will show him the considerable advantages to be derived from the enterprise, and the riches contained in the islands and lands within the Spanish demarcation.

RESPONSE: The king requested that they provide him with this information.

ARTICLE 8: Should one of the two captains die during the voyage, His Majesty promises to assign the aforementioned privileges to the survivor and to the successors and heirs of the deceased, as if both chiefs were alive.

RESPONSE: The king approved this clause.

The second part of the document stipulates the following conditions in the event that the partners would have to furnish the capital for financing the expedition:

1. The overlordship, government, and commerce of all the islands and lands discovered would belong to the partners or their appointed agents; only one fifth of the proceeds would be paid to the king.

2. All ships, even those of His Majesty, would be forbidden to trade in the new regions; their cargoes would be confiscated should this stipulation be violated.

3. For the first ten years, the king would not grant license to anyone to go to these discoveries without the consent of the partners.

These last three stipulations proved superfluous. The enterprise was approved as a Crown-financed project. The royal *capitulación* (contract) was issued on March 22, 1518.

In September 1519, Magellan sent a memorandum to the king stating the distances and geographic coordinates of the Moluccas and of certain lands and capes relating to the demarcation of Tordesillas. The following is a direct translation of the AGI material in Navarrete (Buenos Aires edition of 1946):

Most Mighty Lord: Because the king of Portugal someday may wish to claim that the Moluccas are within his demarcation and might ask you to reveal the coastal routes and ocean traverses [a long the route], and as no one understands these things as I understand and know them, for your convenience here are the latitudes and longitudes of the principal lands and capes; and with this statement Your Highness will be advised that should I perish, you will know the truth.

ITEM. The island of Sant Anton, one of the Cape Verde [islands] off the coast of Guinea, from which is measured the demarcation between these kingdoms and that of Portugal, is 22 degrees east of the line of demarcation.

ITEM. The latitude of the westernmost point of this island is 17 degrees [north].

ITEM. Cape Sant Agustin in the land of Brazil, which is within the Portuguese demarcation, is at 8 degrees of latitude [south] and 20 degrees of longitude [west] of the line of demarcation.

ITEM. Cape Santa María, which is in the same land of Brazil [belonging to] Portugal, is at 35 degrees [south] latitude and 6¼ degrees of longtitude [west] of that island [Sant Anton].

ITEM. The Cape of Good Hope and Cape Santa María lie on an east-west line and the Cape of Good Hope is at 35 degrees of latitude [south] and 65 degrees of longitude east of the line.

ITEM. The said Cape of Good Hope lies on an east northeast, west southwest line with Malacca, and it is 1,600 leagues from that cape to the port of Malacca.

ITEM. The said port of Malacca is one degree north of the equator, and from it to the other line of demarcation to the east is 17½ degrees [of longitude].

ITEM. The Molucca Islands are five in number; the three farthest from the second line of demarcation lie north-south at two and a half degrees of longitude and the island in the middle is on the equator.

ITEM. The other two islands, like the first two, lie north-south, and at 4 degrees east of the second line of demarcation, according to the Portuguese pilots who discovered them.

And this memorandum I send very well guarded to Your Highness because there will come a time when you will need it to support your arguments; and this I state with a clear conscience and the intention to tell nothing but the truth.

Appendix 6 Magellan's Will

For many years it was believed that Magellan had left two wills. The first, dated December 17, 1504 in Belem, Portugal, is now believed by Portuguese scholars to have been either a forgery or to have been executed by a different Fernão de Magalhães. Court records indicate that there were several minor noblemen with that name in sixteenth-century Portugal. The following English translation of Magellan's last will and testament (executed in Seville on August 24, 1519) is from F.H.H. Guillemard, *The Life of Ferdinand Magellan and the First Circumnavigation of the Globe; 1480–1521* (New York: Dodd Mead, 1890).

In the name of the Most High and Mighty God our Lord, who is without beginning and reigns without end, and of the most favored Glorious Virgin, Our Lady, Holy Mary, His blessed Mother, whom all we Christians own as Queen and Advocate in all our actions; to their honor and service, and that of all the Saints of the courts of Heaven. Amen.

Know all ye by these presents, that I, Hernando de Magallanes, Comendador, His Majesty's Captain-general of the Armada bound for the Spice Islands, husband of Doña Beatriz Barbosa, and inhabitant of this most noble and loyal city of Seville, in the precinct of Santa María, being well and in good health, and possessed of such my ordinary senses and judgment as God our Lord has, of His mercy and will thought fit and right to endow me; believing firmly and truly in the Holy Trinity, the Father, Son and Holy Ghost — three persons and one only true God, as every faithful Christian holds and believes, and ought to hold and believe, and being in fear of death, which is a natural thing from which no man can escape; being willing and desirous of placing my soul in the surest and most certain path that I can discern for its salvation, to commit unto the mercy and forgiveness of God, our Lord, that He, who made and created it, may have compassion and pity upon it, and redeem and save it, and bring it to His glory and His heavenly kingdom.

Whereas I am about to proceed in the king's service in the said Armada, by these presents I make known and declare that I make and ordain this my Will, and these my bequests, as well of my goods as of my body and soul, for the salvation of my soul and the satisfaction of my heirs. Firstly, the debts owed by me and to me owing: they are such as will be found written in my book of accounts, the which I confirm and approve and acknowledge as correct. The following are the legacies bequeathed by me: —

Firstly, I commend my soul to God our Lord, who made and created it, and redeemed me with His precious blood, and I ask and beseech of the ever-glorious Virgin Mary, Our Lady, His blessed Mother, that, with all the Saints of the heavenly kingdom, she may be my intercessor and supplicant before her precious Son for my soul, that He may pardon my sins and shortcomings, and receive me to share His glory in the kingdom of heaven. And when this, my present life shall end for the life eternal, I desire that if I die in this city of Seville my body may be buried in the Monastery of Santa María de la Vitoria in Triana — ward and precinct of the city of Seville — in the grave set apart for me; And if I die in this said voyage, I desire that my body may be buried in a church dedicated to Our Lady, in the nearest spot at which death seize me and I die; And I bequeath to the expenses of the chapel of the Sagrario of the Holy Church of Seville, in grateful remembrance of the Holy Sacraments which from said church I have received, and hope to receive, if it be the will of God, our Lord, one thousand maravedis; And I bequeath to the Holy Crusade a real of silver; And I bequeath to the Orders of the Holy Trinity and Santa María de la Merced of this city of Seville, in aid of the redemption of such faithful Christians as may be captives in the country of the Moors, the enemies of our holy Catholic faith, to each order a real of silver; and I bequeath to the Infirmary of San Lázaro without the city, as alms, that they may pray to God our Lord for my soul, another real of silver; And I bequeath to the hospital de Las Bubas of this city of Seville, to gain its intercession, another real of silver; And I bequeath to the Holy Church of Faith in Seville another real of silver, to gain its intercession; And I desire that on the said day of my burial thirty masses may be said over my body—two cantadas and twenty-eight rezadas, and that they shall offer for me the offering of bread and wine and candles that my executors desire; And I desire that in the said monastery of Santa María de la Vitoria a thirty-day mass may be said for my soul, and that the accustomed alms may be given therefore; And I desire that on the said day of my burial three poor men may be clothed—such as I have indicated to my executors—and that to each may be given a cloak of gray stuff, a shirt, and a pair of shoes, that they may pray to God for my soul; And I also desire that upon the said day of my burial food may be given to the said three paupers, and to twelve others, that they may pray to God for my soul; And I desire that upon the said day of my burial a gold ducat may be given as alms for the souls in purgatory. And I confess—to speak the truth before God and the world and to possess my soul in safety—that I received and obtained in dowry and marriage with the said Doña Beatriz Barbosa, my wife, six hundred thousand maravedis, of which I made acknowledgment before Bernal Gonzales de Vallecillo, notary public of Seville; and I desire that before everything the said Doña Beatriz Barbosa, my wife, may be paid and put in possession of the said six hundred thousand maravedis, her dowry, together with the arras that I gave her.

And forasmuch as I am proceeding in the king's service in the said Armada, and since all of the gain and profit which with the help of God our Lord may result therefrom (save and excepting the first charges of the king), the share allotted to me is one fifth of the whole, in addition to that which I may acquire from the merchandise which I take with me in the said Armada—of all this which I acquire from the said Armada I desire to set aside one-tenth part, touching which, by this will and testament, I desire and order, and it is my wish, that the said tenth may be expended in the manner following:—

Firstly, I desire and order that one third of the said tenth part may be given to the said monastery of N.S. Santa María de la Vitoria in Triana, for the construction of the chapel of the said monastery, and that the monks of the said monastery may henceforth forever engage to pray to God for my soul.

Furthermore, I desire, and it is my wish, that the remaining two-thirds of the said tenth part shall be divided into three equal parts, of which one part shall be given to the monastery of N.S. Santa María de Monserrat, in the city of Barcelona; another to the monastery of San Francisco in the town of Aranda de Duero, for the benefit of the said monastery; and the third to the monastery of S. Domingo de las Dueñas, in the city of Oporto, in Portugal, for such things as may be most necessary for the said monastery; and this bequest I make that they may pray to God for my soul.

Furthermore, I will and desire, and it is my wish, that half of the rest of my estate of the said Armada belonging unto me, together with that of the other estate of which I am possessed in this said city of Seville, one-fifth part may be set aside to fulfil these necessities of this my will and testament, and whatever more may seem fitting unto them for the repose of my soul and conscience.

I desire, moreover, that there may be paid to Cristóbal Robelo, my page, the sum of thirty *thousand maravedis from my estate, the which I bequeath unto him for the services he has rendered unto me, and that he may pray to God for my soul.*

And by this my present will and testament, I declare and ordain as free and quit of every obligation of captivity, subjection, and slavery, my captured slave Enrique, mulatto, native of the city of Malacca, of the age of twenty-six years more or less, that from the day of my death thenceforward forever the said Enrique may be free and manumitted, and quit, exempt, and relieved of every obligation of slavery and subjection, and that he may act as he desires and thinks fit; and I desire that of my estate there may be given to the said Enrique the sum of ten thousand maravedis in money for his support; and this manumission I grant because he is a Christian, and that he may pray to God for my soul.

And whereas His Majesty the King has granted unto me, my sons, and my heirs in tail male the governorship of certain lands and islands that I may discover with the said Armada, according to the terms in the Capitulación *made with His Majesty, together with the title of* Adelentado *of the said lands and islands discovered, and also the twentieth part of their produce, and other benefits contained in the said* Capitulación; *by these presents, and by this my will and testament, I declare and name for this* mayorazgo — *in order that, upon my decease, he may succeed to the above—Rodrigo de Magallanes, my legitimate son, and the legitimate son of the said Doña Beatriz de Barbosa, my wife, and thereafter unto any legitimate son that God may grant him; and should he have no legitimate sons born in wedlock to have and inherit the above* mayorazgo, *I desire and command that the other legitimate son or daughter whom God may give me [Beatriz was pregnant at the time the will was written] may inherit, and so successively from father to son; And if by chance a daughter should hold the* mayorazgo, *in such a case I desire that the son whom God may give her to inherit the said* mayorazgo, *shall take the name of Magallaes [sic], and bear my arms without quartering them with any others; And should he fail to take the name of Magallaes and to bear my arms, in such case I desire and order, and it is my wish, that a son or nephew or nearer relation of my lineage may inherit the said* mayorazgo, *and that he may live in Castile, and bear my name and arms; And if—by which may God forbid—the said Rodrigo de Magallaes my son should die without leaving sons or daughters born in wedlock, and that I should beget no other sons or daughters to succeed to the* mayorazgo, *I desire and order, and it is my wish, that Diego de Sosa, my brother, who is now living with His Serene Majesty the King of Portugal, may inherit the above, and come and live in this kingdom of Castile, and marry in it, and that he adopt the name of Magallaes, and bear the arms of Magallaes, as I bear them—the arms of Magallaes e Sosa; And if the said Diego de Sosa, my brother have neither sons nor daughters born in holy wedlock to inherit the aforesaid* mayorazgo, *I desire and order, and it is my wish, that Isabel de Magallaes, my sister, may inherit the said* mayorazgo, *provided that she call herself Magallaes, and bear my arms, and come to reside and marry in this kingdom of Castile.*

And furthermore, I desire and order, and it is my will, that if the said Diego de Sosa, my brother, or the said Isabel de Magallaes, my sister, succeed to the aforesaid mayorazgo, *they shall be obliged to assist the said Doña Beatriz Barbosa, my wife, with the fourth part of all that the said my* mayorazgo *produces, fairly and justly, and without let or hindrance soever; And I desire that the Comendador Diego de Barbosa, my father-in-law, may undertake the charge of the person, goods and* mayorazgo *of the said Rodrigo de Magallaes, my son, and of the child or children with whom the said Doña Beatriz de Barbosa, my wife, is now pregnant, until they reach the age of eighteen years, and that during this period the said Comendador Diego Barbosa may receive and collect all the produce and rents which the said estate and* mayorazgo *may produce, and give and deliver to the said Doña Beatriz de Barbosa, my wife, his daughter, the fourth part of all that may therefrom result, until such time as my sons aforesaid be of the age stated; the said my wife, Doña Beatriz Barbosa, living widowed and chastely; And if she should marry, I desire that there be given and paid to her the sum of two thousand Spanish doubloons, over and above her dowry and arras, and half the accumulations thereon.*

Furthermore, I desire, and it is my will, that the said Comendador Diego Barbosa may take and receive, as his own property, one fourth part; and that he may expend the remainder in the maintenance and education of my sons; and likewise, I desire and order, and it is my wish, that if the said Diego de Sosa, my brother, or the said Isabel de Magallaes, my sister, inherit the aforesaid my mayorazgo, *that above and beyond that which I have desired may be given each year to the said Doña Beatriz Barbosa, my wife, they shall be obliged to give each year to the said Comendador Diego Barbosa, for the remainder of his life, two hundred ducats of gold, to be paid from the estate of the said* mayorazgo.

Furthermore, I desire that, if the said Comendador Diego Barbosa collect the aforesaid my estate, he may give of it to the said Isabel de Magallaes, my sister, for her marriage, such as seems fitting to the said Comendador Diego Barbosa.

Furthermore, I desire that of the fifty thousand maravedis that I have for my life and that of the said Doña Beatriz Barbosa, my wife, from the Casa de Contratación *of the Indies of this city of Seville, the said Doña Beatriz, my wife, may give to the said Isabel de Magallaes, my sister, the sum of five thousand maravedis per annum until the arrival of my estate resulting from this my present voyage, when the said Comendador Diego Barbosa can give her that which I have arranged and desired in this my will that he should give her for her marriage.*

And this my will and testament having been fulfilled and discharged, together with the bequests and clauses therein contained, relating to the aforesaid my possessions, whether fixtures, movables, or livestock, in compliance with that herewith prescribed and expressed, I desire that all and everything of the said possessions which may remain over and above may be had and inherited by the said Rodrigo de Magallaes, my legitimate son by the said Doña Beatriz, my wife, and by the child or children of which the said Dona Beatriz is now pregnant, being born and living for the period that the law requires, whom — the said Rodrigo de Magallaes, my son, and the child or children of which the said my wife is pregnant — I appoint and establish as my legal residuary legatees, equally the one with the other; And if, which God may forbid, the said my son or child borne by my wife, die before attaining the proper age for the succession, I desire that the said Doña Beatriz Barbosa, my wife, may inherit the said estate, save and excepting that of the mayorazgo, *and I appoint and establish her as my residuary legatee.*

And for the discharge and quitment of this my will and testament, and of the bequests and clauses concerning the said my estate therein contained, in compliance with that herewith prescribed and expressed, I hereby appoint as my executors for the payment and distribution of the said my estate, without hurt to them or theirs, Doctor Sancho de Matienzo, Canon of Seville, and the said Comendador Diego Barbosa, my father-in-law; And I bequeath to the said Doctor Sancho de Matienzo for the burden thus laid upon him in the fulfillment and discharge of this my will the sum of thirty gold ducats and two pesos. [Then followed the conclusion in formal legal terms].

Done in Seville in the king's Customs of this city of Seville, Wednesday, the twenty-fourth day of the month of August, in the year of the birth of our Saviour Jesus Christ one thousand five hundred and nineteen. And I, the said Comendador Hernando de Magallaes, sign and confirm it with my name in the register, in the presence of the witnesses Diego Martínez de Medina, Juan Rodríguez de Medina, and Alfonso Fernández, notaries of Seville.

Appendix 7 Timelines

3000 B.C.   Egypt: 3rd to 6th dynasties (Old Kingdom). Maritime expedition to Punt leads to shipments of gold and precious metals from mines of Zimbabwe.

Phoenicians settle in Levant.

Austronesians (ancestral Polynesians) emigrate from Asian mainland to Taiwan and northern Philippines; expand into Malay Archipelago, Marianas, Micronesia, and western Polynesia.

Minoan culture arises in Crete.

Hammurabi rules in Babylon.

2000 B.C.   Greeks migrate from the Caspian Sea region to the shores of the Aegean Sea.

Austronesians reach Tonga, Samoa, Madagascar.

Moses leads Jews out of Egypt.

Phoenicians vie with Minoans for maritime supremacy in Mediterranean.

Shang, Chou dynasties in China.

1000 B.C.   David, and then Solomon rule in Israel; latter promotes Phoenician voyage to Punt.

Greeks establish colonies in Italy, Sicily, Spain.

Phoenicians voyage around Africa, reach Atlantic islands, Britain.

Life of Gautama, Prince Siddhartha (Buddha).

500 B.C.   Grecian civilization: Age of Pericles.

Austronesians reach Marshall Islands.

Beginning of Roman civilization in Italy.

Alexander of Macedon conquers Greece, Egypt, Babylon, and Persia; invades India.

Ptolemaic kingdoms in Egypt develop maritime trade with India; with conquest of Ptolemaic Egypt, Romans enter Indian trade.

Eratosthenes estimates Earth's circumference.

Punic Wars (Carthage vs. Rome).

Pythias's voyage to Britain and Thule.

Chinese expedition to "Isles of the Blessed" (Japan?).

Conquests of Julius Caesar; end of Roman Republic

0   Jesus of Nazareth provokes secular and religious authorities in Pales-
             tine; Paul of Tarsus lays foundations of Christianity.

             Roman conquest of Britain

             Roman Empire assaulted from periphery, seat of empire moved to Con-
             stantinople. Huns invade Europe. Angles, Saxons, Jutes invade Britain.

             Polynesians reach Hawaii, Easter Island.

             Attila defeated by Romans and Visigoths; Huns withdraw from Europe.

A.D. 500   Age of Arthur, Romano-British warlord, legendary British king whose
             final battle (Camlann) is commonly dated 537; however, Geoffrey Ashe,
             The Age of Arthur (New York: Anchor/Doubleday, 1985), places the his-
             torical Arthur in mid- to late-fifth century.

             Muhammad lays foundations of Islam.

             Buddhism introduced into Japan; Christianity into Britain.

             Irish monks settle on islands north of Britain, reach Iceland.

             Arabs adopt Indian numerals.

             Charlemagne becomes first Holy Roman Emperor.

             Polynesians reach New Zealand.

             Expansion of Arab maritime trade in Indian Ocean and China Seas; Ar-
             abs invade Iberian Peninsula, then cross Pyrenees to be repulsed by
             Charles Martel at Tours and Poitiers.

             Danes and Norwegians assault Britain; Alfred, King of Wessex, defeats
             Danes at Edington, preventing extension of Danelaw to southern Brit-
             ain.

             Alfonso III of Castile begins reconquest of Spain.

             Scandinavians penetrate Russia, establish principalities of Novgorod
             and Kiev.

             Norwegians settle in Iceland and Greenland; Leif Ericsson, following an
             earlier sighting by Bjarni Herjolfsson, lands at northern Newfoundland.

A.D. 1000   Sung dynasty in China, magnetic compass in use on seagoing junks.

             Canute rules in Denmark, Norway, and England.

             Macbeth murders King Duncan, assumes throne of Scotland.

1405   Death of Timur the Lame (Tamerlane), a Tatar warlord, who had over-
             run much of Central Asia and the Middle East.

1415   Henry V's English archers and foot soldiers defeat French armored cav-
             alry at Battle of Agincourt.

             Portuguese expeditionary force captures Ceuta from the Moors. From
             his estate at Sagres, Prince Henry ("the Navigator") of Portugal
             (1394–1460) sponsors maritime exploration (the Atlantic islands and
             along the African coast) in search of gold and the Kingdom of Prester
             John.

1405–33   Led by Admiral Zheng He (Chêng Ho), Chinese fleets pay diplomatic
             visits to ports on the Indian Ocean, Persian Gulf, and Red Sea.

Joan of Arc (1412–31) lifts siege of Orléans. Later captured by Burgundians, then tried and convicted by church inquisitors, she was turned over to the English in Rouen and burned at the stake.

1434–35   Gil Eannes, one of Prince Henry's captains, returns to Portugal from West Africa with 200 black slaves; profitability from their sale stimulates slave trade.

1441–44   Death of Jan Van Eyck, Dutch painter; birth of Sandro Botticelli, Italian painter.

1456–57   In Germany, Johann Gutenberg invents printing press, prints forty-two-line Bible and Psalter.

1469   Ferdinand of Aragon and Isabella of Castile wed, create a united Spain, and encourage Inquisition to persecute converted Jews suspected of heresy.

1473   Pining and Pothorst, German mariners employed by the Danish crown, and João Corte Real representing the Portuguese crown, report sighting a wooded "stockfish land" (Labrador, Newfoundland?) in the northwestern Atlantic.

1475   Births of Ferdinand Magellan in Portugal (c. 1470–80) and Michelangelo Buonarotti in Italy.

1479   Treaty of Alcáçovas ends war between Portugal and Castile, confirms Castile's claim to Canary Islands.

1482–83   Columbus travels to Elmina (Gold Coast, West Africa) on a Portuguese ship; upon return to Portugal, petitions João II for ships to sail westward to Asia; proposal rejected.

1482–86   Diogo Cão, a Portuguese captain, enters mouth of Congo River, continues south to Cape Santa María (13° 26′ S), returns to Portugal claiming to have reached Africa's terminal cape. On second voyage (c. 1485–86) Cão leaves marker at Kaap Kruis (21° 50′ S), then disappears with ship and all hands.

1487   The Royal House of Hapsburg begins borrowing from the Fuggers (a family of weavers who founded a merchant banking house in Augsburg, Germany).

1488   Bartolomeu Dias, Portuguese navigator, doubles Cape of Good Hope.

1492   Granada, last Moorish kingdom in Spain, submits to Ferdinand and Isabella; Jews forced to accept Christianity or leave Spain; Columbus sails from Palos with ships provided by Catholic Sovereigns, landing in Bahamas, Cuba, and Hispaniola, then returns to Spain.

1493   Alexander VI (the Borgia Pope) divides unexplored world between Spain and Portugal; papal line of demarcation in Atlantic shifted 370 leagues west by Treaty of Tordesillas.

1495   Manuel I (the Fortunate) succeeds João II as King of Portugal.

1497   John Cabot sails to N. America; Vasco da Gama sails around Africa to India.

Leonardo da Vinci's "The Last Supper."

1498–99   Savonarola, Italian religious reformer, burned at the stake in Florence; Erasmus, Dutch humanist, teaches at Oxford; Michelangelo completes "Pietà;" Ojeda, Vespucci explore coast of South America.

A.D. 1500   Birth of Archduke Charles in Flanders (grandson of Ferdinand and Isabella of Spain). Michelangelo's "David."

1505   Magellan sails for India with Almeida's fleet.

1507   Martin Luther ordained a Roman Catholic priest; Martin Waldseemüller, Alsatian cartographer, names the landmass in the western Atlantic "America" after Amerigo Vespucci, describing it as distinct from Asia.

1508–12   Michelangelo paints ceiling frescoes in Sistine Chapel. Magellan participates in Portuguese seizure of Malacca (1511). Martin Luther earns doctorate, begins teaching (1512).

1513   Vasco Nuñez Balboa views Pacific Ocean from a peak in Darien (1513); Magellan sails for Morocco with Portuguese expeditionary force.

1514   Copernicus (Mikolai Kopernik), Polish astronomer, serves as canon of the cathedral of Frauenberg, practices medicine, and undertakes the study of planetary motions.

1515–17   Magellan humiliated at court by King Manuel (1515); renounces Portuguese citizenship and arrives in Seville (October 20, 1517). Eleven days later in Wittenburg, Germany, Luther nailed his arguments against the sale of indulgences to a church door.

1519   On death of his grandfather, Maximilian I, Charles I of Spain becomes Charles V, Holy Roman Emperor. Captain general of a royal Spanish fleet, Magellan sails for the Moluccas. Hernán Cortez begins conquest of Mexico. Death of Leonardo da Vinci.

1521   Magellan killed in the Philippines. Manuel I of Portugal dies, succeeded by João III.

1522   *Victoria*, last surviving ship of Magellan's fleet, arrives in Seville, completing first circumnavigation of the earth.

1525–27   Luther marries (1525). Albrecht Dürer, German painter, completes "The Four Apostles" (1526). Survivors of Magellan's *Trinidad* return to Spain (1527).

Endnotes

Chapter 1. Early Seafarers

1. Paul Herrmann, *Conquest by Man*, trans. Michael Bullock (New York: Harper's, 1954), pp. 55-59.
2. Edward Dodd, *Polynesian Seafaring*, Ring of Fire, Vol. II (New York: Dodd, Mead, 1972), p. 18; Peter Bellwood, "The Austronesian Dispersal and the Origin of Languages," *Scientific American* (July, 1991), 88-93.
3. Bellwood, *The Polynesians: Prehistory of an Island People* (London: Thomas & Hudson, 1978), 23-27.
4. Ibid., p. 52.
5. Ibid., pp. 11-12; Janet Davidson, *The Prehistory of New Zealand* (Auckland: Longman Paul, 1984), pp. 26-28.
6. B. R. Finney, *Hokule'a: The Way to Tahiti* (New York: Dodd, Mead, 1979); "Voyaging into Polynesia's Past," *J. Pacific Society*, 13 (3), Oct. 1990.
7. Dodd, pp. 49-63, 161-168, 174-176.
8. Herrmann, pp. 55-59.
9. Ibid., p. 61.
10. Ibid., pp. 68-69. The Phoenicians got the better of the deal. After the first voyage, they made many others on their own. The Israelites, without suitable ships or trained seamen, were unable to continue the trade.
11. E. G. R. Taylor, *The Haven Finding Art* (London: Hollis & Carter, 1956), p. 46.
12. Ibid., p. 46; Herrmann, p. 79.
13. Herrmann, pp. 106-109.
14. Taylor, p. 46; Herrmann, p. 80.
15. Herrmann, p. 109, cited Fritjof Nansen, who opted for Norway.
16. Taylor, p. 45, suggested that the brash ice described by Pythias fits Iceland better than Norway.
17. Ibid., pp. 53-56.
18. Daniel J. Boorstin, *The Discoverers* (New York: Random House, Vintage Ed., 1985), pp. 95-96; Taylor, p. 105.
19. Taylor, p. 57.
20. Herrmann, p. 137; Boorstin, p. 180.
21. John A. Garraty and Peter Gay, eds., *The Columbia History of the World* (New York: Harper & Row, 1984), p. 359; Peter Bellwood, "The Austronesian Dispersal and the Origin of Languages," *Scientific American* (July, 1991), 88-93.
22. Herrmann, p. 190, cited Gabriel Ferrand and Eberhard Stechow.
23. Garraty and Gay, p. 359.
24. J. H. Parry, *The Discovery of the Sea* (New York: Dial Press, 1974), p. 20.
25. Peter Kemp, *The History of Ships* (London: Orbis, 1983), p. 54.
26. Alan Villiers, *Men, Ships and the Sea* (Washington, D.C.: National Geographic Society, 1973), p. 54.
27. Jorma Pohjanpolo, *The Sea and Man*, trans. Diana Tullberg (New York: Stein & Day, 1970), p. 59.
28. Boorstin, p. 113.
29. Garraty and Gay, p. 320.
30. Taylor, p. 92.
31. Boorstin, pp. 137-138.
32. Garraty and Gay, p. 326.
33. Boorstin, pp. 190-194.
34. Haraprasad Ray, "The Eighth Voyage of the Dragon That Never Was: An Enquiry into the Causes of the Cessation of Voyages During the Ming Dynasty," *China Report*, vol. 23, no. 2 (New Delhi, 1987), pp. 157-158.
35. Garraty and Gay, p. 431.
36. Boorstin, p. 179.
37. Ibid., p. 180.
38. Allama Syed Sulaiman Nadvi, *The Arab Navigators*, trans. Abdur Rahman, M. A. (Lahore, Pakistan:

Sh. Muhammad Ashraf), p. 98. The Arab navigators' name for Japan was *Waqwaq*.

39. Kemp, pp. 54-55.
40. Nadvi, p. 123.
41. Parry, p. 23.
42. Boorstin, p. 183.
43. Ibid., pp. 121, 179.
44. Ibid., pp. 181-182; Nadvi, pp. 140-144.
45. Nadvi, pp. 100-102.
46. Taylor, p. 65.
47. Ibid., p. 70.
48. Ibid., p. 76.
49. Herrmann, pp. 174-179.
50. Boorstin, p. 215.

51. Kemp, pp. 45-47.
52. Boorstin, pp. 216-217; TAYLOR, PP. 77-80; Parry, p. 38.
53. Taylor, p. 77.
54. Gianni Granzotto, *Christopher Columbus*, trans. Stephen Sartelli (Norman: Univ. of Oklahoma Press, 1987), pp. 26-27.
55. Robert H. Fuson, trans., *The Log of Christopher Columbus* (Camden, Maine: International Marine Publishing, 1987).
56. G. Blakemore Evans, ed., *The Riverside Shakespeare* (Boston: Houghton Mifflin, 1974), p. 1198.
57. Boorstin, pp. 137-138.

Chapter 2. The Iberians

1. Boorstin, p. 142.
2. Herrmann, pp. 405-406. 1 gold ducat = 3.53 grams; 300,000 ducats = 1,059,000 grams. 1,059,000 g. × .032 = 33,888 troy oz.; 1990 gold price = $355/troy oz; 33,888 troy oz. × $355 = $12,030,000.
3. Parry, p. 91.
4. Boorstin, p. 160.
5. Parry, p. 101.
6. Herrmann, p. 364.
7. Charles McKew Parr, *So Noble a Captain: The Life and Times of Ferdinand Magellan* (New York: Crowell, 1953; reprinted, Westport, Conn.: Greenwood Press, 1975), p. 13 (1975 ed.).
8. Boorstin, p. 165.
9. Herrmann, pp. 78-82, 162.
10. Boorstin, pp. 163-164. Cites Gomes Eannes de Zurara, *The Chronicles of the Discovery and Conquest of Guinea*, trans. Edgar Prestage, ed. C. Raymond Beazley (London: Hakluyt Soc., 1896).
11. Ibid., pp. 167-168.
12. Parry, p. 12.
13. Ibid., p. 113. Cites Gian Battista Ramusio, *Delle Navigatione e Viaggi* (Venice: L. Giunti, 1550).
14. Herrmann, pp. 291-292.
15. Parry, p. 233.
16. Ibid., p. 122. 700 kilos of gold =

22,400 troy oz. = $7,952,000 at 1990 gold prices.
17. Ibid., p. 119.
18. Granzotto, p. 46.
19. Herrmann, p. 416.
20. Ibid. The legend on a globe by Martin Behaim states that, for the second expedition, Cão had orders to sail ". . . out beyond the pillars which Hercules set in Africa, always towards the south and always towards the rising sun as far as they could." The instruction to sail ". . . towards the rising sun . . ." indicates that King João wanted Cão to sail east (into the Indian Ocean).
21. Parry, p. 136.
22. Boorstin, pp. 170-172; Parry, pp. 138-139; Herrmann, p. 425; F. Alvarez, *Portuguese Embassy to Abyssinia*, trans. Baron Stanley of Alderley (London: Hakluyt Soc., 1881).
23. Boorstin, pp. 170-172; Parry, pp. 138-139; Edmund Ullendorf, "Covilhão, Pedro de," Encyclopedia Brittanica, 1967, Vol. 6, p. 679.
24. Bjorn Landstrom, *Bold Voyagers and Great Explorers* (first published in English as *The Quest for India*), trans. Michael Phillips and Hugh Stubbs (New York: Doubleday, 1964), p. 221.
25. Granzotto, p. 56.

26. Parry, p. 202.
27. Kirkpatrick Sale, "What Columbus Died Believing: The *True* Geographic Concepts of the Great Discoverer," *Terrae Incognitae*, XXI (1989), 9-16.

28. Barbara W. Tuchman, *The March of Folly* (New York: Alfred A. Knopf, 1984), pp. 75-90.
29. Boorstin, p. 248.
30. Ibid., pp. 248-249.

Chapter 3. Magellan's Early Years

1. Many nineteenth and twentieth-century writers have accepted 1480 as the year of Magellan's birth, and Sabrosa, a village in Tras os Montes (a mountainous district east of Nobrega), as his birthplace. This unsubstantiated version of Magellan's origins started with Diego Barros-Arana's *Vida y Viages de Hernando de Magallanes* (Santiago, Chile: 1864). Henry Edward John Stanley, Baron of Alderley, ed., *The First Voyage Around the World by Magellan* (London: Hakluyt Society, LII, 1874); Francis Henry Hill Guillamard, *The Life of Ferdinand Magellan and the First Circumnavigation of the Globe: 1480-1521* (New York: Dodd, Mead, 1890); Jean Denucé, *La Question des Moluques et la Première* Circumnavigation du Globe (Brussels: Hayez, 1911); Samuel Eliot Morison, *The European Discovery of America: The Southern Voyages* (New York: Oxford Press, 1974), and Mauricio Obregon, *Argonauts to Astronauts* (New York: Harper & Row, 1980), are among the more distinguished authors who accepted the year and place of birth for Magellan given by Barros Arana.

Two prominent historians who did not were José Toribio Medina, *El Descubrimiento del Océano Pacífico: Vasco Nuñez de Balboa, Hernando de Magallanes y sus Compañeros* (Santiago, Chile: Imprenta Universitaria, 1920), and João A. de Mascarenhas Judice, Visconde de Lagôa, *Fernão de Magalhães, A Sua Vida e A Sua Viagem* (Lisbon: Seara Nova, 1938), Vol. I. If, as Medina reasoned on p. XV of *Descubrimiento . . .* , Magellan began service as Queen Leonor's page in 1486, and royal pages were recruited at 13 or 14 years of age, Magellan would have been born in 1472 or 1473. Lagôa, pp. 92-97, noted that the idea that Sabrosa was Magellan's birthplace was derived from a will filed in 1504 by a Fernão de Magalhães. The family details given in that will are at variance with a later will known to be authentic, and with those in a 1567 claim against the discoverer's estate by a nephew from the Nobrega branch of the family, Lourenço de Magalhães. As there were several noblemen with the name Fernão de Magalhães on the palace payroll in 1504, the author of the earlier will probably was a homonym from Sabrosa, home to another branch of the Magellan clan.

2. A study of Magellan genealogy by Charles McKew Parr, *So Noble a Captain: The Life of Ferdinand Magellan* (New York: Crowell, 1953) convinced him that the birthplace of Ferdinand Magellan was the Quinta de Magalhães, a farmstead near Ponte da Barca.

3. Martín Fernández de Navarrete, *Colección De Los Viages Y Descubrimientos Que Hicieron Por Mar Los Españoles Desde Fines Del Siglo XV* (Buenos Aires: Editorial Guaranía, 1946), p. XXVII (first published in Madrid: 1825-1837), Medina, pp. IV-IX, and Lagôa, p. 104, accepted Pôrto as Magellan's birthplace.

4. Parr, pp. 2, 32.
5. Denucé, pp. 98-99.
6. Lagôa, Magellan Genealogy (table between pp. 12-13).
7. Barros Arana, p. 18, cited Bartolomé Juan de Leonardo y Argensola, *Con-*

quista de las Islas Molucas al Rey Felipe II (Madrid: 1609, English translation by John Stevens, London: 1708); Medina, p. XIV, cited Leonardo y Argensola and Jerónomo de Zurita y Castro, Anales de la Corona de Aragón (Zaragoza: 1562-1580).

8. Barros-Arana, p. 17.
9. H. V. Livermore, A New History of Portugal (Cambridge: 1966), p. 106.
10. Ibid., p. 132; Parr, pp. 46-47.
11. Armando Cortesão, The Mystery of

Vasco da Gama (Lisbon, Coimbra: Junta de Investigacões do Ultramar, 1973), p. 33.
12. Medina, p. XVII, cited A. Braancamp Freire, Emmenata da Casa da India, Bol. Soc. Geog. (Lisbon, 1907).
13. Lagôa, p. 119.
14. Charles E. Nowell, ed., Magellan's Voyage Around the World: Three Contemporary Accounts (Evanston: Northwestern University Press, 1962), p. 62.

Chapter 4. Indian Ocean Campaigns

1. Elaine Sanceau, The Reign of the Fortunate King, 1495-1521 (Hamden, Connecticut: Archon Books, 1969), p. 7; Livermore, p. 132; Parr, p. 49.
2. Bailey W. Diffie and George D. Winius, Foundations of the Portuguese Empire, 1415-1580 (Minneapolis: Univ. of Minnesota Press, 1977), p. 176, cited João de Barros, Decadas da Asia, Hernani Cidade and Manuel Murias, eds., 4 vols. (Lisbon: 1945-1946) I, lib. 4, cap. 1. (first published in Lisbon, 1552-1563, and Madrid, 1615).
3. Sanceau, pp. 17-18; Livermore, p. 134; Howell, p. 68.
4. Diffie and Winius, pp. 177-178.
5. Ibid., p. 181; Sanceau, p. 29.
6. Diffie and Winius, pp. 187-188; Sanceau, p. 29.
7. Diffie and Winius, p. 198.
8. Denucé, p. 102; Lagôa, p. 125, cited Braancamp-Freire and Gaspar Correia, Lendas da India, Rodrigo José de Lima-Felner, ed., (Lisbon: Academia Real das Ciências, 1858-1866).
9. The Portuguese chroniclers: Barros, Fernão Lopes de Castanheda, Historia do descobrimento e conquista da India pelos portugueses (Coimbra: Imprensa da Universidade, 1924-1933), Correia and Antonio Galvao, Tratado dos varios e diversos caminhos . . . , (Lisbon: 1731), provide accounts of the events with which Magellan was associated during his period of service with Portuguese forces in the Indian Ocean. Martin Torodash, "Magellan Histori-

ography," Hispanic American Historical Review, p. 51 (May, 1971) and Nowell pointed out that Galvão, not an official court historian, was the only one of these who was temperate in his treatment of Magellan, who was despised as a defector by most historians of that era.
10. Lagôa, p. 126.
11. Denucé, pp. 102, 104 and Medina, p. XX. Both cited Correia and interpreted his statement about Magellan having been wounded at Calicut as having referred to the Battle of Diu in 1509, as does Parr. Lagôa cited part of Correia's statement, but did not mention the wounding incident. It seems more likely that Correia was referring to the Battle of Cananore in 1506, which was waged against an enemy fleet from Calicut. The Battle of Diu, in which Magellan also was wounded, occurred three years later. Denucé, p. 102 and Medina, p. XIX, cited Barros, dec. II, lib. I, cap. V, who stated quite clearly that Serrão distinguished himself at the Battle of Cananore.
12. Lagôa, p. 127.
13. Ibid.; Denucé, p. 105.
14. Lagôa, p. 128; Parr, p. 83.
15. Barros-Arana, p. 20. Lagôa, pp. 127-128, wrote that Afonso Dornelas and "various historians" accepted Barros-Arana's idea that Magellan was in Portugal in 1508, but that he (Lagôa) considered it unfounded, citing Cor-

reia, Barros and Damião de Góis, *Crónica do sereníssimo senhor Rei Dom Manoel*, 7 vols. (Coimbra: Imprensa da Universidade, 1949-1955) III, Ch. I.

16. Lagôa, p. 128.
17. Ibid.
18. Denucé, p. 104, cited Correia, t. II, p. 28; Medina, pp. XIX-XX.
19. Parr, p. 92-93.
20. Denucé, p. 104.
21. Ibid., p. 105.
22. Lagôa, p. 129.
23. Denucé, p. 104; Medina, p. XX; Lagôa, p. 129. Barros, dec. II, liv. IV, cap. III, and Góis, Parte III, cap. I. were the primary sources.
24. Lagôa, p. 129, cited Castanheda, lib. II, cap. CXII.
25 Ibid., pp. 129-131; Denucé, p. 106.
26. Lagôa, p. 131, cited Castanheda, lib. II, cap. CXVI.
27. Denucé, p. 107, wrote that the Portuguese lost 60 men, not counting those taken prisoner. Parr, p. 103, wrote that 30 men were killed, 30 taken prisoner, and that 40 escaped in the boats. Medina, p. XXI, merely claimed that ". . . not a few were taken prisoner." The primary sources for this episode are Castanheda, lib. II, cap. CXVI, and Barros, dec. II, lib. IV, cap. IV.
28. Denucé, p. 107.
29. Ibid., pp. 107-108.
30. Lagôa, p. 131, cited Castanheda, lib. II, cap. CXIV and Góis, Parte III, cap. II.
31. William Manchester, *Goodbye Darkness* (Boston: Little Brown, 1979), p. 391.
32. Lagôa, p. 132.
33. Denucé, p. 108, and Medina, p. XXI, cited Correia, t. II, p. 28; Lagôa, p. 132.
34. Denucé, p. 109, cited Antonio de Herrera, *Historia general de las Indias Occidentales y de los hechos de los castellanos en las islas y tierra firme del mar océano*, 4 vols., (Madrid: 1601-1615); Medina, pp. XXII-XXIII; Lagôa, pp. 133-135. Barros, Castanheda, Góis

and Correia are the primary sources.
35. Medina, p. XXII, cited Herrera, dec. II, lib. II, cap. XIX.
36. Denucé, p. 109; Lagôa, p. 135. Both cited Barros, dec. II, cap. I, p. 61.
37. Denucé, p. 109-110. It is not clear whether or not Magellan participated in the attack on Goa. Barros-Arana stated flatly that he did. Guillemard did not think that the evidence warranted that assumption, while Lagôa, p. 136, argued that it did.
38. Denucé, p. 110, cited Afonso de Albuquerque, *Commentaries of Afonso Dalboquerque*, (translated by W. De Gray Birch, London: Hakluyt Society, 1880, t. II, p. 91, from documents in the Arquivo da Torre do Tombo, Lisbon.
39. Ibid., p. 114, cited J. Gråberg da Hemsö, *Littera di Giovanni da Empoli a Leonardo sua padre . . .* (Firenze, Italy: Archivo Storico Italiano, 1846), t. III, appendix, p. 40.
40. Lagôa, p. 136, cited Correia, t. II, cap. XII, and Albuquerque, Parte II, cap. XXXI.
41. Denucé, p. 112, cited Antonio Baião, *Fernão de Magalhães. O problema de sua naturalidade* (Lisbon: Memorias da Academia das Ciências, t. XIV).
42. Lagôa, p. 144, cited Arquivo da Torre do Tombo, Corpo Cronológico, parte II, maço (bundle) 65, doc. 19.
43. Guillemard.
44. Denucé, p. 115, cited Herrera, dec. II, lib. II, cap. XIX.
45. Ibid., p. 118, cited Bartolomé Juan de Leonardo y Argensola, *Conquista de las islas Molucas al rey Felipe II*, (Madrid, 1609).
46. Ibid., p. 121, cited Góis, Castanheda and Correia.
47. Lagôa, p. 147.
48. Denucé, p. 122.
49. Ibid., p. 123.
50. Denucé, p. 124, stated that they were the first Europeans in the Moluccas, but on p. 102 he wrote that in 1506 Lorenzo de Almeida had been advised by the Italian traveler, Ludovico

di Varthema, of an impending attack on the Portuguese fleet. E.M.J. Campbell, "Varthema, Lodovico di" *Encyclopedia Brittanica*, 1967, XXII, p. 903, stated that about 1505, Varthema, traveling on Arab ships, had visited the Moluccas. Citing Gabriel Rebello, *Informacão das cousas de Maluco dadas ao Senhor dom Constan-* *tino* (Lisbon: Coleccão de noticias para a história de geografia das nacões ultramarinas, 1839), t. V, no. 2, Denucé named Diogo Lopes, Diogo Cão, Diogo Afonso, Pero Fernandes, Álvaro da Costa and Antoneto Ceziliano (Siciliano?) as the Portuguese who accompanied Serrão to the Moluccas.

Chapter 5. Humiliation and Disgrace

1. Lagôa, p. 148, note 1.
2. Denucé, p. 130.
3. Ibid.; Medina, p. XXXI.
4. Lagôa, p. 149, cited "Noticia da conquista da cidade de Azamor," in *Alguns documentos da Torre do Tombo* (Lisbon: Sept. 19, 1513); pp. 149-150, cited Antonio Baiâo, "Rol de pagamento de pâo que se deo a gente de cavalo que serviu na cidade de Azamor no ano 1514," *Arquivo Histórico Português*.
5. Lagôa, p. 149, note 3. 400 reis = 1 cruzado = $30.00 U.S.; 3,700 reis = $277.50 U.S. (for Magellan's horse); 13,000 reis = $975.00 U.S. (for other officers' horses).

   It is possible that Magellan, unable to afford better, had purchased an old nag. If he knew the animal, the quartermaster may have offered him what he thought it was worth.
6. Denucé, pp. 130-131 and Medina, p. XXXII, cited Barros, Dec. III, Parte I, Lib. V, Cap. VIII; Lagôa, p. 150.
7. Denucé, p. 131 and Parr, p. 141 assumed that João de Meneses and João Soares were two different people. Medina, p. XXXII and Lagôa, p. 150 referred only to João Soares as the officer who replaced the Duke of Braganza as commander at Azamor. There probably was but one individual, João Soares, Count de Meneses.
8. Lagôa, p. 150.
9. Denucé, p. 131; Lagôa, p. 151, cited Schaffer, *História do Portugal*, Vol. III.
10. Ibid.
11. Lagôa, p. 151, stated that Barros, Góis and Fr. Luis de Sousa cited 200 reis ($15 U.S.) as the monthly increase Magellan requested, and that Correia and Manuel de Faria e Sousa, *Asia Portuguesa*, trans. (Span. to Port.) Vitoria Garcia Santos Ferreira (Oporto: Livraria Civilizacão, 6 vols.: 1945-1947), put the amount at 100 reis. Góis wrote that Magellan asked for 200 reis and that Manuel offered 100, which Magellan declined. One hundred reis would be equivalent to about $7.50 in today's U.S. currency. It was not the monetary value of the raise that mattered to Magellan. Among the nobility, the *moradia* was regarded as a measure of royal esteem. Magellan was desperate for some indication that the king valued his services.
12. Medina, p. XXXIV, cited Barros, Dec. III, Parte I, Liv. V, Cap. VIII.
13. Denucé, p. 132; Medina, p. XXXIV; Lagôa, p. 152.
14. Ibid.
15. Medina, p. XXXIV, cited Faria e Sousa, I, p. 14, as having stated ". . . to gain five reales [reis] in cash is to gain many grades in quality." Lagôa, p. 151, cited the same source.
16. Medina, p. CVI, cited Fr. Bartolomé de las Casas, "Historia de las Indias" in *Colección de documentos inéditos para la historia de España* (Madrid: 1875-1876), T. III, pp. 376-378, who had this to say of his meeting with Magellan in Valladolid: "This Hernando de Magallanes must have been a spirited man, intellectually bold and capable of undertaking great things although his person did not convey much authority, for he was short and didn't look like much, neither was there [about him] any hint of lack of pru-

dence that might lead one to expect to be able to take advantage of him, for he seemed [both] modest and courageous."

17. Medina, pp. CVII-CXI, stated that the portraits appearing in the Spanish works on Magellan, with few exceptions, were based on a copper engraving made for Don José de Vargas Ponce by Fernando Selma. It was inserted in the *Relación del último viage al Estrecho de Magallanes de la fragata de S.M. "Santa María de la Cabeza,"* (Madrid: 1788). Medina thought that it was copied from a painting in the portrait gallery of the Giovio Museum in Como, Italy, dated prior to 1568.

The fine portrait used by Lagôa and Morison is from the Kunsthistorisches Museum in Vienna. The artist is unknown, but it was painted in the sixteenth century.

18. Denucé, p. 138, cited Correia, Vol. I, Parte II, Cap. IX.

19. Ibid., p. 134, cited Barros, Dec. III, Parte I, Lib. V, Caps. VI, VIII and Castanheda, Lib. II, Cap. LXXXVI.

20. Denucé, p. 78, cited Navarrete, T. III, Num. XXXVI, p. 130.

21. Ibid., p. 135, cited Barros, Dec. III, Lib. V, Cap. VIII.

22. Denucé, p. 137, note 1; Lagôa, p. 153. Both cited Correia.

Chapter 6. Conception

1. Medina, p. XXXV

2. If he did, it was an extraordinarily quick visit, for his recorded itinerary leaves too little time for a journey of such length. Boies Penrose, *Travel and Discovery in the Renaissance, 1420-1620* (New York: Atheneum, 1962), pp. 37-41, stated that Varthema arrived in Malacca from India in the spring of 1506, then claimed to have sailed from there to the Moluccas and returned to India with a two-week stopover in Java, arriving in Calicut in the summer of the same year.

3. Lagôa, p. 156, cited statements in the letters of Afonso de Albuquerque for evidence of Serrão's loyalty to Portugal.

4. Denucé, p. 71; Medina, p. LIX.

5. Nowell, pp. 13-14.

6. Denucé, p. 136, cited Barros, Dec. II, Lib. V, Cap. VIII: *"prazendo a Deos, cedo se veria com elle, e que quando não fosse per via de Portugal, seria via de Castella, porque em tal estado andavão suas cosas: por tanto que o esperasse la, porque ja se conhecião da pousada pera elle esperar que ambos se averião bem."*

7. Medina, p. XCIX.

8. Denucé, p. 133.

9. José Toribio Medina, *Juan Díaz de*

Solís, Estudio Historico (Santiago, Chile: 1897), p. XXXIX.

10. Medina, *Descubrimiento* . . . , p. XXXV.

11. Ibid., quoted Barros (translated into Spanish): *". . . siempre andaba con pilotos, cartas de marear y altura de Leste-Oeste."*

12. Henry Harisse, *The Discovery of North America* (Paris: 1892), p. 137; Denucé, p. 67, hinted that Solís may have joined French pirates in attacking a Portuguese caravel returning from Guinea, robbing it of 20,000 gold doubloons.

13. Denucé, p. 61, cited Harisse, p. 721 and J.I. Brito Rebello, *João de Lisboa, Livro de Marinharia, Tratado da agulha de marear* (Lisbon: 1903), p. XLI.

14. Denucé, p. 75, accorded that honor to Solís, but Medina, pp. LXV-LXVI, note 44, claimed that Solís, having been in Spain from late 1513 to early 1514, could not have been the pilot of the Haro expedition described in *Copia der Newe Zeytung aus Presilg Land*. Medina included a Spanish translation of that German-language company newsletter on p. 1 of the documents appended to his *Descubrimiento*. . . .

15. Medina, p. LXXXI, note 6. His sig-

nature shows that Faleiro spelled his given name *Rodriguo*, rather than the more common *Rodrigo*.

16. Ibid., p. LXXXII.
17. Denucé, p. 140, cited Herrera, dec. II, lib. II, cap. XIX.
18. Ibid., p. 141.
19. Medina, p. LXXXIII
20. Ibid., p. LXXXIV.
21. Ibid., pp. LXXXIV-LXXXV, note 20 states that in Seville in 1535 Juan Cromberger published Francisco Faleiro's *Tratado del Esephera y del arte del marear con el regimiêto de las alturas; cõ alguas reglas nuevamente escritas muy necessarias.*
22. Denucé, p. 139.
23. Ibid., p. 150. These studies were undertaken by Denucé with the Reinel portulans in the *Bibliotheque Nationale* in Paris.
24. Medina, p. LXXX, note 4, cited an

eye-witness report in a letter to King Manuel from the Portuguese consul in Seville.

25. Denucé, pp. 143-144, cited *Cartas de Afonso de Albuquerque*, t. I, p. 433.
26. Ibid., p. 144.
27. Parr, p. 180; Denucé, p. 146 refers to the pirate as *Insart*.
28. Medina, p. LXXXV, note 22. On November 6, 1518, Magellan testified in Seville that Juan de Aranda had written to Diego de Haro and a Haro employee named Covarrubias, in Lisbon, ". . . who knew this witness . . . ," requesting information about him.
29. Ibid. , pp. 137-138, cited Góis, t. IV, cap. XXXVII: ". . . *se disnaturou do regno, tomando disso stromentos publicos.*"
30. Medina, pp. XCI-XCII, note 26.

Chapter 7. Birth

1. Lagôa, p. 161.
2. Parr, p. 193.
3. Helmut George Koenigsberger, "Ferdinand II," *Encyclopedia Britannica*, 1967, IX, 179.
4. Lagôa, p. 164.
5. Lagôa, p. 170. Although some authors have claimed that Barbosa was related to Magellan, the genealogies of the two families reveal no such relationship.
6. Medina, pp. XCV-XCVI.
7. Denucé, p. 168, cited Barros, Dec. III, Lib. V, Cap. VIII.
8. Medina, p. XCVI, cited Diego Ortiz de Zuñiga for the statement that Dom Alvaro was a favorite of the Catholic Sovereigns.
9. Ibid.; Denucé, p. 168.
10. Parr, p. 209; Lagôa, p. 176.
11. Lagôa, p. 173; Eric Hugo Hassinger, "Charles V," *Encyclopedia Brittanica*, 1967, V, 294-298.
12. Lagôa, p. 180; Medina, p. XCIII.
13. Medina, p. XCVIII.
14. Medina, p. XCIX, wrote that Aranda had contacted Diego de Haro and Diego Covarrubias; Lagôa, p. 171, re-

ferred to Corrubias, *mercador*, and Diego de Haro, *mercador*.

15. Lagôa, p. 171.
16. Ibid.
17. Ibid., p. 173; Parr, p. 207.
18. Although Magellan never set foot in it, the name of this city (and its district of Flanders in the Burgundian Netherlands) keeps cropping up in his story like a fateful thread in the fabric of history. Magellan himself was descended from a Burgundian crusader who had settled in Portugal. The Magellan name seems to have been derived from an old family name in Ghent. Queen Philippa of Portugal (a daughter of John of Gaunt (Ghent), was the mother and teacher of Prince Henry the Navigator, who set Portugal on the path to becoming a nation of seafarers. Charles of Ghent, as king of Spain, provided Magellan with the means to carry out the greatest single feat of navigation in history. Planted on the Iberian Peninsula, seeds from Ghent (a city of weavers) sprouted historic feats of navigation.
19. Hassinger, p. 295.

20. Lagôa, p. 176, note 1. The treaty (in settlement of a Franco-Aragonese dispute) obliged Spain to pay an annual indemnity of 100,000 crowns. Although this was supposed to guarantee a French princess as a bride for King Charles, the princess was but one year old. The treaty also gave France the right to take up arms against Spain, should the latter not restore the throne of Navarre to its ancient ruling house.
21. Ibid.
22. Medina, pp. XCIII, C.
23. Ibid.
24. Ibid. Note 19 cited a notarized statement of Magellan's included in Medina's *Documentos Inéditos . . .* , T. II, p. 300.
25. Lagôa, p. 181, deduced this from Magellan's will of 1519.
26. Denucé, p. 165; Lagôa, p. 180.
27. Medina, p. XCIX.
28. Ibid.
29. Parr, p. 213, stated that Magellan's wife, already pregnant, accompanied her husband on the trip to Valladolid. Magellan's will of August 14, 1519 (Navarrete, *Colección . . .* , t. IV, LXXIV) states that his son, Rodrigo, was six months old. This would place the date of his birth in February 1519. Unless the infant had been born prematurely, conception would have occurred in May 1518. Medina (pp. CXXIX-CXXX), stated that Magellan and Faleiro left the court at Zaragoza in mid-April and returned to Seville in May 1518. Rodrigo probably was conceived in Seville after his father's return from Zaragoza. Concerned over the danger from Portuguese agents, it is unlikely that Magellan would have permitted Beatriz to accompany him to Valladolid.
30. Domingo Ramos Pérez, *"Magallanes en Valladolid: La Capitulación,"* in *A viagem de Fernão de Magalhães e a Questão das Molucas,* ed. by A. Teixeira da Mota (Lisbon: Actas do II Coloquio Luso-Espanhol de Historia Ultramarina, Junta de Investigacões Científicas do Ultramar, 1975), p. 216; Denucé, p. 171; Lagôa, p. 183; Medina, p. CI. Denucé and Lagôa cited Gómara as the source of the information on the two slaves.
31. Medina, p. CI: ". . . que quisiese ir a su Corte, porque él deseaba de le conocer para le hacer mercedes.
32. Ibid.; Lagôa, p. 186, cited Asensio, p. 38, for the quotation: "Ya no estaréis quejosas de lo que tengo escrito al Gran Chanciller, antes por ello e por lo que yo faré en decir a su Alteza la información que vos tengo de Portugal, me debriades de dar parte de lo que Dios vos ficiere."
33. Denucé, p. 172.
34. Medina, p. CII, note 27: ". . . among these favors one must recognize that he [Aranda] had furnished Faleiro with money . . . as Magellan himself so noted '. . . e así ofrecerles dineros para ella [la empresa que tenían entre manos], se les hobiesen menester como cree este que depone que los presto a Ruy Faleiro . . .'." (". . . and thus offered them money for it [the enterprise they had brought with them] as they might need it, this deponent believes that he [Aranda] loaned [money] to Rui Faleiro . . .").
35. Ibid., note 28.
36. At that time, the Spanish court was a traveling circus, moving back and forth between the capitals of the former Gothic kingdoms of Castile and Aragon.
37. Medina, p. CIII, included the entire document in his *Colección . . .* ; Denucé, p. 172; Lagôa, p. 186.
38. Denucé, p. 172.

Chapter 8. Royal Support

1. Domingo Ramos Pérez, Magallanes en Valladolid: La Capitulación," in *A Viagem de Fernão de Magalhães e a Questão das Molucas,* ed. by A. Teixeira da Mota (Lisbon: Actas do II Coloquio Luso-Espanhol de Historia

Ultramarina, 1975), p. 215. Charles's entourage numbered over 6,000 persons.

2. Ibid., p. 216; Denucé, p. 177. It is relevant to note that Charles was at this same time engaged to Princess Isabella of Portugal, then only a child. They were married in 1526, and later these bilateral intermarriages resulted in a temporary union of Spain and Portugal.

3. Ramos Pérez, p. 216. Cited *Información levantada en Sevilla . . . , primera declaracion, (Magallanes)*, AGI 56: "*. . . viendo queste negocio era grande e questava en la corte de su Alteza embaxador del rey de Portugal que los podría estorvar, . . .*"

4. Denucé, p. 173.

5. Lagôa, p. 187, called Sauvage an "imbecile." Denucé, p. 174, wrote, "*. . . Sauvage, que tous les espagnols ont eu en horreur.*"

6. Medina, p. CV; Lagôa, p. 187; Denucé, p. 174. Columbus, Balboa, Cortez, and Las Casas all suffered the sting of Fonseca's disapproval.

7. Denucé, p. 175, cited Peter Martyr, another court prelate, who wrote to Eleanor of Austria (King Charles's sister) that the success of Magellan's enterprise would transfer to Spain the benefits of the commerce in spices and precious stones now enjoyed by the Orientals and the king of Portugal.

8. Ibid., p. 176; Lagôa, p. 189.

9. Lagôa, p. 188, note 2, wrote that Fonseca frequently consulted the geographer Antonio de Nobrija.

10. Denucé, p. 176, note 1.

11. Ibid., p. 222.

12. Medina, p. CXIII.

13. Denucé, pp. 144-145, 176-177. By 1514, merchant ships had sailed along the coast of China much farther than had been reported in official Portuguese documents. In his letters to King Manuel, Albuquerque mentioned "*. . . homems que emvia nas naos de Mallaca, que vao aos chyns.*" ("*. . . men who sent ships from Malacca*

that went to [the lands of] the Chinese.*"). The first official Portuguese expedition to China left Malacca in 1515; the Italian merchant, Giovanni da Empoli, went along as an observer.

14. Ibid., p. 72; Ramos Pérez, p. 193. In 1513, Haro outfitted two small ships to reconnoiter the coast of Brazil with Joao de Lisboa as chief pilot. They returned in October 1514, having noted the westerly trend of the coastline as they followed it south. Beyond Cape Santa Maria, they entered an opening to the west at a position reported as 40° S, west of the Treaty Line and *only six hundred leagues from Malacca!* When a storm prevented them from exploring the waterway (the La Plata Estuary or the Gulf of San Matías?), the expedition returned to Portugal. A garbled report of this expedition, entitled *Die Copia der Newen Zeytung aus Presillg Land*, written in bad German (probably by a Portuguese agent of the Welser Company of Augsberg), was found in Germany in 1895. The expedition's leaders apparently thought that the opening to the west was a strait. It is quite possible that in the library of India House in Lisbon, Magellan's perusal of the reports of the expedition's pilots inspired his expectation that he would find a strait south of Cape Santa Maria.

15. Torodash, p. 323. Transylvanus's letter was published in Rome in 1523 as *De Moluccis Insulis*. An English translation appears in Nowell.

16. José Toribio Medina, *Esteban Gómez al Servicio de España* (Santiago, Chile: Imprenta Elzeviriana, 1908), pp. 9-11; Denucé, pp. 248-249.

17. Denucé, p. 176; Lagôa, p. 189. Both cited Góis: "*por fallar melhor nas cousas do mar que Faleiro.*"

18. Las Casas' impressions of Magellan are discussed in Medina, p. CVI, and Ramos Pérez, p. 204.

19. Lagôa, p. 189, cited Barros: "*El rey de Castella estava namorado das cartas e pomas de marear que Fernão de Ma-*

*galhães lhe tinha mostrado, e princi-
palmente da carta que Francisco Serrão
escreveo a elle Fernão de Magalhães de
Maluco."* (The king of Castile was impressed by the nautical charts and
globes that Magellan showed him,
and especially the letter that Francisco Serrão had written to Magellan
from the Moluccas.) Las Casas and
Herrera said that Magellan brought a
globe. Leonardo y Argensola wrote
that it was a *"planisferio dibuxado por
Pedro Reynel."* Whether Magellan
brought a globe, a planisphere, or
both, they probably were made for
him by Pedro Reinel.

20. Ramos Pérez, p. 184, cited Juan Man-
zano, *La Incorporación de las Indias a
la Corona de Castilla* (Madrid: Edi-
ciones Cultura Hispánica, 1948), pp.
23-26; Granzotto, pp. 196-197.

The second *Inter Caetera* of July
1493, issued by Pope Alexander VI,
modified an earlier bull issued in 1456
that gave Portugal the right to extend
its territories *". . . usque ad Indos"* (all
the way to India) to read *". . . versus
Indiam"* (up to [but not including] India), and established a line of partition 100 leagues west of the Azores
and Cape Verde. *Dudum Sequidem* (a
bull of extension issued in September
1493) gave Castile the rights to unexplored lands to the west of the line of
partition *up to and including India*. In
the Treaty of Tordesillas, the line of
partition in the Atlantic was changed

to *a line extending from pole to pole*, 370
leagues west of the Cape Verde Islands. The idea of a Far Eastern antimeridian was considered in neither
the bulls nor the treaty.

21. Lagôa, pp. 175-176, cited Peter Martyr.

22. Medina, p. CVI. On pp. 12-20 of the
Documentos appended to this work are
those parts of Las Casas' *Historia . . .*
(published prior to 1561) that pertain
to Magellan.

23. Ibid. In note 30, Medina argued that
this assertion by Las Casas is self-
contradictory. If the space on the
globe where the strait was supposed
to have been had been left blank on
purpose, that in itself would have indicated where Magellan supposed it
to be. Medina believed that the South
American coast was depicted as far as
Cape Santa Maria, the southern limit
of exploration at that time. South of
the cape, all was blank.

24. Ibid., p. 184.

25. Denucé, p. 179.

26. Ibid.

27. Medina, p. CVI.

28. Lagôa, p. 193.

29. Denucé, pp. 182-185, cited Arch. de
Indias, 1,2,1/1, no. 7, in Vicente
Llorens Asensio, *La Primera vuelta al
mundo. . .* (Seville, 1903), p. 17; Medina, *Colección . . .*, t. I, p. 5. *See* Appendix 5 for an English summary of
the memorandum and the king's
comments on it.

Chapter 9. The Fleet

1. Medina, pp. CXXI-CXXII.

2. Denucé, p. 145. Cited *Archivo de las
Indias*, 1, 1, 2, 1/1, num. 3. Details
about Lequios are given in Denucé,
"Les Isles Lequios (Formose et Riu-
Kiu) et Ophir," *Bull. Soc. Royale Belge
de Géogr.* (Bruxelles: 1907, No. 6);
Barbosa, Odoardo, *O Livro de
Odoardo Barbosa*, in *Colecção de Noti-
cias para a História e Geografia das
Nações Ultramarinas que Vivem nos
Dominios Portuguêses* (Lisbon: Real
Acad. Ciências, 1867). An English

version of *O Livro . . .* is available as
The Book of Duarte Barbosa, ed. Man-
sel Longworth Dames (London:
Hakluyt Society, 1918-21).

3. Denucé, Les Iles Lequios . . . , p.
439. Cited Lisbon edition of *O Livro
. . .*: ". . . *dizem hos de Malaca que
saom hos daquuy melhores homeins, mais
riquos mercadores, e honrados que hos
chins . . .*" The question of whether
the author of *O Livro . . .* was the
same Duarte Barbosa as Magellan's
brother-in-law was discussed by

Denucé, p. 4 and Lagôa, pp. 280-281. There were several homonyms in India at the time the book was written who could have been the author. There is no evidence that Magellan's brother-in-law had been in India, nor any to prove that he had not. The issue remains unresolved.

4. Ibid. ". . . *das quaes gentes ateguora nos temos muyta enformaçam, porque non vieram ainda ha Malaca depois que he del Rey noso Senhor.*" (". . . of which folk we don't have much information, because they haven't come to Malacca since [the Portuguese] arrived.") At the Prefectural Museum and Library in Shuri City, Okinawa, old texts confirm that sixteenth-century Okinawan merchants stopped sending their ships to Malacca because they had heard of the savagery of the Portuguese.

5. Information in the *Guidebook of the Okinawa Prefectural Museum* (Naha, 1987-1988), shows that from the fourteenth through the sixteenth centuries, Okinawan trading ships visited ports in Honshu, Kyushu, Korea, Indochina, Siam, the Malay Peninsula, Sumatra, and Java.

6. Fuson, p. 23. Fiske's mercator projection of Behaim's globe of 1492 shows *Cipango* lying between 5° and 15° North.

7. Herrmann, pp. 28, 70.

8. Denucé, pp. 187-189; Lagôa, pp. 202-203, cited *Archivo de las Indias*, 41, 4, 1/30, liv. 1, fls. 42, 43. A maravedi was a small copper coin worth about eleven and one-half U.S. cents.

9. Ibid., p. 188, cited Peter Martyr d'Anghiera, *De Orbe Novo*, (Alcalá de Henares: 1530), dec. 5, ch. VII. ". . . Juan de Cartagena, confidant of the Bishop of Burgos who, with royal consent, had been assigned to Magellan as a fellow officer and named second in command of the expedition . . ." Medina, p. CCCLXXI.

10. Medina, pp. CXXXII-CXXXIII; Lagôa, p. 210. Both cited Gois: ". . .

escreveo huma carta a el rei que eu vi, que ho devia de recolher por ser homem de grandes espíritos, e muito prático nas cousas do mar. . . ."

11. Denucé, pp. 192-193.

12. Ibid., Lagôa, p. 209, cited Sousa Viterbo, *Os Trabalhos Náuticos dos Portuguezes nos Séculos XVI e XVII* (Lisbon: 1898), vol. I, p. 61.

13. Medina, pp. CXXXIII-CXXXIV.

14. Lagôa, p. 206.

15. Medina, pp. CXXVII-CXXIX, cited *Archivo de las Indias*, 139.1-15. The pilots mentioned specifically by the king were: Sebastian Cabot, Juan Vespuche (Vespucci), Andrés de Morales and Andrés de San Martín. See also Denucé, p. 189.

16. Medina, p. CXXIX.

17. Denucé. p. 191; Medina, pp. CXXX, note 6.

18. Medina, p. CXXXII. López de Recalde, *contador* (paymaster) of the Casa, also was called to court to explain the Casa's foot dragging on *all* aspects of the preparation of the fleet.

19. Ibid., p. CXXXV-CXXXVI, cited Las Casas for statements about walking in shadows and the escort provided by Fonseca.

20. Medina, p. CXXXVI. This must have occurred in the summer of 1518, since Fonseca referred to both Magellan and Faleiro as *Caballeros de Santiago* (Knights of St. James) in a memorandum to the Casa dated in July of that year.

21 Denucé, p. 200.

22. Ibid., cited AGI, 2, 5, 1/6, num. 9, (Asensio No. 7).

23. Lourdes Díaz-Trechuelo, "La Organización del Viaje Magellanico: Financión, Enganches, Acopios y Preparativos," in *A Viagem de Fernão de Magalhães e a Questião das Molucas*, ed. by A. Teixeira da Mota (Lisbon: Actas do II Colóquio Luso-Espanhol de História Ultramarina, Junta de Investigacões do Ultramar, 1975), pp. 267-314. Cited AGI, Contratación 5090, t.IV, fls. 8-9.

24. Ibid., pp. 270-271, cited Indiferente

General 419, t. VII, fl. 84; Guillemard, *loc. cit.*, stated that of the 16,000 ducats contributed by the Crown, 10,000 were borrowed from the House of Fugger, bankers of Augsburg, Germany.

25. Medina, p. CXLI and *Colección* . . . , I, p. 118. The tonnages given were reported as *toneles* by the scribes of the Casa. They have been variously interpreted as Biscayan *toneles* or as *toneladas* of Seville. João da Gama Pimentel Barata, "A Armada de Fernão de Magalhães," in A. Teixeira da Mota (ed.), *loc. sit.*, argued that the Biscayan *tonel* was not used in Magellan's time as a measure of capacity, and that the *tonel* used in the Casa records to describe Magellan's ships probably referred to the unit called the *tonelada* in the *Ordenanzas* (Ordinances) of

1553, the space occupied by a box with sides 9 × 4 × 3 *palmos* long. Since one *palmo* was about 0.21 meters, the volume of the 1553 *tonelada* works out to about one cubic meter.

26. Díaz-Trechuelo, p. 274.
27. Medina, p. CXLI, note 32.
28. Denucé, p. 203.
29. Lagôa, p. 216.
30. Medina, pp. CXLI-CXLII.
31. Lagôa, p. 216.
32. Medina, pp. CXLII-CXLIII. The complete text of Magellan's letter is reproduced in Medina's *Colección* . . . , I, pp. 18-21.
33. Ibid., pp. CXLIII-CXLIV, cited AGI 139-1.5.
34. Ibid., pp. CXXXVI. The first notice in which the title of *Comendador* was given to Magellan occurred on November 6, 1518.

Chapter 10. Recruiting and Final Preparations

1. Denucé, p. 203; Medina, p. CLXII.
2. Rolando A. Laguarda Trías, "Las Longitudes Geográficas de la Membranza de Magallanes y del Primer Viaje de Circunnavegación," in A. Teixeira da Mota (ed.), loc. cit., pp. 135-176. Ruy Faleiro's manual was among the papers from the *Trinidad* seized by Admiral Brito in the Moluccas. Long believed lost, A. Teixeira da Mota identified it with papers discovered in the *Archivo General de las Indias* (AGI) in Seville. Francisco Faleiro included his brother's system for determining longitude from compass variation in his *Tratado del Esfera i del Arte de Marear* (Seville: 1535).

3. Lagôa, p. 158.
4. Laguarda Trías, p. 155.
5. Díaz-Trechuelo, p. 271, cited AGI, Patronato 34, No. 2.
6. Medina, p. CCCLXXI.
7. Lagôa, p. 234, cited AGI (Asensio), pp. 153, 158.
8. Ibid.
9. Ibid.
10. Ibid., p. 235; Denucé, pp. 210-15, cited Navarrete IV, p. 181; Guillemard, p. 126, cited Medina, *Colección* . . . , p. 234; Medina, *Descubrimiento* . . . , p. CXLV; Díaz-Trechuelo, p. 272. The contributions of each investor for which there are records are shown in the following table:

Investor	ducats	maravedis	U.S.$
The Crown			
Treasury funds	6,000[1]	2,250,000	240,750
Borrowed from House of Fugger	10,000[2]	3,750,000	401,250
Total	16,000[2]	6,000,000	642,000
Haro	5,104	1,880,126[1]	201,173
	4,311	1,616,781[3]	172,996
			(continued)

(Table Continues) Investor	ducats	maravedis	U.S.$
Gutiérrez	420[1]	157,500	16,852
	35	12,014[3]	1,285
Cartagena	129	48,217[4]	5,159

1 ducat = 3.53 grams gold = 0.113 troy oz. = $40.10 (U.S.) @ $355/troy oz. (1990 gold price); 375 maravedis = 1 ducat; 1 maravedi = $0.107 (U.S.).

Sources: 1. Denucé; 2. Guillemard; 3. Díaz-Trechuelo; 4. Lagôa.

11. Lagôa, pp. 236-238. Cited Herrera, who suggested that Magellan's reluctance to reveal the route was because he wished to avoid interception by Portuguese naval forces.

12. Ibid., p. 238.

13. Medina, p. CXLVII. In note 5, he quotes a royal decree dated April 18, 1519: "Fernando de Magallanes came here . . ."

14. Denucé, p. 219. Cited AGI 41, 6, 2/ 25 (Asensio 91).

15. Ibid. Cited AGI (Asensio 94) and *Alguns documentos da Torre do Tombo* (ADTT), p. 430.

16. Lagôa, p. 239. Cited AGI 41, 6, 2/25 (Asensio). Regarding the guarantee of security for the personal possessions of the crew, the wording of the decree couldn't have been stronger: ". . . no one may remove from their lodgings clothes or any other household goods, not even the King, Queen or the Royal Princes."

17. Denucé, pp. 230-31.

18. Ibid., pp. 231-32.

19. Ibid., p. 231.

20. Parr, pp. 229-30.

21. Denucé, p. 231. Cited Herrera, dec. III, lib. IV, cap. XXI.

22. Medina, p. CXLIX; Lagôa, p. 240, cited AGI 46, 4, 1/30 (Asensio 157).

23. Denucé, p. 220. Cited AGI 41, 6, 2/ 25 (Asensio 95).

24. Medina, pp. CXLIX-CL. The date was deduced from the fact that the first payment of Magellan's salary was made in Seville on May 1, and that he left Barcelona around April 18, the date of the royal decree addressed by King Charles to the Casa, which contained the statement: ". . . as you see by the letters that he [Magellan] brings . . ."

25. Denucé, pp. 207-8, cited *Arquivo Histórico Portugês* (Lisbon: 1906), p. 445; Lagôa, pp. 237-38, cited ADTT, *corpo cronólogico*, Part I, bundle 10, doc. 31.

26. Medina, pp. CXLIX-CL, allowed Magellan a week to 10 days for travel between Barcelona and Seville.

27. Lagôa, p. 240, cited AGI 41, 6, 2/25; Denucé, p. 220, cited ADTT, p. 423; Medina, pp. CCCCXI-CCCCXII, cited Castanheda as his source for giving Granada as the home town of Mendoza. The AGI has yielded no information about the backgrounds of either Mendoza or Quesada, and very little about Cartagena. The latter had a daughter, Catalina, who in 1538 managed to recover 48,217 maravedis of her father's investment. Medina reproduced the pertinent documents in the *Anexo* to his *Descubrimiento* . . . , pp. 287-89. See also Guillemard, p. 107; Navarrete, t. IV, p. 128; AGI (Asensio 89).

28. Lagôa, p. 240. Cited royal decree of April 6, 1519 (AGI 139, 6, liv. VIII, fl. 54 (Asensio 154).

29. Medina, p. CCCLXXIII.

30. Parr, p. 233.

31. Medina, p. CCCLXXIII.

32. Denucé, p. 222. Cited AGI 46, 4, 1/ 30, fl. 54 (Asensio 156).

33. Ibid., cited AGI 41, 6, 2/25 (Asensio 96); Medina, p. CCCLXXXIX. In a declaration made on August 9, 1519, Espinosa said that he was thirty years old ". . . a little more or less." In a

statement made in 1527 he said that he was forty; in another, made in 1537, he gave his age as fifty-two. In 1519, his age would have been between thirty and thirty-three.

34. Ibid., cited Navarrete, t. IV, p. 201.

35. Medina, p. CCCXCIII.

36. Navarrete, pp. 12-22, and Díaz Trechuelo, pp. 313-14, provide useful lists of the supernumeraries and their classifications.

37. Díaz-Trechuelo, pp. 297-307.

38. Medina, pp. CCCCXXIV-CCCCXVI. Cited L. Hugues, ed., *Raccolta di documenti e studi pubblicati dalla Reale Commissione Colombiana* (Rome: 1892-1893), Part V, vol. I, p. 94.

39. Lagôa, p. 265.

40. Medina, p. CLII.

41. Ibid., p. CLIII.

42. Ibid.

43. Medina, p. CLIII.

44. Ibid.; Denucé, p. 238.

45. Medina, p. CLIV.

46. Ibid., ". . . *que ellos no impidan a los dichos portugueses sus parientes e criados, porque él non los tiene de dejar, sino cuando el mismo quedaré.*"

47. Ibid.

48. Medina, p. CLV.

49. Denucé, p. 239. Cited AGI 129, 1, 6, fl. 53 (Asensio 168), 1, 2, 1, num. 14, Herrera dec. II, lib. IV, cap. IX. ". . . *i que Magallanes no llevase consigo a Martín de Mezquita ni a Pedro de Abreu, por tenerlos inquietos.*" (". . . and Magellan didn't take [them] with him, since doing so would have upset [the Casa]."

50. Denucé, p. 238; Guillemard, p. 137, cited an *información* of August 9, 1519, sent by Magellan to the Casa, providing the testimony of five recruiters of good character. One of these was Juan Sebastián del Cano.

51. Medina, p. CLVIII. More precisely, ". . . couldn't swallow . . ." (the verb was *tragar*).

52. Ibid., pp. CLV-CLVII. As recently as 1975, Díaz-Trechuelo, working with material from the AGI, arrived at an estimate of 237. Medina used the same source plus a broad array of others, including sixteenth-century chroniclers and documents uncovered in the *Torre do Tombo* in Lisbon, to arrive at his estimate of 270.

53. Medina, p. CLVIII. Note 15 states that the royal decree of 26 July is only known by reference, and that a letter from the king to the Casa, dated July 16, contains the first mention of Faleiro's replacement.

54. Hassinger, Erich Hugo, "Charles V," *Encyclopedia Brittanica*, 1967, V, 294-95.

55. Lagôa, p. 247. Cited Leonardo y Argensola, *Historia de las Molucas*, liv. I, and *Anales de Aragón*, liv. I; Barros, dec. III, liv. V, p. 631; F. López de Gómara, *Histoire générale des Indes occidentalles et terres neuves, qui jusques à present ont esté descouvertes* (Paris: 1587), cap. XC; Antonio Pigafetta, *Primo Viaggio Intorno Al Globo . . .*, ed. Carlos Amoretti (Milan: 1800); Ferdinand Denis and others.

56. Ibid. Cited Herrera, dec. II, liv. III, cap. IX, and Leonardo y Argensola, *Anales . . .*, liv. II, cap. LXXXIV, p. 740.

57. Medina, p. CLVIII.

58. Ibid., p. CLX.

59. Denucé, p. 227. Cited ADTT, p. 431; Stanley, Appendix X.

60. Translation based on Guillemard (pp. 130-33), Medina (pp. CLXVI-CLXVII), and Denucé (pp. 227-29).

61. A spiked wheel used for torture. In the fourth century, the martyred Saint Catherine of Alexandria was said to have been put to death on it.

62. Magellan was referring, cynically, to a hermit's life in the mountains. Guillemard, (p. 131) suggested that the irony was lost on Álvares, who took the statement at face value.

63. This suggests that Magellan was wondering whether a royal invitation for him to return to Portugal was indeed being offered.

64. These talks with Ribeiro and Mendes

took place in Barcelona. The two diplomats appear to have told Magellan that King Manuel would invite him to return to Portugal. Had such an invitation been proffered, Magellan might have been tempted, but it is doubtful that he would have accepted. It appears more likely that in this last interview with Álvares, he was was merely toying with the earnest Portuguese diplomat.

65. In a note to his translation, Guillemard observed that this statement was patently false. It contradicts the first sentence of the letter.

66. Denucé (p. 230) suggested that the letter which Magellan awaited so anxiously probably was a directive from King Charles clarifying the authority granted to Cartagena. Magellan was worried about the extent to which it would encroach on his command. Cartagena may have brought the letter with him when he arrived in Seville, and it seems to have satisfied Magellan that Cartagena's authority did not conflict with his, for he so advised the Casa.

67. A familiar spirit was a personal demon. Álvares was suggesting a supernatural cause for Faleiro's apparent madness.

68. This was a damnation, for the Cortereal brothers (Gaspar in 1501 and Miguel in 1502) had sailed toward Newfoundland in search of a northwest passage. They disappeared into the North Atlantic with their ships and crews, never to return.

69. This suggests that these orders were communicated to Magellan, not by the king, but by Cartagena. Magellan may have had doubts about their authenticity.

70. Medina, pp. CLXX, CCCCXLI. Although his birth date is not known, Serrano probably was about Magellan's age. As a young man in 1499-1500, he had sailed to Brazil in a squadron led by Alonzo Vélez de Guevara. He was commissioned a royal pilot by King Ferdinand in 1514. Most Portuguese writers have claimed that Serrano was Portuguese (Serrão). Medina made a strong case for his having been a Castilian. Among other arguments, he cited the sixteenth-century Portuguese chronicler, Lopes de Castanheda, to show that Serrano was born in Frejenal de la Sierra, in Extremadura, Castile.

71. Ibid., p. CCCCXLIV-CCCCXLVII. San Martín bad been employed in the outfitting of the fleet that took Dávila to Darien in 1514. After the fleet departed, bills for its expenses amounting to 300 gold ducats remained outstanding. He was given only 200 ducats to pay them off, leaving 100 ducats for which he was held responsible. To get him to sail with Magellan, the king promised San Martín that, upon his return from the voyage, the Crown would pay the outstanding debt.

72. Denucé, p. 240.

73. Ibid.; Guillemard, p. 135; Medina, p. CLXXIX, note 61.

74. Díaz-Trechuelo, p. 308 (extracted from records in the AGI).

75. Medina, p. CLXXIII; Diaz-Trechuelo, p. 275.

76. Díaz-Trechuelo, p. 295.

77. Although his surname is spelled Gómez in Spanish documents, I have used the Portuguese spelling to avoid confusion with Gómez de Espinosa, and because he was a native of Portugal.

78. Medina, pp. CCCCXXI-CCCCXII.

79. Ibid., Colección . . . , pp. 57-73

80. Ibid., Descubrimiento. . ., pp. CLXXVII-CLXXIX; Parr, pp. 260-61

81. Medina, p. CLXXIX.

82. Guillemard, Denucé, Asensio, and Parr refer to this official as Sancho Martínez de Leiva. However, in a letter from the Casa to King Charles (AGI, Asensio, 94-5) his signature appears as "Doctor Matienço." Medina, who consistently referred to him as

Doctor Sancho de Matienzo, reproduced the letter on p. 21 of the *Anexo* to his *Descubrimiento.*

83. Medina, p. CLXXIX. Note 62 cites payroll records reproduced in the *Anexo* to Medina's *Descubrimiento* . . . , p. 108.

84. Ibid., p. CLXXX. Cited Herrera and Article 45 of the Royal Instructions. These are reproduced in Medina's *Colección* . . . , vol. 1, p. 72.

85. Ibid. Cited Manuel de la Puente y Olea, "Primer Viaje Alrededor del Mundo," in *Los Trabajos de la Casa de Contratación* (Seville: 1900), which contains an engraving depicting the delivery of the royal standard to Magellan.

86. Ibid., p. CLXXXII. Over the years, there has been some confusion over the date of departure of Magellan's fleet from Seville. The Spanish historian, Oviedo, claimed that Pigafetta was wrong in this, giving a later date that corresponds to the departure from San Lúcar. The records of the Casa show that the fleet left Seville on Wednesday, August 10, 1519. Pigafetta gave the correct date, but erred on the day of the week; he said it was on a Monday.

87. Denucé, p. 241.

88. Navarrete, t. IV, pp. 188-89; Medina, *Colección* . . . , p. 112; Guillemard, p. 139; Denucé, p. 242.

Chapter 11. The Atlantic

1. Admiral J. Freitas Ribeiro, "Estudio náutico do roteiro da viagem de Magalhãis," in Lagôa, vol. II, p. 217; Medina, p. CXCI. Pigafetta gave the date of departure as September 20. The Genoese Pilot, "Navegaçam e vyagem que fez Fernam de Magalhães de Sevilha pero Maluco no anno de 1519" in *Collecção de noticias para a história e geografia* . . . (Lisbon, Acad. Sci.: 1825) Vol. IV., (English version in Stanley), said it was September 21. The departure probably occurred before dawn on the 21st.

2. Parr, p. 61.

3. Medina, pp. CXCI-CXCII.

4. Ibid., p. CXCIII, note 19.

5. Denucé, p. 257, wrote that the caravel carried *poix* (pitch). This makes more sense than the *pez* (fish) reported by other authors, since pitch is an essential naval store used in caulking. I have reconstructed the incident so that Magellan was loading locally produced pitch at Monte Rojo when the caravel carrying the message from his father-in-law caught up with him. It seems to me unlikely that the fleet, freshly loaded with food supplies, would have been taking on fish, a perishable commodity, when heading for the tropics.

6. Medina, pp. CXCII-CXCIII, cited Corrêa, Barros, and Argensola; Denucé, p. 257, and Guillemard, p. 149, cited Corrêa and Argensola.

7. Denucé, p. 257; Medina, CXCIII. Both cited Corrêa. Medina also noted (citing Argensola) that when Magellan got the warning from his father-in-law, he kept quiet about it, and ". . . *anduvo muy sobre sí*" (kept his guard up).

8. Medina, p. CXCIV.

9. Ibid.

10. Ibid., pp. CXCIV-CXCV, cited Herrera.

11. Denucé, p. 258, cited Juan Sebastián del Cano in Navarrete, t. IV, doc. XXV, pp. 286-88.

12. J. Freitas Ribeiro, in Lagôa II, p. 217-18.

13. Medina, p. CXCVI, cited Pigafetta.

14. Denucé, p. 258.

15. Medina, pp. CXCVI-CXCVIII and Denucé, pp. 259-60, drew their accounts of these incidents from two sources: a letter, dated May 12, 1521, from López Recalde to Bishop Fonseca, telling him of the return to

Spain of the *San Antonio* after its separation from Magellan's fleet; and a deposition given by Cano in Valladolid on October 18, 1522, after the *Victoria* had completed its historic circumnavigation. The two accounts differ slightly in some details, but not in essentials.

16. Medina, p. CXCVII.
17. Ibid.

18. J. Freitas Ribeiro, in Lagôa II, p. 218.
19. Ibid., cited Pigafetta.
20. Francisco Albo, "Diario ó derrotero del viaje de Fernando de Magallanes desde el cabo de San Agustín en el Brasil hasta el regreso a Espana de la nao *Victoria*," in Navarrete, t. IV.
21. Medina, p. CXCIX, note 28.
22. Denucé, p. 260; J. Freitas Ribeiro, in Lagôa II, p. 219.

Chapter 12. Brazil

1. Denucé, pp. 260-61.
2. Max Justo Guedes, in Mota, p. 365, cited Navarrete, p. 186, and López Recalde's report on the return to Spain of the *San Antonio*. Since Gomes had engineered the desertion of the *San Antonio* in the Strait of Magellan, the deposition he gave Recalde could have been self-serving.
3. Ibid., p. 365, cited Ernest Mouchet, *Les Côtes de Brésil* (Paris: Challamel Ainé, 1876).
4. Morison, p. 360.
5. Denucé, p. 260, cited Orville A. Derby, "Os Mappas Mais Antigos do Brasil," in *Revista do Instituto Histórico de São Paulo* (São Paulo: 1903) vol. III, p. 24, note 1).
6. Morison, pp. 280-82.
7. Guedes, in Mota, p. 363.
8. Denucé, p. 261; *Indians of South America* (a map by the National Geographic Society, Washington, D.C., 1982).
9. Antonio Pigafetta, "A Primeira Viagem de Circunnavegação . . . ," in Lagôa, II, p. 22. (See Sources in this book for references to Pigafetta documents and translations).
10. Medina, p. CCII.
11. Pigafetta, in Lagôa, II, p. 27.
12. Quotation from Pigafetta in Medina, p. CCII, note 29. This incident suggests the high value placed by these natives on articles of iron, a substance

not long known to them.
13. Medina, p. CCIII, quoted his *Colección . . .* , vol. I, p. 171: "*En el martes* [December 20, 1519], *fué sentenciado a muerte Antón Salamón, maestre que fué de la nao [Victoria], por somético, la cual sentencia fué ejecutada este dicho día en el puerto de Santa Lucía, ques en la costa del Brasil.*"
14. Parr, pp. 283-84.
15. Morison, pp. 361-62.
16. Medina, p. CCIII.
17. Guedes, in Mota, p. 376, cited Lagôa, I, p. 21, who cited two surviving eye-witnesses, Martín de Ayamonte and Ginés de Mafra.
18. Morison, p. 361.
19. Medina, p. CCII, cited Herrera.
20. Ibid., p. CCIII, note 34; Freitas-Ribeiro in Lagôa, II, p. 219.
21. Medina, p. CCIV; Freitas-Ribeiro in Lagôa, II, p. 219; Denucé, p. 262.
22. Medina, p. CCIV; Freitas-Ribeiro in Lagôa, II, p. 219.
23. Ibid.; Morison, pp. 300-01. Medina and Lagôa gave similar accounts of this leg of Magellan's voyage. Medina's, which contains more detail, was derived from Herrera. Morison cited Laguarda Trías who identified João de Lisboa as the pilot of a Portuguese caravel that, according to the *Newen Zeitung* newsletter of 1514, reached Cape Santa María in 1511-12.

Chapter 13. Storms and Mutiny

1. Magellan's view seems to have been shared by Portuguese officials. Medina, p. CCV, note 40, cited Brito's letter to King Manuel: "The ships of Your Majesty have discovered as far as this river [the La Plata]."

2. Medina, p. CCVI.
3. Morison, p. 263, identified this hill as the 1,640-foot Cerro las Ánimas.
4. Lagôa, vol. II, p. 220, noted that Pigafetta used the expression, *monte vidi* (I saw a mountain). Medina, p. CCV, stated that ". . . one of the pilots of the fleet" wrote that they named the hill behind Cape Santa María "*Montevidi*."
5. Medina, p. CCVI; Lagôa, vol. II, p. 219.
6. Medina, p. CCVII.
7. Ibid., note 43, cited Brito for the fifty-league statement.
8. Denucé, p. 264.
9. Ibid., p. 265, note 1; Map, *Indians of South America* (Washington, D. C. National Geographic Society, 1982).
10. Medina, p. CCVIII.
11. Denucé, p. 265.
12. Medina, pp. CCVIII-CCIX.
13. Ibid., p. CCIX; Lagôa II, p. 220. Denucé, p. 266, suggested that Cape San Antonio was the locale where repairs were made to the *San Antonio*.
14. The information on course headings and the location of the various anchorages is derived from the study by Admiral J. Freitas Ribeiro (Lagôa II, p. 220). The story about the near grounding of the *Victoria* is from Medina, p. CCIX. He described the bumps on the keel as "*culadas*," which Morison translated as "arse hits."
15. Lagôa, vol. II, p. 221, cited the Genoese Pilot; Medina, P. CCIX, quoted Herrera, p. 353: ". . . *y habiendo hallado una bahía muy hermosa, quiso Hernando de Magallanes entrar en ella, para ver si estrecho.*"
16. Morison, p. 366, without providing evidence, claimed that Magellan's fleet anchored for several days in Golfo Nuevo. The itinerary suggested by Freitas Ribeiro presents a reasonable reconstruction from the often disparate accounts by participants in the expedition.
17. The location of the Bahía de los Patos cannot be readily determined. Morison, p. 366, suggested that it may have been a shallow bay just south of Cabo Dos Bahías (45° S). Medina, p, CCIX, suggested that it was near two islands called "Pengüines" and "Leones" near Puerto Deseado at 47° 47' S (modern charts show an Isla Pingüino and a Punta Lobos at that location). Since Albo gave its latitude as 44°, Medina's choice seems too far south. As the fleet's next anchorage was probably at Puerto Deseado, Morison's guess seems reasonable.
18. Medina, p. CCX, cited Herrera, who transcribed the story from a pilot's diary (since lost along with the identity of the pilot).
19. Ibid., pp. CCX-CCXI. Such vows and promises in times of great stress were commonplace among sailors on Spanish ships in those times. In Canto XVI of his epic poem *La Araucana*, the Spanish soldier-poet Alonso de Ercilla y Zúñiga, recalling a great storm that struck his ship at Talcahuano, Chile, included the following lines:

> *Quién a publicas voces se confiesa*
>
> *Y a Dios perdón de sus errores pide;*
> *Quien hace voto expreso, quien promesa . . .*

> Who publicly confesses
>
> And asks God's pardon for his sins;
> Who makes explicit vows, who promises

Yet fulfillment of those vows, made under stress, was another matter. As another great Spanish poet, Lope de Vega, put it:

> *Allí sí que los votos y promesas*
> *Dichos tan bien, pero tan mal cumplidas . . .*

> There indeed the vows and promises
> So earnestly pledged, but so poorly fulfilled . . .

20. Based on Freitas Ribeiro's analysis of Magellan's route, Lagôa, (vol. II, p.

221) was confident that this haven was Puerto Deseado (47° 47′ S).

21. Medina, p. CCXI, wrote that they subsisted on shellfish; Denucé, that fish had been cast up by the waves. Mussels, abundant on the Patagonian coast, seem the most likely.

22. Ibid. (see note 18 above for Medina's source).

23. Lagôa, vol. II, p. 222, cited the Genoese Pilot and Herrera. Albo stated that the fleet entered the harbor of San Julián on March 2, but he (or his transcriber) must have been mistaken. With the slow progress against storms and headwinds from its position on February 29 (45° 20′ S), the fleet could not have reached Port San Julián by March 2. He probably meant April 2.

24. Morison, p. 367.

25. Denucé, p. 271.

26. Ibid., pp. 271-272, cited Maximilian Transylvanus, Herrera, Oviedo and Faria e Sousa (who called it a pompous harangue); Nowell, pp. 286-287; O.H.K. Spate, *The Spanish Lake* (Minneapolis: University of Minnesota Press, 1979), p. 43; Morison, p. 370. While there is ample evidence that Magellan did exhort his men thus, his actual words can only be conjectured from second-hand accounts.

27. Denucé, p. 272, cited Barros, III, lib. V, cap. IX.

28. Medina, pp. CCXIII-CCXIV, cited a letter of López Recalde (included in Medina's *Colección . . . I*, p. 165), and Cano's declaration of 18 October, 1522 (*Colección . . . I*, p. 301).

29. Spate, p. 304, note 47. By the Julian calendar in use in 1520, Easter Sunday fell on April 1.

30. Medina, pp. CCXIII-CCXIV.

31. Denucé, p. 272.

32. Medina, p. CCXV.

33. Ibid.

34. Ibid., p. CCXVI, note 5.

35. Well-annotated descriptions of this episode on the *San Antonio* can be found in Medina, pp. CCXVI-CCXVII, and in Denucé, pp. 272-73. Medina's account is more detailed.

36. Medina, p. CCXVI, note 7, cited the eye-witness testimony of Ortiz de Goperi (Gopeguy): ". . . and I saw how the supplies were used without regard to either weight or measure; anything was available to whomever wanted it, because Gaspar Quesada threatened this witness, who was in charge of stores on that ship, [saying] that no restrictions were to be imposed on anyone, but that I should issue anything for which [anyone] might ask. . . ."

37. Ibid., p. CCXVII, note 8. Medina ascribed the story of the skiff to Herrera who got it from a pilot's diary.

38. Ibid., pp. CCXVII-CCXVIII, note 9.

39. Ibid.

40. Ibid., p. CCXVII.

41. Ibid., p. CCXVIII; Denucé, p. 274; Parr, p. 298; Morison, p. 371.

42. Corrêa, in Nowell, p. 318.

43. Denucé, p. 274.

44. Medina, p. CCXVIII, note 12, cited Castanheda and Cano, who declared that Magellan rewarded Espinosa for his night's work with twelve ducats, "and those who accompanied him [to the *Victoria*] received six, taken from the effects of Quesada and Mendoza."

45. Ibid., p. CCXIX.

46. Ibid.; Denucé, p. 274.

47. Corrêa, in Nowell, p. 318. Corrêa badly scrambled the names of the mutinous captains. Morison, p. 372, also used the idea of a loyal seaman cutting the anchor cable. However, he put this action on the *Concepción*, with Quesada on deck as captain. Parr, p. 299, used the cable-cutting incident in a scenario that adheres more closely to the evidence presented by Medina.

48. Medina, p. CCXIX; Denucé, pp. 274-75.

49. Ibid.

50. Medina, p. CCXIX, cited Herrera, p. 359.

51. Denucé, p. 275; Medina, p. CCXX, note 16. Although he found no record of such a court martial in the Spanish archives, taking his cue from Herrera, Medina believed that there must have been such a trial. By Spanish law, all cases involving the death penalty required it.

52. Corrêa, in Nowell, p. 319.

Chapter 14. Winter in Patagonia

1. Morison, p. 374.

2. Medina, p. CCXXV, cited Hernando de la Torre, "Derrotero del viaje y navegación de la armada de Loaisa," in *Colección* . . . (Santiago de Chile: 1888), vol. III, p. 92. Torre mentioned the islet in his description of Puerto San Julián.

3. Morison, p. 374; Parr, pp. 302-03.

4. Edmundo Pisano, *La Vida en los Parques Nacionales de Magallanes* (Punta Arenas, Chile: Instituto de la Patagonia, 1973).

5. Medina, p. CCXXV. Note 2 cites J. F. Chaigneau, *Jeografía Nautica de la República Arjentina.*

6. Denucé, pp. 277-78. Note 1 cites Herrera, vol. II, lib. IX, cap. XIII, p. 188.

7. Medina, p. CCXXXII, note 41.

8. Ibid., and Supplement, p. 171.

9. Rolando A. Laguarda Trías, "Las Longitudes Geográficas de la Membranza de Magallanes y del Primer Viaje de Circunnavegación," in *Mota* (ed.), (Lisbon: 1975), p. 163.

10. Medina, p. CCXXVI.

11. Boorstin, pp. 52-3.

12. Denucé, p. 275, cited Cano's deposition of October 18, 1522; Medina, p. CCXXI, in note 17, cited Fray Gaspar de San Augustín, *Conquista de las Islas Filipinas* (Madrid: 1698). From this work, Medina reproduced Chapters II, III and IV in the document supplement to *Descubrimiento.* . . . The pertinent passage is in Ch. III, p. 75. The priest marooned with Cartagena also has been called Pedro Sánchez de Reina. Medina, p. CCCLXIII, argued that this was another name for Bernard Calmette, a Frenchman born in Lectoure,

France, chaplain of the *San Antonio.*

13. Medina, pp. CCXXVI-CCXXVII; Denucé, p. 278, cited Herrera as his source.

14. Medina, p. CCXXVII.

15. Denucé, p. 279, wrote that the loss of the sails and rudder occurred three miles beyond the bar; Medina, p. CCXXVII, Lagôa, p. 223, and Morison, p. 374, wrote that it was three leagues. Since it took the survivors four days to walk from the site of the wreck to the estuary at Santa Cruz, the latter estimate is probably correct.

16. From personal experience, I can testify that the huge barnacles from the south of Chile, called *lapas*, make very good eating. They taste much like crab, and probably were what kept the survivors alive at the site of the wreck of the *Santiago.*

17. Medina, p. CCXXVII, cited Herrera. Denucé, p. 279, stated that the trip from from the shipwreck site to the river took five days.

18. Denucé, p. 279. The fish probably were *róbalo*, abundant in the estuaries of subantarctic South America. They have been described by Leonardo Guzman and Italo Campodónico, "*Biologiá de Eleginops maclovinus*," in *Anales del Instituto de la Patagonia* (Punta Arenas, Chile: 1973), vol. IV, 1-3, pp. 343-44.

19. Medina, p. CCXXVIII.

20. Ibid., note 32.

21. Morison, p. 374, quoted the anonymous author of the Leiden narrative (probably Vasquito Galego, an apprentice seaman on the *Trinidad*), who wrote that Serrano was ". . . an industrious man who never rested."

22. Medina, pp. CCXXVIII-CCXXIX; Denucé, pp. 280-81. The natives of this region were Tehuelches, the South American counterparts of the bison-hunting Indians of the North American Great Plains. They were nomadic hunters whose principal quarry was guanaco, the wild llama of Patagonia.

23. Denucé, p. 281, note 1; Medina, p. CCXXIX, in note 33, stated that Darwin gave six feet as the average height of the Patagonians, and that Muster, a later traveler in those parts, agreed, stating that some of them reached a height of six feet, four inches.

24. This is from Nowell, p. 102, who used the 1906 Robertson translation of the manuscript in the Ambrosian Library in Milan. The Portuguese translation of MS 5650 of the National Library in Paris, used by Lagôa, is similar, but varies in minor details.

25. Pigafetta wrote that Magellan gave the name *Patagoni* to the natives. Rodrigue Lévesque, *The Philippines (Pigafetta's Story of Their Discovery by Magellan)* (Quebec: Les Editions Lévesque Publications, 1980), suggested its derivation from Magellan's Portuguese *pata de cão*. As a naturalized Castilian and leader of a Spanish fleet, it seems more likely that, except for the Portuguese with him on the *Trinidad*, Magellan communicated with the men of the fleet in Castilian.

26. Shakespeare must have read Pigafetta's story. In the Tempest, Act I, Scene II, he has the savage, Caliban, invoke the name of *Setebos*.

27. The encounter with Patagonian natives is exhaustively treated by Pigafetta. Herrera's more terse version is similar in most details. Medina, pp. CCXXVIII-CCXXXI, used both sources, but evidently preferred Herrera for specifics. Neither Pigafetta nor Herrera gave the name of the seaman killed in the fracas with the natives, but Medina, p. CCXXX, figured it out by matching the date of the seaman's death (from Herrera) with payroll records in the archives in Seville.

28. Denucé, p. 283.

29. Laguarda Trías, in Mota (ed.), pp. 163-168. The Portuguese chroniclers Barros and Castanheda were the sources for the 43° and 46° longitide values for San Julián. Barros was responsible for the charge of deliberate falsification.

30. Medina, p. CCXXXI.

31. Denucé, p. 283.

32. Medina, p. CCCCXXXI, note 29; Morison, pp. 642-43.

33. Medina, p. CCXXXIV.

34. Ibid.

35. Ibid.

Chapter 15. The Strait

1. There is a legend that St. Ursula, a fourth-century British princess, led 11,000 virgins on a pilgrimage to Rome. On their return journey they were waylaid near Cologne, raped, and then slaughtered by an army of Huns.

2. Francisco Albo, "Diario o Derrotero del Viage de Magallanes," ed. Navarrete, *Colección* . . . (Madrid: 1837) Vol. IV. English translation in Stanley (London: Hakluyt Soc., 1874) Vol. LII, pp. 209-247. See also Medina, CCXXXV-CCXXXVI, note 11.

3. Medina, p. CCXXXVI, note 12. Across the mouth of the strait from Punta Dungeness is Punta Catalina. It marks the eastern end of Bahía Lomas with its immense sand banks, also noted by Albo.

4. Denucé, pp. 285-86. Mateo Martinić (Instituto de la Patagonia, Universidad de Magallanes, Punta Arenas, Chile) thinks that the hill climbed by

Carvalho was the 348-foot Monte Dinero, on the northern shore of the strait, just inside Punta Dungeness.

5. Medina, pp. CCXXXVI-CCXXX-VII; Lagôa II, p. 223.

6. Martinić, personal communication.

7. Medina, p. CCXXXVII, cited Pigafetta (Nowell, p. 114).

8. Lagôa II, p. 223.

9. Medina, p. CCXXXVII.

10. Nowell, p. 115. This scenario, in which the *San Antonio* alone first explored deep within the strait, was suggested by Lagôa, who derived it from Herrera's comment that the *San Antonio* and the *Concepción* took separate routes. Medina noted Herrera's observation, but glossed over its implications. Denucé ignored Herrera and followed Pigafetta, who only saw the two ships returning together, and reported that the *San Antonio* and the *Concepción* had jointly explored the strait.

11. Denucé, p. 286; Medina, p. CCXX-VIII. Herrera reported that the shore party discovered 200 graves. Martinić (personal communication) states that on both sides of the strait there rarely were more than several native graves (*chenques*) at any one burial site. Herrera must have reported information that had been either misconstrued or exaggerated. Curiously, the area about three nautical miles back of the shore south-southwest of Caleta Munición, appears on Chilean military maps as *Campo Piramide* (Pyramid Field).

12. Denucé, p. 287.

13. Lagôa II, p. 224, cited Herrera, who wrote that the fleet had anchored three leagues west of Cape San Severin, at latitude 52° 56' S. If this were the cape now called San Vicente, three leagues west-southwest of it would place the anchorage behind Isabel Island in Paso Real. Denucé wrote that Herrera had derived his information from the notes of San Martín. The latitude given by

Herrera was read by Denucé as 53° 30' S, which would have placed the anchorage off Dawson Island. Of the two interpretations, Lagôa's better matches the narrative accounts. Mateo Martinić, in his *Historia del Estrecho de Magallanes* (Santiago, Chile: Editorial Andrés Bello, 1977) p. 43, and personal communication, suggests that the anchorage may have been a few nautical miles to the southwest in Pelican Roads or Bahía Shoal (Ensenada Baja on some maps), on the Brunswick Peninsula.

14. Lagôa II, pp. 224-25; Medina, p. CCXLIX.

15. Nowell, p. 115.

16. Martinić, Historia . . . , p. 43.

17. Ibid., personal communication.

18. Lagôa II, p. 225, cited The Genoese Pilot. The three waterways visible from the northern end of Dawson Island are: to the east, Bahía Inútil (Useless Bay), to the south southeast, Canal Whiteside, and to the southwest, Paso del Hambre (Famine Reach).

19. Mateo Martinić, "Panorama de la Colonización en Tierra del Fuego Entre 1881 y 1900," *Anales del Instituto de la Patagonia* (Punta Arenas, Chile: 1973), Vol. IV, Nos. 1, 3. For a summary account, in English, of the history of European settlement around the Strait of Magellan, see R. D. Talbott, *A History of the Chilean Boundaries* (Iowa State University Press: 1974).

20. Lagôa II, pp. 225-26, cited Herrera, who wrote that only the *San Antonio* was sent on that mission. Medina and Morison, following Pigafetta, wrote that both the *San Antonio* and the *Concepción* were sent to investigate the waterways to the east of Dawson Island. Magellan's order to Mesquita to rendezvous with the other ships ". . . at the foot of some snow-covered heights . . . ," was related by Ginés de Mafra, "Descubrimiento del Estrecho de Magallanes," *Real Sociedad Geo-*

gráfica (Madrid: 1921), p. 194.

The surviving accounts of Magellan's voyage through the strait are so vague that it is difficult to reconstruct from them the movements of the various units of his fleet. Historians and biographers rarely agree on all details. In this reconstruction, I have attempted to fit the events portrayed in the often contradictory accounts to the time available to the explorers. Many of the basic elements of this scenario are derived from the analysis in Mateo Martinić's *Historia* . . . of Magellan's route through the strait. Recollections of a 1976 fishery assessment cruise (courtesy of the Chilean Navy), close study of that navy's excellent hydrographic charts, and the maps published by the Military Geographic Institute of Chile were also helpful in developing this reconstruction.

21. Medina, pp. CCXLVII-CCXLVIII, cited testimony given by the crew of the *San Antonio* after their return to Spain.

22. Denucé, pp. 291-92, cited *Archivo de las Indias*, 1, 2, 1/1: 13, 14 (1521); Herrera II, IX, Ch. XV. Medina, pp. CCXLIX-CCLI, cited the letter to Charles V from López Recalde and Dr. Sancho de Matienzo, reporting on the return to Spain of the *San Antonio*, in Arch. Ind. 1, 2, 1/1: 14. Medina also cited Herrera, Oviedo and Maximilian Transylvanus.

23. Medina, p. CCXXI (in note 16, beginning on p. CCXX).

24. Ibid., p. CCLIV.

25. Martinić, *Historia* . . . , p. 45. Morison and Ribeiro (Lagôa II), both with naval backgrounds, also opted for Bahía Fortescue. Medina, p. CCXXIX, suggested Bahía Woods. Since this shallow bay offers little protection from storms, it seems more likely that, after investigating it, Magellan moved on in search of a better anchorage. According to Leonardo Guzmán and Italo Campodónico, hydrobiologists at the Instituto de la Patagonia, four species of small fish that could be called sardines are found in the strait. They usually inhabit open waters, but occasionally take refuge in coastal inlets when chased by predators. Magellan may have entered Bahía Fortescue on such an occasion.

26. The fragrant wood was channel cypress, *Pilgerodendron uviferum*. When burned, it gives off a delightful fragrance (Martinić, personal communication). It is described on p. 30 of the *Manual de Identificación de Especies Lenosas del Bosque Húmido de Chile*, published by the Corporación Nacional Forestal, in Chile.

27. At the northwest end of English Reach, Carlos III Island blocks the view from the southeast into Crooked Reach.

28. Medina, p. CCXL. It was the custom in sixteenth century Spain to reward carriers of news of exceptional value to the crown with money. The prizes were known as *albricias*.

29. Ibid., p. CCXLI; Nowell, p. 117; Martinić, *Historia* . . . , pp. 47-48.

30. Medina, pp. CCXLI-CCXLII, note 27, cited Herrera.

31. The basic elements of this scenario were proposed by Mateo Martinić, in his *Historia* . . . , p. 48.

32. The summit of Cerro El Morrión is 330 meters, or 1083 feet. Add 5 feet for the height above sea level of Roldán's eyes to get 1088 feet. The distance to the horizon = $1.17 \times \sqrt{1088} = 38.6$ nautical miles. To the northwest (if the day was clear) from the summit of Cerro El Morrión, Roldán's horizon was in Ocean Reach beyond its junction with Long Reach.

33. Except for Herrera's mention of Roldán, there is no direct evidence revealing the names of other members of the shallop's crew. Medina suggested that Hernando de Bustamente and Bocacio Alonso also were in that crew, basing his supposition on records showing that they were paid

the *albricias* promised by Magellan. How they were earned, however, was not recorded.

34. Medina, pp. CCXLV-CCXLVI (see especially note 32).

35. Ibid., p. CCXLV, notes 30, 31.

36. Ibid., p. CCXLVI, note 32 (from previous page).

37. Martinić, *Historia* . . . , p. 49. Lagôa II, p. 226, suggested that the anchorage was in Bahía San Miguel (the inner cove at Bahía Cordes). During a visit in 1976, I observed that a shallow sill at the entrance precluded its entry by vessels of deeper draft than a longboat. Except at high tide, it is doubtful that Magellan's ships could have passed over the sill. With a shallow bank extending south-southeast from the sill, room for maneuvering sailing vessels is limited. It does not seem a likely place for Magellan to have anchored.

38. Medina, p. CCXLVII, note 33 (beginning on p. CCXLVI).

39. Medina, Document Supplement to *Descubrimiento* . . ., pp. 27-28. Barros, a Portuguese chronicler, translated both statements from Castilian into Portuguese. Medina translated them back into Spanish. Presented here, therefore, are twice-copied, thrice-translated statements. Magellan's was dictated to the clerk, Ezpeleta, who may have modified the captain general's heavily accented Castilian. Medina translated the Portuguese of Barros into Spanish, and I have rendered Medina's Spanish into English.

It is indeed puzzling that San Martín seemed to have been unaware of the discovery made by the scouting party led by Roldán. Reluctant to sail into an unknown ocean with a reduced fleet and depleted supplies, yet fearful of expressing opposition to Magellan's obvious determination to press forward, he may have deliberately ignored the possibility that the ocean lay just ahead, and tried to draw Magellan's attention to the dangers of remaining in high latitudes beyond summer. The two channels that he mentioned, one leading east and the other east northeast, also are puzzling. Perhaps they refer to the Paso de los Boquerones and Bahía Inútil, northeast of Dawson Island.

The name, *Canal de Todos los Santos* (All Saints' Channel), used by Magellan, was not thought by Medina to refer to the strait as a whole, but only to that part northwest of Cape Froward. The name probably was given on November 1 (All Saints' Day). On that date, the fleet was in Broad Reach, somewhere to the north of Dawson Island. Since Magellan also used the same name to describe his location on November 21, when he was anchored at the *Río del Isleo* off Carlos III Island, it appears that he used that name for the entire strait.

40. Medina, p. CCLVI, attributed this interpretation to Barros. However, the response of San Martín (the most scholarly of Magellan's officers) was not an unqualified endorsement of Magellan's plans. Unfortunately, there is no record of the response of Serrano, a pilot of vast experience whose comments Magellan surely would have valued. Pigafetta's treatment of Magellan was far better than that of Barros, which reflected the attitudes of the Portuguese court and was less than charitable toward a man regarded as a defector.

41. Ibid.

42. Lagôa II, p. 227. These dates are not documented. Lagôa derived them by interpolating between known events on November 21 and 28, taking into account the time needed for intervening events, and the distance traveled.

43. Medina, p. CCLVI, note 53, cited Maximilian Transylvanus for the observation about sailors thinking that they were hearing surf, and Guillemard for the information on Schouten and Le Maire.

44. Morison, p. 396.

45. Medina, p. CCLVIII, cited Pigafetta: ". . . we sailed out of the strait to enter the great sea to which we immediately gave the name Pacific."

Chapter 16. The Pacific

1. Thrice, if Marco Polo is counted. In 1292, the Polos escorted a Mongol princess from China to Persia by sea. En route, they sailed through the South China Sea, an arm of the Pacific Ocean. While the Polos may have been the first Europeans to see that ocean, they did not recognize it as a distinct geographical entity, and cannot, therefore, be considered to have "discovered" it.

2. Lagôa II, p. 227; Denucé, p. 296.

3. Pigafetta, in Nowell, p. 119, and Lagôa II, p. 63. As do many tellers of fish stories, Pigafetta exaggerated in describing the size of the albacore and bonito he saw. They rarely exceed four feet in length.

4. Denucé, Plate V, facing p. 294, Lagôa II, facing p. 228, and Morison, pp. 406-409, used Albo's log to reconstruct Magellan's track across the Pacific, with only minor variations in their results. In plotting the squadron's positions, Morison and and his associate, Thomas Keller, assumed that Albo's headings were corrected for compass variation. The Genoese Pilot wrote, ". . . we northeasted the compass box by two points." This easterly correction of 22.5° is not much different from the variation observed for that region today. Morison and Keller checked Albo's course between Guam and the entrance to Leyte Gulf, and found it to be within 2.8° of the true bearing.

A variation on the Albo track has been proposed: After passing inside the Juan Fernández Islands on December 18, rather than changing course to the west-northwest, Magellan continued to follow the American coast to the north and northwest, across the equator to nearly 20° N, before turning west. According to George E. Nunn, "Magellan's Route in the Pacific," *Geographical Review*, XXIV (1935), pp. 615-33, and Nowell, pp. 124-25, the two islands sighted in mid-Pacific were Clipperton (10° 17' N) and Clarion (18° N). This astounding departure from the positions recorded by Albo was taken to justify the theory that Magellan was striking for a landfall in the Ryukyu Islands, and to explain why he encountered but two islands between the strait and Guam. This departure from Albo's log is unnecessary for defending the Ryukyus theory, which is not unreasonable. As for the dearth of islands along the route, subsequent expeditions traveling the same route experienced the same phenomenon in an ocean filled with islands.

5. Morison, p. 407.

6. Denucé, p. 297, cited Brito.

7. Denucé, p. 298; Morison, p. 410; Albo, in Stanley, pp. 221-22.

8. Denucé, p. 298; Lagôa II, p. 228; Morison, pp. 410-12.

9. Lagôa II, p. 228; Morison, p. 412.

10. Denucé, p. 299, cited Maximilian Transylvanus and Herrera.

11. Lagôa, p. 228.165° W according to Denucé, p. 300.

12. Medina, pp. CCLXVIII-CCLXIX, note 8.

13. Lagôa II, p. 228.

14. W. A. R. Richardson, "Piloting a Toponymic Course through Sixteenth-Century Southeast Asian Waters," *Terrae Incognitae*, XX (1988), pp. 1-15.

15. Jean Denucé, "Les Îles Lequios (Formose et Riu-Kiu) et Ophir," *Bull. Soc. Royale Belge de Géographie*, (Brussels: 1907), No. 6.

16. Denucé, p. 304, quoting Pigafetta, also cited De Orbis Situ, édition de L. Gallois, and *De Orontis Finnaeo-Gallico Geographico* (Paris: 1890); Nowell, p. 127.

17. Barros, dec. III, lib. V, cap. X, as

cited by Denucé, p. 302, wrote that the fleet's course across the Pacific was proof of Magellan's incompetence, adding that when he reached 21° N, he was frantic because the Asiatic mainland had not been sighted. On questioning San Martín, Magellan became convinced that the former had lost his ability to navigate. In panic, Magellan ". . . abandoned astronomy and turned to astrology," which suggests that in sixteenth-century Portugal, astrology already had begun to be regarded as humbug.

Denucé, pp. 302-03, cited Castanheda, lib. VI, cap. VIII, who reported that Magellan and his pilots were filled with consternation at not finding the Moluccas when they reached the equator. "The admiral affirmed," he wrote, "along with the astronomer and the pilots (as is manifest by the papers we Portuguese found at Ternate) that they had navigated so far to the west after leaving the strait, the ships had crossed the boundary of Castile's domain and had entered the Portuguese hemisphere. For fear of falling into our hands, and also being in dire need of fresh water, they decided to abandon the route they had been following and sail north until they reached 10° N latitude." This account lacks the strong bias of most Portuguese chroniclers of that period.

Portuguese chroniclers had access to papers taken from the *Trinidad*, and in citing them, all but Castanheda attempted to discredit Magellan. These captured papers were not made available to the Conference of Badajoz-Elvas on the Portuguese-Spanish frontier, which convened in 1524 to settle the issue of the boundary between Portuguese and Spanish dominions in the Far East, nor have they been found in Portuguese archives. The likelihood of deliberate bias in the unsupported statements about Magellan's voyage in sixteenth-century Portuguese chronicles is too

great to be ignored. Of the Conference of Badajoz-Elvas, Nowell, p. 336, wrote: "Neither side wanted an accurate decision for its own sake. Each desired the islands [Moluccas] and was willing to resort to any falsification or misrepresentation to obtain them."

18. Pigafetta, in Nowell, p. 131.
19. Medina, p. CCLXXII, cited Herrera, p. 373.
20. Ibid., pp. CCLXI-CCLXII, cited Albo; Denucé, p. 306.
21. Denucé, p. 306.
22. Nowell, p. 129.
23. Medina, p. CCLXII, cited Maximilian Transylvanus; Denucé, p. 307, speculated that they might have been referring to Leyte, in the Philippines.
24. Paul Carano and Pedro C. Sanchez, *A Complete History of Guam* (Rutland, Vermont, and Tokyo, Japan: Tuttle, 1964), pp. 62-3.
25. Ibid., p. 17.
26. Lagôa II, p. 229.
27. Pigafetta, in Nowell, pp. 129-30.
28. Morison, p. 418.
29. Medina, p. CCCXLVI.
30. Denucé, p. 307. The latitude given in the *Roteiro* of the Anonymous Portuguese was 11° N, exactly right for the southern tip of Samar. Albo recorded 9° 40' N, not one of his best shots.
31. Morison, p. 418.
32. Medina, p. CCLXXIII.
33. Ibid.; Pigafetta (Portuguese translation) in Lagôa II, pp. 79-80.
34. Denucé, p. 308, cited the *Roteiro* of the Anonymous Portuguese.
35. Pigafetta (Portuguese translation) in Lagôa II, p. 76.
36. Ibid., pp 77-80.
37. Rolando A. Laguarda Trías, "Las Longitudes Geográficas de la Membranza de Magallanes y del Primer Viaje de Circunnavegación," in A. Teixeira da Mota, pp. 135-78. The following, extracted from Table V, p. 170, shows the estimated error in Albo's longitude for Suluan-Homonhon: (1) Island: Suluan-Homonhon; (2) Pertinent page in Navarrete, Tome

IV: 220; (3) Albo's longitude west of Tordesillas Treaty line (47° W): 189° W; (4) Longitude east of Greenwich: 126° E; (5) Longitude west of Greenwich: 234° W; (6)

Longitude west of the Treaty Line: 187°; (7) Error: (3) minus (6) = plus 2° (W)

38. Denucé, p. 309.

39. Morison, p. 435.

Chapter 17. The Fatal Alliance

1. Pigafetta, in Nowell, p. 137; Denucé, p. 309; Medina, p. CCLXXIV.

2. Denucé, p. 310.

3. Pigafetta called the fish *orade*, probably for dorado. Some translations of Pigafetta say that the rice was delivered raw in porcelain jars (Nowell, p. 138); in others, cooked, served on porcelain platters (Denucé, p. 310).

4. Denucé, p. 310; Morison, p. 422.

5. Nowell, p. 138.

6. Ibid., pp. 140-141.

7. Denucé, p. 310. Pigafetta reported that Siaui ruled over Butuan and Calagan. Butuan Bay is on the northwest coast of Mindanao.

8. Nowell, p. 142.

9. Peter Martyr d'Anghiera, *Opus Epistolarum*, (Amsterdam: 1670) Ep. DC-CLXX, cited by Denucé, p. 311.

10. Medina, pp. CCLXXIV-CCLXXV, cited Covarrubias, *Tesoro de la Lengua Castellana*.

11. Ibid., p. CCLXXV, note 19.

12. Denucé, p. 311.

13. Ibid., p. 312.

14. Nowell, p. 147.

15. Denucé, p. 312; Medina, p. CCLXVI.

16. Medina, p. CCLXXVI; Nowell, pp. 148-149. Medina wrote that Enrique went ashore with "someone" in whom Magellan had confidence. Pigafetta stated that "The captain sent a *foster* son of his to the King of Zubu with the interpreter." Medina, p. CCCCXVII, argued that Revêlo was Magellan's *natural* son.

17. Ibid.

18. Ibid., p. CCLXXVII.

19. Pigafetta, in Nowell, p. 150.

20. Ibid., pp. 150-151.

21. Medina, p. CCLXXVIII, cited Pigafetta (Paris manuscript).

22. Ibid.

23. Ibid.

24. Denucé, p. 313.

25. Medina, p. CCLXXVII, notes 20, 21.

26. Denucé, p. 313.

27. Medina, p. CCLXXIX.

28. Pigafetta, in Nowell, p. 157.

29. Ibid., p. 159.

30. Ibid., p. 158.

31. Denucé, p. 313.

32. Denucé, pp. 313-14, stated that the image was given to the ranee by Pigafetta. Pigafetta (Nowell, p. 160) said only that "she asked us to give her the little child, Jesus, to keep in place of her idols." Morison, p. 425, wrote that "Magellan gave the lady a small image of a smiling Christ child." Because of the religious rapture he was experiencing at that time, and since the Holy Virgin was the principal source of his religious inspiration, it is quite possible that Magellan was the donor.

33. Morison, p. 436; Mairin Mitchell, *Friar Andrés de Urdaneta*, O.S.A. (London: MacDonald & Evans, 1964) p. 126. Mitchell noted that the image preserved in Cebu does not precisely match the description given by Pigafetta.

34. Nowell, p. 160.

35. Denucé, p. 314, cited Maximilian Transylvanus.

36. Nowell, p. 167.

37. Morison, p. 435, cited Tom Harrison, "The Palang, Its History and Protohistory in West Borneo and the Philippines, *Journal of the Malaysian Branch, Royal Asiatic Society*, XXXVII (1964) Part 2, pp. 162-174; and, for il-

lustrations, Theodor De Bry, *Tertia Pars Indiae Orientalis*, (1628), pp. 23, 109.

38. Ibid., p. 423.

39. Medina, p. CCCCXXVII, item 107, note 2, cited the testimony of Nicolás de Napolés (a seaman on the *Victoria*) in an unsuccessful lawsuit filed against the Crown by Jaime, a son of Diego Barbosa.

40. See note 16.

41. The story of the burning of the village of Bulaya has been synthesized from the accounts given by Pigafetta and Antonio Herrera in his *Historia General* . . . . José Ibañez Cerda, in A. Teixeira da Mota, p. 428, suggested that Herrera's story was derived from an account taken from the notes of Andrés de San Martín. Denucé's scenario (p. 315) also synthesized from several sources, is very similar to the one presented here.

42. Denucé, p. 316.

43. These quotations from Pigafetta are from Nowell, pp. 169-172, who used the Robertson translation of the Milan manuscript.

44. Antonio Herrera, *Historia General*. . . . The pertinent excerpts are given by Ibañez Cerda, in Mota, pp. 428-30.

45. Father Rodrigo Agánduru Moriz, cited by Medina, pp. CCLXXXVII-CCLXXXVIII.

46. Denucé, p. 318, cited Navarrete, *Colección* . . . , t. IV, pp. 65-66, and Brito, who reported that in addition to Magellan, six Europeans were killed. As for the fifteen Mactanese reported to have been killed, enemy body counts by troops under fire tend to be grossly exaggerated.

47. Medina, p. CCLXXXIX, quoted Herrera.

48. Denucé, pp. 319-324.

49. Medina, pp. CCLXXXVI-CCLXXX-VII.

50. Denucé, p. 324.

51. Medina, pp. CCC-CCCI. The numbers of Spaniards reported to have attended the banquet vary. Pigafetta's twenty-six is in accord with the official casualty lists.

52. Morison, p. 439, cited the *Roteiro* of the Anonymous Portuguese.

53. Medina, pp. CCCI-CCCII, noted that in 1528, a survivor of the Loaísa expedition, rescued by a ship of Saavedra's fleet, told Francisco Ganado, the rescue ship's notary, that after his ship had been wrecked, he had been captured by natives on Mindanao and made the slave of a rajah. Accompanying the rajah on a trip to Cebu, he had learned that "up to eight" of Magellan's men had survived the May 1, 1521 massacre, and that they had been sold into slavery in China.

Chapter 18. The Wanderers

1. Medina, p. CCCLXXXII. The approximate positions of the fleet on the dates given by Medina for the deaths of crew members were estimated from the reconstruction of Magellan's route by Admiral J. Freitas Ribeiro (Lagôa II).

2. Medina, p. CCCCXLI.

3. Ibid., p. CCCLXXXVI.

4. Ibid., p. CCCLIII.

5. Ibid., p. CCCCXXIV.

6. Ibid., p. CCCI, note 2.

7. Estimates of the number of survivors at this point range from 180 (Barros) to 108 (The Genoese Pilot). Gómara and Denucé estimated 115, Guillemard, 120.

8. Lagôa II, p. 231, note 1.

9. Denucé, p. 327, note 2, cited Stanley, p. 252, who stated that Corrêa suspected that Espinosa was elected captain of the *Victoria* because he was related to the deceased pilot, San Martín. Medina's biographical studies of San Martín and Espinosa revealed no such family linkage.

10. Lagôa II, p. 231.
11. Ibid., cited Albo.
12. Denucé, p. 327.
13. Nowell, pp. 182-3 Pigafetta's "Lozon" was obviously Luzon. Lequian (Ryukyuan) ships called there regularly.
14. Denucé, p. 327.
15. Nowell, p. 183.
16. Denucé, p. 328.
17. Lagôa II, p. 231.
18. Medina, p. CCCII.
19. Pigafetta, The Genoese Pilot, and the *Roteiro* all give such garbled spellings of the name of this port that it is impossible to identify it with any modern names. However, the configuration of the coast at the latitude given by the pilots (9° 30′ N) strongly suggests Puerto Princesa.
20. Denucé, p. 329.
21. Lagôa II, p. 232.
22. Denucé, pp. 330-1.
23. Pigafetta, in Nowell, pp. 185-6.
24. Ibid., p. 189.
25. Medina, p. CCCIV. Denucé, pp. 332-3, cited Brito. Denucé gave the names of the Greek deserters as Juan and Mateo Griego. According to Medina (pp. CCCXCII-CCCXCIII), Mateo's surname was listed as *Gorfo* (probably a Spanish scribe's rendering of Corfu).
26. Denucé, p. 232.
27. Ibid.
28. Medina, p. CCCIV. The crewman killed was Nicolás de Capua, an able seaman on the *Victoria*.
29. Ibid.; Denucé, p. 332.
30. Denucé, p. 332
31. Medina, p. CCCIV.
32. Ibid.; Pigafetta (Nowell, p. 191). Corrêa (Nowell, p. 324) stated that when the Spaniards found that Carvalho had slept with the women hostages, they ". . . were near killing him," and that they were not deceived when Carvalho blamed the watch for the escape of the Luzon prince during the night.
33. Pigafetta, in Nowell, pp. 191-2.
34. Denucé, p. 333, cited Herrera, Corrêa, and The Genoese Pilot.

35. Pigafetta, in Nowell, p. 194.
36. Ibid.
37. Denucé, p. 334.
38. Ibid.; Medina, p. CCCIV. Both authors reported a latitude of 7° N, but failed to give their sources for this information. Pigafetta's latitude of 8° 07′ N, would place the anchorage at Balabac Island, off the southern end of Palawan.
39. Denucé, p. 334, cited E. Gelsich, "Zwei Briefe Über die Magalhäesche Weltumsgelung," *Sitzungberichte D. Acad. Wiss.*, CXVII (Vienna, 1888) p. 7. Medina (p. CCCIV) and Lagôa II (p. 232) wrote that Gómez de Espinosa was made captain general. Although his strength of character undoubtedly was respected by his shipmates, Espinosa knew nothing of navigation. The claim by Juan Bautista de Polcevera, in his letter from Tidore of December 21, 1521, that he had been given overall command of the fleet, makes sense. He was the most experienced mariner among the survivors, had admirably performed his duties as master of the *Trinidad*, had remained steadfastly loyal to Magellan throughout the voyage, and had kept out of fleet politics. According to Medina (p. CCCIV), Bautista's claim that he was given overall charge of the fleet is supported by Brito's letter to King Manuel concerning the capture of the *Trinidad* by the Portuguese.
40. Medina, p. CCCIV.
41. Ibid., pp. CCCIV-CCCV.
42. Pigafetta, in Nowell, p. 195.
43. Denucé, p. 335.
44. Ibid.
45. Ibid., cited The Genoese Pilot (Paris manuscript).
46. Pigafetta, in Nowell, p. 197.
47. Ibid., p. 198, wrote that the native vessel was a *bigniday*, like a prau (a double-hulled vessel), containing eighteen men, of whom seven were killed. He did not mention any casualties among the Europeans. Denucé (pp. 336-7) cited the *Roteiro* by the

Anonymous Portuguese for the statement that the vessel attacked was a large junk (a single-hulled vessel), and that 20 of its crew were killed and 30 captured. According to this report, of the 60 Europeans who attacked the junk in two longboats, two were killed.

48. Here, the two accounts cited in the note above are also divergent. Pigafetta wrote that the man who told them the way to the Moluccas was ". . . a brother of the king of Maingdanao." This could have been a town near the mouth of the Mindanao River, near the present town of Cotaboto. Denucé (pp. 336-7), citing the *Roteiro*, stated that the information came from the pilots of the captured junk. Perhaps there is no discrepancy

here. The brother of the rajah could have been the pilot of the junk (or was it a prau?). Denucé also cited the *Roteiro* for the story that the chief had been at the house of Francisco Serrão in Ternate.

49. Nowell, p. 198, cited Andrea da Mosto, *Raccolta* . . . , (1894) V, III, 91, who noted the custom of heart eating by the Manobo tribe of eastern Mindanao.

50. Denucé, p. 338.

51. Ibid.

52. Ibid, p. 339.

53. Medina, p. CCCV.

54. Denucé, p. 339. Among the many bits of false information spread by the Portuguese concerning the Moluccas was that fresh water there was in short supply.

Chapter 19. Maluco

1. The principal islands of the Moluccas are Ternate, Tidore, Motir, Makian, and Batjan.

2. Twenty-seven months less two days, according to Pigafetta (Nowell, p. 200).

3. Denucé calculated that when the fleet left Cebu there were 115 survivors. Between Cebu and Borneo five more perished. With the three abandoned at Brunei, when the *Trinidad* and the *Victoria* arrived in the Moluccas, 107 (not counting Malay captives) remained.

4. R. A. LaGuarda Trías, in Mota (ed.), p. 170 (based on data previously published in Navarrete).

5. Navarrete, Vol. IV, pp. 209-247.

6. Pigafetta, in Nowell, pp. 201-202.

7. Ibid., p. 204. On p. 262, Nowell cited Armando Melón y Ruiz de Gordejuela, *Los primeros tiempos de colonización* . . . (Barcelona, Madrid, Buenos

Aires, Mexico, Rio de Janeiro: 1952) for another version in which Serrão was poisoned, not by the rajah of Tidore, but by a native woman at the instigation of the Portuguese.

8. Ibid., p. 205.

9. Ibid., pp. 205-206.

10. Medina, p. CCCVII.

11. Pigafetta, in Nowell, pp. 209-210. With only a single ship, Faria may have unwilling to confront Magellan's fleet, believing it to consist of five well-armed vessels.

12. Medina, p. CCCVIII.

13. Ibid.

14. Pigafetta, in Nowell, pp. 206-207.

15. Morison, p. 450.

16. Pigafetta, in Nowell, p. 214.

17. Medina, p. CCCIX.

18. Pigafetta, in Nowell, p. 224.

19. Medina, p. CCCIX.

20. Pigafetta, in Nowell, pp. 224-225.

21. Medina, pp. CCCX-CCCXI.

Chapter 20. The Last Voyage of the *Trinidad*

1. Mairin Mitchell, *Friar Andrés de Urdaneta, O.S.A.* (London: MacDonald and Evans, 1964), p. 33.

2. Medina, p. CCCXXIX.

3. Ibid.

4. Ibid., pp. CCCXXX-CCCXXXI, note 3.

5. Denucé, p. 366. 1,800 leagues ac-

cording to Espinosa; 2,000 according to The Genoese Pilot.

6. Ibid., pp. 366-367.
7. Medina, p. CCCXXXII.
8. Ibid., cited Espinosa's letter to King Charles, dated in Cochin, January 12, 1525.
9. Denucé, p. 369.
10. Medina, p. CCCXXXIII, cited Herrera.
11. Denucé, p. 369.
12. Ibid., pp. 369-370. In note 2, cited Galvão for the story about the sighting of seals and tuna. The coincidence of tuna and seals would not be unusual off northeastern Japan, where the warm waters of the Japan Current merge with the cold Kamchatka Current. The Ribeiro world map of 1529 places the northernmost point attained by the *Trinidad* on the same meridian as the Marshall Islands.
13. Medina, p. CCCXXXIV, cited Oviedo in note 68.
14. Ibid.
15. Ibid., and pp. CCCCLIII-CCCCLIV, cited Agánduru Moriz and a letter from Albuquerque to King João III, dated at Malacca January 1, 1524, for elements of this story. However, the letter refers to the presence on Borneo of a "*vizcaino*" from Magellan's fleet. It has been assumed by some

that this was Vigo, but if so, how could he have been on Saipan in 1526?
16. Ibid., p. CCCXXXV. This count does not include Lorosa, his wife, nor two natives who sailed from Tidore with the *Trinidad*.
17. Ibid., p. CCCXXXIV. The apprentice seamen suffered the greatest number of casualties, followed by the able seamen. The only officer to succumb was Juan Morales, the ship's surgeon.
18. Possibly the village of Sahoe shown on Defense Mapping Agency Chart No. 524.
19. Denucé, p. 373. In note 1, concluded that Brito had been given seven ships to intercept and destroy Magellan's fleet in the Moluccas.
20. Ibid.; Navarrete IV, pp. 95-97.
21. Denucé, p. 372, cited Barros.
22. Ibid.
23. Medina, p. CCCXXXVI. Possibly the modern town of Djailolo.
24. Ibid., p. CCCXXXVII, cited Espinosa's declaration in Valladolid, made after his return to Spain.
25. Navarrete, IV, p. 347, declaration given at Valladolid by León Pancaldo.
26. Medina, p. CCCXXXVIII, cited Castanheda, who got Lorosa's name wrong.

Chapter 21. The World Encompassed

1. Medina, p. CCCXII.
2. Albo, in Stanley, p. 230. "Motil is on the Line and is in the longitude of the meridian of 191° 45'." Laguarda Trías, pp. 169-70, proposed that the Tordesillas Treaty line west of the Azores was the reference meridian on which Albo based this value, placing the Moluccas west of the extended line of demarcation, in Portuguese territory.
3. Morison, p. 457.
4. Ibid., cited Albo.
5. Pigafetta, in Stanley, p. 151.
6. Ibid., pp. 150-151.
7. Pigafetta, in Nowell, p. 247.

8. Nowell, p. 247.
9. Medina, p. CCCXIII, cited payroll records of the Casa de Contratación. The port at which they deserted was called Batatara (possibly modern Barate, near the western end of Timor).
10. Ibid. Note 11 cited Oviedo and López de Gómara. The former reported that several crewmen were executed at Timor for their part in a mutiny. The latter wrote that "many" were killed in a brawl. Lagôa, p. 234, cited Herrera for the story of a brawl in which "some" crewmen were killed.

11. Morison, p. 458, following a quotation from Pigafetta. However, Pigafetta made no mention of it, nor did he ever mention Cano (whom he apparently despised) in his narrative. Morison did not cite a source for the statement about sandalwood being carried to Spain on the *Victoria*, although it is quite possible that Cano brought a sample of the valuable wood to present to the emperor.

12. Albo called it "Manvai" (Stanley, pp. 232-233). Medina, p. CCCXIII, spelled it "Mombay."

13. Reflecting the spelling conventions of his native Italian, Pigafetta spelled it "Laut Chidol."

14. Stanley, pp. 233-234. Albo's island was Amsterdam, in the South Indian Ocean. Its actual latitude is 37° 48′ S.

15. Lagôa II, p. 234, cited Albo. The latitude of the Cape of Good Hope is 34° 21′ S. Cape Agulhas, the southernmost point of Africa, is at 34° 50′ S.

16. Albo, in Stanley, p. 234. Albo's Río del Infante was the Great Fish River.

17. Pigafetta, in Stanley, p. 160.

18. Albo, in Stanley, p. 235.

19. Lagôa II, p. 235.

20. Corrêa, cited by Medina, pp. CCCXIV-CCCXV and Lagôa II, p. 235.

21. Medina, p. CCCXV.

22. Ibid., cited Albo.

23. Stanley, p. 161.

24. Medina, p. CCCXV, cited Albo.

25. Stanley, p. 161.

26. Medina, p. CCCXV, cited the depositions given by Cano, Albo, and Bustamente upon their return to Spain.

27. Lagôa II, p. 235.

28. Albo, in Stanley, p. 235.

29. Medina, p. CCCXVII.

30. Nowell, p. 308.

31. Stanley, p. 162.

32. Medina, p. CCCXVIII.

33. Ibid. On pp. 95-99 of his appended *Documentos* (II, No. IX), Medina provided a transcript of Burgos' declaration.

34. Ibid., p. CCCXIX.

Epilogue

1. Medina, p. CCCXX, cited Peter Martryr (Asensio translation). The names of the European survivors are listed in the appendices.

2. Ibid.

3. Ibid., note 27.

4. Ibid., p. CCCXXII. In note 30, Medina stated that the original of Cano's letter was lost. A copy, in Italian, of the Castilian original was found by J. Gelcich in the archives of the city of Ragusa.

5. Denucé, p. 360.

6. Pigafetta, in Nowell, p. 259. Medina, p. CCCXXV, note 34, provided evidence that the pledges made by the survivors at the shrine of Nuestra Señora de la Victoria were paid in July, 1523.

7. Medina, p. CCCXXVI. In his *Colección* . . . , Vol. I, p. 298, Medina reproduced the entire text of the royal order.

8. Nowell, p. 333, cited Navarrete IV, pp. 263-8.

9. Ibid.; Medina, pp. CCCXLIII-CCCXLIV, CCCLVIII-CCCLXI, note 5.

10. Herrera, cited by Medina, p. CCCXVI, note 36.

11. Nowell, p. 332.

12. Medina, p. CCCXXVI, note 37.

13. Morison, p. 490.

14. Medina, p. CCCLXXXVIII, item 106. See Medina, *Estéban Gómez al Servicio de España* (Santiago, Chile, Imprenta Elzeviriana: 1908) p. 28 for the brief imprisonment of Gomes, Guerra, and two others from the crew of the *San Antonio*. Mesquita remained in jail after they were released.

15. Parr, p. 394.
16. Ibid.
17. Medina, p. X.
18. Ibid., p. CCCXXV, note 33; Denucé, pp. 362-3.
19. Lagôa I, pp. 235-6.
20. Medina, p. CCCLXIV. Denucé, p. 377, suggested that Campos escaped from Ternate in a native junk.
21. Denucé, p. 377.
22. Medina, p. CCCCXXV, cited Brito's letters to the king (Arquivo da Torre do Tombo).
23. Ibid., p. CCCLXXXIX.
24. Denucé p. 378.

25. Ibid., p. 379, note 1.
26. Medina, p. CCCCXXXIX.
27. Ibid., P. CCCCXXV. The original letters, addressed to a church official, are in the Arquivo da Torre do Tombo in Lisbon. They have been reproduced in *Raccolta Colombiana*, Part V, Vol. I, pp. 284-6.
28. Medina, *Algunas Noticias de León Pancaldo . . .Estudio Histórico* (Santiago, Chile: Imprenta Elzeviriana, 1908) pp. 15-18.
29. Medina, p. CCCXXIV, cited Oviedo, *Historia de las Indias*.

Bibliography

Agánduro Moriz, Fr. Rodrigo. "Historia general de las Islas Occidentales a la Asia adyacentes, llamadas Philipinas," in Tomo LXXVII, *Colección de documentos inéditos para la historia de España*, ed. by Martín Fernández de Navarrete, Miguel Salvá, and Pedro Sainz de Baranda (Madrid: 1842).

Albo, Francisco. "Diario ó derrotero del viage de Magallanes," in *Colección de los viages y descubrimientos que hicieron por mar los Españoles desde fines de siglo XV*, ed. by Martín Fernández de Navarrete (Madrid: 1825–1837, Buenos Aires: 1945–1946). Partial English translation in *The First Voyage Around the World by Magellan*, ed. and trans. by Henry Edward John Stanley (London: Hakluyt Soc., 1874) Ser. I, Vol. LII.

Albuquerque, Afonso de. *Comentarios de Afonso de Albuquerque*. Translated into English from the Portuguese document in the Arquivo da Torre do Tombo in Lisbon by W. de Gray Birch for the Hakluyt Society (London: 1880).

Álvarez, F. *Verdadera informaçam das terras do Preste Joam* (Lisbon: 1540). Translated by Stanley as *Portuguese Embassy to Abyssinia* (London: 1881).

Asensio, Vicente Llorens. *La Primera Vuelta al Mundo. Relación documentada de viaje de Hernando de Magallanes y Juan Sebatián del Cano, 1519–1522* (Seville: 1903), pp. 89–179.

Ayamonte, Martín de. This *roteiro* of the Magellanic voyage is included among the documents of the Arquivo Nacional da Torre do Tombo published in *Arquivo Histórico de Portugal*, vol. 1, fasc. 5, 6.

Baião, Antonio. "Fernão de Magalhães: O problema da sua naturalidade," in *Memorias da Academia das Ciências* (Lisbon: 1936–), t. XIV.

Barbosa, Odoardo. "O livro de Odoardo Barbosa," in *Colecção de noticias para a história e geografia das nacões ultramarinas* (Lisbon: 1813). English translation, London: Hakluyt Soc., 1866.

Barros, João de. *Decadas da Asia*, (Lisbon: 1552–1563, Madrid: 1615), 4 vols. Modern edition by Hernani Cidade and Manuel Murias (Lisbon: 1945–1946), 4 vols.

Barros Arana, Diego de. *Vida y Viages de Hernando de Magallanes* (Santiago, Chile: 1864). Reprinted as *Vida y Viajes de Magallanes* (Buenos Aires: 1945).

Baumgarten. *Geschichte Karls V*, Tome I (Stuttgart: 1885).

Bellwood, Peter. *The Polynesians: Prehistory of an Island People* (London: Thomas and Hudson, 1978, 1987).

Boorstin, Daniel J. *The Discoverers* (New York: Random House, 1978, 1987).

Braamcamp-Freire, A. *Emmenata da Casa da India*, (Lisbon: Bol. Soc. Geog, 1907).

Bromsen, Maury A. ed., *José Toribio Medina, Humanist of the Americas: An Appraisal* (Washington, D.C.: Pan American Union, 1960).

Casas, Fr. Bartolomé de las. "Historia de las Indias," in *Colección de documentos inéditos para la historia de España* (Madrid: 1875–1876), 4 vols. Partial English translation by George Sanderlin entitled *Bartolomé de las Casas; A Selection of His Writings* (New York: Knopf, 1971).

Castanheda, Fernão Lopes de. *História do descobrimento e conquista da India pelos por-*

tugueses (Coimbra: 1551–1561), 8 vols. Reprinted (Coimbra: 1924–1933), 4 vols.

Cinthio, Geraldi. *Hecatomminthi* (Venice: 1565), III, 7.

Corrêa, Gaspar. *Lendas de India* (Lisbon: Lima Felner, 1856–1866), 8 vols.

Cortesão, Armando. *The Mystery of Vasco da Gama* (Lisbon, Coimbra: Junta de Investigações do Ultramar, 1973).

Davidson, Janet. *The Prehistory of New Zealand* (Auckland: Longman Paul, 1984).

Denis, Ferdinand. *Nouvelle Biographie Générale* (Paris: 1853).

Denucé, Jean. (1) *La Question des Molcuques et la Première Circumnavigation du Globe* (Brussels: Hayez, 1911). (2) "Les Îles Lequios (Formose et Riu-Kiu)" *Bull. Soc. Roy. Belge de Géog.* (Brussels: 1907), No. 6, pp. 435–461.

Díaz-Trechuelo, Lourdes. "La Organización del Viaje Magellanico," in *A Viagem de Fernão de Magalhães e a Questião das Molucas*, Actas do II Colóquio Luso-Espanhol de História Ultramarina (Lisbon: Junta de Investigações do Ultramar, 1975), pp. 267–314.

Dicuil. *De Mensura Orbis*, ed. by G. Parthey, 1870.

Diffie, Bailey W. and George D. Winius. *Foundations of the Portuguese Empire, 1415–1580* (Minneapolis: U. of Minnesota Press, 1977).

Dodd, Edward. *Polynesian Seafaring* (New York: Dodd, Mead, 1972), vol. II.

Evans, G. Blakemore, ed., *The Riverside Shakespeare* (Boston: Houghton Mifflin, 1974).

Faria e Sousa, Manuel de. *Asia Portuguesa*, trans. Maria Vitoria Garcia Santos Ferreira (Oporto: Livraria Civilização, 1945–1947). English translation entitled *The Portuguese Asia* by Captain John Stevens (London: C. Brome, 1695) and Gregg (Farnborough, England: 1971).

Ferrand, Gabriel. "La K'ouen-Louen et les anciennes navigations dans les mers du Sud," *J. Asiatique* (Paris: 1919).

Finney, B. R. *Hokule'a: The Way to Tahiti.* (New York: Dodd Mead, 1979).

Fuson, Robert H., trans. *The Log of Christopher Columbus* (Camden, Maine: International Marine, 1987).

Galvão, António. *Tratado dos varios e diversos caminhos . . . e todos os descobrimentos antigos e modernos que são feitos até á era de 1550 . . .* (Lisbon: 1563, 1731; reprinted Oporto: 1944). English translation by Charles Drinkwater Bethune, entitled *The Discoveries of the World . . .* (London: Hakluyt Soc., 1862) Ser. I, Vol. XXX.

Garraty, John A. and Peter Gay, eds. *The Columbia History of the World* (New York: Harper & Row, 1972; reprinted 1981, 1984).

Goís (Goes), Damião de. *Chronica do felicíssimo Rei Dom Emanuel . . .* (Lisbon: 1566–1567; corrected in 1619; reprinted Coimbra: 1926) 4 vols. Republished (Coimbra: 1949–1955), 7 vols.

Gomara, F. Lopez de. *Histoire générale des Indes occidentalles et terres neuves qui jusques à présent ont esté descouvertes* (Paris: 1587).

Granzotto, Gianni. *Christopher Columbus,* trans. Stephen Sartelli (Norman, OK and London: U. of Oklahoma Press, 1987).

Guillemard, Francis Henry Hill. *The Life of Ferdinand Magellan and the First Circumnavigation of the Globe: 1480–1521* (New York: Dodd, Mead, 1890).

Harrisse, Henry. *The Discovery of North America* (Paris: 1892); *Christophe Colomb* (Paris: 1884).

Hemsö, J. Gråberg da. *Littera di Giovanni da Empoli a Leonardo sua padre intorno al viaggio da lui fatto a Malacca e framenti di altre lettere del medesimo* (Florence: Archivo Stòrico Italiano, 1846).

Herrera, Antonio de. *Historia general de los hechos de los Castellanos en las Islas y tierra firme del Mar óceano* (Madrid: 1601–1615, 1726–1730); *Descripción de las Indias occidentales* (Madrid: 1730).

Herrmann, Paul. *Conquest by Man*, trans. Michael Bullock (New York: Harper, 1954). First published as *Sieben Vorbei und Acht Verweht* (Germany: 1952).

Hugues, L., ed. *Raccolta di documenti e studi publicati dalla Reale Commissione Colombiana* (Rome: 1892–1893).

Irving, Washington. *The Life and Voyages of Christopher Columbus* (Paris: 1828).

Jorge, Ricardo. *O óbito de Dom João II* (Lisbon: 1922).

Kemp, Peter. *The History of Ships* (London: Obis, 1978).

Koenigsberger, Helmut George. "Ferdinand II," *Encyclopedia Brittanica*, 1967, IX, 178–179.

Lagôa, Visconde de (João A. de Mascarenhas Judice). *Fernão de Magalhãis (A Sua Vida e A Sua Viagem)* Lisbon: Seara Nova, 1938.

Laguarda Trías, Rolando A. "Las Longitudas Geográficas de la Membranza de Magallanes y del Primer Viaje de Circunnavigación," in *A Viagem . . .* , ed. by A. Teixeira da Mota (Lisbon: 1975), pp. 135–176.

Landström, Björn. *Vägen til Indien*, translated into English as *The Quest for India* by Michael Phillips and Hugh Stubbs (1964). Republished as *Bold Voyagers and Great Explorers* (New York: Doubleday, 1964).

Leonardo y Argensola, Bartolomé Juan de (Argensola). *Conquista de las islas Molucas al Rey Felipe II* (Madrid: 1609). French edition: *Histoire des Molucques* (Amsterdam: 1707).

Livermore, H. V. *A New History of Portugal* (Cambridge: 1966).

Mafra, Ginés de. *Libro que trata del descubrimiento y principio del Estrecho que se llama de Magallanes*, eds. Antonio Blaz-

quez and Delgado Aguilera (Madrid: R. Soc. Geográfica, 1920).

Manchester, William. *Goodbye Darkness* (Boston: Little, Brown, 1979).

Martinić, Mateo. "Panorama de colonización en Tierra del Fuego entre 1881 y 1900," *Anales del Instituto de la Patagonia*, IV, 1, 3, (Punta Arenas, Chile: 1973). *Historia del Estrecho de Magallanes* (Santiago, Chile: Editorial Andrés Bello, 1977).

Medina, José Toribio. *Colección de Documentos Inéditos para la Historia de Chile* (Santiago, Chile: 1888). *El Descubrimiento del Océano Pacífico: Vasco Nuñez Balboa, Hernando de Magallanes y Sus Compañeros* (Santiago, Chile: Imprenta Universitaria, 1920).

Morison, Samuel Eliot. *The European Discovery of America: The Southern Voyages* (New York: Oxford, 1974).

Mota, A. Teixeira de, ed., *A Viagem de Fernão de Magalhães e A Questão das Molucas (Actas do II Colóquio Luso-Espanhol de História Ultramarina)* (Lisbon: Junta de Investigações do Ultramar, 1975).

Nadvi, Allama Syed Sulaiman. *The Arab Navigators*, trans. Abdur Rahman, M. A. (Lahore, Pakistan: Sh. Muhammad Ashraf, 1966).

Navarrete, Martín Fernández de. *Colección de los viages y descubrimientos que hicieron por mar los Españoles desde fines de siglo XV* (Madrid: 1825–1837; Buenos Aires: 1945–1946).

Nowell, Charles E. *A History of Portugal* (New York: 1952); ed. *Magellan's Voyage Around the World: Three Contemporary Accounts* (Evanston: Northwestern U. Press, 1962).

Osorius, Heironimus. *De Rebus Emmanuelis Regis Lusitaniae* (Lisbon: 1571).

Oviedo y Valdez, Gonzalo Fernández de. *Historia general y natural de las Indias* (Valladolid: 1556; Madrid: 1851–1855, 1959; Asunción: Editorial Guaranía, 1944–1945).

Parr, Charles McKew. *So Noble a Captain: The Life and Times of Ferdinand Magellan* (New York: Crowell, 1953; Westport, CT: Greenwood Press, 1975).

Parry, J. H. *The Discovery of the Sea* (New York: Dial Press, 1974).

Peres, Damião. *História dos Descobrimentos Portugueses* (Oporto: 1943; a second ed. privately printed in 1960).

Pigafetta, Antonio (detailed reference in Sources, pp. 1–2).

Pimentel Barata, João de Gama. "A Armada de Fernão de Magalhães (Estudio de Arqueologia Naval)," in Mota, pp. 109–133.

Pohjanpolo, Jorma. *The Sea and Man*, trans. from the Finnish *Meri ja Ihminen* by Diana Tullberg (New York: Stein and Day, 1970).

Queiroz Velloso, José Maria de. *Fernão de Magalhães: a Vida e a Viagem* (Lisbon: 1941). First published as "Fernão de Magalhães: sa Vie et son Voyage," in *Revue d'histoire Moderne*, XIV (Aug.–Sept., 1939), 417–515.

Ramos Pérez, Demetrio. "Magallanes en Valladolid: la Capitulación," in Mota, pp. 179–241.

Ramusio, Gian Battista. *Delle Navigationi e Viaggi* . . . (Venice: L. A. Giunti, 1550).

Ray, Haraprasad. "The Eighth Voyage of the Dragon that Never Was: An Enquiry into the Causes of Cessation of Voyages During the Early Ming Dynasty," *China Report* XXV, no. 2 (New Delhi: 1987), 157–178.

Rebello, Gabriel. "Informações das Cousas de Maluco dadas as Senhor dom Constantino," in *Colecção de Noticias para a História das Nações Ultramarinas*, t. V, no. 2 (Lisbon: 1839).

Rustichello (Rusticiano) of Pisa. *Marco Polo, Il Milione*, trans. A. Ricci (London: 1931).

Sanceau, Elaine. *The Reign of the Fortunate King, 1495–1521* (Hamden, CT: Archon Books, 1969).

Serrão, Joel. *Diccionário de História de Portugal* (Lisbon: 1963–1971) 4 vols.

Silverberg, Robert. *The Longest Voyage: Circumnavigators in the Age of Discovery* (Indianapolis and New York: Bobbs-Merrill, 1972).

Spate, O. H. K. *The Spanish Lake* (Minneapolis: U. of Minnesota Press, 1979).

Stanley, Henry Edward John, Third Baron of Alderley (complete reference in note 6, Sources).

Stechow, Eberhard. "Wann kamen die Malaien zuerst nach Madagaskar?" *Forschungen und Fortschritte*, No. 18 (Berlin: 1944).

Talbott, R. D. *A History of the Chilean Boundaries* (Ames: Iowa State U. Press, 1974).

Taylor, E. G. R. *The Haven Finding Art* (London: Hollis & Carter, 1956).

Torodash, Martin. "Magellan Historiography," *Hispanic American Historical Review*, LI (May, 1971) 313–335.

Tuchman, Barbara. *The March of Folly* (New York: Alfred A. Knopf, 1984), pp. 51–126.

Varthema, Ludovico di. *Itinerario di Ludovico di Varthema, Bolognese* (Rome: 1510).

Villiers, Alan. *Men, Ships and the Sea* (Washington, D.C., Nat. Geogr. Soc., 1962, 1973).

Zurara, Gomes Eannes de. *The Chronicles of the Discovery and Conquest of Guinea*, trans. Edgar Prestage, ed. C. Raymond Beazley (London: Hakluyt Soc., 1890).

Zurita y Castro, Jerónimo de. *Anales de la Corona de Aragón* (Zaragoza: 1562–1580).

Zweig, Stefan (complete reference in note 41, Sources).

Sources

Firsthand Accounts

Antonio Pigafetta

The most detailed account by a survivor of the Magellan expedition, Pigafetta's original manuscript was probably written in a mixture of the author's native Italian and Castilian.[1] While the original has not survived, four early copies have been preserved. Three are written in French, the fourth in Italian. Two of the French versions are in the Bibliothèque Nationale in Paris; the third is at Yale University's Beinecke Library in New Haven, Connecticut. The Biblioteca Ambrosiana in Milan holds the Italian copy. Among the various published editions and translations derived from these copies, the following merit the attention of the genuinely curious:

1. Andrea da Mosto (ed.), *Il primo viaggio intorno al globo di Antonio Pigafetta*, (Rome: Raccolta di Documenti e Studi Publicati dalla R. Commissione Colombiana, 1894) Part V, vol. III, presents the Milan document in modern Italian. An English translation of Mosto's work can be found in James Alexander Robertson (ed.), *Magellan's Voyage Around the World by Antonio Pifagetta: the Original Text of the Ambrosian Manuscript, with English Translation, Notes, Bibliography and Index* (Cleveland: 1906), 3 vols. A limited edition featuring Robertson's annotated translation also was published in Vols. I and II of the *The Philippine Islands* (Cleveland: 1903–1909), which Robertson co-edited with Emma H. Blair. A non-annotated version can be found in Charles E. Nowell (ed.) *Magellan's Voyage Around the World: Three Contemporary Accounts* (Evanston, IL: Northwestern University Press, 1962).

2. In England, Baron (Henry Edward John) Stanley of Alderley's edited translation of Pigafetta's account was published by the Hakluyt Society in 1874 as *The First Voyage Around the World by Magellan*. It was based on Italian and French editions of the Milan document published around 1800 by Carlo Amoretti. In Chile, José Toribio Medina (Santiago: 1920) published a Spanish translation of the French Amoretti.[2]. Neither the Amoretti editions nor translations of them are as precise as the later Mosto edition and its derivatives.[3]

3. Jean Denucé (ed.), *Antonio Pigafetta: Relation du Première Voyage Autour du Monde par Magellan, 1519–1522* (Antwerp and Paris: 1923). This extensively annotated version in modern French was based on Document No. 5650 in the Bibliothèque Nationale in Paris, and collated with the other three extant copies of Pigafetta's account.

4. R. A. Skelton (ed. and trans.) *Magellan's Voyage: A Narrative Account of the First Circumnavigation* (New Haven: Yale University Press, 1969). Published in two volumes, the first is Skelton's English translation of the Beinecke Library's French-language manuscript: *Navigation et descouvrement de la Inde supérieure et isles de Malucques ou naissant les cloux de Girofle*. The second volume is a color facsimile of that document.

5. Paula Spurlin Page (trans.) *The Voyage of Magellan: The Journal of Antonio Pigafetta* (Englewood Cliffs, NJ: 1969). A facsimile and English translation of a French edition entitled *Le voyage et nauigation faict par les Espaignolz es Iles de Molluques . . .* (Paris:

Colines, 1525–1536), abridged and translated by Jacques Fabre from an Italian copy of Pigafetta's account. It is not annotated. The facsimile and translation are held by the William L. Clements Library in Ann Arbor, Michigan.

Francisco Albo

This priceless navigational record of Magellan's voyage by the Greek officer who completed the circumnavigation as pilot of the *Victoria* is preserved in the Archivo General de las Indias in Seville. Entitled *Diario ó derrotero del viaje de Magallanes desde el cabo de San Agustín en el Brasil, hasta el regreso a España de la nao Victoria*, it has been published in Spanish in two document collections: those of Navarrete[4] and Medina.[5] Stanley provided an English translation.[6]

Albo started his logbook on November 29, 1519, as the fleet approached Cape Santo Agostinho on the coast of Brazil. Probably it was then that Magellan promoted him to acting pilot. Albo had begun the voyage as master's mate on the *Trinidad*. Once he started his *Diario*, Albo faithfully recorded estimates of his position until, as pilot of the *Victoria* on September 4, 1522, he sighted Cape St. Vincent on the European mainland.

Since the art of celestial navigation was still in its infancy when Albo took his measurements, his determinations of latitude at sea were susceptible to significant errors. The determination of longitude by means other than dead reckoning from a known point of departure was beyond his capability. However, the fleet's astrologer-pilot Andrés de San Martín was capable of precise observations of celestial bodies when he was able to set up his instruments ashore. His skill with mathematics and the use of astronomical tables made it possible for him to convert some of these observations into estimates of longitude. Several times during the voyage, San Martín was able to make multiple observations of the position of the moon and planets. At Port San Julián in Patagonia, and on Homonhon Island in the Philippines, he achieved longitude estimates of surprising precision.[7] Albo recorded these estimates in his logbook and used them as points of departure for dead reckoning.

After his return to Spain, Albo probably was pressured to adjust his logbook entries to favor Spanish territorial claims. Did unwillingness to compromise his professional integrity by doing so cause him to leave Spain? Whatever the cause, Albo disappears from history following his appearance at court in the autumn of 1522. There are no records to indicate whether he ever received payments from the pension granted to him by the Emperor. His *Diario* remained undiscovered in the Spanish archives until 1788. Since then it has served as the best single source of navigational data for reconstructing the voyage of Magellan.

The Genoese Pilot

Another important source of information on the navigation of Magellan's fleet, especially on the last voyage of the *Trinidad*, is an anonymous document entitled *Navegaçam a vyagem que fez Fernam de Magalhães de Sevilha pero Maluco no anno de 1519*. The author, usually referred to as The Genoese Pilot, probably was Léon Pancaldo, a native of Saona in Genoa who sailed from San Lúcar on the *Trinidad* as an able seaman. After Albo transferred to the *Victoria*, Pancaldo assisted his Genoese countryman, Giovanni Battista, master of the *Trinidad*, with the piloting duties. The document was among the papers from the *Trinidad* seized by the Portuguese in the Moluccas.

While the original document has disappeared, three copies have survived. One is held by the Library of São Francisco da Cidade in Lisbon, another by the Academy of History in Madrid, and a third by the National Library in Paris. It was published in Lisbon in 1826 by the Royal Academy of Sciences in *Coleccão de Notícias para a História e Geografia das Nacões Ultramarinas* . . . , vols. IV and VI. Two translations have been made from this edition: one in Italian by Hugues,[8] the other in English by Stanley.[9]

Ginés de Mafra

An account ascribed to Ginés de Mafra, one of the five *Trinidad* survivors, was included by Navarrete in his *Colección* . . . , vol. IV (1837) and in the *Libro que trata del descubrimiento y principio del Estrecho que se llama de Magallanes, por Ginés de Mafra*, (Antonio Blazqez and Delgado Aguilera for the Royal Geographic Society of Madrid: 1920–1921). In the prologue to the latter edition, there is a statement to the effect that it was based on a handwritten document in the National Library in Madrid, copied from the original in 1542 "by a curious person."

When Mafra arrived in Lisbon in 1527, he was imprisoned. Among his possessions were navigational papers that had belonged to Andrés de San Martín. The papers were confiscated by Portuguese authorities before Mafra was released to return to Spain. It seems likely that at least part of the information in the account was derived from Mafra's memory of the content of San Martín's papers. Mafra was an accomplished, literate mariner who subsequently served as a royal pilot in Spanish exploratory fleets. His account has proved a useful adjunct to those of Albo and the Genoese Pilot for reconstructing the track of Magellan's voyage.[10]

The Anonymous Portuguese

Vasquito Galego, an apprentice seaman who returned to Spain with the *Victoria*, and whose father had been pilot of that ship, probably was the author of this brief (two-folio) account of the voyage of circumnavigation. An Italian translation entitled *Narratione di un Portoghese Compagno di Odoardo Barbosa, qual fu supra la nave Vittoria del Anno MDXIX*, was included in the 1554 edition of Ramusio's *Delle Navigatione et viaggi* . . . . There is a Spanish translation in Medina's *Colección* . . . , and an English translation in Stanley's *First Voyage* . . . , pp. 30–32.

At the University of Leiden in the Netherlands is an anonymous document possibly derived from the same source. Consisting of fourteen folios, it is longer and more detailed than the *Narratione* . . . in the Ramusio collection. It is thought to have been dictated to a scribe in the second half of the sixteenth century by a Portuguese survivor of the Magellan voyage. Except for Simon de Burgos, who consistently denied his Portuguese origin, Vasquito Galego was the only Portuguese among the survivors. The son of one of the expedition's pilots, young Galego seems the most likely source of the Leiden document. It was printed in 1937 under the title *Viagem de Fernão de Magalhães, escripta p hum homem q foi na cõpanhia*, by M. de Jong for publication by the German Institute of the University of Coimbra in Portugal.[11]

Martín Méndez

Records prepared by the *contador* (ship's clerk) of the *Victoria* between September 6 and December 17, 1521, detail the pacts concluded by the leadership of the Magellan expedition with chieftans and sultans of islands from Palawan to the Moluccas. At this

time two ships, the *Trinidad* and the *Victoria*, remained to the survivors of the expedi-
tion, then led by a triumvirate of two captains, Gonzalo Gómez de Espinosa and Juan
Sebastián del Cano, and the master of the *Trinidad*, Juan Bautista. These records, lost
for nearly 500 years, were discovered among uncatalogued documents in the *Archivo
General de las Indias* in Seville by Mauricio Obregón, acting on a hint from Katherine
Romoli. Photocopies and a transcription of Méndez's records have been published in
Dr. Obregón's *La Primera Vuelta al Mundo* (Bogotá: 1984).

Martín de Ayamonte

This is the least significant of the surviving eye-witness accounts. Ayamonte was one of
the two crewmen from the *Victoria* who deserted off Timor by swimming ashore at
night. Both were apprehended by Portuguese and taken to Malacca, where they were
questioned. A document of four folios in the National Archives of Portugal provides a
record of their interrogation, and signed by Jorge Dalboquerque and Lopo Cabra
Bernardes in the first quarter of the sixteenth century, it provides a brief account of the
voyage of Magellan. Ayamonte (a Portuguese registered as a Castilian in the enrollment
records of the expedition) must have done most of the talking, for the document states
that he was the author of the account.[12] It was published in 1933 by Antonio Baião in
Arquivo Histórico de Portugal, vol. I, fasc. 5, 6.

Other Derivatives of Firsthand Accounts

An Italian translation of the letter (now missing) written by Cano to Charles V, informing him of the return of the *Victoria*,[13] and an account by Martín Méndez of the treaties
concluded with the Moluccan princes[14] have been published. Except for interesting
specifics in the latter, they add little to the accounts of other participants.

Secondary Sources

1. Detailed accounts by contemporary writers with access to first-hand reports.

Antonio de Brito

The commander of a Portuguese naval squadron dispatched to the Moluccas, Brito
seized the *Trinidad* on its return from its attempt to sail across the Pacific to Panama.
After confiscating its papers and interrogating the survivors, Brito sent a long letter to
King Manuel, reporting on what he had learned about the Magellan expedition. The
letter was dated February 11, 1523. A duplicate, dated May 6, 1523, also was dispatched, probably to enhance the probability that the information would reach Portugal. The first copy was published in 1894 in Mosto's *Raccolta Colombiana*, Part V, No. 2.
The second, entitled *Carta escrita de S. João de Ternate, em 6 de Maio de 1523, a D. Manuel I*, was reproduced in *Alguns documentos do Arquivo Nacional da Torre do Tombo* (Lisbon: 1892) pp. 464–478. When Brito wrote the letter, news of Dom Manuel's death on
December 13, 1521, and the succession of João III, had not yet reached the Moluccas.
In Brito's letter are passages apparently copied directly from the *roteiro* of the Genoese
Pilot, which was among the papers seized from the *Trinidad*.[15]

Pietro Martire d'Anghiera (Peter Martyr)

An apostolic protonotary and longtime representative of the Vatican at the royal court
of Spain, Martire had been chaplain to Queen Isabella. Having served as Secretary of

the Council of the Indies in 1518, he had been privy to the hearings at which Magellan and Faleiro presented their proposal to King Charles and his counsellors. After the return of the *Victoria* in 1522, Martire, aided by Maximilian Transylvanus, interviewed Cano, Albo, Bustamente, and others of its crew who were summoned to court. He therefore had unparalleled access to inside information about the Magellan expedition.

Perhaps because of the diplomatically sensitive nature of this information, Martire restricted his writing about it to Chapter VII, *De Orbe Ambito*, in the fifth of the eight decades in his *De Orbe Novo*, completed in 1530,[16] and to brief comments in his personal correspondence.[17]

Maximilian Transylvanus

In spite of his name, Transylvanus was not from Transylvania. He probably was raised in Flanders.[18] A secretary to Charles V and married to a niece of Cristóbal de Haro, he was well positioned to acquire knowledge of the Magellan expedition. When the crew of the *Victoria* arrived in Valladolid following their successful circumnavigation, Transylvanus with his mentor, Pietro Martire, questioned them closely about the events of the voyage.

On October 24, 1522, Transylvanus wrote a letter to his father, Matthäus Lang, archbishop of Salzburg, describing what he had learned about the voyage. The letter, written in Latin, is the source of the first printed report of the circumnavigation. Published in Cologne in January 1523, the identifying part of its ponderous title is *De Moluccis Insulis* . . . . Other editions have been published in Italian, Spanish, and English.[19] While Transylvanus clearly had a lively interest in his subject, the quality of his information is diminished somewhat by the young courtier's uncritical acceptance of testimony from informants with cause for bias, and by his haste to get his letter published.

2. Brief comments on the Magellan expedition by contemporary writers.

Bartolomé de las Casas

A missionary priest who had returned to Spain from Hispaniola to complain of the brutal exploitation of natives in the Caribbean colonies, Las Casas was present at court in 1518 when Magellan was promoting his enterprise. In his *Historia de las Indias* completed between 1547 and 1561 (published in Madrid 1875–1876), Tome III, pp. 376–378, Las Casas reported a brief conversation with Magellan in the anteroom to Chancellor Sauvage's chambers. An English translation by George Sanderlin (New York: Alfred A. Knopf, 1971) contains the material on Magellan.

Gaspar Contarini

The Venetian ambassador to the court of Charles V, Contarini was a witness to the arrival at court of Cano and his fellow officers from the *Victoria*. In a dispatch dated in Valladolid on September 24, 1522, he commented that the return of the *Victoria* would encourage Spain to dispute Portugal's sovereignty in the Moluccas, and predicted the outbreak of war between the two kingdoms.[20]

Pedro Mexia

One of the chroniclers at the court of Charles V, Mexia had been a witness to the departure of Magellan's fleet from Seville, and to the return of the *Victoria*. His observations were recorded without commentary as *Coloquio del Sol* in his *Silva de Varia . . .* , published in Seville in 1540.[21]

3. Reports of contemporary or near-contemporary writers with access to first-hand documents.

João de Barros

A prolific writer, Barros entered the Portuguese civil service during the reign of João III. In 1522 he was sent to Guinea as a colonial administrator. After his return to Portugal, he served as treasurer (1525–1528), and factor (1533–1567) of the *Casa da India e da Guinea*. During those years he used the information stored in that agency's archives for compiling the history of Portugal's maritime discoveries and its conquests in Asia between 1495 and 1528. Known as *Decadas da Asia*, this four-volume work was published between 1552 and 1615. A classic of Portuguese maritime history, it has been republished many times, most recently in four volumes edited by Hernani Cidade and Manuel Múrias (Lisbon: 1945–1946). Fortescue's translation of part of the work into English was published in 1571; a French translation by Claude Gruget in 1580.

Barros had access to viceregal reports concerning the Indian Ocean campaigns in which Magellan had participated, the papers confiscated from the *Trinidad* and the correspondence between Magellan and Serrão. Although he considered him a renegade, Barros' coverage of Serrão's discovery of the Moluccas is the most complete on record. He held Magellan in low esteem and scoffed at the scientific competence of Faleiro and San Martín. His harsh treatment of Magellan should not be surprising. Like most Portuguese of his time, Barros despised Magellan as a traitor whose defection to Spain he considered inexcusable.

Fernão Lopes de Castanheda

In his *História do descobrimento e conquista da India pelos portugueses* (Coimbra: 1551–1561, reprinted 1924–1933) this Portuguese chronicler provided detailed accounts of Portuguese discoveries and conquests. In Lisbon he had access to the confiscated navigational notes of San Martín. Like Barros, he had little use for Magellan. It was Castanheda who initiated the story that Faleiro owed his mathematical skills to a "familiar demon."

Gaspar Corrêa

Secretary to Afonso de Albuquerque from 1510 to 1515, Corrêa was familiar with many of the events with which Magellan was involved while he served in India and Malacca. Corrêa's *Lendas da India* focuses on Portuguese activities in India from 1497 to 1550 and contains information concerning Magellan's participation in the Indian Ocean campaigns of Almeida and Albuquerque.[22] These chronicles are valuable history, but should be treated with caution. Critical readers will detect in Corrêa's writing the influence of a very lively imagination.

Damião de Góis

This renowned humanist was the most erudite of the Portuguese royal chroniclers of the sixteenth century. From 1523 to 1529 he served as an attaché at the Portuguese

Trade Bureau in Flanders, where he became an intimate of Erasmus.[23] After his return to Portugal, he was commissioned to write the history of the reign of Manuel I, resulting in the four-part *Crónica do felicíssimo Rei Dom Emanuel* (Lisbon: 1566–1567). Like Barros, Góis had unlimited access to a wealth of archival material pertinent to Magellan. His circumspect treatment of the expatriate Portuguese discoverer is notable for its lack of prejudice.[24]

Antonio Galvão

The so-called "Apostle of the Moluccas," Galvão held no royal commission for his history of the Portuguese conquest of the East Indian Spice Islands.[25] Perhaps because he was not obliged to any prince when he produced his work, he was even more temperate in his treatment of Magellan's defection than the fairminded Góis.[26] Like Pigafetta, however, he reported with uncritical enthusiasm the tall tales told by the natives of the Moluccas.[27]

Gonçalo Fernández de Oviedo y Váldes

A chronicler at the court of Charles V, Book XX, Part II of his *Historia de las Indias* (Valladolid: 1557) contains a discussion of Magellan's voyage based on the report of Juan Sebatián del Cano.[28]

Antonio de Herrera

Appointed official chronicler at the Spanish royal court in 1596, Herrera had access to first-hand material on the Magellan expedition, including the precious papers of San Martín that Portuguese authorities seized from the *Trinidad* in the Moluccas. They were brought to Spain from Portugal after the union of the two kingdoms under Philip II in 1580. While much of this material since has been lost, Herrera copied extensively from it for his *Historia general* . . . .[29]

Collections of Sources

Martín Fernández de Navarrete

A wealth of information on Magellan, his voyage and its aftermath is contained in Volume IV of this eminent historian's five-volume collection of accounts of Spanish voyages of discovery.[30] Some of this information was based on Spanish sources brought to light by the archival researches of Navarrete's contemporary, Muñoz.[31] Martin Torodash, an American historiographer, considered Navarrete's *Colección* . . . to be ". . . absolutely indispensable, the very basis of modern historical writing on the discovery period."[32]

Medina, José Toribio

A prolific writer, this distinguished Chilean historian was designated "Humanist of the Americas" by his admirers at the Pan American Union.[33] Between 1888 and 1902 he published a remarkable collection of unedited documents relating to the Spanish discovery and colonization of Chile, including many reprinted from Navarrete.[34] Volumes II and III of this collection deal with Magellan, with whom the recorded history of Chile began. In 1920, Medina published an exhaustive study of Magellan containing much biographical material, a detailed analyses of the conception and development of his enterprise, the voyage, and a wealth of information on the crews of the expedition's ships.[35] An appendix to this work contains a valuable list of documentary sources and an excellent bibliography.

Henry Edward John Stanley

Lord Stanley, the third Baron of Alderley, edited and translated into English six contemporary accounts of Magellan's voyage, to which he added other documentary materials and a short biography of Magellan.[36] It is a useful compilation for readers of English, but was written before the adoption of the rigorous standards of modern historical scholarship.

Vicente Llorens Asensio

La Primera Vuelta del Mundo (Seville: 1903) contains a brief account of Magellan's voyage and a useful list of documents in the Archivo General de las Indias pertaining to it.

Emma H. Blair and James Alexander Robertson (eds.)

A valuable source containing translations into English of many documents pertaining to the Magellan voyage can be found in Volume I of their fifty-five volume work, *The Philippine Islands: 1493–1893* (Cleveland: 1903–1909).

Charles E. Nowell (ed.)

This American scholar has translated into English three contemporary accounts of the Magellan voyage. To these he has added an instructive Introduction.[37] In a summary entitled *Aftermath*, Nowell presented a map showing that Magellan crossed the Pacific Ocean by the route suggested in 1934 by George E. Nunn.[38] In the eastern Pacific, this route lies far to the north of the tracks reconstructed from the data of Albo and The Genoese Pilot.

Biographies

Diego Barros Arana

Reasonably accurate as far as it goes, but somewhat limited in scope, Barros Arana's *Vida i Viajes de Hernando de Magellanes* (Santiago, Chile: 1864) was the first of the Magellan biographies. It was reprinted in 1945 by Editorial Futuro in Buenos Aires as *Vida y Viajes de Magallanes*.

Francis Henry Hill Guillemard

By far the best of the English-language biographies of Magellan, Guillemard's *The Life of Ferdinand Magellan and the First Circumnavigation of the Globe: 1480–1521*, appeared in the series *The World's Great Explorers* (New York: Dodd, Mead, 1890). A professor at Cambridge University, Guillemard had traveled over much of Magellan's route in a sailing yacht, bringing to his study of Magellan a professional geographer's expertise and an intimate knowledge of the sea and its dangers. He made good use of the information available to him in the waning years of the nineteenth century. At that time, clarifications of the genealogy and early years of Magellan made by Portuguese scholars in the first half of the twentieth century had not yet appeared.

Jean Denucé

In 1911, this Belgian scholar published an outstanding study, in French, of Magellan and his celebrated voyage.[39] In addition to a penetrating analysis of the geographical concepts on which Magellan based his enterprise, it provides detailed accounts of Magellan's early career, the conception of his enterprise, the preparations for the voyage, and the voyage itself. Denucé also presented a well-reasoned hypothesis concerning Magellan's motives for sailing west in the Pacific 12–14° north of the equator, a choice that produced landfalls at Guam and the Philippines.

José Toribio Medina

Written in Spanish, the great Chilean historian's *El Descubrimiento del Océano Pacífico* . . . contains a well-documented biographical study of Magellan.[40] Any serious study of Magellan and his enterprise must include this informative product of Medina's exhaustive archival research.

João A. Mascarenhas Judice, Visconde de Lagôa

Volume I of Lagôa's two-volume *Fernão de Magalhãis (A Sua Vida e A Sua Viagem)* (Lisbon: Seara Nova, 1938) contains a fine biographical study of the great navigator by a Portuguese scholar. For the second volume, Admiral J. Freitas Ribeiro carefully reconstructed Magellan's route from navigational records left by Albo and The Genoese Pilot, both professional mariners who served in Magellan's fleet. As with several other fine studies of Magellan by European scholars, Lagôa's work has not been translated into English.

Stefan Zweig

In 1938, the same year that Lagôa's masterful work was published, Zweig's *Conquerer of the Seas: the Story of Magellan* was published in German, Portuguese and English editions.[41] A highly romanticized psycho-biography, it makes interesting reading, but is not suitable for historical study. Zweig, a Viennese, was a writer of popular biographies.

Charles McKew Parr

In *So Noble a Captain*, a well-researched biography of Magellan, Parr allowed his unbounded admiration for his subject to color his text so that it became more of a panegyric than a historical study of the great navigator.[42] Desperate to credit his hero with a circumnavigation of the globe, Parr included in his story an episode in which, as captain of a Portuguese ship in 1511, Magellan sailed from Malacca into the South China Sea and then northwest to islands (the Philippines) that ". . . he later was to discover while sailing westward across the Pacific." Parr probably got his idea from Leonardo y Argensola's unsupported claim that Magellan had commanded one of the ships in the squadron of Simón de Abreu that sailed to Banda in 1511.[43] Parr's ideas on how economic competition between rival banking houses in Germany and Venice affected the financing and staffing of Magellan's expedition are intriguing. While his book makes good reading, its lack of adequate documentation can be frustrating.

Morison, Samuel Eliot

A distinguished Harvard historian with a naval background, Morison included a chapter on Magellan in his *The European Discovery of America: The Southern Voyages* (New York:

Oxford University Press, 1974). It contains some good biographical material, although Morison rejected the views of modern Portuguese scholars concerning Magellan's birthplace. He favored the location indicated in a will thought to have been either a forgery or the testament of a homonym. Morison's treatment of the voyage is superb. The nautical charts showing Magellan's track (as reconstructed by Admiral J. Freitas Ribeiro) are especially instructive. So too is Morison's reconstruction of the movements of Magellan's ships during the mutiny at Port San Julián. While close reading of the documents describing the mutiny reveals that Morison's reconstruction is not entirely accurate, the errors are minor. His diagram of the maneuvers of the five ships during the mutiny adds much to the understanding of that critical event. At the end of the chapter, Morison provided a useful bibliographic survey. Together with the longer, earlier work by Guillemard, Morison's chapter provides a readily accessible, reliable source of information on Magellan in English.

Mauricio Obregón
In this writer's fascinating *Argonauts to Astronauts* (New York: Harper and Row, 1980), there is a fine chapter on Magellan, notable for the insights the author gained by traveling over much of the route of the first circumnavigation, viewing key locations from light aircraft and from the decks of ships. In this chapter, the author modestly reports finding, in the Archives of the Indies in Seville, thirty pages of the lost *Paces*, treaties with Moluccan sultans signed by members of the expedition who, after Magellan's death, succeeded in reaching the Spice Islands. The treaties were notarized by Martín Méndez, the clerk of the *Victoria*. With twelve others of his ship's crew, Méndez was seized by the Portuguese in the Cape Verde Islands and later returned to Spain. As notarized eyewitness accounts, the discovery of these pages represents a significant contribution to the documented history of the first circumnavigation of the earth.

Other Biographical Accounts
The works of Benson,[44] Daniel,[45] and Cameron[46] can be found in many public libraries in the United States. Like those of Zweig and Parr, their value lies in the entertainment provided by a powerful story, rather than in their reliability as history.

Comment
The above listing is by no means complete. It includes most of the best and a few of the least reliable sources directly or indirectly consulted for this study. An expanded list, not annotated, can be found in the Bibliography.

Notes
1. Jean Denucé, *La Question des Molucques et la Première Circumnavigation du Globe* (Brussels: Hayez, 1911).
2. In José Toribio Medina, *Colección de Documentos Inéditos para la Historia de Chile* (Santiago, Chile: 1888).
3. Martin Torodash, "Magellan Historiography," *Hispanic American Historical Review*, 51 (2) (May, 1971); Denucé, *loc. sit.*, p. 12.
4. Martín Fernández de Navarrete, *Colección de las viages y descubrimientos que hicieron por mar los Españoles desde fines del siglo XV* (Madrid: 1825–1837, Buenos Aires: 1945–1946).
5. Medina, *Colección . . .* , *loc. cit.*
6. Henry Edward John Stanley, Third Baron of Alderley (ed. and trans.) *The First Voyage Around the World by Magellan* (London: Hakluyt Soc., 1874), Ser. I, LII. (Reprinted, New York: 1964).

7. Rolando A. Laguarda Trías, "Las Longitudes Geográficas de la Membranza de Magallanes y del Primer Viaje de Circumnavigatión," in *A Viagem de Fernão de Magalhães e a Questião das Molucas*, ed. by A. Teixeira da Mota (Lisbon: Actas do II Colóquio Luso-Espanhol de História Ultramarina, 1975), pp. 135–178.
8. In Raccolta di Documenti e Studi Publicati dalla R. Commissione Colombiana, (Rome: 1975), V (2), p. 258.
9. Stanley, *op. cit.*, pp. 1–30.
10. Admiral J. Freitas Ribeiro used it for his *Estudio Nautico do Roteiro da Viagem de Fernão de Magalhãis*, on pp. 217–136 of Lagôa II, *op. cit.* (p. 17, this text).
11. Lagôa I, *op. cit.*, p. 286.
12. Ibid., p. 287.
13. Denucé, *op. cit.*, p. 22, cited an Italian translation by Gaspare Contarini (Venetian ambassador to the court of Charles V) included in Raccolta Colombiana, Part III (1), 103.
14. Ibid., cited P. Pastills, *Labor Evangélica . . . de le Compañía de Jesus en las Islas Filipinas* (Barcelona: 1900), Part I, Tome I, Book I, Chapters XIX, XXIII.
15. Denucé, *loc. cit.*, p. 26.
16. Gian Battista Ramusio, *Delle Navigatione et Viaggi . . .* , (Venice: 1536–1583). English translations by Richard Eden in *Decades of the Newe Worlde*, (London: 1558) and Francis McNutt (New York and London: 1912). Martire's original manuscript; dedicated to Pope Clement VII, was lost in the sack of Rome in 1527 by mutinous soldiers of a Hispano-German army.
17. Denucé, *op. cit.*, p. 29, cited Pual Gaffarel et Louvot, "Lettres Inédites de P. Martyr d'Anghiera," *Revue de Géographie*, (Paris: 1884–1885), and E. Gelcich, "Aus den Briefen Peter Martyr Anghiera," *Zeitschr. Ges. Erdkunke*, (Berlin: 1891).
18. Denucé, *loc. cit.*, p. 28.
19. English translations in Stanley, *op. cit.*, pp. 179–210, Emma H. Blair and James Alexander Robertson (eds.), *The Philippine Islands*, (Cleveland: 1903–1909), I, pp. 305–337, and in Charles R. Nowell (ed.), *Magellan's Voyage Around the World: Three Contemporary Accounts*, (Evanston, IL: 1962), pp. 269–309.
20. Denucé, *loc. cit.*, cited Franz von Wieser, "Ein Bericht des Gasparo Contarini . . . ," *Mitteil. Inst. Oesterr. Geschichts-Forschung*, (Vienna: 1884), Tome V, p. 447.
21. Ibid., stated that Mexia's *Coloquio del Sol* can be found on p. CII of the 1547 edition.
22. (Lisbon: Royal Academy of Sciences, 1588 and 1866). An English translation is provided by Nowell, *op. cit.*, pp. 312–328.
23. Denucé, *loc. cit.*, p. 33.
24. Ibid., p. 34.
25. Antônio Galvão, *Tratado dos Varios e Diversos Caminos . . . ate a Era de 1550 . . .* , (Lisbon: 1731). There is an English translation in Charles Drinkwater Bethune (ed.), *Discoveries of the World . . .* , (London: Hakluyt Soc., 1862) Ser. I, Vol. XXX.
26. Charles E. Nowell, *loc. cit.* (note 19 above), p. 7.
27. Denucé, *loc. cit.*, p. 33.
28. José Toribio Medina, *El Descubrimiento del Océano Pacífico*, (Santiago, Chile: 1920).
29. Antonio de Herrera, *Historia General de los Hechos de los Castellanos en las Islas y Tierra Firme del Mar Océano*, (Madrid: 1601–1615), 4 vols. Reprinted in 17 vols., (Madrid: 1934–1937).
30. Navarrete, *op. cit.* Most of the original manuscript is in London in the British Museum.
31. Denucé, *op. cit.*, p. 8.
32. Martin Torodash, "Magellan Historiography," *Hispanic American Historical Review*, 51 (2) (May, 1951), pp. 313–335.
33. Murray Bromsen, ed., *José Toribio Medina, Humanist of the Americas* (Washington, D.C.: Pan American Union, 1960).
34. Medina, *Colección . . .* , *op. cit.* The material on Magellan is in Vols. II and III.
35. Ibid., *Descubrimiento . . .* , *op. cit.*
36. Stanley, *op. cit.*
37. Nowell, *op. cit.*, pp. 3–76.
38. George E. Nunn, "Magellan's Route Across the Pacific," *Geographical Review*, XXIV (4) (October, 1934), 602.
39. Denucé, *loc. cit.*
40. Medina, *Descubrimiento, loc. cit.*

41. Stefan Zweig, *Conquerer of the Seas: The Story of Ferdinand Magellan*, ed. and trans. Eden and Cedar Paul (London and New York: 1938). Portuguese edition, *Fernão de Magalhães* (Rio de Janeiro: 1938). German edition, *Magellán: Der Man und Seine Tat*, (Vienna: 1938).

42. Charles McKew Parr, *So Noble A Captain* (New York: Crowell, 1953). Reprinted (Westport, CT: Greenwood Press, 1973).

43. Bartolomé de Leonardo y Argensola, *Conquista de las Islas Malucas al Rey Felipe II* (Madrid: 1609). French translation (Amsterdam: 1707).

44. Edward F. Benson, *Ferdinand Magellan* (London: 1929, New York: 1930).

45. Hawthorne Daniel, *Ferdinand Magellan* (Garden City, NY: 1964).

46. Ian Cameron (Donald Gordon Paine), *Magellan and the First Circumnavigation of the World* (New York: Saturday Review Press, 1973).

Index